Data Algorithms with Spark

Recipes and Design Patterns for Scaling Up Using PySpark

Mahmoud Parsian

Beijing • Boston • Farnham • Sebastopol • Tokyo

Data Algorithms with Spark

by Mahmoud Parsian

Published by O'Reilly Media, Inc., 1005 Gravenstein Highway North, Sebastopol, CA 95472.

O'Reilly books may be purchased for educational, business, or sales promotional use. Online editions are also available for most titles (*http://oreilly.com*). For more information, contact our corporate/institutional sales department: 800-998-9938 or *corporate@oreilly.com*.

Acquisitions Editor: Jessica Haberman
Development Editor: Melissa Potter
Production Editor: Christopher Faucher
Copyeditor: Rachel Head
Proofreader: Justin Billing
Indexer: Potomac Indexing, LLC
Interior Designer: David Futato
Cover Designer: Karen Montgomery
Illustrator: Kate Dullea

April 2022: First Edition

Revision History for the First Edition

2022-04-08: First Release

See *http://oreilly.com/catalog/errata.csp?isbn=9781492082385* for release details.

978-1-492-08238-5

[LSI]

This book is dedicated to my

family: Behnaz, Maral, and Yaseen

parents: Bagher and Monireh

brother: Ahmad

sister: Nayerazam

Table of Contents

Part III. Data Design Patterns

Foreword

When I started the Apache Spark project a decade ago, one of my main goals was to make it easier for a wide range of users to implement parallel algorithms. New algorithms acting on large-scale data are having a profound impact in all areas of computing, and I wanted to help developers implement such algorithms and reason about their performance without having to build a distributed system from scratch.

I am therefore very excited to see this new book by Dr. Mahmoud Parsian on data algorithms with Spark. Dr. Parsian has extensive research and practical experience with large-scale data-parallel algorithms, including developing new algorithms for bioinformatics as the lead of Illumina's big data team. In this book, he introduces Spark through its Python API, PySpark, and shows how to implement a wide range of useful algorithms efficiently using Spark's distributed computing primitives. He also explains the workings of the underlying Spark engine and how to optimize your algorithms through techniques such as controlling data partitioning. This book will be a great resource for both readers looking to implement existing algorithms in a scalable fashion and readers who are developing new, custom algorithms using Spark.

I am also thrilled that Dr. Parsian has included working code examples for all the algorithms he discusses, using real-world problems where possible. These will serve as a great starting point for readers who want to implement similar computations. Whether you intend to use these algorithms directly or build your own custom algorithms using Spark, I hope that you enjoy this book as an introduction to the open source engine, its inner workings, and the modern parallel algorithms that are having such a broad impact across computing.

— *Matei Zaharia*
Assistant Professor of Computer Science, Stanford
Chief Technologist, Databricks
Original Creator of Apache Spark

Preface

Spark has become the de facto standard for large-scale data analytics. I have been using and teaching Spark since its inception nine years ago, and I have seen tremendous improvements in Extract, Transform, Load (ETL) processes, distributed algorithm development, and large-scale data analytics. I started using Spark with Java, but I found that while the code is pretty stable, you have to write long lines of code, which can become unreadable. For this book, I decided to use PySpark (a Python API for Spark) because it is easier to express the power of Spark in Python: the code is short, readable, and maintainable. PySpark is powerful but simple to use, and you can express any ETL or distributed algorithm in it with a simple set of transformations and actions.

Why I Wrote This Book

This is an introductory book about data analysis using PySpark. The book consists of a set of guidelines and examples intended to help software and data engineers solve data problems in the simplest possible way. As you know, there are many ways to solve any data problem: PySpark enables us to write simple code for complex problems. This is the motto I have tried to express in this book: keep it simple and use parameters so that your solution can be reused by other developers. My aim is to teach readers how to think about data and understand its origins and final intended form, as well as showing how to use fundamental data transformation patterns to solve a variety of data problems.

Who This Book Is For

To use this book effectively it will be helpful to know the basics of the Python programming language, such as how to use conditionals (`if-then-else`), iterate through lists, and define and call functions. However, if your background is in another programming language (such as Java or Scala) and you do not know Python, you will still be able to use the book as I have provided a reasonable introduction to Spark and PySpark.

This book is primarily intended for people who want to analyze large amounts of data and develop distributed algorithms using the Spark engine and PySpark. I have provided simple examples showing how to perform ETL operations and write distributed algorithms in PySpark. The code examples are written in such a way that you can cut and paste them to get the job done easily.

The sample code provided on GitHub (*https://github.com/mahmoudparsian/data-algorithms-with-spark*) is a great resource to get you started with your own data projects.

How This Book Is Organized

The book consists of 12 chapters, organized into three parts:

Part I, "Fundamentals"
: The first four chapters cover the fundamentals of Spark and PySpark and introduce data transformations such as mappers, filters, and reducers. They contain many practical examples to get you started on your own PySpark projects. Approximately 95% of all data problems can be tackled by using simple PySpark data transformations (such as `map()`, `flatMap()`, `filter()`, and `reduceByKey()`) introduced in the first four chapters of this book. Here's a closer look at what you'll find here:

  - Chapter 1, "Introduction to Spark and PySpark", provides a high-level overview of data algorithms and introduces the use of Spark and PySpark for solving data analytics problems.
  - Chapter 2, "Transformations in Action", shows how to use Spark transformations (mappers, filters, and reducers) to solve real data problems.
  - Chapter 3, "Mapper Transformations", introduces the most frequently used mapper transformations: `map()`, `filter()`, `flatMap()`, and `mapPartitions()`.
  - Chapter 4, "Reductions in Spark", focuses on reduction transformations (such as `reduceByKey()`, `groupByKey()`, and `combineByKey()`), which play a very important role in grouping data by keys. Many simple but useful examples are given to make sure that you'll be able to use these reductions effectively.

Part II, "Working with Data"
: The next four chapters cover partitioning data, graph algorithms, reading/writing data from/to many different data sources, and ranking algorithms:

- Chapter 5, "Partitioning Data", presents functions to physically partition data on specific data columns. This partitioning will enable your SQL queries (e.g., in Amazon Athena or Google BigQuery) to analyze a slice of the data rather than the whole dataset, which will improve query performance.
- Chapter 6, "Graph Algorithms", introduces one of the most important external Spark packages, GraphFrames, which can be used to analyze large graphs in Spark's distributed environment.
- Chapter 7, "Interacting with External Data Sources", shows you how to read data from and write it to a variety of data sources.
- Chapter 8, "Ranking Algorithms", presents two important ranking algorithms, PageRank (used in search engines) and rank product (used in gene analysis).

Part III, "Data Design Patterns"
: The final four chapters cover practical data design patterns, which are presented in an informal way with solid examples:

- Chapter 9, "Classic Data Design Patterns", introduces a selection of fundamental data design patterns, or reusable solutions, that are commonly used to solve a variety of data problems. Examples include Input-Map-Output and Input-Filter-Output.
- Chapter 10, "Practical Data Design Patterns", introduces common and practical data design patterns, for tasks such as combining, summarizing, filtering, and organizing data. These patterns are presented informally, with practical examples.
- Chapter 11, "Join Design Patterns", presents simple patterns for joining two or more datasets; some performance criteria are discussed to improve the efficiency of join algorithms.
- Chapter 12, "Feature Engineering in PySpark", presents the most common feature engineering techniques used in developing machine learning algorithms.

Bonus Chapters
: Since I did not want to make this book too bulky, I have included additional material on topics such as TF-IDF, correlation, and k-mers as bonus chapters in the book's GitHub repository (*https://github.com/mahmoudparsian/data-algorithms-with-spark*).

Conventions Used in This Book

The following typographical conventions are used in this book:

Italic
: Indicates new terms, URLs, email addresses, filenames, and file extensions.

`Constant width`
: Used for program listings, as well as within paragraphs to refer to program elements such as variable or function names, databases, data types, environment variables, statements, and keywords.

`Constant width bold`
: Shows commands or other text that should be typed literally by the user.

`Constant width italic`
: Shows text that should be replaced with user-supplied values or by values determined by context.

This element signifies a tip or suggestion.

This element signifies a general note.

This element indicates a warning or caution.

Using Code Examples

Supplemental material (code examples, exercises, etc.) is available for download at *https://github.com/mahmoudparsian/data-algorithms-with-spark*.

If you have a technical question or a problem using the code examples, please send email to *mahmoud.parsian@yahoo.com*.

This book is here to help you get your job done. In general, if example code is offered with this book, you may use it in your programs and documentation. You do not need to contact us for permission unless you're reproducing a significant portion of the code. For example, writing a program that uses several chunks of code from this book does not require permission. Selling or distributing examples from O'Reilly books does require permission. Answering a question by citing this book and quoting example code does not require permission. Incorporating a significant amount of example code from this book into your product's documentation does require permission.

We appreciate, but generally do not require, attribution. An attribution usually includes the title, author, publisher, and ISBN. For example: "*Data Algorithms with Spark* by Mahmoud Parsian (O'Reilly). Copyright 2022 Mahmoud Parsian, 978-1-492-08238-5."

If you feel your use of code examples falls outside fair use or the permission given above, feel free to contact us at *permissions@oreilly.com*.

O'Reilly Online Learning

O'REILLY®

For more than 40 years, *O'Reilly Media* has provided technology and business training, knowledge, and insight to help companies succeed.

Our unique network of experts and innovators share their knowledge and expertise through books, articles, conferences, and our online learning platform. O'Reilly's online learning platform gives you on-demand access to live training courses, in-depth learning paths, interactive coding environments, and a vast collection of text and video from O'Reilly and 200+ other publishers. For more information, please visit *http://oreilly.com*.

How to Contact Us

Please address comments and questions concerning this book to the publisher:

O'Reilly Media, Inc.
1005 Gravenstein Highway North
Sebastopol, CA 95472
800-998-9938 (in the United States or Canada)
707-829-0515 (international or local)
707-829-0104 (fax)

We have a web page for this book, where we list errata, examples, and any additional information. You can access this page at *https://oreil.ly/data-algorithms-with-spark*.

Email *bookquestions@oreilly.com* to comment or ask technical questions about this book.

For more information about our books, courses, conferences, and news, see our website at *http://www.oreilly.com*.

Find us on LinkedIn: *https://linkedin.com/company/oreilly-media*

Follow us on Twitter: *http://twitter.com/oreillymedia*

Watch us on YouTube: *http://youtube.com/oreillymedia*

Acknowledgments

This idea for this book was initiated by Jess Haberman (Senior Acquisitions Editor at O'Reilly Media). I am so grateful to her for reaching out—thank you very much, Jess! I am indebted to Melissa Potter (Content Development Editor at O'Reilly Media), who has worked tirelessly with me since the start of this project and has helped me so much to make it a better book. Thank you very much, Melissa! Thank you so much to the copyeditor, Rachel Head, who has done a tremendous job in editing the whole book; if you can read and understand this book, then it is because of Rachel. I want to say a big thank you to Christopher Faucher (the Production Editor) for doing a great job and making sure that deadlines were met and everything is in its proper place. Taking a book through production is not an easy job at all, but Christopher has done a superb job.

Thank you so much to technical reviewers Parviz Deyhim and Benjamin Muskalla for their very careful review of my book, and for the comments, corrections, and suggestions that ensued. I would also like to say a special thank you to my PhD advisor and dear friend, Dr. Ramachandran Krishnaswamy, from whom I have learned so much; I will cherish my friendship with him forever.

To add to the PySpark solutions I have provided for all chapters on GitHub, Deepak Kumar and Biman Mandal have provided Scala solutions, which is a great resource for readers. Thank you very much, Deepak and Biman. Last but not least, I want to give a huge, sparkling thank you to Dr. Matei Zaharia (creator of Apache Spark) for writing a foreword to my book; I am honored and humbled for his kind words.

PART I

Fundamentals

CHAPTER 1

Introduction to Spark and PySpark

Spark is a powerful analytics engine for large-scale data processing that aims at speed, ease of use, and extensibility for big data applications. It's a proven and widely adopted technology used by many companies that handle big data every day. Though Spark's "native" language is Scala (most of Spark is developed in Scala), it also provides high-level APIs in Java, Python, and R.

In this book we'll be using Python via PySpark, an API that exposes the Spark programming model to Python. With Python being the most accessible programming language and Spark's powerful and expressive API, PySpark's simplicity makes it the best choice for us. PySpark is an interface for Spark in the Python programming language that provides the following two important features:

- It allows us to write Spark applications using Python APIs.
- It provides the *PySpark shell* for interactively analyzing data in a distributed environment.

The purpose of this chapter is to introduce PySpark as the main component of the Spark ecosystem and show you that it can be effectively used for big data tasks such as ETL operations, indexing billions of documents, ingesting millions of genomes, machine learning, graph data analysis, DNA data analysis, and much more. I'll start by reviewing the Spark and PySpark architectures, and provide examples to show the expressive power of PySpark. I will present an overview of Spark's core functions (transformations and actions) and concepts so that you are empowered to start using Spark and PySpark right away. Spark's main data abstractions are resilient distributed datasets (RDDs), DataFrames, and Datasets. As you'll see, you can represent your data (stored as Hadoop files, Amazon S3 objects, Linux files, collection data structures, relational database tables, and more) in any combinations of RDDs and DataFrames.

Once your data is represented as a Spark data abstraction, you can apply transformations on it and create new data abstractions until the data is in the final form that you're looking for. Spark's transformations (such as `map()` and `reduceByKey()`) can be used to convert your data from one form to another until you get your desired result. I will explain these data abstractions shortly, but first, let's dig a little deeper into why Spark is the best choice for data analytics.

> **Source Code**
>
> Complete programs for this chapter are available in the book's GitHub repository (*https://oreil.ly/Aurk4*).

Why Spark for Data Analytics

Spark is a powerful analytics engine that can be used for large-scale data processing. The most important reasons for using Spark are:

- Spark is simple, powerful, and fast.
- Spark is free and open source.
- Spark runs everywhere (Hadoop, Mesos, Kubernetes, standalone, or in the cloud).
- Spark can read/write data from/to any data source (Amazon S3, Hadoop HDFS, relational databases, etc.).
- Spark can be integrated with almost any data application.
- Spark can read/write data in row-based (such as Avro) and column-based (such as Parquet and ORC) formats.
- Spark has a rich but simple set of APIs for all kinds of ETL processes.

In the past five years Spark has progressed in such a way that I believe it can be used to solve any big data problem. This is supported by the fact that all big data companies, such as Facebook, Illumina, IBM, and Google, use Spark every day in production systems.

Spark is one of the best choices for large-scale data processing and for solving MapReduce problems and beyond, as it unlocks the power of data by handling big data with powerful APIs and speed. Using MapReduce/Hadoop to solve big data problems is complex, and you have to write a ton of low-level code to solve even primitive problems—this is where the power and simplicity of Spark comes in. Apache Spark (*http://spark.apache.org*) is considerably faster than Apache Hadoop (*http://hadoop.apache.org*) because it uses in-memory caching and optimized execution for fast performance, and it supports general batch processing, streaming analytics, machine learning, graph algorithms, and SQL queries.

For PySpark, Spark has two fundamental data abstractions: the RDD and the DataFrame. I will teach you how to read your data and represent it as an RDD (a set of elements of the same type) or a DataFrame (a table of rows with named columns); this allows you to impose a structure onto a distributed collection of data, permitting higher-level abstraction. Once your data is represented as an RDD or a DataFrame, you may apply transformation functions (such as mappers, filters, and reducers) on it to transform your data into the desired form. I'll present many Spark transformations that you can use for ETL processes, analysis, and data-intensive computations.

Some simple RDD transformations are represented in Figure 1-1.

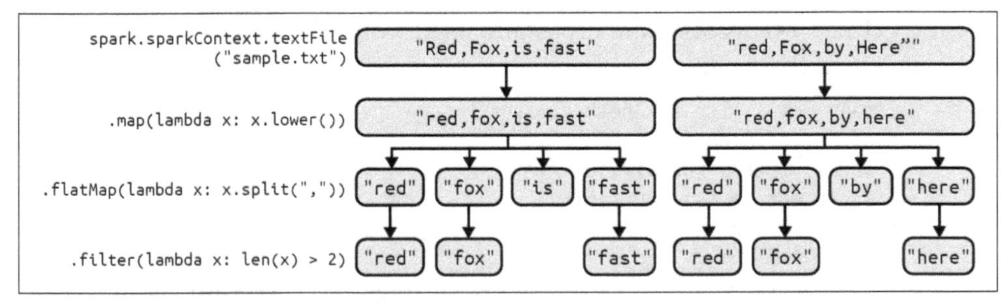

Figure 1-1. Simple RDD transformations

This figure shows the following transformations:

1. First we read our input data (represented as a text file, *sample.txt*—here, I only show the first two rows/records of input data) with an instance of `SparkSession`, which is the entry point to programming Spark. The `SparkSession` instance is represented as a `spark` object. Reading input creates a new RDD as an `RDD[String]`: each input record is converted to an RDD element of the type `String` (if your input path has *N* records, then the number of RDD elements is *N*). This is accomplished by the following code:

    ```
    # Create an instance of SparkSession
    spark = SparkSession.builder.getOrCreate()
    # Create an RDD[String], which represents all input
    # records; each record becomes an RDD element
    records = spark.sparkContext.textFile("sample.txt")
    ```

2. Next, we convert all characters to lowercase letters. This is accomplished by the `map()` transformation, which is a 1-to-1 transformation:

    ```
    # Convert each element of the RDD to lowercase
    # x denotes a single element of the RDD
    # records: source RDD[String]
    ```

```
# records_lowercase: target RDD[String]
records_lowercase = records.map(lambda x: x.lower())
```

3. Then, we use a `flatMap()` transformation, which is a 1-to-many transformation, to convert each element (representing a single record) into a sequence of target elements (each representing a word). The `flatMap()` transformation returns a new RDD by first applying a function (here, `split(",")`) to all elements of the source RDD and then flattening the results:

```
# Split each record into a list of words
# records_lowercase: source RDD[String]
# words: target RDD[String]
words = records_lowercase.flatMap(lambda x: x.split(","))
```

4. Finally, we drop word elements with a length less than or equal to 2. The following `filter()` transformation drops unwanted words, keeping only those with a length greater than 2:

```
# Keep words with a length greater than 2
# x denotes a word
# words: source RDD[String]
# filtered: target RDD[String]
filtered = words.filter(lambda x: len(x) > 2)
```

As you can observe, Spark transformations are high-level, powerful, and simple. Spark is by nature distributed and parallel: your input data is partitioned and can be processed by transformations (such as mappers, filters, and reducers) in parallel in a cluster environment. In a nutshell, to solve a data analytics problem in PySpark, you read data and represent it as an RDD or DataFrame (depending on the nature of the data format), then write a set of transformations to convert your data into the desired output. Spark automatically partitions your DataFrames and RDDs and distributes the partitions across different cluster nodes. Partitions are the basic units of parallelism in Spark. Parallelism is what allows developers to perform tasks on hundreds of computer servers in a cluster in parallel and independently. A partition in Spark is a chunk (a logical division) of data stored on a node in the cluster. DataFrames and RDDs are collections of partitions. Spark has a default data partitioner for RDDs and DataFrames, but you may override that partitioning with your own custom programming.

Next, let's dive a little deeper into Spark's ecosystem and architecture.

The Spark Ecosystem

Spark's ecosystem is presented in Figure 1-2. It has three main components:

Environments
: Spark can run anywhere and integrates well with other environments.

Applications
: Spark integrates well with a variety of big data platforms and applications.

Data sources
: Spark can read and write data from and to many data sources.

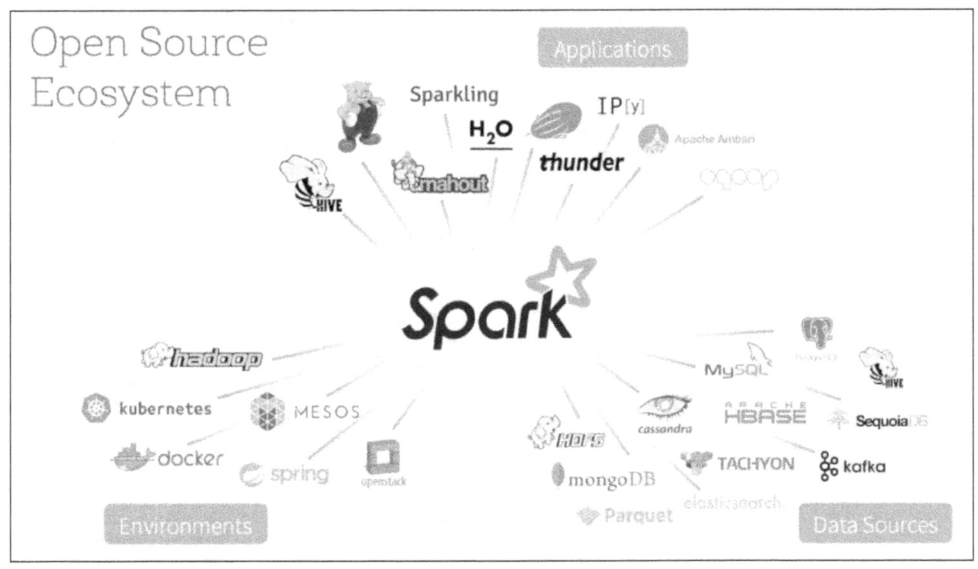

Figure 1-2. The Spark ecosystem (source: Databricks)

Spark's expansive ecosystem makes PySpark a great tool for ETL, data analysis, and many other tasks. With PySpark, you can read data from many different data sources (the Linux filesystem, Amazon S3, the Hadoop Distributed File System, relational tables, MongoDB, Elasticsearch, Parquet files, etc.) and represent it as a Spark data abstraction, such as RDDs or DataFrames. Once your data is in that form, you can use a series of simple and powerful Spark transformations to transform the data into the desired shape and format. For example, you may use the `filter()` transformation to drop unwanted records, use `groupByKey()` to group your data by your desired key, and finally use the `mapValues()` transformation to perform final aggregation (such as finding average, median, and standard deviation of numbers) on the grouped data. All of these transformations are very possible by using the simple but powerful PySpark API.

Spark Architecture

When you have small data, it is possible to analyze it with a single computer in a reasonable amount of time. When you have large volumes of data, using a single computer to analyze and process that data (and store it) might be prohibitively slow, or even impossible. This is why we want to use Spark.

Spark has a core library and a set of built-in libraries (SQL, GraphX, Streaming, MLlib), as shown in Figure 1-3. As you can see, through its DataSource API, Spark can interact with many data sources, such as Hadoop, HBase, Amazon S3, Elasticsearch, and MySQL, to mention a few.

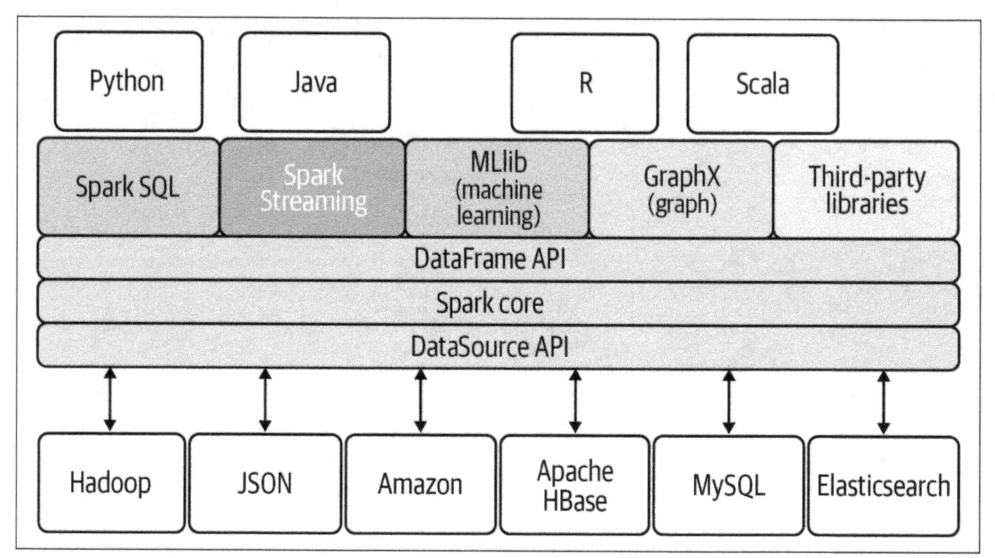

Figure 1-3. Spark libraries

This figure shows the real power of Spark: you can use several different languages to write your Spark applications, then use rich libraries to solve assorted big data problems. Meanwhile, you can read/write data from a variety of data sources.

Key Terms

To understand Spark's architecture, you'll need to understand a few key terms:

`SparkSession`
: The `SparkSession` class, defined in the `pyspark.sql` package, is the entry point to programming Spark with the Dataset and DataFrame APIs. In order to do anything useful with a Spark cluster, you first need to create an instance of this class, which gives you access to an instance of `SparkContext`.

PySpark (*https://oreil.ly/fSTe9*) has a comprehensive API (comprised of packages, modules, classes, and methods) to access the Spark API. It is important to note that all Spark APIs, packages, modules, classes, and methods discussed in this book are PySpark-specific. For example, when I refer to the `SparkContext` class I am referring to the `pyspark.SparkContext` Python class, defined in the `pyspark` package, and when I refer to the `SparkSession` class, I am referring to the `pyspark.sql.SparkSession` Python class, defined in the `pyspark.sql` module.

`SparkContext`
: The `SparkContext` class, defined in the `pyspark` package, is the main entry point for Spark functionality. A `SparkContext` holds a connection to the Spark cluster manager and can be used to create RDDs and broadcast variables in the cluster. When you create an instance of `SparkSession`, the `SparkContext` becomes available inside your session as an attribute, `SparkSession.sparkContext`.

Driver
: All Spark applications (including the PySpark shell and standalone Python programs) run as independent sets of processes. These processes are coordinated by a `SparkContext` in a driver program. To submit a standalone Python program to Spark, you need to write a driver program with the PySpark API (or Java or Scala). This program is in charge of the process of running the `main()` function of the application and creating the `SparkContext`. It can also be used to create RDDs and DataFrames.

Worker
: In a Spark cluster environment, there are two types of nodes: one (or two, for high availability) master and a set of workers. A worker is any node that can run programs in the cluster. If a process is launched for an application, then this application acquires executors at worker nodes, which are responsible for executing Spark tasks.

Cluster manager
: The "master" node is known as the cluster manager. The main function of this node is to manage the cluster environment and the servers that Spark will leverage to execute tasks. The cluster manager allocates resources to each application. Spark supports five types of cluster managers, depending on where it's running:

1. Standalone (Spark's own built-in clustered environment)
2. Mesos (*http://mesos.apache.org*) (a distributed systems kernel)
3. Hadoop YARN (*https://oreil.ly/SICSG*)

4. Kubernetes (*https://kubernetes.io*)
5. Amazon EC2 (*https://aws.amazon.com/ec2*)

While use of master/worker terminology is outmoded and being retired in many software contexts, it is still part of the functionality of Apache Spark, which is why I use this terminology in this book.

Spark architecture in a nutshell

A high-level view of the Spark architecture is presented in Figure 1-4. Informally, a Spark cluster is comprised of a master node (the "cluster manager"), which is responsible for managing Spark applications, and a set of "worker" (executor) nodes, which are responsible for executing tasks submitted by the Spark applications (your applications, which you want to run on the Spark cluster).

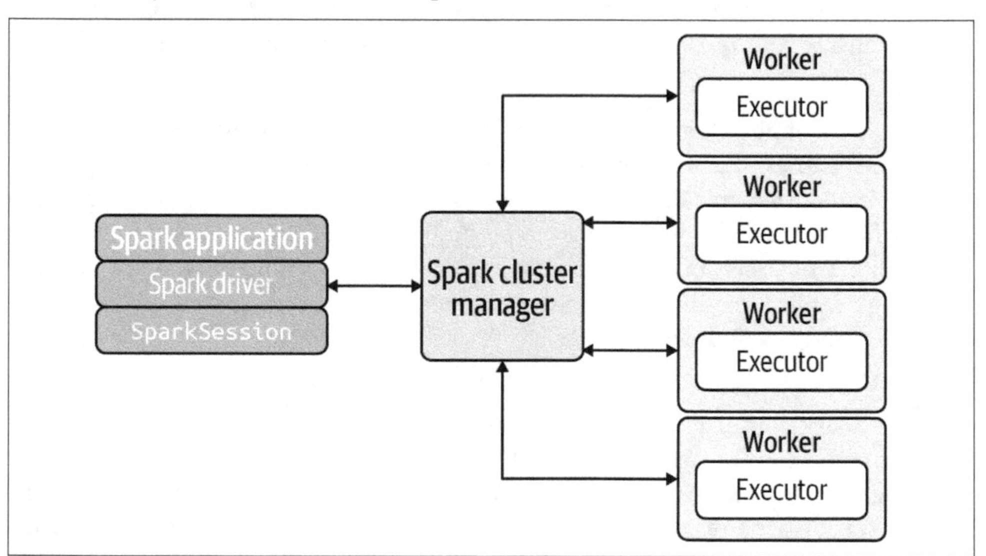

Figure 1-4. Spark architecture

Depending on the environment Spark is running in, the cluster manager managing this cluster of servers will be either Spark's standalone cluster manager, Kubernetes, Hadoop YARN, or Mesos. When the Spark cluster is running, you can submit Spark applications to the cluster manager, which will grant resources to your application so that you can complete your data analysis.

Your cluster may have one, tens, hundreds, or even thousands of worker nodes, depending on the needs of your business and your project requirements. You can run Spark on a standalone server such as a MacBook, Linux, or Windows PC, but typically for production environments Spark is run on cluster of Linux servers. To run a Spark program, you need to have access to a Spark cluster and have a driver program, which declares the transformations and actions on RDDs of data and submits such requests to the cluster manager. In this book, all driver programs will be in PySpark.

When you start a PySpark shell (by executing `<spark-installed-dir>/bin/pyspark`), you automatically get two variables/objects defined:

`spark`
: An instance of `SparkSession`, which is ideal for creating DataFrames

`sc`
: An instance of `SparkContext`, which is ideal for creating RDDs

If you write a self-contained PySpark application (a Python driver, which uses the PySpark API), then you have to explicitly create an instance of `SparkSession` yourself. A `SparkSession` can be used to:

- Create DataFrames
- Register DataFrames as tables
- Execute SQL over tables and cache tables
- Read/write text, CSV, JSON, Parquet, and other file formats
- Read/write relational database tables

PySpark defines `SparkSession` as:

```
pyspark.sql.SparkSession (Python class, in pyspark.sql module)
class pyspark.sql.SparkSession(sparkContext,jsparkSession=None)

SparkSession: the entry point to programming Spark with the RDD
and DataFrame API.
```

To create a `SparkSession` in Python, use the builder pattern shown here:

```
# import required Spark class
from pyspark.sql import SparkSession ❶

# create an instance of SparkSession as spark
spark = SparkSession.builder \ ❷
  .master("local") \
  .appName("my-application-name") \
  .config("spark.some.config.option", "some-value") \ ❸
  .getOrCreate() ❹

# to debug the SparkSession
print(spark.version) ❺
```

```
# create a reference to SparkContext as sc
# SparkContext is used to create new RDDs
sc = spark.sparkContext ❻

# to debug the SparkContext
print(sc)
```

❶ Imports the `SparkSession` class from the `pyspark.sql` module.

❷ Provides access to the Builder API used to construct `SparkSession` instances.

❸ Sets a `config` option. Options set using this method are automatically propagated to both `SparkConf` and the `SparkSession`'s own configuration. When creating a `SparkSession` object, you can define any number of `config(<key>, <value>)` options.

❹ Gets an existing `SparkSession` or, if there isn't one, creates a new one based on the options set here.

❺ For debugging purposes only.

❻ A `SparkContext` can be referenced from an instance of `SparkSession`.

PySpark defines `SparkContext` as:

```
class pyspark.SparkContext(master=None, appName=None, ...)

SparkContext: the main entry point for Spark functionality.
A SparkContext represents the connection to a Spark cluster,
and can be used to create RDD (the main data abstraction for
Spark) and broadcast variables (such as collections and data
structures) on that cluster.
```

`SparkContext` is the main entry point for Spark functionality. A shell (such as the PySpark shell) or PySpark driver program cannot create more than one instance of `SparkContext`. A `SparkContext` represents the connection to a Spark cluster, and can be used to create new RDDs and broadcast variables (shared data structures and collections—kind of read-only global variables) on that cluster. Figure 1-5 shows how a `SparkContext` can be used to create a new RDD from an input text file (labeled `records_rdd`) and then transform it into another RDD (labeled `words_rdd`) using the `flatMap()` transformation. As you can observe, `RDD.flatMap(f)` returns a new RDD by first applying a function (*f*) to all elements of the source RDD, and then flattening the results.

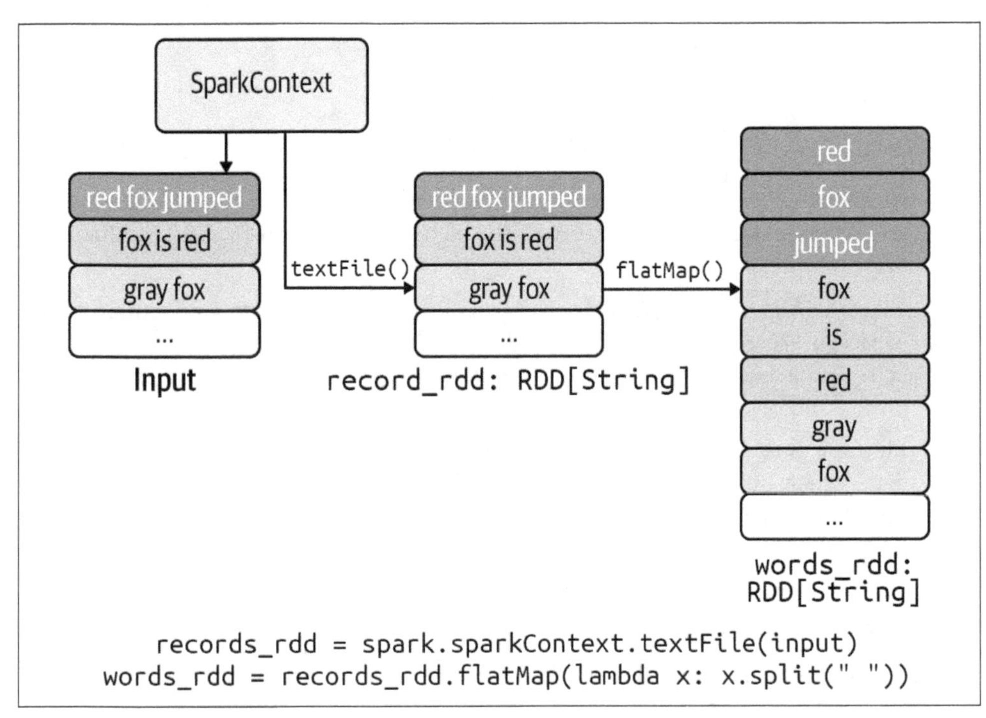

Figure 1-5. Creation of RDDs by `SparkContext`

To create `SparkSession` and `SparkContext` objects, use the following pattern:

```
# create an instance of SparkSession
spark_session = SparkSession.builder.getOrCreate()

# use the SparkSession to access the SparkContext
spark_context = spark_session.sparkContext
```

If you will be working only with RDDs, you can create an instance of `SparkContext` as follows:

```
from pyspark import SparkContext
spark_context = SparkContext("local", "myapp");
```

Spark Usage

Here are some examples of how big companies use Spark:

- Facebook (*https://oreil.ly/OUpG3*) processes 60 TB of data on a daily basis. Spark and MapReduce are at the heart of the algorithms used to process production data.
- Viacom (*https://oreil.ly/GnLc7*), with its 170 cable, broadcast, and online networks in around 160 countries, is transforming itself into a data-driven enterprise, collecting and analyzing petabytes of network data to increase viewer loyalty and revenue.
- Illumina (*https://www.illumina.com*) ingests thousands of genomes (this is big data, which cannot fit on or be processed by one server) using Spark, PySpark, MapReduce, and distributed algorithms.
- IBM uses Spark, MapReduce, and distributed algorithms on a daily basis to scale out its computations and operations.

Now that you know the basics of Spark, let's dive a little deeper into PySpark.

The Power of PySpark

PySpark is a Python API for Apache Spark, designed to support collaboration between Spark and the Python programming language. Most data scientists already know Python, and PySpark makes it easy for them to write short, concise code for distributed computing using Spark. In a nutshell, it's an all-in-one ecosystem that can handle complex data requirements with its support for RDDs, DataFrames, GraphFrames, MLlib, SQL, and more.

I'll show you the amazing power of PySpark with a simple example. Suppose we have lots of records containing data on URL visits by users (collected by a search engine from many web servers) in the following format:

```
<url_address><,><frequency>
```

Here are a few examples of what these records look like:

```
http://mapreduce4hackers.com,19779
http://mapreduce4hackers.com,31230
http://mapreduce4hackers.com,15708
...
https://www.illumina.com,87000
https://www.illumina.com,58086
...
```

Let's assume we want to find the average, median, and standard deviation of the visit numbers per key (i.e., `url_address`). Another requirement is that we want to drop any records with a length less than 5 (as these may be malformed URLs). It is easy to express an elegant solution for this in PySpark, as Figure 1-6 illustrates.

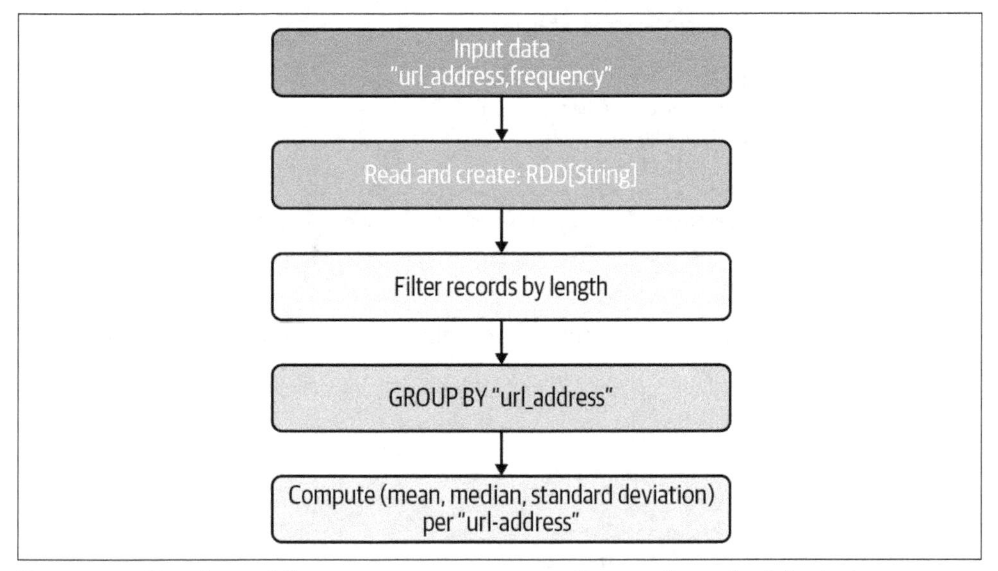

Figure 1-6. Simple workflow to compute mean, median, and standard deviation

First, let's create some basic Python functions that will help us in solving our simple problem. The first function, `create_pair()`, accepts a single record of the form `<url_address><,><frequency>` and returns a (key, value) pair (which will enable us to do a `GROUP BY` on the key field later), where the key is a `url_address` and the value is the associated `frequency`:

```
# Create a pair of (url_address, frequency)
# where url_address is a key and frequency is a value
# record denotes a single element of RDD[String]
# record: <url_address><,><frequency>
def create_pair(record): ❶
    tokens = record.split(',') ❷
    url_address = tokens[0]
    frequency = tokens[1]
    return (url_address, frequency) ❸
#end-def
```

❶ Accept a record of the form `<url_address><,><frequency>`.

❷ Tokenize the input record, using the `url_address` as a key (`tokens[0]`) and the `frequency` as a value (`tokens[1]`).

❸ Return a pair of (url_address, frequency).

The next function, compute_stats(), accepts a list of frequencies (as numbers) and computes three values, the average, median, and standard deviation:

```
# Compute average, median, and standard
# deviation for a given set of numbers
import statistics ❶
# frequencies = [number1, number2, ...]
def compute_stats(frequencies): ❷
       average = statistics.mean(frequencies) ❸
       median = statistics.median(frequencies) ❹
       standard_deviation = statistics.stdev(frequencies) ❺
       return (average, median, standard_deviation) ❻
#end-def
```

❶ This module provides functions for calculating mathematical statistics of numeric data.

❷ Accept a list of frequencies.

❸ Compute the average of the frequencies.

❹ Compute the median of the frequencies.

❺ Compute the standard deviation of the frequencies.

❻ Return the result as a triplet.

Next, I'll show you the amazing power of PySpark in just few lines of code, using Spark transformations and our custom Python functions:

```
# input_path = "s3://<bucket>/key"
input_path = "/tmp/myinput.txt"
results = spark ❶
        .sparkContext ❷
        .textFile(input_path) ❸
        .filter(lambda record: len(record) > 5) ❹
        .map(create_pair) ❺
        .groupByKey() ❻
        .mapValues(compute_stats) ❼
```

❶ spark denotes an instance of SparkSession, the entry point to programming Spark.

❷ sparkContext (an attribute of SparkSession) is the main entry point for Spark functionality.

❸ Read data as a distributed set of `String` records (creates an `RDD[String]`).

❹ Drop records with a length less than or equal to 5 (keep records with a length greater than 5).

❺ Create `(url_address, frequency)` pairs from the input records.

❻ Group the data by keys—each key (a `url_address`) will be associated with a list of frequencies.

❼ Apply the `compute_stats()` function to the list of frequencies.

The result will be a set of (key, value) pairs of the form:

```
(url_address, (average, median, standard_deviation))
```

where `url-address` is a key and `(average, median, standard_deviation)` is a value.

The most important thing about Spark is that it maximizes concurrency of functions and operations by means of partitioning data. Consider an example:

If your input data has 600 billion rows and you are using a cluster of 10 nodes, your input data will be partitioned into *N* (> 1) chunks, which are processed independently and in parallel. If *N*=`20,000` (the number of chunks or partitions), then each chunk will have about 30 million records/elements (600,000,000,000 / 20,000 = 30,000,000). If you have a big cluster, then all 20,000 chunks might be processed in one shot. If you have a smaller cluster, it may be that only every 100 chunks can be processed independently and in parallel. This process will continue until all 20,000 chunks are processed.

PySpark Architecture

PySpark is built on top of Spark's Java API. Data is processed in Python and cached/shuffled in the Java Virtual Machine, or JVM (I will cover the concept of shuffling in Chapter 2). A high-level view of PySpark's architecture is presented in Figure 1-7.

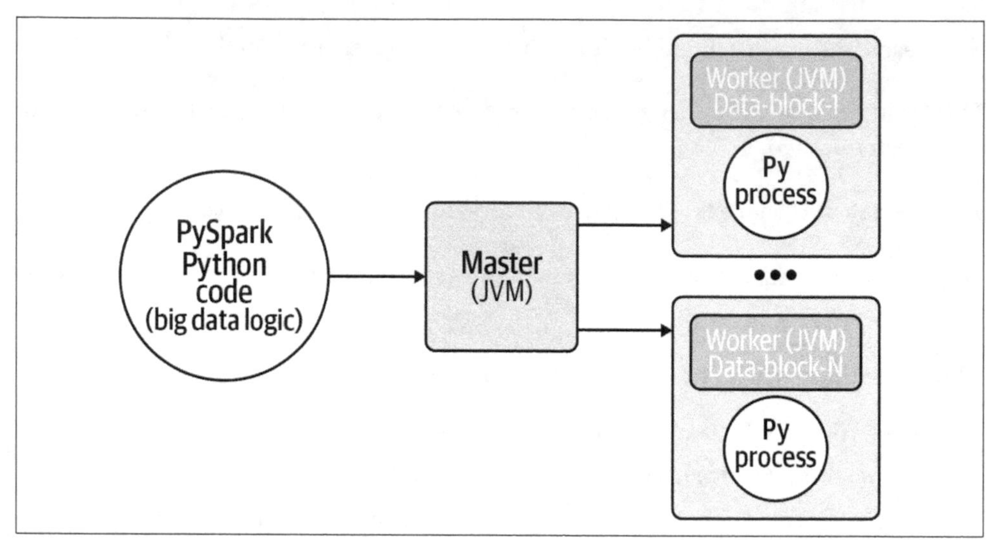

Figure 1-7. PySpark architecture

And PySpark's data flow is illustrated in Figure 1-8.

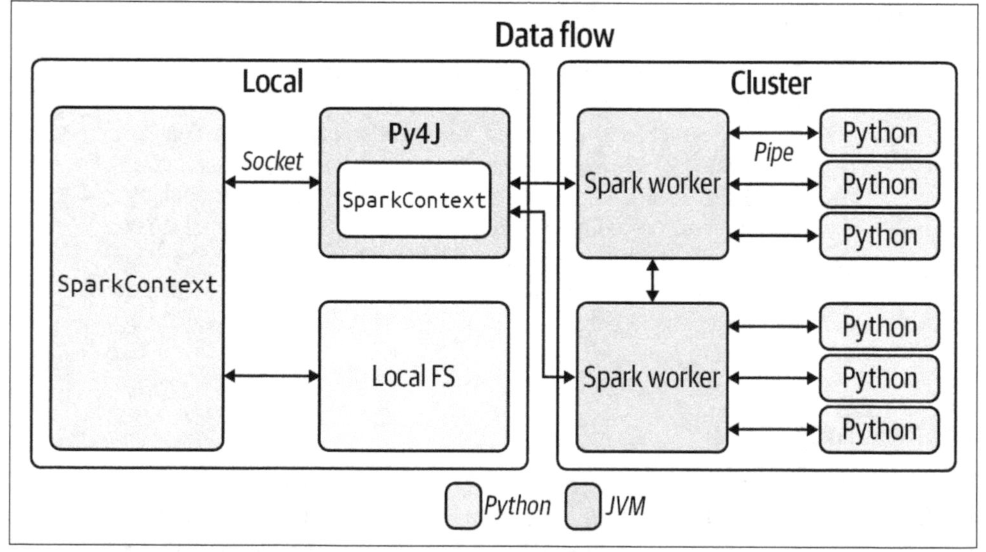

Figure 1-8. PySpark data flow

In the Python driver program (your Spark application in Python), the `SparkContext` uses Py4J (*https://www.py4j.org*) to launch a JVM, creating a `JavaSparkContext`. Py4J is only used in the driver for local communication between the Python and Java `SparkContext` objects; large data transfers are performed through a different mechanism. RDD transformations in Python are mapped to transformations on `PythonRDD` objects in Java. On remote worker machines, `PythonRDD` objects launch Python subprocesses and communicate with them using pipes, sending the user's code and the data to be processed.

Py4J enables Python programs running in a Python interpreter to dynamically access Java objects in a JVM. Methods are called as if the Java objects resided in the Python interpreter, and Java collections can be accessed through standard Python collection methods. Py4J also enables Java programs to call back Python objects.

Spark Data Abstractions

To manipulate data in the Python programming language, you use integers, strings, lists, and dictionaries. To manipulate and analyze data in Spark, you have to represent it as a Spark dataset. Spark supports three types of dataset abstractions:

- RDD (resilient distributed dataset):
  - Low-level API
  - Denoted by `RDD[T]` (each element has type `T`)
- DataFrame (similar to relational tables):
  - High-level API
  - Denoted by `Table(column_name_1, column_name_2, ...)`
- Dataset (similar to relational tables):
  - High-level API (not available in PySpark)

The Dataset data abstraction is used in strongly typed languages such as Java and is not supported in PySpark. RDDs and DataFrames will be discussed in detail in the following chapters, but I'll give a brief introduction here.

RDD Examples

Essentially, an RDD represents your data as a collection of elements. It's an immutable set of distributed elements of type `T`, denoted as `RDD[T]`.

Table 1-1 shows examples of three simple types of RDDs:

`RDD[Integer]`
: Each element is an `Integer`.

`RDD[String]`
: Each element is a `String`.

`RDD[(String, Integer)]`
: Each element is a pair of `(String, Integer)`.

Table 1-1. Simple RDDs

RDD[Integer]	RDD[String]	RDD[(String, Integer)]
`2`	`"abc"`	`('A', 4)`
`-730`	`"fox is red"`	`('B', 7)`
`320`	`"Python is cool"`	`('ZZ', 9)`
...	...	...

Table 1-2 is an example of a complex RDD. Each element is a (key, value) pair, where the key is a `String` and the value is a triplet of `(Integer, Integer, Double)`.

Table 1-2. Complex RDD

`RDD[(String, (Integer, Integer, Double))]`
`("cat", (20, 40, 1.8))`
`("cat", (30, 10, 3.9))`
`("lion king", (27, 32, 4.5))`
`("python is fun", (2, 3, 0.6))`
...

Spark RDD Operations

Spark RDDs are read-only, immutable, and distributed. Once created, they cannot be altered: you cannot add records, delete records, or update records in an RDD. However, they can be transformed. RDDs support two types of operations: transformations, which transform the source RDD(s) into one or more new RDDs, and actions, which transform the source RDD(s) into a non-RDD object such as a dictionary or array. The relationship between RDDs, transformations, and actions is illustrated in Figure 1-9.

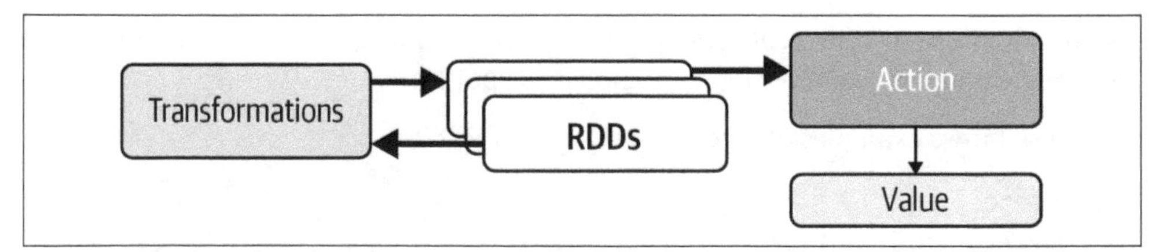

Figure 1-9. RDDs, transformations, and actions

We'll go into much more detail on Spark's transformations in the following chapters, with working examples to help you understand them, but I'll provide a brief introduction here.

Transformations

A transformation in Spark is a function that takes an existing RDD (the source RDD), applies a transformation to it, and creates a new RDD (the target RDD). Examples include: `map()`, `flatMap()`, `groupByKey()`, `reduceByKey()`, and `filter()`.

Informally, we can express a transformation as:

```
transformation: source_RDD[V] --> target_RDD[T] ❶
```

❶ Transform `source_RDD` of type `V` into `target_RDD` of type `T`.

RDDs are not evaluated until an action is performed on them: this means that transformations are lazily evaluated. If an RDD fails during a transformation, the data lineage of transformations rebuilds the RDD.

Most Spark transformations create a single RDD, but it is also possible for them to create multiple target RDDs. The target RDD(s) can be smaller, larger, or the same size as the source RDD.

The following example presents a sequence of transformations:

```
tuples = [('A', 7), ('A', 8), ('A', -4),
          ('B', 3), ('B', 9), ('B', -1),
          ('C', 1), ('C', 5)]
rdd = spark.sparkContext.parallelize(tuples)

# drop negative values
positives = rdd.filter(lambda x: x[1] > 0)
positives.collect()
[('A', 7), ('A', 8), ('B', 3), ('B', 9), ('C', 1), ('C', 5)]

# find sum and average per key using groupByKey()
sum_and_avg = positives.groupByKey()
    .mapValues(lambda v: (sum(v), float(sum(v))/len(v)))

# find sum and average per key using reduceByKey()
# 1. create (sum, count) per key
sum_count = positives.mapValues(lambda v: (v, 1))
# 2. aggregate (sum, count) per key
sum_count_agg = sum_count.reduceByKey(lambda x, y:
     (x[0]+y[0], x[1]+y[1]))
# 3. finalize sum and average per key
sum_and_avg = sum_count_agg.mapValues(
    lambda v: (v[0], float(v[0])/v[1]))
```

The `groupByKey()` transformation groups the values for each key in the RDD into a single sequence, similar to a SQL `GROUP BY` statement. This transformation can cause out of memory (OOM) errors as data is sent over the network of Spark servers and collected on the reducer/workers when the number of values per key is in the thousands or millions.

With the `reduceByKey()` transformation, however, data is combined in each partition, so there is only one output for each key in each partition to send over the network of Spark servers. This makes it more scalable than `groupByKey()`. `reduceByKey()` merges the values for each key using an associative and commutative reduce function. It combines all the values (per key) into another value with the exact same data type (this is a limitation, which can be overcome by using the `combineByKey()` transformation). Overall, the `reduceByKey()` is more scaleable than the `groupByKey()`. We'll talk more about these issues in Chapter 4.

Actions

Spark actions are RDD operations or functions that produce non-RDD values. Informally, we can express an action as:

```
action: RDD => non-RDD value
```

Actions may trigger the evaluation of RDDs (which, you'll recall, are evaluated lazily). However, the output of an action is a tangible value: a saved file, a value such as an integer, a count of elements, a list of values, a dictionary, and so on.

The following are examples of actions:

`reduce()`
: Applies a function to deliver a single value, such as adding values for a given `RDD[Integer]`

`collect()`
: Converts an `RDD[T]` into a list of type `T`

`count()`
: Finds the number of elements in a given RDD

`saveAsTextFile()`
: Saves RDD elements to a disk

`saveAsMap()`
: Saves `RDD[(K, V)]` elements to a disk as a `dict[K, V]`

Don't collect() on Large RDDs

In this book, I have often used the `RDD.collect()` action for testing, debugging, educational, and demonstration purposes. However, as a general rule you should avoid using this on the production servers unless you really have a requirement for it.

When a `collect()` operation is called on an RDD, the entire RDD is copied to the driver program. If the dataset is too large to fit in memory, a memory exception will be thrown. If this is a risk, you should use the `take()` or `takeSample()` actions instead of `collect()`. For example `RDD.take(`*N*`)` returns the first *N* elements of the RDD and `DataFrame.take(`*N*`)` returns the first *N* rows of the DataFrame as a list of `Row` objects.

To summarize, `RDD.collect()` returns a list that contains all of the elements in this RDD. According to the Spark documentation, "this method should only be used if the resulting array is expected to be small, as all the data is loaded into the driver's memory." Using `collect()` on a large RDD might cause an OOM exception.

If you need to manipulate all of your RDD elements, rather than using `collect()`, consider whether you can use transformations such as `map()`, `filter()`, `flatMap()`, or `foreach(`*func*`)`.

DataFrame Examples

Similar to an RDD, a DataFrame in Spark is an immutable distributed collection of data. But unlike in an RDD, the data is organized into named columns, like a table in a relational database. This is meant to make processing of large datasets easier. DataFrames allow programmers to impose a structure onto a distributed collection of data, allowing higher-level abstraction. They also make the processing of CSV and JSON files much easier than with RDDs.

The following DataFrame example has three columns:

```
DataFrame[name, age, salary]
name: String, age: Integer, salary: Integer

+-----+----+---------+
| name| age|   salary|
+-----+----+---------+
|  bob|  33|    45000|
| jeff|  44|    78000|
| mary|  40|    67000|
|  ...| ...|      ...|
+-----+----+---------+
```

A DataFrame can be created from many different sources, such as Hive tables, Structured Data Files (SDF), external databases, or existing RDDs. The DataFrames API was designed for modern big data and data science applications, taking inspiration from DataFrames in R and pandas in Python. As we will see in later chapters, we can execute SQL queries against DataFrames.

Spark SQL comes with an extensive set of powerful DataFrame operations that includes:

- Aggregate functions (min, max, sum, average, etc.)
- Collection functions
- Math functions
- Sorting functions
- String functions
- User-defined functions (UDFs)

For example, you can easily read a CSV file and create a DataFrame from it:

```
# define input path
virus_input_path = "s3://mybucket/projects/cases/case.csv"

# read CSV file and create a DataFrame
cases_dataframe = spark.read.load(virus_input_path,format="csv",
   sep=",", inferSchema="true", header="true")

# show the first 3 rows of created DataFrame
cases_dataframe.show(3)
+-------+-------+-----------+--------------+---------+
|case_id|country|       city|infection_case|confirmed|
+-------+-------+-----------+--------------+---------+
|  C0001|    USA|   New York|       contact|      175|
+-------+-------+-----------+--------------+---------+
|  C0008|    USA| New Jersey|       unknown|       25|
+-------+-------+-----------+--------------+---------+
|  C0009|    USA|  Cupertino|       contact|      100|
+-------+-------+-----------+--------------+---------+
```

To sort the results by number of cases in descending order, we can use the `sort()` function:

```
# We can do this using the F.desc function:
from pyspark.sql import functions as F
cases_dataframe.sort(F.desc("confirmed")).show()
+-------+-------+-----------+--------------+---------+
|case_id|country|       city|infection_case|confirmed|
+-------+-------+-----------+--------------+---------+
|  C0001|    USA|   New York|       contact|      175|
+-------+-------+-----------+--------------+---------+
```

```
| C0009|    USA|  Cupertino|         contact|       100|
+-------+-------+-----------+----------------+----------+
| C0008|    USA| New Jersey|         unknown|        25|
+-------+-------+-----------+----------------+----------+
```

We can also easily filter rows:

```
cases_dataframe.filter((cases_dataframe.confirmed > 100) &
                       (cases_dataframe.country == 'USA')).show()

+-------+-------+-----------+----------------+----------+
|case_id|country|       city|infection_case|confirmed|
+-------+-------+-----------+----------------+----------+
| C0001|    USA|   New York|         contact|       175|
+-------+-------+-----------+----------------+----------+
...
```

To give you a better idea of the power of Spark's DataFrames, let's walk through an example. We will create a DataFrame and find the average and sum of hours worked by employees per department:

```
# Import required libraries
from pyspark.sql import SparkSession
from pyspark.sql.functions import avg, sum

# Create a DataFrame using SparkSession
spark = SparkSession.builder.appName("demo").getOrCreate()
dept_emps = [("Sales", "Barb", 40), ("Sales", "Dan", 20),
             ("IT", "Alex", 22), ("IT", "Jane", 24),
             ("HR", "Alex", 20), ("HR", "Mary", 30)]
df = spark.createDataFrame(dept_emps, ["dept", "name", "hours"])

# Group the same depts together, aggregate their hours, and compute an average
averages = df.groupBy("dept")
   .agg(avg("hours").alias('average'),
        sum("hours").alias('total'))

# Show the results of the final execution
averages.show()
+-----+-------+------+
| dept| average| total|
+-----+-------+------+
|Sales|    30.0|  60.0|
|   IT|    23.0|  46.0|
|   HR|    25.0|  50.0|
+-----+-------+------+
```

As you can see, Spark's DataFrames are powerful enough to manipulate billions of rows with simple but powerful functions.

Using the PySpark Shell

There are two main ways you can use PySpark:

- Use the PySpark shell (for testing and interactive programming).
- Use PySpark in a self-contained application. In this case, you write a Python driver program (say, *my_pyspark_program.py*) using the PySpark API and then run it with the `spark-submit` command:

  ```
  export SUBMIT=$SPARK_HOME/bin/spark-submit
  $SUBMIT [options] my_pyspark_program.py <parameters>
  ```

  where *<parameters>* is a list of parameters consumed by your PySpark (*my_pyspark_program.py*) program.

For details on using the `spark-submit` command, refer to "Submitting Applications" (*https://spark.apache.org/docs/latest/submitting-applications.html*) in the Spark documentation.

In this section we'll focus on Spark's interactive shell for Python users, a powerful tool that you can use to analyze data interactively and see the results immediately (Spark also provides a Scala shell). The PySpark shell can work on both single-machine installations and cluster installations of Spark. You use the following command to start the shell, where `SPARK_HOME` denotes the installation directory for Spark on your system:

```
export SPARK_HOME=<spark-installation-directory>
$SPARK_HOME/bin/pyspark
```

For example:

```
export SPARK_HOME="/home/spark" ❶
$SPARK_HOME/bin/pyspark ❷
Python 3.7.2

Welcome to Spark version 3.1.2
Using Python version 3.7.2
SparkSession available as spark.
SparkContext available as sc
>>>
```

❶ Define the Spark installation directory.

❷ Invoke the PySpark shell.

When you start the shell, PySpark displays some useful information including details on the Python and Spark versions it is using (note that the output here has been shortened). The `>>>` symbol is used as the PySpark shell prompt. This prompt indicates that you can now write Python or PySpark commands and view the results.

To get you comfortable with the PySpark shell, the following sections will walk you through some basic usage examples.

Launching the PySpark Shell

To enter into a PySpark shell, we execute `pyspark` as follows:

```
$SPARK_HOME/bin/pyspark ❶
Welcome to
      ____              __
     / __/__  ___ _____/ /__
    _\ \/ _ \/ _ `/ __/  '_/
   /__ / .__/\_,_/_/ /_/\_\   version 3.1.2
      /_/

SparkSession available as 'spark'.
SparkContext available as 'sc'.
>>> sc.version ❷
'3.1.2'
>>> spark.version ❸
'3.1.2'
```

 Executing `pyspark` will create a new shell. The output here has been shortened.

❷ Verify that `SparkContext` is created as `sc`.

❸ Verify that `SparkSession` is created as `spark`.

Once you enter into the PySpark shell, an instance of `SparkSession` is created as the `spark` variable and an instance of `SparkContext` is created as the `sc` variable. As you learned earlier in this chapter, the `SparkSession` is the entry point to programming Spark with the Dataset and DataFrame APIs; a `SparkSession` can be used to create DataFrames, register DataFrames as tables, execute SQL over tables, cache tables, and read CSV, JSON, and Parquet files. If you want to use PySpark in a self-contained application, then you have to explicitly create a `SparkSession` using the builder pattern shown in "Spark architecture in a nutshell" on page 8. A `SparkContext` is the main entry point for Spark functionality; it can be used to create RDDs from text files and Python collections. We'll look at that next.

Creating an RDD from a Collection

Spark enables us to create new RDDs from files and collections (data structures such as arrays and lists). Here, we use `SparkContext.parallelize()` to create a new RDD from a collection (represented as `data`):

```
>>> data = [ ❶
    ("fox", 6), ("dog", 5), ("fox", 3), ("dog", 8),
    ("cat", 1), ("cat", 2), ("cat", 3), ("cat", 4)
]

>>># use SparkContext (sc) as given by the PySpark shell
>>># create an RDD as rdd
>>> rdd = sc.parallelize(data) ❷
>>> rdd.collect() ❸
[
 ('fox', 6), ('dog', 5), ('fox', 3), ('dog', 8),
 ('cat', 1), ('cat', 2), ('cat', 3), ('cat', 4)
]
>>> rdd.count() ❹
8
```

❶ Define your Python collection.

❷ Create a new RDD from a Python collection.

❸ Display the contents of the new RDD.

❹ Count the number of elements in the RDD.

Aggregating and Merging Values of Keys

The `reduceByKey()` transformation is used to merge and aggregate values. In this example, `x` and `y` refer to the values of the same key:

```
>>> sum_per_key = rdd.reduceByKey(lambda x, y : x+y) ❶
>>> sum_per_key.collect() ❷
[
 ('fox', 9),
 ('dog', 13),
 ('cat', 10)
]
```

❶ Merge and aggregate values of the same key.

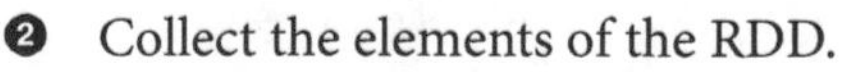

❷ Collect the elements of the RDD.

The source RDD for this transformation must consist of (key, value) pairs. reduceByKey() merges the values for each key using an associative and commutative reduce function. This will also perform the merging locally on each mapper before sending the results to a reducer, similarly to a "combiner" in MapReduce. The output will be partitioned with numPartitions partitions, or the default parallelism level if numPartitions is not specified. The default partitioner is HashPartitioner.

If T is the type of the value for (key, value) pairs, then reduceByKey()'s func() can be defined as:

```
# source_rdd : RDD[(K, T)]
# target_rdd : RDD[(K, T)]
target_rdd = source_rdd.reduceByKey(lambda x, y: func(x, y))
# OR you may write it by passing the function name
# target_rdd = source_rdd.reduceByKey(func)
# where
#      func(T, T) -> T
# Then you may define `func()` in Python as:
# x: type of T
# y: type of T
def func(x, y):
  result = <aggregation of x and y: return a result of type T>
  return result
#end-def
```

This means that:

- There are two input arguments (of the same type, T) for the reducer func().
- The return type of func() must be the same as the input type T (this limitation can be avoided if you use the combineByKey() transformation).
- The reducer func() has to be associative. Informally, a binary operation f() on a set T is called associative if it satisfies the associative law, which states that the order in which numbers are grouped does not change the result of the operation.

Associative Law

```
f(f(x, y), z) = f(x, f(y, z))
```

Note that the associative law holds for addition (+) and multiplication (*), but not for subtraction (-) or division (/).

- The reducer func() has to be commutative: informally, a function f() for which f(x, y) = f(y, x) for all values of x and y. That is, a change in the order of the numbers should not affect the result of the operation.

Commutative Law

    f(x, y) = f(y, x)

The commutative law also holds for addition and multiplication, but not for subtraction or division. For example:

$5 + 3 = 3 + 5$ but $5 - 3 \neq 3 - 5$

Therefore, you may not use subtraction or division operations in a `reduceByKey()` transformation.

Filtering an RDD's Elements

Next, we'll use the `filter()` transformation to return a new RDD containing only the elements that satisfy a predicate:

```
>>> sum_filtered = sum_per_key.filter(lambda x : x[1] > 9) ❶
>>> sum_filtered.collect() ❷
[
 ('cat', 10),
 ('dog', 13)
]
```

❶ Keep the (key, value) pairs if the value is greater than 9.

❷ Collect the elements of the RDD.

Grouping Similar Keys

We can use the `groupByKey()` transformation to group the values for each key in the RDD into a single sequence:

```
>>> grouped = rdd.groupByKey() ❶
>>> grouped.collect() ❷
[
 ('fox', <ResultIterable object at 0x10f45c790>), ❸
 ('dog', <ResultIterable object at 0x10f45c810>),
 ('cat', <ResultIterable object at 0x10f45cd90>)
]
>>>
>>># list(v) converts v as a ResultIterable into a list
>>> grouped.map(lambda (k,v) : (k, list(v))).collect() ❹
[
 ('fox', [6, 3]),
 ('dog', [5, 8]),
 ('cat', [1, 2, 3, 4])
]
```

❶ Group elements of the same key into a sequence of elements.

❷ View the result.

❸ The full name of `ResultIterable` is `pyspark.resultiterable.ResultIterable`.

❹ First apply `map()` and then `collect()`, which returns a list that contains all of the elements in the resulting RDD. The `list()` function converts `ResultIterable` into a list of objects.

The source RDD for this transformation must be composed of (key, value) pairs. `groupByKey()` groups the values for each key in the RDD into a single sequence, and hash-partitions the resulting RDD with `numPartitions` partitions, or with the default level of parallelism if `numPartitions` is not specified. Note that if you are grouping (using the `groupByKey()` transformation) in order to perform an aggregation, such as a sum or average, over each key, using `reduceByKey()` or `aggregateByKey()` will provide much better performance.

Aggregating Values for Similar Keys

To aggregate and sum up the values for each key, we can use the `mapValues()` transformation and the `sum()` function:

```
>>> aggregated = grouped.mapValues(lambda values : sum(values)) ❶
>>> aggregated.collect() ❷
[
 ('fox', 9),
 ('dog', 13),
 ('cat', 10)
]
```

 `values` is a sequence of values per key. We pass each value in the (key, value) pair RDD through a mapper function (adding all `values` with `sum(values)`) without changing the keys.

❷ For debugging, we return a list that contains all of the elements in this RDD.

We have several choices for aggregating and summing up values: `reduceByKey()` and `groupByKey()`, to mention a few. In general, the `reduceByKey()` transformation is more efficient than the `groupByKey()` transformation. More details on this are provided in Chapter 4.

As you'll see in the following chapters, Spark has many other powerful transformations that can convert an RDD into a new RDD. As mentioned earlier, RDDs are read-only, immutable, and distributed. RDD transformations return a pointer to a new RDD and allow you to create dependencies between RDDs. Each RDD in the dependency chain (or string of dependencies) has a function for calculating its data and a pointer (dependency) to its parent RDD.

Serverless Spark

If you do not have the budget to set up your own dedicated Spark cluster, then you can use either Amazon's AWS Glue or Databricks's Serverless Spark. Both these options reduce operational complexity and costs for big data and interactive data science applications.

For example, you can use AWS Glue to create a PySpark job and then submit it to a dynamic cluster. You don't own the cluster; you just pay for the compute time of your PySpark job.

Serverless Spark can help reduce operational costs by using a predefined pool of clusters provided by cloud services such as Amazon and Databricks.

It is expected that most cloud services will provide Serverless Spark as a service.

Data Analysis Tools for PySpark

Jupyter (http://jupyter.org)
: Jupyter is a great tool to test and prototype programs. PySpark can also be used from Jupyter notebooks; it's very practical for explorative data analysis.

Apache Zeppelin (https://zeppelin.apache.org)
: Zeppelin is a web-based notebook that enables data-driven, interactive data analytics and collaborative documents with SQL, Python, Scala, and more.

ETL Example with DataFrames

In data analysis and computing, ETL is the general procedure of copying data from one or more sources into a destination system that represents the data differently from the source(s) or in a different context than the source(s). Here I will show how Spark makes ETL possible and easy.

For this ETL example, I'll use 2010 census data in JSON format (*census_2010.json*):

```
$ wc -l census_2010.json
101 census_2010.json

$ head -5 census_2010.json
{"females": 1994141, "males": 2085528, "age": 0, "year": 2010}
{"females": 1997991, "males": 2087350, "age": 1, "year": 2010}
{"females": 2000746, "males": 2088549, "age": 2, "year": 2010}
{"females": 2002756, "males": 2089465, "age": 3, "year": 2010}
{"females": 2004366, "males": 2090436, "age": 4, "year": 2010}
```

This data was pulled from U.S. Census Bureau data, which at the time of writing this book only provides the binary options of male and female. We strive to be as inclusive as possible, and hope that in the future national data sets such as these will provide more inclusive options.

Let's define our ETL process:

Extraction
: First, we create a DataFrame from a given JSON document.

Transformation
: Then we filter the data and keep the records for seniors (`age > 54`). Next, we add a new column, `total`, which is the total of males and females.

Loading
: Finally, we write the revised DataFrame into a MySQL database and verify the load process.

Let's dig into this process a little more deeply.

Extraction

To do a proper extraction, we first need to create an instance of the `SparkSession` class:

```
from pyspark.sql import SparkSession
spark = SparkSession.builder \
    .master("local") \
    .appName("ETL") \
    .getOrCreate()
```

Next, we read the JSON and create a DataFrame:

```
>>> input_path = "census_2010.json"
>>> census_df = spark.read.json(input_path)
>>> census_df.count()
101
>>> census_df.show(200)
+---+-------+-------+----+
|age|females|  males|year|
+---+-------+-------+----+
|  0|1994141|2085528|2010|
|  1|1997991|2087350|2010|
|  2|2000746|2088549|2010|
...
| 54|2221350|2121536|2010|
| 55|2167706|2059204|2010|
| 56|2106460|1989505|2010|
...
```

```
| 98|  35778|   8321|2010|
| 99|  25673|   4612|2010|
+---+-------+-------+----+
only showing top 100 rows
```

Transformation

Transformation can involve many processes whose purpose is to clean, format, or perform computations on the data to suit your requirements. For example, you can remove missing or duplicate data, join columns to create new columns, or filter out certain rows or columns. Once we've created the DataFrame through the extraction process, we can perform many useful transformations, such as selecting just the seniors:

```
>>> seniors = census_df[census_df['age'] > 54]
>>> seniors.count()
46
>>> seniors.show(200)
+---+-------+-------+----+
|age|females|  males|year|
+---+-------+-------+----+
| 55|2167706|2059204|2010|
| 56|2106460|1989505|2010|
| 57|2048896|1924113|2010|
...
| 98|  35778|   8321|2010|
| 99|  25673|   4612|2010|
|100|  51007|   9506|2010|
+---+-------+-------+----+
```

Next, we create a new aggregated column called `total`, which adds up the numbers of males and females:

```
>>> from pyspark.sql.functions import lit
>>> seniors_final = seniors.withColumn('total',
  lit(seniors.males + seniors.females))
>>> seniors_final.show(200)
+---+-------+-------+----+-------+
|age|females|  males|year|  total|
+---+-------+-------+----+-------+
| 55|2167706|2059204|2010|4226910|
| 56|2106460|1989505|2010|4095965|
| 57|2048896|1924113|2010|3973009|
...
| 98|  35778|   8321|2010|  44099|
| 99|  25673|   4612|2010|  30285|
|100|  51007|   9506|2010|  60513|
+---+-------+-------+----+-------+
```

Loading

The loading process involves saving or writing the final output of the transformation step. Here, we will write the seniors_final DataFrame into a MySQL table:

```
seniors_final\
  .write\
  .format("jdbc")\
  .option("driver", "com.mysql.jdbc.Driver")\
  .mode("overwrite")\
  .option("url", "jdbc:mysql://localhost/testdb")\
  .option("dbtable", "seniors")\
  .option("user", "root")\
  .option("password", "root_password")\
  .save()
```

The final step of loading is to verify the load process:

```
$ mysql -uroot -p
Enter password: <password>
Your MySQL connection id is 9
Server version: 5.7.30 MySQL Community Server (GPL)

mysql> use testdb;
Database changed
mysql> select * from seniors;
+------+--------+--------+-----+--------+
| age  | females | males  | year | total   |
+------+--------+--------+-----+--------+
|   55 | 2167706 | 2059204 | 2010 | 4226910 |
|   56 | 2106460 | 1989505 | 2010 | 4095965 |
|   57 | 2048896 | 1924113 | 2010 | 3973009 |
...
|   98 |   35778 |    8321 | 2010 |   44099 |
|   99 |   25673 |    4612 | 2010 |   30285 |
|  100 |   51007 |    9506 | 2010 |   60513 |
+------+--------+--------+-----+--------+
46 rows in set (0.00 sec)
```

Summary

Let's recap some key points from the chapter:

- Spark is a fast and powerful unified analytics engine (up to one hundred times faster than traditional Hadoop MapReduce) due to its in-memory operation, and it offers robust, distributed, fault-tolerant data abstractions (called RDDs and DataFrames). Spark integrates with the world of machine learning and graph analytics through the MLlib (machine learning library) and GraphX (graph library) packages.

- You can use Spark's transformations and actions in four programming languages: Java, Scala, R, and Python. PySpark (the Python API for Spark) can be used for solving big data problems, efficiently transforming your data into the desired result and format.
- Big data can be represented using Spark's data abstractions (RDDs, DataFrames, and Datasets—all of these are distributed datasets).
- You can run PySpark from the PySpark shell (using the `pyspark` command from a command line) for interactive Spark programming. Using the PySpark shell, you can create and manipulate RDDs and DataFrames.
- You can submit a standalone PySpark application to a Spark cluster by using the `spark-submit` command; self-contained applications using PySpark are deployed to production environments.
- Spark offers many transformations and actions for solving big data problems, and their performance differs (for example, `reduceByKey()` versus `groupByKey()` and `combineByKey()` versus `groupByKey()`).

The next chapter dives into some important Spark transformations.

CHAPTER 2

Transformations in Action

In this chapter, we will explore the most important Spark transformations (mappers and reducers) in the context of data summarization design patterns, and examine how to select specific transformations for targeted problems.

As you will see, for a given problem (we'll use the DNA base count problem here) there are multiple possible PySpark solutions using different Spark transformations, but the efficiency of these transformations differs due to their implementation and shuffle processes (when the grouping of values by key happens). The DNA base count problem is very similar to the classic word count problem (finding the frequency of unique words in a set of files/documents), with the difference that in DNA base counting you find the frequencies of DNA letters (`A`, `T`, `C`, `G`).

I chose this problem because in solving it we will learn about data summarization, condensing a large quantity of information (here, DNA data strings/sequences) into a much smaller set of useful information (the frequency of DNA letters).

This chapter provides three complete end-to-end solutions in PySpark, using different mappers and reductions to solve the DNA base count problem. We'll discuss the performance differences between them, and explore data summarization design patterns.

Source Code

Complete programs for this chapter are available in the book's GitHub repository (*https://oreil.ly/ogZEA*).

The DNA Base Count Example

The purpose of our example in this chapter is to count DNA bases in a given set of DNA strings/sequences. Don't worry, you don't need to be an expert in DNA, biology, or genomics to understand this example. I'll cover the basics, which should be all you need to get the idea.

Human DNA consists of about 3 billion bases, and more than 99% of those bases are the same in all people. To understand DNA base counting, we need to first understand DNA strings. DNA strings are constructed from the alphabet `{A, C, G, T}`, whose symbols represent the bases adenine (`A`), cytosine (`C`), guanine (`G`), and thymine (`T`). Our DNA is composed of a set of DNA strings. The question we want to answer is how many times each base letter occurs in a set of DNA strings. For example, if we have the DNA string `"AAATGGCATTA"` and we ask how many times the base `A` occurs in this string, the answer is 5; if we ask how many times the base `T` occurs in this string, the answer is 3. So, we want to count the number of occurrences of each base letter, ignoring case. Since DNA machines might produce uppercase and lowercase letters, we will convert all of them to lowercase.

For this problem, I will provide three distinct solutions using different combinations of powerful and efficient Spark transformations. Even though all the solutions generate the same results, their performance will be different due to the transformations used.

Figure 2-1 illustrates the process of solving the DNA base count problem using Spark. For each solution, we will write a driver program in Python using the PySpark API (a series of Spark transformations and actions) and submit the program to a Spark cluster. All the solutions will read input (FASTA files format, to be defined shortly) and produce a dictionary, where the key is a DNA letter and the value is the associated frequency.

These three solutions will show that we have choices in selecting Spark transformations for solving this problem (and any data problem you are trying to solve) and that the performance of the different transformations varies. A summary of the three PySpark solutions is provided in Table 2-1.

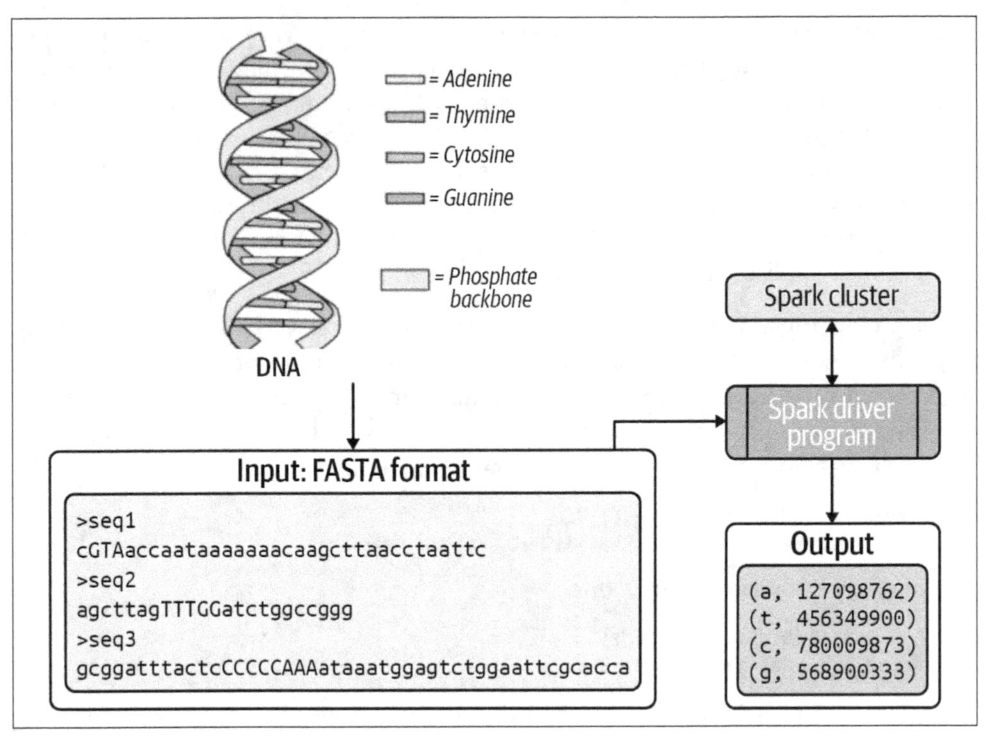

Figure 2-1. Solving the DNA base count problem

Table 2-1. Solutions for the DNA base count problem

	Solution 1	Solution 2	Solution 3
Program	*dna_bc_ver_1.py*	*dna_bc_ver_2.py*	*dna_bc_ver_3.py*
Design pattern	*Basic MapReduce*	*In-mapper combiner*	*Mapping partitions*
Transformations	`textFile()`	`textFile()`	`textFile()`
	`flatMap()`	`flatMap()`	`mapPartitions()`
	`reduceByKey()`	`reduceByKey()`	`reduceByKey()`

As Table 2-2 shows, the three programs performed very differently on my machine (a MacBook with 16 GB RAM, a 2.3 GHz Intel processor, and a 500 GB hard disk). Note I used the default parameters with the `$SPARK_HOME/bin/spark-submit` command for all of them; no optimization was done for any solution.

Table 2-2. Performance of the three solutions

Input data (in bytes)	Version 1	Version 2	Version 3
253,935,557	72 seconds	27 seconds	18 seconds
1,095,573,358	258 seconds	79 seconds	57 seconds

What does this basic performance table tell you? When you write your PySpark applications, you have a lot of choices. There are no hard and fast rules for which transformations or actions to use; this will depend on the specifics of your data and your program. In general, when you write a PySpark application, you can choose from a variety of arrangements of transformations and actions that will produce the same results. However, not all these arrangements will result in the same performance: avoiding common pitfalls and picking the right combination can make a world of difference in an application's performance.

For example, for a large set of (key, value) pairs, using `reduceByKey()` or `combineByKey()` is typically more efficient than using the combination of `groupByKey()` and `mapValues()`, because they reduce the shuffling time. If your RDD (represented by the variable `rdd`) is an `RDD[(String, Integer)]` (an RDD where each element is a pair of `(key-as-String, value-as-Integer)`), then this:

```
# rdd: RDD[(String, Integer)]
rdd.groupByKey().mapValues(lambda values : sum(values))
```

will produce the same results as this:

```
# rdd: RDD[(String, Integer)]
rdd.reduceByKey(lambda x,y: x+y)
```

However, the `groupByKey()` operation will transfer the entire dataset across the cluster network (incurring a large performance penalty), while the `reduceByKey()` operation will compute local sums for each key in each partition and combine those local sums into larger sums after shuffling. Therefore, `reduceByKey()` will transfer much less data across the cluster network than `groupByKey()`, which means that in most situations `reduceByKey()` will outperform the combination of `groupByKey()` and `mapValues()`.

Now, let's dig into a little more detail on our DNA base count problem.

The DNA Base Count Problem

The goal of this example is to find the frequencies (or percentages) of the letters `A`, `T`, `C`, `G`, and `N` (the letter `N` denotes any letter other than `A`, `T`, `C`, or `G`—i.e., an error) in a given set of DNA sequences. As I mentioned earlier, `{'A', 'T', 'C', 'G'}` stand for the four nitrogenous bases associated with DNA.

DNA sequences can be huge—for example, the human genome consists of three billion DNA base pairs, while the diploid genome (found in somatic cells) has twice the DNA content—and can contain both uppercase and lowercase letters. For consistency, we will convert all letters to lowercase. The goal of DNA base counting for our example is to generate the frequencies for each DNA base. Table 2-3 shows the result for the example sequence "ACGGGTACGAAT". Note that I am using the key z to find the total number of DNA sequences processed.

Table 2-3. DNA base count example

Base	Count
a	4
t	2
c	2
g	4
n	0
z	1 (the total number of DNA sequences)

FASTA Format

DNA sequences can be represented in many different formats, including FASTA (*https://oreil.ly/wF0fe*) and FASTQ. These are popular text-based formats where the input is given as a text file. Our solutions will only handle FASTA format, since it is much easier to read FASTA files. Both the FASTA and FASTQ formats store sequence data and sequence metadata. With some minor modifications to the presented solutions, you can use them with inputs in FASTQ format; a FASTQ solution is provided on GitHub (*https://oreil.ly/ogZEA*).

A sequence file in FASTA format can contain many DNA sequences. Each sequence begins with a single-line description, followed by one or many lines of sequence data. According to the FASTA format specification, the description line must begin with a greater-than symbol (>) in the first column. Note that the description line may be used for counting the number of sequences and does not contain any DNA sequence data.

Sample Data

We'll use the *sample.fasta* file, available in the book's GitHub repository (*https://oreil.ly/qQLCq*), as a test case for our PySpark programs. This small FASTA file contains four sample DNA sequences (remember, the case of the characters is irrelevant):

```
$ cat sample.fasta
>seq1
cGTAaccaataaaaaaacaagcttaacctaattc
>seq2
agcttagTTTGGatctggccgggg
>seq3
gcggatttactcCCCCCAAAAANNaggggagagcccagataaatggagtctgtgcgtccaca
gaattcgcacca
AATAAAACCTCACCCAT
agagcccagaatttactcCCC
```

```
>seq4
gcggatttactcaggggagagcccagGGataaatggagtctgtgcgtccaca
gaattcgcacca
```

To test the DNA base count programs provided in this chapter with larger files, you can download FASTA data from the University of California, Santa Cruz website (*https://oreil.ly/sv3fs*).

Next, we'll walk through three distinct PySpark solutions for the DNA base count problem, using different Spark transformations. Remember that while the outcome of all the solutions is the same (they produce the same results), the performance of each solution will differ due to the nature of the data and the transformations used.

DNA Base Count Solution 1

The first version I'll present is a very basic solution for the DNA base count problem. The high-level workflow is shown in Figure 2-2.

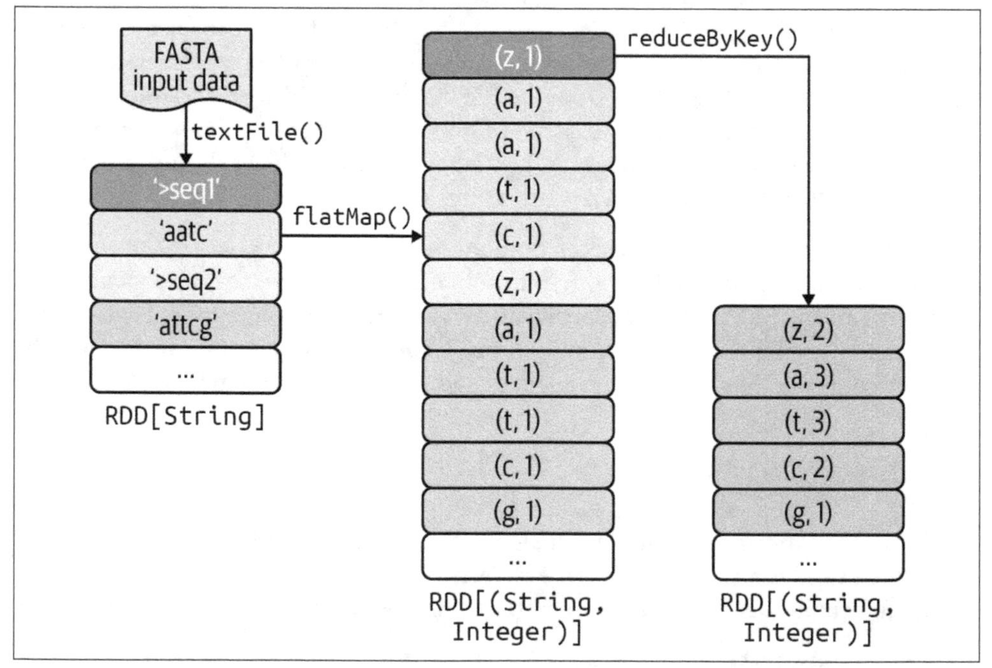

Figure 2-2. DNA base count solution

It consists of three simple steps:

1. Read FASTA input data and create an RDD[String], where each RDD element is a FASTA record (it can be either a comment line or an actual DNA sequence).
2. Define a mapper function: for every DNA letter in a FASTA record, emit a pair of (dna_letter, 1), where dna_letter is in {A, T, C, G} and 1 is a frequency (similar to a word count solution).
3. Sum up the frequencies for all DNA letters (this is a reduction step). For each unique dna_letter, group and add all frequencies.

To test this solution, I will use the *sample.fasta* file presented earlier.

Step 1: Create an RDD[String] from the Input

The SparkContext.textFile() function is used to create an RDD[String] for input in FASTA text-based format. textFile() can be used to read a text file from HDFS, Amazon S3, a local filesystem (available on all Spark nodes), or any Hadoop-supported filesystem URI, and return it as an RDD[String]. If spark is an instance of the SparkSession class, then to create a FASTA records RDD (as denoted by records_rdd), we have at least two options. We can use the SparkSession:

```
>>># spark: instance of SparkSession
>>> input_path = "./code/chap02/sample.fasta" ❶
>>> records_rdd = spark.read
                       .text(input_path)
                       .rdd.map(lambda r: r[0]) ❷
```

❶ Define the input path.

❷ Use the DataFrameReader interface (accessed with spark.read) to create a DataFrame and then convert it to an RDD[String].

DataFrameReader and DataFrameWriter

Spark's DataFrameReader class is an interface to read data from external data sources—such as text, CSV, and JSON files, Parquet and ORC files, Hive tables, or Java Database Connectivity (JDBC)-compliant database tables—into a DataFrame. Its DataFrameWriter class is an interface to write a DataFrame into an external data source.

Or we can use the SparkContext:

```
>>> input_path = "./code/chap02/sample.fasta" ❶
>>># Let 'spark' be an instance of SparkSession
```

```
>>> sc = spark.sparkContext ❷
>>> records_rdd = sc.textFile(input_path) ❸
```

❶ Define the input path.

❷ Create an instance of `SparkContext` (as `sc`).

❸ Use the `SparkContext` to read input and create an `RDD[String]`.

The second option is preferable, because it is easy and efficient. The first one works too, but it's less efficient because it first creates a DataFrame, then converts it to an RDD, and eventually performs another mapper transformation.

Next we'll examine the contents of the created RDD. Each RDD element (as a `String`) is denoted by `u'<element>'`:

```
>>> records_rdd.collect()
[
 u'>seq1',
 u'cGTAaccaataaaaaaacaagcttaacctaattc',
 u'>seq2',
 u'agcttagTTTGGatctggccgggg',
 u'>seq3',
 u'gcggatttactcCCCCCAAAAANNaggggagagcccagataaatggagtctgtgcgtccaca',
 u'gaattcgcacca',
 u'AATAAAACCTCACCCAT',
 u'agagcccagaatttactcCCC',
 u'>seq4',
 u'gcggatttactcaggggagagcccagGGataaatggagtctgtgcgtccaca',
 u'gaattcgcacca'
]
```

The `RDD.collect()` method is used here to get the content as a list of `String` objects and display it. As mentioned in Chapter 1, for large RDDs you should not use `collect()`, which might cause OOM errors as well as incurring a performance penalty. To just view the first *N* elements of an RDD, you may use `RDD.take(N)`.

Step 2: Define a Mapper Function

To map RDD elements into a set of pairs `(dna_letter, 1)`, we'll need to define a Python function that will be passed to the `flatMap()` transformation. `flatMap()` is a 1-to-many transformation; it returns a new RDD by first applying a function to all elements of the source RDD and then flattening the results. For example, if the Python function we pass to the `flatMap()` transformation returns a list as $[V_1, V_2, V_3]$, then that will be flattened into three target RDD elements, V_1, V_2, and V_3. Informally, we can write this as:

1. Create an iterable list:

```
single_RDD_element() -> [V1, V2, V3]
```

2. Flatten the list into many elements (here, three target elements):

```
[V1, V2, V3] -> V1, V2, V3
```

For this solution we'll define a function, `process_FASTA_record()`, that accepts an RDD element (a single record of the FASTA file as a `String`) and returns a list of pairs as `(dna_letter, 1)`. For example, given the input record `"AATTG"`, it will emit the following (key, value) pairs (recall that we're converting all the DNA letters to lowercase):

```
(a, 1)
(a, 1)
(t, 1)
(t, 1)
(g, 1)
```

If the input is a description record (which contains no sequence data and begins with `>seq`), then we emit `(z, 1)`. This will enable us to find the number of sequences as well. If the input is a DNA sequence we first tokenize it by characters and then, for each DNA letter (denoted by `dna_letter`), we emit `(dna_letter, 1)`. Finally, we return a list of these pairs. The function definition follows. Note that I have included some `print` statements for debugging purposes, but in a production environment these should be removed as they will cause performance penalties:

```
# Parameter: fasta_record: String (a single FASTA record)
#
# Output: a list of (key, value) pairs, where key
#         is a dna_letter and value is a frequency
#
def process_FASTA_record(fasta_record):
    key_value_list = [] ❶

    if (fasta_record.startswith(">")):
        # z counts the number of FASTA sequences
        key_value_list.append((z, 1)) ❷
    else:
        chars = fasta_record.lower()
        for c in chars:
            key_value_list.append((c, 1)) ❸

    print(key_value_list) ❹
    return key_value_list ❺
#end-def
```

❶ Create an empty list, to which we will add (key, value) pairs (this is our output from this function).

❷ Append `(z, 1)` to the list.

❸ Append `(c, 1)` to the list, where `c` is a DNA letter.

❹ For debugging purposes only.

❺ Return a list of (key, value) pairs, which will be flattened by the `flatMap()` transformation.

Now, we will use this function to apply the `flatMap()` transformation to the `records_rdd` (`RDD[String]`) we just created:

```
>>># rec refers to an element of records_rdd
>>># Lambda is a notation that defines input and output
>>>#   input: "rec" as a records_rdd element ❶
>>>#   output: result of process_FASTA_record(rec)
>>> pairs_rdd = records_rdd.flatMap(lambda rec: process_FASTA_record(rec)) ❷
```

 The source RDD (`records_rdd`) is an `RDD[String]`.

❷ We use a lambda expression, where `rec` denotes a single element of `records_rdd`. The target RDD (`pairs_rdd`) is an `RDD[(String, Integer)]`.

Alternatively, we can write it as follows (without using a lambda expression):

```
>>> pairs_rdd = records_rdd.flatMap(process_FASTA_record)
```

For example, if an element of `records_rdd` contains the DNA sequence as "`gaattcg`", then it will be flattened into the following (key, value) pairs:

```
(g, 1)
(a, 1)
(a, 1)
(t, 1)
(t, 1)
(c, 1)
(g, 1)
```

If an element of `records_rdd` contains `>seq`, then it will be flattened into the following (key, value) pair (recall that we use the key `z` to find the total number of DNA sequences for a given input):

```
(z, 1)
```

Step 3: Find the Frequencies of DNA Letters

`pairs_rdd` now contains a set of (key, value) pairs where the key is a DNA letter and the value is its frequency (`1`). Next, we apply the `reduceByKey()` transformation to `pairs_rdd` to find the aggregated frequencies for all DNA letters.

The `reduceByKey()` transformation merges the values for each unique key using an associative and commutative reduce function (we'll use addition as our reduction function). Therefore, we can now see that we are simply taking an *accumulated value* for the given key and summing it with the *next value* of that key. In other words, if key `K` has five pairs in the RDD, `(K, 2)`, `(K, 3)`, `(K, 6)`, `(K, 7)`, and `(K, 8)`, then the `reduceByKey()` transformation will transform these five pairs into a single pair, `(K, 26)` (because 2 + 3 + 6 + 7 + 8 = 26). If these five pairs were stored on two partitions, each partition would be processed in parallel and independently:

```
Partition-1: {
               (K, 2),
               (K, 3)
             }

   (K, 2), (K, 3) => (K, 2+3) = (K, 5)
   Result of Partition-1: (K, 5)

Partition-2: {
               (K, 6),
               (K, 7),
               (K, 8)
             }

   (K, 6), (K, 7)  => (K, 6+7) = (K, 13)
   (K, 8), (K, 13) => (K, 8+13) = (K, 21)
   Result of Partition-2: (K, 21)
```

And then the partitions would be merged:

```
Merge Partitions:
  => Partition-1, Partition-2
  => (K,5), (K, 21)
  => (K, 5+21) = (K, 26)

  Final result: (K, 26)
```

To produce the final result, we use the `reduceByKey()` transformation:

```
# x and y refer to the frequencies of the same key
# source: pairs_rdd: RDD[(String, Integer)]
# target: frequencies_rdd: RDD[(String, Integer)]
frequencies_rdd = pairs_rdd.reduceByKey(lambda x, y: x+y)
```

Note that the source and target data types for `reduceByKey()` are the same. That is, if the source RDD is an `RDD[(K, V)]` then the target RDD will also be an `RDD[(K, V)]`. Spark's `combineByKey()` transformation does not have the data type restrictions for values imposed by `reduceByKey()`.

There are several ways that you can view the final output. For example, you can use the `RDD.collect()` function to get the final RDD's elements as a list of pairs:

```
frequencies_rdd.collect()
[
  (u'a', 73),
  (u'c', 61),
  (u't', 45),
  (u'g', 53),
  (u'n', 2),
  (u'z', 4)
]
```

Or you can use the `RDD.collectAsMap()` action to return the result as a hash map:

```
>>> frequencies_rdd.collectAsMap()
{
  u'a': 73,
  u'c': 61,
  u't': 45,
  u'g': 53,
  u'n': 2,
  u'z': 4
}
```

You can also use other Spark transformations to aggregate frequencies of DNA letters. For example, you could group the frequencies (using `groupByKey()`) by DNA letter and then add all the frequencies together. This solution is, however, less efficient than using the `reduceByKey()` transformation:

```
grouped_rdd = pairs_rdd.groupByKey() ❶
frequencies_rdd = grouped_rdd.mapValues(lambda values : sum(values)) ❷
frequencies_rdd.collect()
```

 `grouped_rdd` is an `RDD[(String, [Integer])]`, where the key is a `String` and the value is a list/iterable of `Integers` (as frequencies).

❷ `frequencies_rdd` is an `RDD[(String, Integer)]`.

For example, if `pairs_rdd` contains four pairs of `('z', 1)`, then `grouped_rdd` will have a single pair of `('z', [1, 1, 1, 1])`. That is, it groups values for the same key. While both of these transformations (`reduceByKey()` and `groupByKey()`) produce the correct answer, `reduceByKey()` works much better on a large FASTA dataset. That's because Spark knows it can combine output with a common key (DNA letter) on each partition before shuffling the data. Spark experts recommend that we avoid `groupByKey()` and use `reduceByKey()` and `combineByKey()` whenever possible, as they scale out better than `groupByKey()`.

If you want to save your created RDD to disk, you can use `RDD.saveAsTextFile(path)`, where *path* is your output directory name.

Pros and Cons of Solution 1

Let's take a look at some of the pros and cons of this solution:

Pros

- The provided solution works and is simple. It uses minimal code to get the job done with Spark's `map()` and `reduceByKey()` transformations.
- There is no scalability issue since we use `reduceByKey()` to reduce all the (key, value) pairs. This transformation will automatically perform the `combine()` optimization (local aggregation) on all worker nodes.

Cons

- This solution emits a large number of (key, value) pairs (one for each letter in the input), which might cause memory problems. If you get an error because too many (key, value) pairs are produced, try adjusting the RDD's `StorageLevel`. By default, Spark uses `MEMORY_ONLY`, but you can set the `StorageLevel` to `MEMORY_AND_DISK` for this RDD.
- Performance is not optimal because emitting a large number of (key, value) pairs will place a high load on the network and prolong the shuffle time. The network will be a bottleneck when scaling this solution.

Next, I'll present a second solution for the DNA base count problem.

DNA Base Count Solution 2

Solution 2 is an improved version of solution 1. In solution 1, we emitted pairs of `(dna_letter, 1)` for each DNA letter in the input DNA sequences. FASTA sequences can be very long, with multiple `(dna_letter, 1)` pairs per DNA letter. So, in this version we will perform an in-mapper combining optimization (a design pattern discussed in much greater depth in Chapter 10) to reduce the number of intermediate (key, value) pairs that are emitted by the mapper. We will aggregate the `(dna_letter, 1)` pairs into a hash map (an unordered collection of (key, value) pairs stored in a hash table, where the keys are unique), then flatten the hash map into a list and finally aggregate the frequencies. For example, given the FASTA sequence record `"aaatttcggggaa"`, the values in column 2 of Table 2-4 will be emitted instead of the values in column 1 (as in solution 1).

Table 2-4. Emitted (key, value) pairs for the sequence "aaatttcggggaa"

Solution 1	Solution 2
(a, 1)	(a, 5)
(a, 1)	(t, 3)
(a, 1)	(c, 1)
(t, 1)	(g, 4)
(t, 1)	
(t, 1)	
(c, 1)	
(g, 1)	
(g, 1)	
(g, 1)	
(g, 1)	
(a, 1)	
(a, 1)	

The advantage of this solution is that it will emit many fewer (key, value) pairs, which will reduce the cluster network traffic and hence improve the overall performance of our program.

Solution 2 can be summarized as follows:

1. Read FASTA input data and create an `RDD[String]`, where each RDD element is a FASTA record. This step is the same as in solution 1.
2. For every FASTA record, create a `HashMap[Key, Value]` (a dictionary or hash table) where the `key` is a DNA letter and the `value` is an aggregated frequency for that letter. Then, flatten the hash map (using Spark's `flatMap()`) into a list of (key, value) pairs. This step is different from solution 1 and enables us to emit fewer (key, value) pairs.
3. For each DNA letter, aggregate and sum all the frequencies. This is a reduction step, and it is the same as in solution 1.

The workflow is presented visually in Figure 2-3.

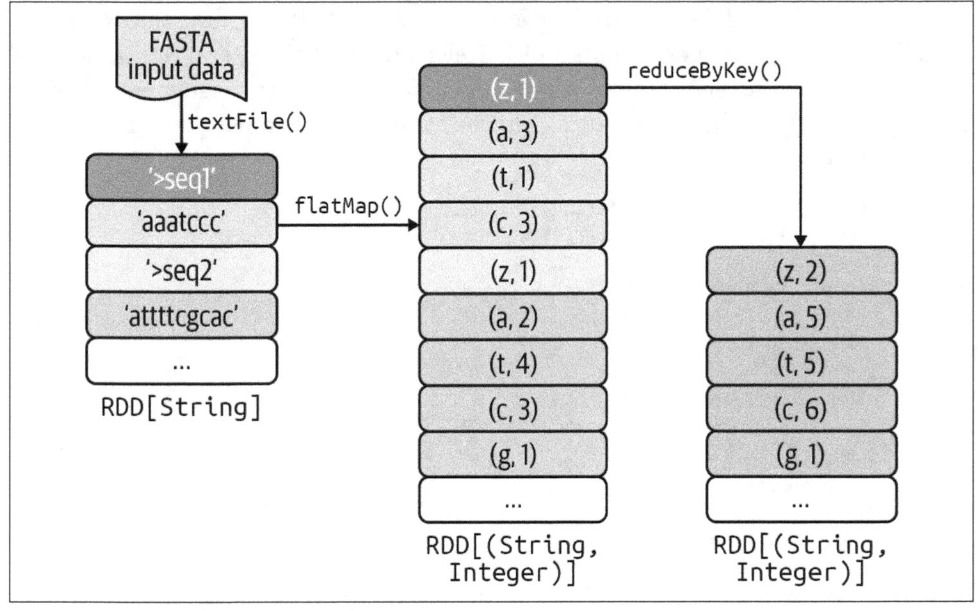

Figure 2-3. DNA base count solution 2

Let's dig into the details of each step.

Step 1: Create an RDD[String] from the Input

The `SparkContext.textFile()` function is used to create an RDD for input in FASTA text-based format. Let `spark` be a `SparkSession` object:

```
>>># spark: an instance of SparkSession
>>> input_path = "./code/chap02/sample.fasta"
>>> records_rdd = spark.sparkContext.textFile(input_path) ❶
```

❶ `records_rdd` is an `RDD[String]`.

Step 2: Define a Mapper Function

Next, we'll map each RDD element (which represents a single FASTA record as a `String`) into a list of (key, value) pairs, where the key is a unique DNA letter and the value is an aggregated frequency for the entire record.

We define a Python function, which is passed to the `flatMap()` transformation to return a new RDD, by first applying a function to all elements of this RDD and then flattening the results.

To process the RDD elements, we'll define a Python function, `process_FASTA_as_hashmap`, which accepts an RDD element as a `String` and returns a list of `(dna_letter, frequency)`. Note that I've included some `print` statements here for debugging and teaching purposes, which should be removed for production environments:

```
# Parameter: fasta_record: String, a single FASTA record
# output: a list of (dna_letter, frequency)
#
def process_FASTA_as_hashmap(fasta_record):
    if (fasta_record.startswith(">")): ❶
        return [("z", 1)]

    hashmap = defaultdict(int) ❷
    chars = fasta_record.lower()
    for c in chars: ❸
        hashmap[c] += 1
    #end-for
    print("hashmap=", hashmap)

    key_value_list = [(k, v) for k, v in hashmap.iteritems()] ❹
    print("key_value_list=", key_value_list)
    return key_value_list ❺
#end-def
```

❶ > indicates a comment line in a DNA sequence.

❷ Create a `dict[String, Integer]`.

❸ Aggregate the DNA letters.

❹ Flatten the dictionary into a list of `(dna_letter, frequency)` pairs.

❺ Return the flattened list of `(dna_letter, frequency)` pairs.

Now, we will use this Python function, to apply the `flatMap()` transformation to the `records_rdd` (an `RDD[String]`) created earlier:

```
>>># source: records_rdd (RDD[String])
>>># target: pairs_rdd (RDD[(String, Integer)])
>>> pairs_rdd = records_rdd.flatMap(lambda rec: process_FASTA_as_hashmap(rec))
```

Alternatively, we can write this as follows without the lambda expression:

```
>>># source: records_rdd (as RDD[String])
>>># target: pairs_rdd (as RDD[(String, Integer)])
>>> pairs_rdd = records_rdd.flatMap(process_FASTA_as_hashmap)
```

For example, if the records_rdd element contains 'gggggaaattccccg', then it will be flattened into the following (key, value) pairs:

```
(g, 6)
(a, 3)
(t, 2)
(c, 4)
```

To enable us to count the total number of DNA sequences, any records_rdd elements that begin with ">seq" will be flattened into the following (key, value) pair:

```
(z, 1)
```

Step 3: Find the Frequencies of DNA Letters

Now, pairs_rdd contains (key, value) pairs where the key is a dna_letter and the value is the frequency of that letter. Next, we apply the reduceByKey() transformation to pairs_rdd to find the aggregated frequencies for all DNA letters. Recall that 'n' is the key used to denote any letter other than a, t, c, or g:

```
# x and y refer to the frequencies of the same key
frequencies_rdd = pairs_rdd.reduceByKey(lambda x, y: x+y) ❶
frequencies_rdd.collect() ❷
[
  (u'a', 73),
  (u'c', 61),
  (u't', 45),
  (u'g', 53),
  (u'n', 2),
  (u'z', 4)
]
```

❶ pairs_rdd is an RDD[(String, Integer)].

❷ frequencies_rdd is an RDD[(String, Integer)].

Alternatively, we can use the collectAsMap() action to return the result as a hash map:

```
>>> frequencies_rdd.collectAsMap()
{
  u'a': 73,
  u'c': 61,
  u't': 45,
  u'g': 53,
  u'n': 2,
  u'z': 4
}
```

Pros and Cons of Solution 2

Let's examine the pros and cons of this solution:

Pros

- The provided solution works and is simple and semi-efficient. It improves on the previous version by emitting many fewer (key, value) pairs—at most six per DNA sequence, since we create a dictionary per input record and then flatten it into a list of (key, value) pairs, where the key is a DNA letter and the value is the aggregated frequency of that letter.
- Network traffic demands are lower due to the reduction in the number of (key, value) pairs emitted.
- There is no scalability issue since we use `reduceByKey()` for reducing all the (key, value) pairs.

Cons

- Performance is not optimal, since we are still emitting up to six (key, value) pairs per DNA string.
- With large datasets or limited resources this solution might still use too much memory due to the creation of a dictionary per DNA sequence.

DNA Base Count Solution 3

This final solution improves on versions 1 and 2 and is an optimal solution with no scalability issues at all. Here, we'll solve the DNA base count problem using a powerful and efficient Spark transformation called `mapPartitions()`. Before I present the solution itself, let's take a closer look at this transformation.

The mapPartitions() Transformation

If the source RDD is `RDD[T]` and the target RDD is `RDD[U]`, the `mapPartitions()` transformation is defined as:

```
pyspark.RDD.mapPartitions(f, preservesPartitioning=False)

mapPartitions() is a method in the pyspark.RDD class.

Description:

    Return a new RDD (called target RDD) by applying a
    function f() to each partition of the source RDD.

    Input to f() is an iterator (of type T), which
    represents a single partition of the source RDD.
    Function f() returns an object of type U.
```

```
f: Iterator<T> --> U ❶

mapPartitions : RDD[T]--f()--> RDD[U] ❷
```

❶ The function `f()` accepts a pointer to a single partition (as an `iterator` of type `T`) and returns an object of type `U`; `T` and `U` can be any data types and they do not have to be the same.

❷ Transform an `RDD[T]` to `RDD[U]`.

To understand the semantics of the `mapPartitions()` transformation, first you must understand the concept of a partition and partitioning in Spark. Informally, using Spark's terminology, input data (in this case, DNA sequences in FASTA format) is represented as an RDD. Spark automatically partitions RDDs and distributes the partitions across nodes. As an example, say that we have 6 billion records, and the Spark partitioner partitions the input data into 3,000 chunks/partitions. Each partition will have roughly 2 million records and will be processed by a single `mapPartitions()` transformation. Therefore, the function `f()` that is used in the `mapPartitions()` transformation will accept an iterator (as an argument) to handle one partition.

In solution 3, we will create one dictionary per partition rather than a dictionary per FASTA record to aggregate DNA letters and their associated frequencies. This is a huge improvement over solutions 1 and 2, as the creation of 3,000 hash tables in a cluster uses very little memory compared to creating a dictionary per input record. This solution is highly scalable and fast, due to the concurrent and independent processing of all partitions in the cluster.

map() Versus mapPartitions()

What are the main differences between Spark's `map()` and `mapPartitions()` transformations? In a nutshell, `map()` is a 1-to-1 transformation: it maps each element of the source RDD into a single element of the target RDD. `mapPartitions()`, on the other hand, can be considered a many-to-1 transformation: it maps each partition (comprising many elements of the source RDD—each partition may have thousands or millions of elements) into a single element of the target RDD.

The `map()` transformation converts each element of the source RDD into a single element of the target RDD by applying a mapper function. `mapPartitions(`*`func`*`)`, where `func()` is a user-provided function, converts each partition of the source RDD into multiple elements of the target RDD (possibly none) by applying `func()` to each partition. Note that the `mapPartitions()` transformation is a map operation over partitions, and not over the elements of the partition (`func()` receives an iterator, which you can iterate over elements of a partition). This transformation is called once for each input RDD partition, unlike `map()` and `foreach()`, which are called for each element in the RDD. The main advantage of this is that it means we can do initialization on a per-partition basis instead of per-element basis (as is done by `map()` and `foreach()`).

The `mapPartitions()` transformation semantics for DNA base count solution 3 are illustrated in Figure 2-4.

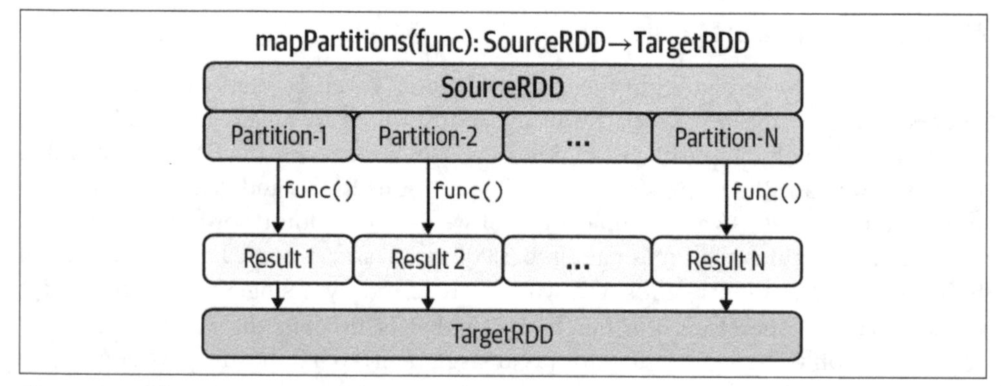

Figure 2-4. The `mapPartitions()` transformation

Let's walk through Figure 2-4:

- The source RDD represents all of our input as an `RDD[String]`, since each record of a FASTA file is a `String` object.
- The entire input is partitioned into *N* chunks or partitions (where *N* can be `100`, `200`, `1000`, …, based on the data size and cluster resources), each of which may hold thousands or millions of DNA sequences (each DNA sequence is a record of type `String`). Partitioning of the source RDD is similar to the Linux `split` command, which splits a file into pieces.
- Each partition is sent to a `mapPartitions()` mapper/worker/executor to be processed by your provided `func()`. Your `func()` accepts a partition (as an iterator of type `String`) and returns at most six (key, value) pairs, where the key is a DNA-letter and the value is the total frequency of that letter for that partition. Note that partitions are processed in parallel and independently.
- Once processing of all partitions is complete, the results are merged into the target RDD, which is an `RDD[(String, Integer)]`, where the key is a DNA letter and the value is the frequency of that DNA letter.

The detailed `mapPartitions()` transformation semantics for the DNA base count problem are presented in Figure 2-5.

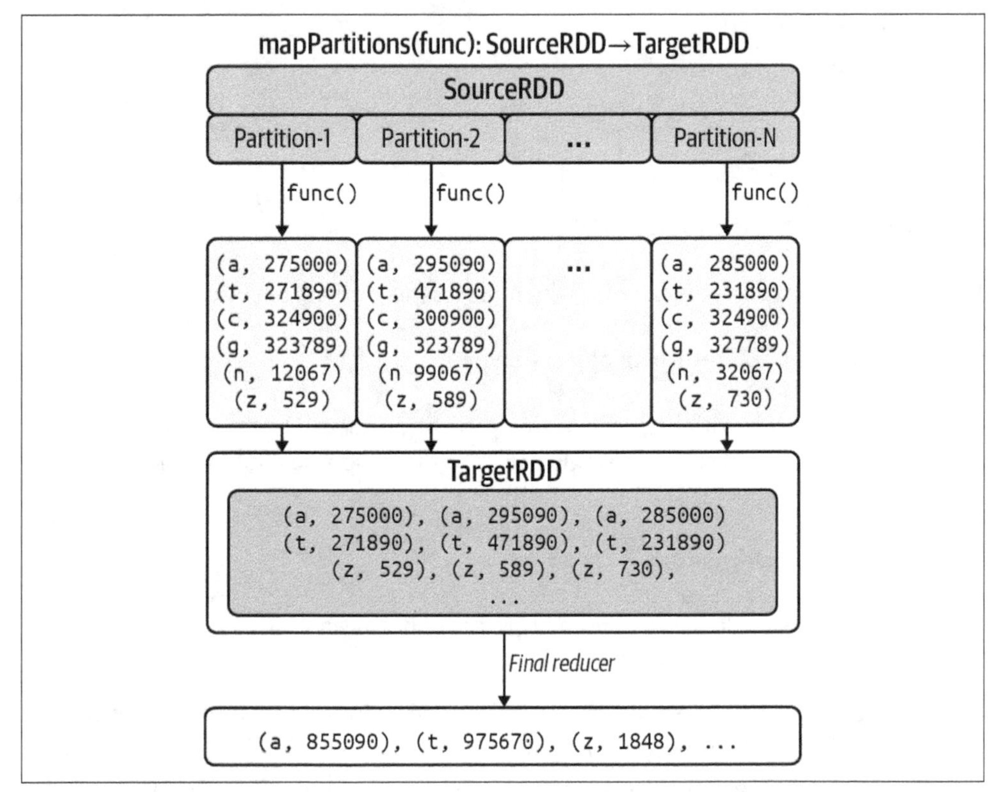

Figure 2-5. Using `mapPartitions()` to solve the DNA base count problem

As this figure shows, our input (FASTA-format data) has been partitioned into `N` chunks/partitions, each of which can be handled by a mapper/worker/executor independently and in parallel. For example, if our input has a total of 5 billion records and `N = 50,000`, then each partition will have about 100,000 FASTA records (5 billion = 50,000 × 100,000). Therefore, each `func()` will process (by means of iteration) about 100,000 FASTA records. Each partition will emit at most six (key, value) pairs, where the keys will be in `{"a", "t", "c", "g", "n", "z"}` (the four letters, `"n"` as a key for non-DNA letters, and `"z"` as a key for the number of processed DNA strings/sequences.

Because the `mapPartitions(func)` transformation runs separately on each partition (block) of the RDD, `func()` must be of type `iterator`:

```
source: RDD[T] ❶

# Parameter p: iterator<T> ❷
def func(p): ❸
   u = <create object of type U by iterating all
        elements of a single partition denoted by p>
```

```
        return u ❹
    #end-def

    target = source.mapPartitions(func) ❺

    target:  RDD[U] ❻
```

❶ Each element of the source RDD is of type `T`.

❷ Parameter `p` is an `iterator<T>`, which represents a single partition.

❸ Each iteration will return an object of type `T`.

❹ Define a `func()`, which accepts a single partition as an `iterator<T>` (an iterator of type `T` that iterates over a single partition of the source `RDD[T]`) and returns an object of type of `U`.

❺ Apply the transformation.

❻ The result is an `RDD[U]`, where each partition has been converted (using `func()`) into a single object type of `U`.

Let's assume that we have a source `RDD[T]`. Therefore, for our example, `T` represents a `String` type (a DNA sequence record) and `U` represents a hash table (a.k.a. dictionary in Python) as `HashMap[String, Integer]`, where the key is a DNA letter (as a `String` object) and the value is the associated frequency (as an `Integer`).

We can define `func()` (as a generic template) in Python as shown here:

```
# Parameter: iterator, which represents a single partition
#
# Note that iterator is a parameter from the mapPartitions()
# transformation, through which we can iterate through all
# the elements in a single partition.
#
# source is an RDD[T]
# target is an RDD[U]

def func(iterator): ❶
   # 1. Make sure that iterator is not empty. If it is empty,
   #    then handle it properly; you cannot ignore empty partitions.

   # 2. Initialize your desired data structures
   #    (such as dictionaries and lists).

   # 3. Iterate through all records in a given partition.
    for record in iterator: ❷
       # 3.1 Process the record
       # 3.2 Update your data structures
```

```
    #end-for

    # 4. If required, post-process your data structures (DS).
     result_for_single_partition = post_process(DS) ❸

    # 5. Return result_for_single_partition.
#end-def
```

 `iterator` is a pointer to a single partition, which you can use to iterate through elements of a partition.

❷ `record` is of type `T`.

❸ `result_for_single_partition` is of type `U`.

Summarization Design Pattern

Spark's `mapPartitions()` transformation can be used to implement the summarization design pattern, which is useful when you're working with big data and you want to get a summary view so you can glean insights that are not available from looking at a localized set of records alone. This design pattern involves grouping similar data together and then performing an operation such as calculating a statistic, building an index, or simply counting.

So when should you use the `mapPartitions()` transformation? It's particularly useful when you want to extract some condensed or minimal amount of information from each partition, where each partition is a large set of data. For example, if you want to find the minimum and maximum of all numbers in your input, using `map()` can be pretty inefficient, since you will be generating tons of intermediate (key, value) pairs but the bottom line is that you want to find just two numbers. It's also useful if you want to find the top 10 (or bottom 10) values in your input. `mapPartitions()` does this efficiently: you find the top (or bottom) 10 per partition, then the top (or bottom) 10 for all partitions. This way, you avoid emitting too many intermediate (key, value) pairs.

For counting DNA bases, the `mapPartitions()` transformation is an ideal solution that scales out very well even when the number of partitions is in the high thousands. Let's say you partition your input into 100,000 chunks (which is a very high number of partitions—typically the number of partitions will not be this high). Aggregating the resulting 100,000 dictionaries (hash maps) is a trivial task that can be accomplished in seconds, with no danger of OOM errors or scalability problems.

I will mention one more tip about using `mapPartitions()` before presenting a complete DNA base count solution using this powerful transformation. Suppose that you will be accessing a database for some of your data transformations, so you need a connection to your database. As you know, creating a connection object is expensive, and it will take some time (maybe a second or two) to create this object. If you create a connection object per source RDD element, then your solution will not scale at all: you will quickly run out of connections and resources. Whenever you have to perform heavyweight initialization (such as creating a database connection object), ideally this should be done once for many RDD elements rather than once per RDD element. If this initialization cannot be serialized (so that Spark can transmit it across the cluster to the worker nodes), as in the case of creating objects from an external library, you should use `mapPartitions()` instead of `map()`. The `mapPartitions()` transformation allows the initialization to be done once per worker task/partition instead of once per RDD data element.

This concept of initialization per partition/worker is presented by the following example:

```
# source_rdd: RDD[T]
# target_rdd: RDD[U]
target_rdd = source_rdd.mapPartitions(func)

def func(partition): ❶
   # create a heavyweight connection object
   connection = <create a db connection per partition> ❷

   data_structures = <create and initialize your data structure> ❸

   # iterate all partition elements
   for rdd_element in partition: ❹
      # Use connection and rdd_element to
      # make a query to your database
      # Update your data_structures
   #end-for

   connection.close() # close db connection here ❺

   u = <prepare object of type U from data_structures> ❻
   return u ❼
#end-def
```

❶ The `partition` parameter is an iterator<T>, which represents a single partition of `source_rdd`; this `func()` returns an object of type `U`.

❷ Create a single `connection` object to be used by all elements in a given partition.

❸ `data_structures` can be a list or dictionary or whatever you desire.

❹ `rdd_element` is a single element of type `T`.

❺ Close the `connection` object (to release allocated resources).

❻ Create an object of type `U` from your created `data_structures`.

❼ Return a single object of type `U` per partition.

Now that you understand the basics of the summarization design pattern (to be implemented by Spark's `mapPartitions()`), let's get into the specifics of using it to solve our DNA base count problem.

The high-level workflow for solution 3 is presented in Figure 2-6. We'll again use the *sample.fasta* file to test this solution.

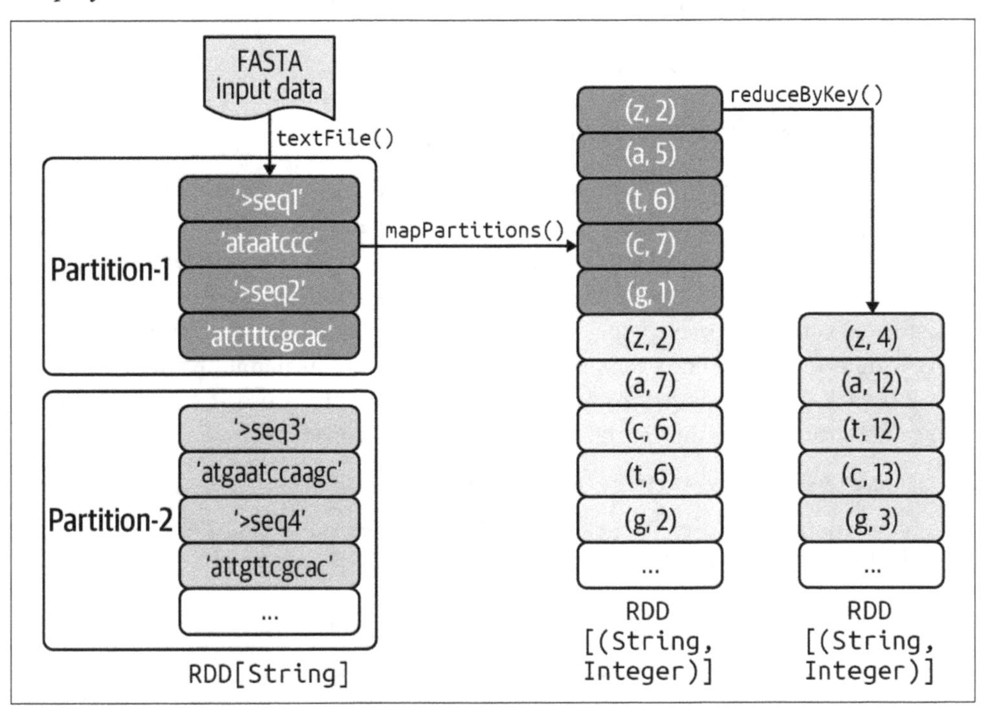

Figure 2-6. DNA base count solution 3

There are a few important points to keep in mind here:

- I show only four records (two FASTA sequences) per partition in this figure, but in reality, each partition may contain thousands or millions of records. If your total input is *N* records and you have *P* partitions, then each partition will have about (*N*/*P*) records.
- If you have enough resources in your Spark cluster, then each partition can be processed in parallel and independently.

- As a general rule, if you have a lot of data but you only need to extract small amount of information from that data, `mapPartitions()` is likely to be a good choice and will outperform the `map()` and `flatMap()` transformations.

With that said, let's look at the main steps of solution 3.

Step 1: Create an RDD[String] from the Input

The `SparkContext.textFile()` function is used to create an RDD for input in FASTA text-based format. This step is identical to step 1 of the previous solutions:

```
input_path = ".../code/chap02/sample.fasta"
>>> records = spark.sparkContext.textFile(input_path) ❶
```

❶ Create records as an `RDD[String]`.

Step 2: Define a Function to Handle a Partition

Let your RDD be an `RDD[T]` (in our example, `T` is a `String`). Spark splits our input data into partitions (where each partition is a set of elements of type `T`—in our example, `T` is `String`) and then executes computations on the partitions independently and in parallel. This is called the divide and conquer model. With the `mapPartitions()` transformation, the source RDD is partitioned into *N* partitions (the number of partitions is determined by the size and number of resources available in the Spark cluster) and each partition is passed to a function (this can be a user-defined function). You can control the number of partitions by using `coalesce()`:

```
RDD.coalesce(numOfPartitions, shuffle=False)
```

which partitions the source RDD into `numOfPartitions` partitions. For example, here we create an RDD and partition it into three partitions:

```
>>> numbers = [1, 2, 3, 4, 5, 6, 7, 8, 9, 10]
>>> numOfPartitions = 3
>>> rdd = sc.parallelize(numbers, numOfPartitions) ❶

>>> rdd.collect()
[1, 2, 3, 4, 5, 6, 7, 8, 9, 10]

>>> rdd.getNumPartitions() ❷
3
```

❶ Create an RDD and set the number of partitions to 3.

❷ Check the number of partitions for the RDD.

Next, I'll define a `scan()` function in Python to iterate a given iterator—you can use this function to debug small RDDs and check the partitioning:

```
>>> def scan(iterator): ❶
... print(list(iterator))
>>>#end-def
>>> rdd.foreachPartition(scan) ❷
1 2 3
===
7 8 9 10
===
4 5 6
===
```

❶ Iterate the elements of a partition.

❷ Apply the `scan()` function to a given partition. From the output, we can see that there are three partitions here.

Do not use `scan()` for production environments; this is for teaching purposes only.

Now let's take a look at the results if we define an `adder()` function in Python that adds the values in each partition:

```
>>> def adder(iterator):
...     yield sum(iterator) ❶
...
>>> rdd.mapPartitions(adder).collect()
[6, 34, 15]
```

 `yield` is a keyword that is used like `return`, except the function will return a generator that can be iterated.

For the DNA base counting problem, to handle (i.e., process all elements in) an RDD partition we'll define a function, `process_FASTA_partition()`, which accepts a single partition (represented as an `iterator`). We then iterate on the `iterator` to process all the elements in the given partition. This produces a dictionary, which we map into a list of `(dna_letter, frequency)` pairs:

```
#-------------------------------------
# Parameter: iterator
# We get an iterator that represents a single
# partition of the source RDD, through which we can
# iterate to process all the elements in the partition.
#
# This function creates a hash map (dictionary) of DNA
# letters and then flattens it into (key, value) pairs.
#-------------------------------------
```

```
from collections import defaultdict

def process_FASTA_partition(iterator): ❶
    hashmap = defaultdict(int) ❷

    for fasta_record in iterator:
        if (fasta_record.startswith(">")): ❸
            hashmap["z"] += 1
        else: ❹
            chars = fasta_record.lower()
            for c in chars:
                hashmap[c] += 1 ❺
    #end-for

    print("hashmap=", hashmap)
    key_value_list = [(k, v) for k, v in hashmap.iteritems()] ❻
    print("key_value_list=", key_value_list)
    return  key_value_list ❼
```

❶ The input parameter `iterator` is a handle/pointer to a single partition.

❷ Create a hash table of `[String, Integer]`.

❸ Handle comments for input data.

❹ Handle a DNA sequence.

❺ Populate the hash table.

❻ Flatten the hash table into a list of `(dna_letter, frequency)` pairs.

❼ Return list of `(dna_letter, frequency)` pairs.

In defining the `process_FASTA_partition()` function, we used a `defaultdict(int)`, which works exactly like a normal dictionary (as an associative array) but is initialized with a function (the "default factory") that takes no arguments and provides the default value for a nonexistent key. In our case, the `defaultdict` is used for counting DNA letters and the default factory is `int` (as in the `Integer` data type), which in turn has a default value of zero. For each character in the list, the value of the corresponding key (a DNA letter) is incremented by one. We do not need to make sure the DNA letter is already a key; if it is not, it will use the default value of zero.

Step 3: Apply the Custom Function to Each Partition

In this step, we apply the `process_FASTA_partition()` function to each partition. I have formatted the output and added some comments to show the output per partition (we have two partitions):

```
>>> records_rdd.getNumPartitions()
2
>>> pairs_rdd = records_rdd.mapPartitions(process_FASTA_partition)

>>># output for partition 1
hashmap= defaultdict(<type 'int'>,
{
 'a': 38, 'c': 28, 'g': 28,
 'n': 2, 't': 24, 'z': 3
})
key_value_list= [
  ('a', 38), ('c', 28), ('g', 28),
  ('n', 2), ('t', 24), ('z', 3)]

>>># output for partition 2
hashmap= defaultdict(<type 'int'>,
{
 'a': 35, 'c': 33,
 't': 21, 'g': 25, 'z': 1,
})
key_value_list= [
 ('a', 35), ('c', 33),
 ('t', 21), ('g', 25), ('z', 1),
]
```

Note that for this solution, each partition returns at most six (key, value) pairs:

```
('a', count-of-a)
('t', count-of-t)
('c', count-of-c)
('g', count-of-g)
('n', count-of-non-atcg)
('z', count-of-DNA-sequences)
```

For our sample data, the final collection from all partitions will be:

```
>>> pairs_rdd.collect()
[
 ('a', 38), ('c', 28), ('t', 24), ('z', 3),
 ('g', 28), ('n', 2), ('a', 35), ('c', 33),
 ('t', 21), ('g', 25), ('z', 1)
]
```

Finally, we aggregate and sum up the output (generated by `mapPartitions()`) for all partitions:

```
>>> frequencies_rdd = pairs_rdd.reduceByKey(lambda a, b: a+b)
>>> frequencies_rdd.collect()
[
 ('a', 73),
 ('c', 61),
 ('g', 53),
 ('t', 45),
 ('n', 2),
```

```
    ('z', 4),
  ]
```

Pros and Cons of Solution 3

Let's examine the pros and cons of solution 3:

Pros

- This is the optimal solution for the DNA base count problem. The provided solution works and is both simple and efficient. It improves on solutions 1 and 2 by emitting the least number of (key, value) pairs, since we create a dictionary per partition (rather than per record) and then flatten it into a list of (key, value) pairs.
- There are no scalability issues since we use `mapPartitions()` for handling each partition and `reduceByKey()` for reducing all the (key, value) pairs emitted by the partitions.
- At most we will create *N* dictionaries, where *N* is the total number of partitions for all the input data (this can be in the hundreds or thousands). This will not be a threat to scalability and will not use too much memory.

Cons

- This solution requires custom code.

Summary

To recap:

- There are usually multiple ways to solve big data problems, using a variety of actions and transformations. Although they all achieve the same result, their performance can differ. When selecting transformations to solve a specific data problem, make sure that you test it with "real" big data rather than toy data.
- For large volumes of (key, value) pairs, overall, the `reduceByKey()` transformation performs better than `groupByKey()` due to different shuffling algorithms.
- When you have big data and you want to extract and aggregate or derive a small amount of information (e.g., finding the minimum and maximum or top 10 values, or counting values like in the DNA base count problem), the `mapPartitions()` transformation is often a good choice.
- Emitting fewer (key, value) pairs improves the performance of your data solutions. This reduces the time required for the sort and shuffle phase of your Spark application.

Next, we'll dig deeper into mapper transformations.

CHAPTER 3

Mapper Transformations

This chapter will introduce the most common Spark mapper transformations through simple working examples. Without a clear understanding of transformations, it is hard to use them in a proper and meaningful way to solve any data problem. We will examine mapper transformations in the context of RDD data abstractions. A mapper is a function that is used to process all the elements of a source RDD and generate a target RDD. For example, a mapper can transform a `String` record into tuples, (key, value) pairs, or whatever your desired output may be. Informally, we can say that a mapper transforms a source `RDD[V]` into a target `RDD[T]`, where `V` and `T` are the data types of the source and target RDDs, respectively. You may apply mapper transformations to DataFrames as well, by either applying DataFrame functions (using `select()` and UDFs) to all rows or converting your DataFrame (a table of rows and columns) to an RDD and then using Spark's mapper transformations.

> **Source Code**
>
> Complete programs for this chapter are available in the book's GitHub repository (*https://oreil.ly/ghCnP*).

Data Abstractions and Mappers

Spark has many transformations and actions, but this chapter is dedicated to explaining the ones that are most often used in building Spark applications. Spark's simple and powerful mapper transformations enable us to perform ETL operations in a simple way.

As I've mentioned, the RDD is an important data abstraction in Spark that is suitable for unstructured and semi-structured data: an immutable, partitioned collection of elements that can be operated on in parallel. The RDD is a lower-level API than Spark's other main data abstraction, the DataFrame (see Figure 3-1). In an RDD, each element may have a data type `T`, denoted by `RDD[T]`.

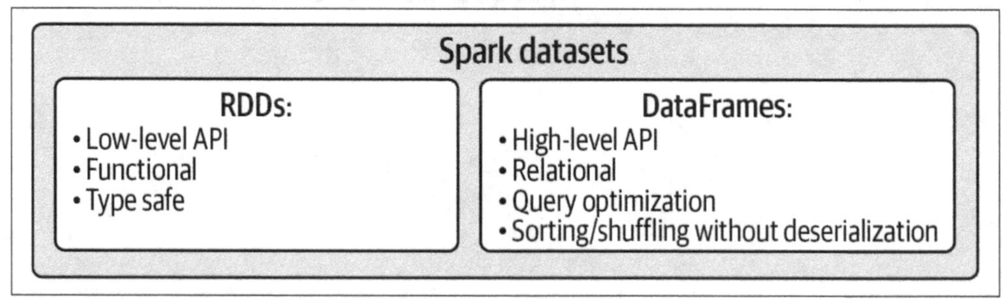

Figure 3-1. Spark's data abstractions

In every data solution, we use mapper transformations to convert one form of data into another desired form of data (for example, converting a record (as a `String`) into a (key, value) form). Spark provides five important mapper transformations that are used heavily in RDD transformations, which are summarized in Table 3-1.

Table 3-1. Mapper transformations

Transformation	Relation type	Description
`map(f)`	1-to-1	Return a new RDD by applying a function (`f()`) to each element of this RDD. Source and target RDDs will have the same number of elements (transforms each element of the source `RDD[V]` into one element of the resulting target `RDD[T]`).
`mapValues(f)`	1-to-1	Pass each value in the (key, value) pair RDD through a `map(f)` function without changing the keys; this also retains the original RDD's partitioning. Source and target RDDs will have the same number of elements (transforms each element of the source `RDD[K, V]` into one element of the resulting target `RDD[K, T]`).
`flatMap(f)`	1-to-many	Return a new RDD by first applying a function (`f()`) to all elements of this RDD, and then flattening the results. Source and target RDDs might not have the same number of elements (transforms each element of the source `RDD[V]` into zero or more elements of the target `RDD[T]`).
`flatMapValues(f)`	1-to-many	Pass each value in the (key, value) pair RDD through a `flatMap(f)` function without changing the keys; this also retains the original RDD's partitioning. Source and target RDDs might not have the same number of elements.
`mapPartitions(f)`	Many-to-1	Return a new RDD by applying a function (`f()`) to each partition of the source RDD. Source and target RDDs might not have the same number of elements (transforms each partition of the source `RDD[V]`, which may be composed of hundreds, thousands, or millions of elements, into one element of the resulting target `RDD[T]`).

We'll dig into each of these later in this chapter with practical examples of their use, but first let's talk some more about what transformations actually are.

What Are Transformations?

A transformation is defined as "a thorough or dramatic change in form or appearance." This exactly matches the semantics of Spark transformations, which transform data from one form to another. For example, a `map()` transformation can transform a record of movie information (as a `String` object of <user_id><,><user name><,><movie_name><,><movie_id><,><rating><,><timestamp><,> <director> <,>...) into a triplet of `(user_id, movie_id, rating)`. Another example of a transformation might be converting a chromosome "chr7:890766:T" into a tuple of `(chr7, 890766, T, 47)`, where 47 (as a derived partition number) is 890766 % 101 (the modulo of 101).

As we learned in Chapter 1, Spark supports two types of operations on RDDs: transformations and actions. As a reminder:

- Most RDD transformations accept a single source RDD and create a single target RDD.
- Some Spark transformations create multiple target RDDs.
- Actions create non-RDD elements (values such as integers, strings, lists, tuples, dictionaries, and files).

There are at least three ways to create a brand new RDD:

1. RDDs can be created from datafiles. You can use `SparkContext.textFile()` or `SparkSession.spark.read.text()` to read datafiles from Amazon S3, HDFS, the Linux filesystem, and many other data sources, as discussed in Chapter 1.
2. RDDs can be created from collections such as a list data structure (e.g., a list of numbers, or a list of strings, or a list of pairs) using `SparkContext.parallelize()`.
3. Given a source RDD, you can apply a transformation (such as `filter()` or `map()`) to create a new RDD.

Spark offers many useful transformations, which are the topic of this chapter. Figure 3-2 illustrates these options.

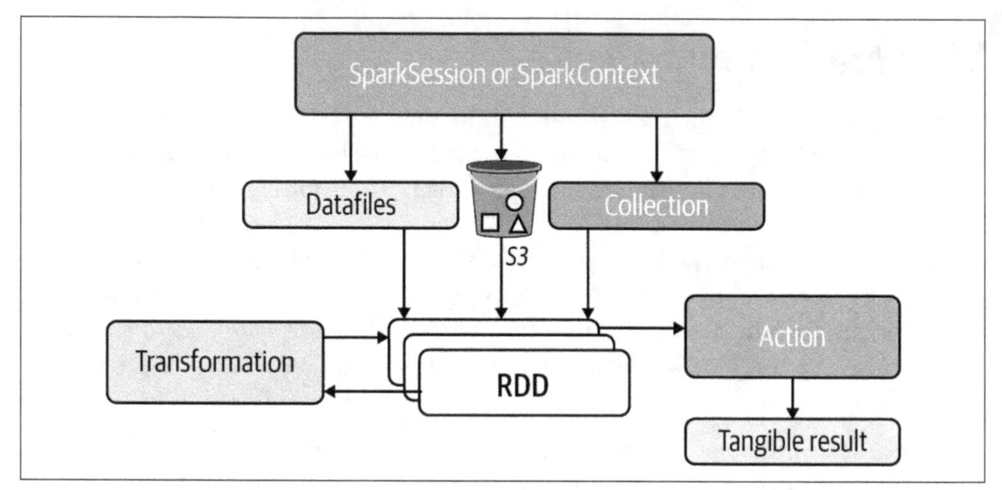

Figure 3-2. Different options for creating RDDs

Informally, the `textFile()` and `parallelize()` operations can be stated as:

```
parallelize : collection --> RDD[T]
# where T is the type of collection elements

textFile : file(s) --> RDD[String]
# reading text files always creates an RDD[String]
```

A transformation (such as `map()` or `filter()`) on a source RDD (with an element type of `U`) creates a new RDD (target RDD [with an element type of `V`]):

```
transformation : RDD[U] --> RDD[V] where
U: data type of source RDD elements
V: data type of target RDD elements
```

An action (such as `collectAsMap()` or `count()`) on a source RDD creates a tangible result (non-RDD) such as integer, string, list, file, or dictionary:

```
acton : RDD[U] --> non-RDD
```

Some basic Spark operations (transformations and actions) are illustrated in Figure 3-3.

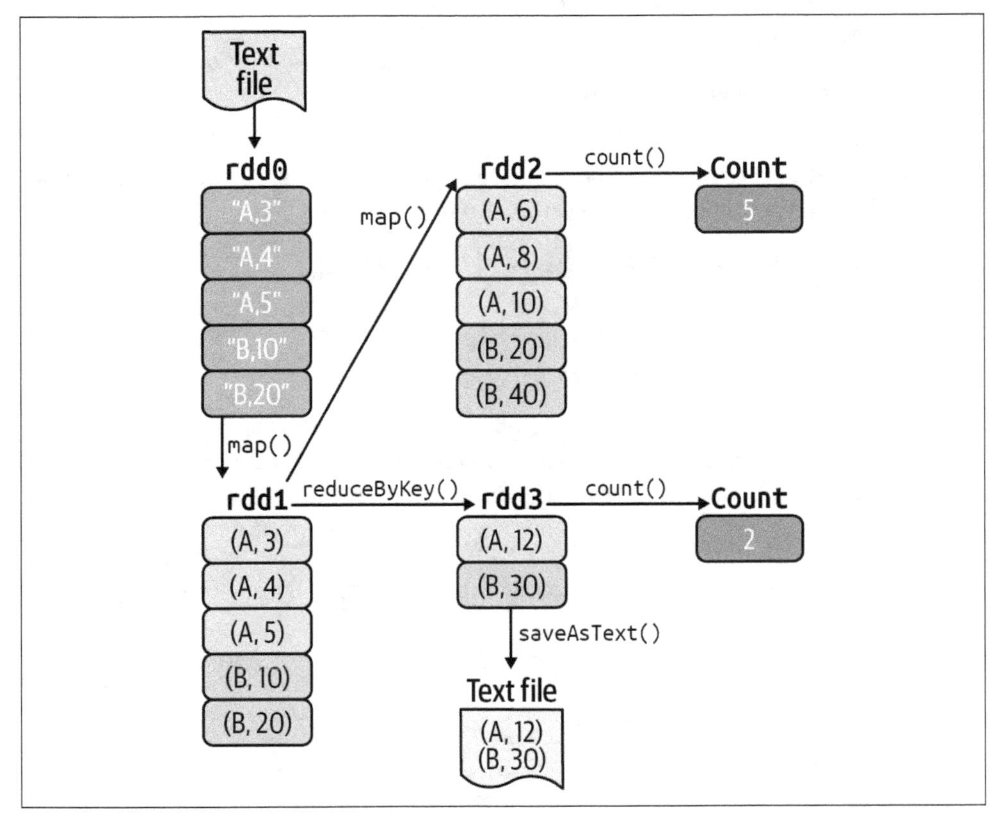

Figure 3-3. Spark transformations and actions

Let's walk through what's happening in Figure 3-3. Four RDDs are created—`rdd0`, `rdd1`, `rdd2`, and `rdd3`—through the following transformations:

Transformation 1

`SparkSession.sparkContext.textFile()` reads our input from a text file and creates the first RDD as `rdd0`:

```
input_path = "sample_5_records.txt"
rdd0 = spark.sparkContext.textFile(input_path)
```

`rdd0` is denoted as `RDD[String]`, meaning that each element of `rdd0` is a `String` object.

Transformation 2

`rdd1` (an `RDD[(String, Integer)]`) is created by the `rdd0.map()` transformation, which maps each element of `rdd0` into (key, value) pairs:

```
def create_pair(record):
    tokens = record.split(",")
    return (tokens[0], int(tokens[1]))
#end-def

rdd1 = rdd0.map(create_pair)
```

Transformation 3

rdd2 (an RDD[(String, Integer)]) is created by rdd1.map(), where the mapper doubles the value part of the (key, value) pairs:

```
rdd2 = rdd1.map(lambda x: (x[0], x[1]+x[1]))

-- OR --

rdd2 = rdd1.mapValues(lambda v: v+v)
```

Transformation 4

rdd3 (an RDD[(String, Integer)]) is created by rdd1.reduceByKey(), where the reducer sums up the values of the same keys:

```
rdd3 = rdd1.reduceByKey(lambda x, y: x+y)
```

Then, the following actions are used to create three additional non-RDD outputs:

Action 1

rdd2.count() is called to count the number of elements of rdd2 (the result is an integer number):

```
rdd2_count = rdd2.count()
```

Action 2

rdd3.count() is called to count the number of elements of rdd3 (again, the result is an integer number):

```
rdd3_count = rdd3.count()
```

Action 3

rdd3.saveAsText() is called to persist the content of rdd3 into a filesystem (the result is a text file):

```
rdd3.saveAsText("/tmp/rdd3_output")
```

Let's take a look at another example, illustrated in Figure 3-4. You can view this sequence of transformations and actions as a directed acyclic graph (DAG), where nodes or vertices represent the RDDs and the edges represent the operations to be applied on the RDDs. As you'll see shortly, Spark uses the DAG to optimize the operations.

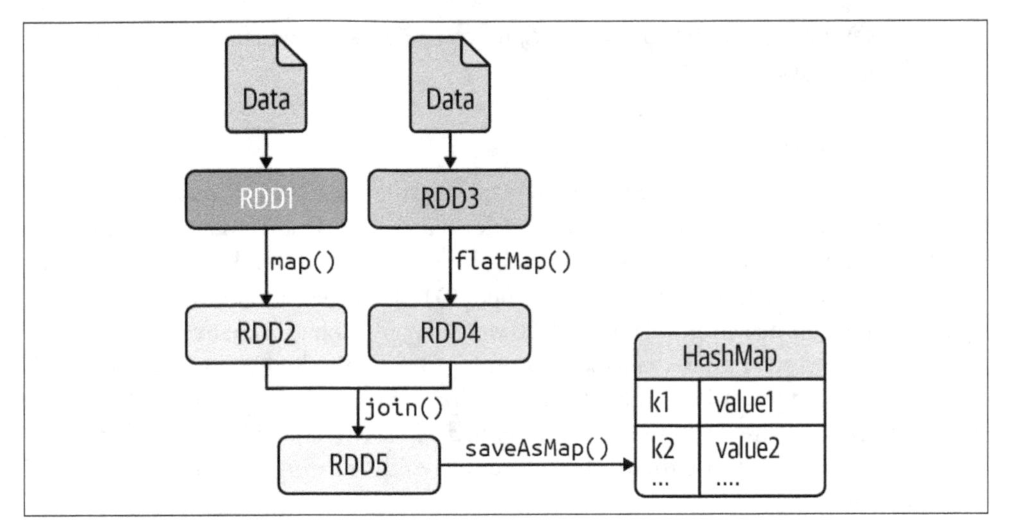

Figure 3-4. Spark operations

Let's walk through what's happening in Figure 3-4:

1. RDD1 and RDD3 are created from text files.

2. RDD2 is created by a `map()` transformation:

```
# source RDD: RDD1[U]
# target RDD: RDD2[V]
RDD2 = RDD1.map(func1)
```

3. RDD4 is created by a `flatMap()` transformation:

```
# source RDD: RDD3[C]
# target RDD: RDD4[D]
RDD4 = RDD3.flatMap(func2)
```

4. RDD5 is created by joining two RDDs (RDD2 and RDD4). The result of this transformation is an RDD containing all pairs of elements with matching keys in RDD2 and RDD4:

```
# source RDDs: RDD2, RDD4
# target RDD: RDD5
# join RDD2 and RDD4 on a common key
RDD5 = RDD2.join(RDD4)
```

5. Finally, the elements of RDD5 are saved as a hash map:

```
# source RDD: RDD5
# action: saveAsMap()
# target: hashmap : dictionary
hashmap = RDD5.saveAsMap()
```

Until the `saveAsMap()` action is executed, no transformation will be evaluated or executed: this is called *lazy evaluation*.

Lazy Transformations

Let's dig a little deeper into Spark's lazy transformations. When running a Spark application (in Python, Java, or Scala), Spark creates a DAG and that graph. Because Spark transformations are lazily evaluated, the execution of the DAG will not start until an action (such as `collect()` or `count()`) is triggered. This means that the Spark engine can make optimization decisions after it has had a chance to look at the DAG in its entirety, rather than looking only at the individual transformations and actions. For example, it is possible to write a Spark program that creates 10 RDDs, 3 of which are never used (these are called *nonreachable RDDs*). The Spark engine does not need to compute those three RDDs, and by avoiding doing so it reduces the total execution time.

As mentioned previously, a DAG in Apache Spark is a set of vertices and edges, where vertices represent the RDDs and the edges represent the operations (transformations or actions) to be applied on the RDDs. In a Spark DAG, every edge is directed from earlier to later in the sequence. On calling of an action (such as `saveAsMap()`, `count()`, `collect()`, or `collectAsMap()`), the created DAG is submitted to Spark's `DAG Scheduler` which further splits the graph into the stages of the task, as illustrated in Figure 3-5.

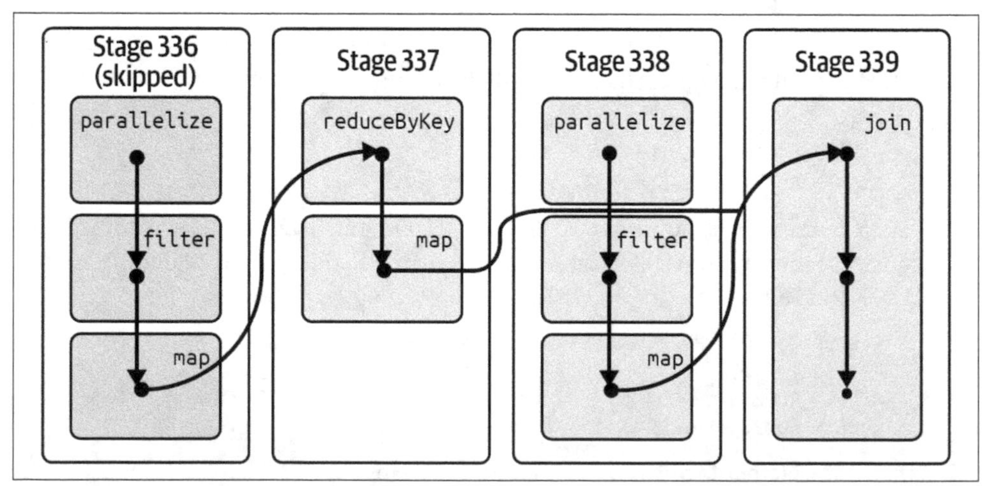

Figure 3-5. Spark's DAG

Every SparkContext launches a web UI (by default on port 4040, with multiple SparkContexts binding to successive ports) that displays useful information about the application, including a visualization of the DAG. You can view the DAG by going to *http://<master>/4040*.

Lazy evaluation in Spark has several benefits. It increases the manageability of transactions, and enables the Spark engine to perform various optimizations. This reduces complexity, saves computation, and increases speed. Reducing the execution time of the RDD operations improves performance, and the lineage graph (DAG) helps Spark achieve fault tolerance by providing a record of the operations performed on the RDDs.

Now that you understand a bit more about transformations, we'll dive into Spark's most common mapper transformations in a little more detail. We'll start with the `map()` transformation, which is the most widely used transformation in any Spark application.

The map() Transformation

The `map()` transformation is the most common transformation in the Spark and MapReduce paradigm. This transformation can be applied to RDDs and Dataframes.

RDD mapper

The goal of `RDD.map()` is to transform every element of the source `RDD[V]` into a mapped element of the target `RDD[T]` by applying a function `f()` to it. This function can be a predefined one or a custom user-defined function. The `map()` transformation is defined as:

```
pyspark.RDD.map (Python method)
map(f, preservesPartitioning=False)

f: V --> T ❶
map: RDD[V] --> RDD[T] ❷
```

 Function `f()` accepts a `V` type element and returns an element of type `T`.

❷ Using function `f()`, the `map()` transformation transforms `RDD[V]` to `RDD[T]`.

This is a 1-to-1 transformation: if your source RDD has *N* elements, then the resulting/target RDD will have exactly *N* elements as well. Bear in mind that the `map()` transformation is not a sequential function. Your source RDD is partitioned into *P* partitions, which are then processed independently and concurrently. For example, if your source RDD has 40 billion elements and *P* = `20,000`, then each partition will have roughly 2 million elements (40 billion = 20,000 x 2 million). If the number of available mappers is 80 (this number depends on the available resources in your cluster), then 80 partitions can be mapped at the same time independently and concurrently.

The function `f()` for the `map()` transformation can be defined as:

```
# v : a data type of V
# return an object of type T
def convert_V_to_T(v):
   t = <convert v to an object of data type T>
   return t
#end-def

# source RDD: source_rdd : RDD[V]
# target RDD: target_rdd : RDD[T]
target_rdd = source_rdd.map(convert_V_to_T)
```

Or you may create your target RDD (`rdd_v`) by using a lambda expression, as follows:

```
target_rdd = source_rdd.map(lambda v : convert_V_to_T(v))
```

Figure 3-6 illustrates the semantics of the `map()` transformation.

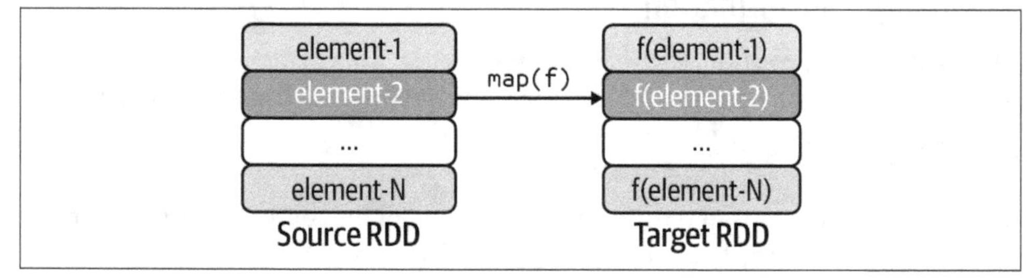

Figure 3-6. The `map()` transformation

The following example shows how to use the `map()` transformation using the PySpark shell. The example maps a source `RDD[Integer]` to a target `RDD[Integer]`: it transforms an RDD that contains a list of numbers into a new RDD in which the value of each positive element has been increased by 5 while all other elements have been changed to 0.

First, let's define our mapper function as `mapper_func()`:

```
>>># define a simple mapper function
>>> def mapper_func(x):
...     if (x > 0):
...             return x+5
...     else:
...             return 0
>>>#end-def
```

Next, we'll apply the a map() transformation and see how it works:

```
>>># spark : SparkSession
>>> data = [1, -1, -2, 3, 4]
>>> rdd = spark.sparkContext.parallelize(data) ❶
>>> rdd.collect()
[1, -1, -2, 3, 4]
>>># use lambda expression
>>> rdd2 = rdd.map(lambda x : mapper_func(x)) ❷
>>> rdd2.collect()
[6, 0, 0, 8, 9]
>>># use a function instead
>>> rdd3 = rdd.map(mapper_func) ❸
>>> rdd3.collect()
[6, 0, 0, 8, 9]
>>>
>>> rdd4 = rdd.map(lambda x : (x, mapper_func(x))) ❹
>>> rdd4.collect()
[(1, 6), (-1, 0), (-2, 0), (3, 8), (4, 9)]
>>> rdd4.count()
5
```

❶ rdd is an RDD[Integer].

❷ rdd2 is an RDD[Integer].

❸ rdd3 is an RDD[Integer].

❹ rdd4 is an RDD[(Integer, Integer)].

Here's another example, which maps an RDD[(String, Integer)] to an RDD[(String, Integer, String)]. This example transforms elements in the form of (key, value) pairs into (key, value, value+100) triplets:

```
>>> pairs = [('a', 2), ('b', -1), ('d', -2), ('e', 3)]
>>> rdd = spark.sparkContext.parallelize(pairs) ❶
>>> rdd.collect()
[('a', 2), ('b', -1), ('d', -2), ('e', 3)]
>>> rdd2 = rdd.map(lambda (k, v) : (k, v, v+100)) ❷
>>> rdd2.collect()
[
 ('a', 2, 102),
 ('b', -1, 99),
 ('d', -2, 98),
 ('e', 3, 103)
]
```

❶ rdd is an RDD[(String, Integer)].

❷ rdd2 is an RDD[(String, Integer, Integer)].

It's also straightforward to create (key, value) pairs from `String` objects:

```
>>> def create_key_value(string):
>>>   tokens = string.split(",")
>>>   return (tokens[0], (tokens[1], tokens[2]))
>>>
>>> strings = ['a,10,11', 'b,8,19', 'c,20,21', 'c,2,8']
>>> rdd = spark.sparkContext.parallelize(strings) ❶
>>> rdd.collect()
['a,10,11', 'b,8,9', 'c,20,21', 'c,2,8']
>>> pairs = rdd.map(create_key_value) ❷
>>> rdd2.collect()
[
 ('a', (10, 11)),
 ('b', (8, 19)),
 ('c', (20, 21)),
 ('c', (2, 8))
]
```

 `rdd` is an `RDD[String]`.

❷ `rdd2` is an `RDD[(String, (Integer, Integer))]`.

Next, I'll discuss custom mapper functions.

Custom mapper functions

When using Spark's transformations, you may use custom Python functions to parse records, perform computations, and finally create your desired output.

Suppose we have a sample dataset, where each record has the following format:

```
<id><,><name><,><age><,><number-of-friends>
```

Our data looks like this:

```
$ cat /tmp/users.txt
1,Alex,30,124
2,Bert,32,234
3,Curt,28,312
4,Don,32,180
5,Mary,30,100
6,Jane,28,212
7,Joe,28,128
8,Al,40,600
```

For each age category, we want to get the average number of friends. We can write our own custom mapper function:

```
# record=<id><,><name><,><age><,><number-of-friends>
# parse record and return a pair as (age, number_of_friends)
def parse_record(record):
    # split record into a list at comma positions
```

```
        tokens = record.split(",")
        # extract and typecast relevant fields
        age = int(tokens[2])
        number_of_friends = int(tokens[3])
        return (age, number_of_friends)
    #end-def
```

Then read our data and use the custom function:

```
users_path = '/tmp/users.txt'
users = spark.sparkContext.textFile(users_path) ❶
pairs = users.map(parse_record) ❷
```

❶ `users` is an `RDD[String]`.

❷ `pairs` is an `RDD[(Integer, Integer)]`, where each record gets sent through `parse_record()`.

For our sample data, `pairs` will be:

```
(30, 124), (32, 234), (28, 312), (32, 180),
(30, 100), (28, 212), (28, 128), (40, 600)
```

To get the average per age category, we first get the sum and the number of entries per age:

```
totals_by_age = pairs \ ❶
  .mapValues(lambda x: (x, 1)) \ ❷
  .reduceByKey(lambda x, y: (x[0] + y[0], x[1] + y[1])) ❸ ❹
```

❶ `pairs` is an `RDD[(Integer, Integer)]`.

❷ Convert the `number_of_friends` field to a `(number_of_friends, 1)` pair.

❸ Perform reduction on age to find `(sum_of_friends, frequecy_count)` per age.

❹ `totals_by_age` is `RDD[(Integer, (Integer, Integer))]`

For our data, `totals_by_age` will be:

```
(30, (124+100, 1+1))         --> (30, (224, 2))
(32, (234+180, 1+1))         --> (32, (414, 2))
(28, (312+212+128, 1+1+1)) --> (28, (652, 3))
(40, (600, 1))               --> (40, (600, 1))
```

Now, to compute the average number of friends for each age, we need to do one more transformation, dividing the sum by the frequency count to get the average:

```
# x = (sum_of_friends, frequency_count)
# x[0] = sum_of_friends
# x[1] = frequency_count
```

```
averages_by_age = totals_by_age.mapValues(lambda x: float(x[0]) / float(x[1]))
averages_by_age.collect()
```

For our data, averages_by_age (an RDD[(Integer, Integer)]) will be:

```
(30, (224 / 2)) = (30, 112)
(32, (414 / 2)) = (32, 207)
(28, (652 / 3)) = (28, 217)
(40, (600 / 1)) = (40, 600)
```

DataFrame Mapper

Spark's DataFrame does not have a map() function, but we can achieve the map() equivalency in many ways: we can add new columns by applying DataFrame.withColumn() and drop existing columns with DataFrame.drop(). The new column values can be computed based on existing row values or other requirements.

Mapper to single DataFrame column

Consider the following DataFrame:

```
tuples3 = [ ('alex', 440, 'PHD'), ('jane', 420, 'PHD'),
            ('bob', 280, 'MS'), ('betty', 200, 'MS'),
            ('ted', 180, 'BS'), ('mary', 100, 'BS') ]

df = spark.createDataFrame(tuples3, ["name", "amount", "education"])
>>> df.show()
+-----+------+---------+
| name|amount|education|
+-----+------+---------+
| alex|   440|      PHD|
| jane|   420|      PHD|
|  bob|   280|       MS|
|betty|   200|       MS|
|  ted|   180|       BS|
| mary|   100|       BS|
+-----+------+---------+
```

Suppose we want to calculate a 10% bonus to the "amount" column and create a new "bonus" column. There are multiple ways to accomplish this mapper task.

To keep all of the columns, do the following:

```
df2 = df.rdd\
    .map(lambda x: (x["name"], x["amount"],
                    x["education"], int(x["amount"])/10))
    .toDF(["name", "amount", "education", "bonus"])

>>> df2 = df.rdd.map(lambda x: (x["name"], x["amount"],
    x["education"], x["amount"]/10))
    .toDF(["name", "amount", "education", "bonus"])
>>> df2.show()
```

```
+-----+-----+--------+-----+
| name|amount|education|bonus|
+-----+-----+--------+-----+
| alex|   440|      PHD| 44.0|
| jane|   420|      PHD| 42.0|
|  bob|   280|       MS| 28.0|
|betty|   200|       MS| 20.0|
|  ted|   180|       BS| 18.0|
| mary|   100|       BS| 10.0|
+-----+-----+--------+-----+
```

You have to map the row to a tuple containing all of the existing columns, then add in the new column(s).

If you have too many columns to enumerate, you could also just add a tuple to the existing row.

```
>>> df3 = df.rdd.map(lambda x: x + \
   (str(x["amount"]/10),)).toDF(df.columns + ["bonus"])
>>> df3.show()
+-----+-----+--------+-----+
| name|amount|education|bonus|
+-----+-----+--------+-----+
| alex|   440|      PHD| 44.0|
| jane|   420|      PHD| 42.0|
|  bob|   280|       MS| 28.0|
|betty|   200|       MS| 20.0|
|  ted|   180|       BS| 18.0|
| mary|   100|       BS| 10.0|
+-----+-----+--------+-----+
```

There is another way to add a `bonus` column with using `DataFrame.withColumn()`:

```
>>> df4 = df.withColumn("bonus", F.lit(df.amount/10))
>>> df4.show()
+-----+-----+--------+-----+
| name|amount|education|bonus|
+-----+-----+--------+-----+
| alex|   440|      PHD| 44.0|
| jane|   420|      PHD| 42.0|
|  bob|   280|       MS| 28.0|
|betty|   200|       MS| 20.0|
|  ted|   180|       BS| 18.0|
| mary|   100|       BS| 10.0|
+-----+-----+--------+-----+
```

Mapper to multiple DataFrame columns

Now, assume that you want to add a `bonus` column, which depends on two columns: "amount" and "education": The `bonus` column is calculated as:

```
bonus = amount * 30% if education = PHD
bonus = amount * 20% if education = MS
bonus = amount * 10% all other cases
```

the simplest way to do this is with a user-defined function (UDF): define a Python function and then register it as a UDF:

```
def compute_bonus(amount, education):
    if education == "PHD": return int(amount * 0.30)
    if education == "MS": return int(amount * 0.20)
    return int(amount * 0.10)
#end-def
```

Now, register your Python function as a UDF:

```
>>> from org.apache.spark.sql.functions import udf
>>> compute_bonus_udf = udf(lambda amount, education:
   compute_bonus(amount, education), IntegerType())
```

Once your UDF is ready, then you can apply it:

```
>>> df5 = df.withColumn("bonus",
   compute_bonus_udf(df.amount, df.education))
>>> df5.show()
+-----+------+---------+-----+
| name|amount|education|bonus|
+-----+------+---------+-----+
| alex|   440|      PHD|  132|
| jane|   420|      PHD|  126|
|  bob|   280|       MS|   56|
|betty|   200|       MS|   40|
|  ted|   180|       BS|   18|
| mary|   100|       BS|   10|
+-----+------+---------+-----+
```

Next, we'll take a look at the `flatMap()` transformation.

The flatMap() Transformation

The `flatMap()` transformation returns a new RDD by applying a function to each element of the source RDD, then flattening the results. This is a 1-to-many transformation: every element of the source RDD can be mapped into 0, 1, 2, or many elements of the target RDD. In other words, The `flatMap()` transforms a source `RDD[U]` of length *N* into a target `RDD[V]` of length *M* (where *M* and *N* can be different), When using `flatMap()`, you need to make sure that the source RDD's elements are iterable (such as a list of items).

For example, if an element of the source RDD is `[10, 20, 30]` (an iterable list of three numbers), then it will be mapped as three elements (`10`, `20`, and `30`) of the target RDD; if an element of the source RDD is `[]` (an empty list, which is iterable), then it will be dropped and will not be mapped to the target RDD at all. If any element of source RDD is not iterable, then an exception will be raised.

Note that whereas `map()` transforms an RDD of length *N* into another RDD of length *N* (the same length), `flatMap()` transforms an RDD of length *N* into a set of *N* iterable collections, then flattens these into a single RDD of results. Therefore, the source and target RDDs may have different sizes.

The `flatMap()` transformation is defined as:

```
pyspark.RDD.flatMap (Python method)
flatMap(f, preservesPartitioning=False)

U: iterable collection of V
source RDD: RDD[U]
target RDD: RDD[V]

f: U --> [V] ❶
flatMap: RDD[U] --> RDD[V]
```

❶ The function `f()` accepts an element of type `U` and converts it into a list of elements of type `V` (this list may have 0, 1, 2, or more elements), which is then flattened. Note that empty lists are dropped. The function `f()` must create an iterable object.

Figure 3-7 shows an example of the `flatMap()` transformation.

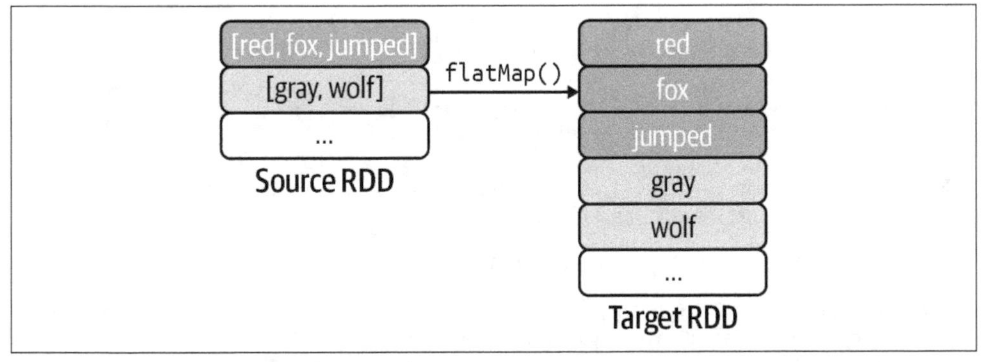

Figure 3-7. The `flatMap()` transformation

In Figure 3-7, each element (a `String`) of the source RDD is tokenized into a list of `Strings` and then flattened into a `String` object. For example, the first element, `"[red fox jumped]"`, is converted into a list of `Strings` as `["red", "fox", "jumped"]` and then the list is flattened into three `String` objects as `"red"`, `"fox"`, and `"jumped"`. The first source element is thus mapped into three target elements.

The following example shows how to use the `flatMap()` transformation:

```
>>> numbers = [1, 2, 3, 4, 5]
>>> rdd = spark.sparkContext.parallelize(numbers)
>>> rdd.collect()
[1, 2, 3, 4, 5]
>>> rdd2 = rdd.flatMap(lambda x: range(1, x))
>>> rdd2.collect()
[1, 1, 2, 1, 2, 3, 1, 2, 3, 4]
>>> rdd3 = rdd.flatMap(lambda x: [(x, x+1), (x+1, x)])
>>> rdd3.collect()
[
 (1, 2), (2, 1),
 (2, 3), (3, 2),
 (3, 4), (4, 3),
 (4, 5), (5, 4),
 (5, 6), (6, 5)
]
>>> rdd3.count()
10
```

Let's examine how `rdd2` is created:

```
Element 1: --maps--> range(1, 1) --flattens--> []
           --> dropped since empty

Element 2: --maps--> range(1, 2) --flattens--> [1]
           --> maps into one element as 1

Element 3: --maps--> range(1, 3) --flattens--> [1, 2]
           --> maps into two elements as 1, 2

Element 4: --maps--> range(1, 4) --flattens--> [1, 2, 3]
           --> maps into three elements as 1, 2, 3

Element 5: --maps--> range(1, 5) --flattens--> [1, 2, 3, 4]
           --> maps into four elements as 1, 2, 3, 4
```

You can also use a function, instead of a lambda expression:

```
>>> numbers = [1, 2, 3, 4, 5]
>>> rdd = spark.sparkContext.parallelize(numbers) ❶
>>> rdd.collect()
[1, 2, 3, 4, 5]
>>> def create_list(x):
...     return [(x, x+1), (x, x+2)]
>>>#end-def
...
>>> rdd4 = rdd.flatMap(create_list) ❷
>>> rdd4.collect()
[
 (1, 2), (1, 3),
 (2, 3), (2, 4),
 (3, 4), (3, 5),
```

```
 (4, 5), (4, 6),
 (5, 6), (5, 7)
]
>>> rdd4.count()
10
```

❶ rdd is an RDD[Integer] with five elements.

❷ rdd4 is an RDD[(Integer, Integer)] with 10 elements.

The following example illustrates how flatMap() can return zero or more elements in the target RDD for each element in the source RDD:

```
>>> words = ["a", "red", "of", "fox", "jumped"]
>>> rdd = spark.sparkContext.parallelize(words)
>>> rdd.count() ❶
5
>>> rdd.collect()
['a', 'red', 'of', 'fox', 'jumped']
>>> def my_flatmap_func(x):
...     if len(x) < 3:
...         return [] ❷
...     else:
...         return [x, x, x] ❸
...
>>> flattened = rdd.flatMap(my_flatmap_func)
>>> flattened.count() ❹
9
>>> flattened.collect()
['red', 'red', 'red', 'fox', 'fox', 'fox', 'jumped', 'jumped', 'jumped']
```

❶ rdd is an RDD[String] with five elements.

❷ Empty lists are dropped.

❸ This will map to three target elements.

❹ flattened is an RDD[String] with nine elements.

The following example clearly shows the difference between map() and flatMap(). As you can see from the outputs, flatMap() flattens its output, while the map() transformation is a 1-to-1 mapping and does not flatten its output:

```
def to_list(x): return [x, x+x, x*x]

# rdd1: RDD[Integer] (element type is Integer)
rdd1 = spark.sparkContext.parallelize([3,4,5]) ❶
            .map(to_list) ❷
rdd1.collect()
# output: notice non-flattened list
```

```
[[3, 6, 9], [4, 8, 16], [5, 10, 25]]
rdd1.count()
3

# rdd2 : RDD[[Integer]] (element type is [Integer])
rdd2 = spark.sparkContext.parallelize([3,4,5]) ❸
                         .flatMap(to_list) ❹
rdd2.collect()
# output: notice flattened list
[3, 6, 9, 4, 8, 16, 5, 10, 25]
rdd2.count()
9
```

❶ Create an `RDD[Integer]`.

❷ Each element of `rdd1` is a list of integer numbers (as `RDD[[Integer]]`).

❸ Create an `RDD[[Integer]]`.

❹ Each element of `rdd2` is an integer number (as `RDD[Integer]`).

A visual representation of the `flatMap()` transformation is presented in the Figure 3-8.

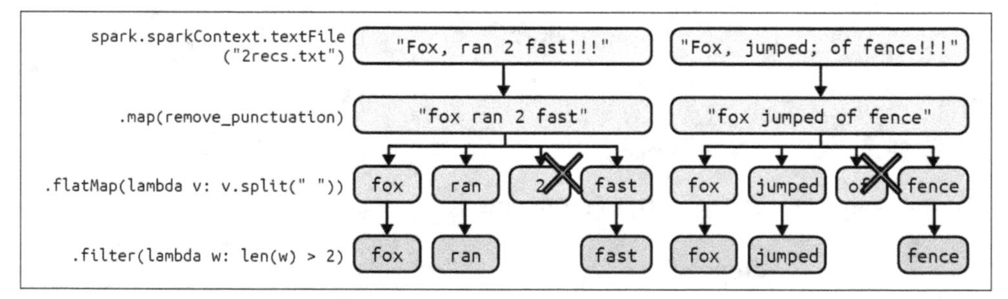

Figure 3-8. A `flatMap()` transformation

Let's walk through what's happening here. We'll start by examining the content of the input file, *2recs.txt*:

```
$ cat 2recs.txt
Fox, ran  2 fast!!!
Fox, jumped; of fence!!!
```

Here are the steps:

1. First, we create an `RDD[String]` with only two records/elements:

```
rdd = spark.sparkCintext.textFile("2recs.txt")
rdd.collect()
[
```

```
 "Fox, ran  2 fast!!!",
 "Fox, jumped; of fence!!!"
]
```

2. Next, we apply a `map()` transformation to all elements of this RDD that removes all punctuation, reduces multiple spaces into a single space, and converts all letters to lowercase. This is accomplished by a simple Python function:

```
import string, re
def no_punctuation(record_str):
    exclude = set(string.punctuation)
    t = ''.join(ch for ch in record_str if ch not in exclude)
    trimmed = re.sub('\s+',' ', t)
    return trimmed
#end-def

rdd_cleaned = rdd.map(no_punctuation)
rdd_cleaned.collect()
[
 "fox ran 2 fast",
 "fox jumped of fence"
]
```

3. We then apply a `flatMap()` transformation to `rdd_cleaned`, first tokenizing the elements of this RDD and then flattening it:

```
flattened = rdd_cleaned.flatMap(lambda v: v.split(" "))
flattened.collect()
['fox', 'ran', '2', 'fast', 'fox', 'jumped', 'of', 'fence']
```

4. Finally, the `filter()` transformation drops elements of the `flattened` RDD, keeping only elements with a length greater than 2.

```
final_rdd = flattened.filter(lambda w: len(w) > 2)
final_rdd.collect()
['fox', 'ran', 'fast', 'fox', 'jumped', 'fence']
```

The filtered-out elements are indicated with an X in Figure 3-8.

map() Versus flatMap()

You've now seen some examples of `map()` and `flatMap()` transformations, but it's important to understand the differences between them. To recap:

`map()`
: This is a 1-to-1 transformation. It returns a new RDD by applying the given function to each element of the RDD. The function in `map()` returns only one item.

`flatMap()`
: This is a 1-to-many transformation. It also returns a new RDD by applying a function to each element of the source RDD, but the function may return 0, 1, 2, or more elements per source element, and the output is flattened.

The difference between `map()` and `flatMap()` is illustrated in Figure 3-9.

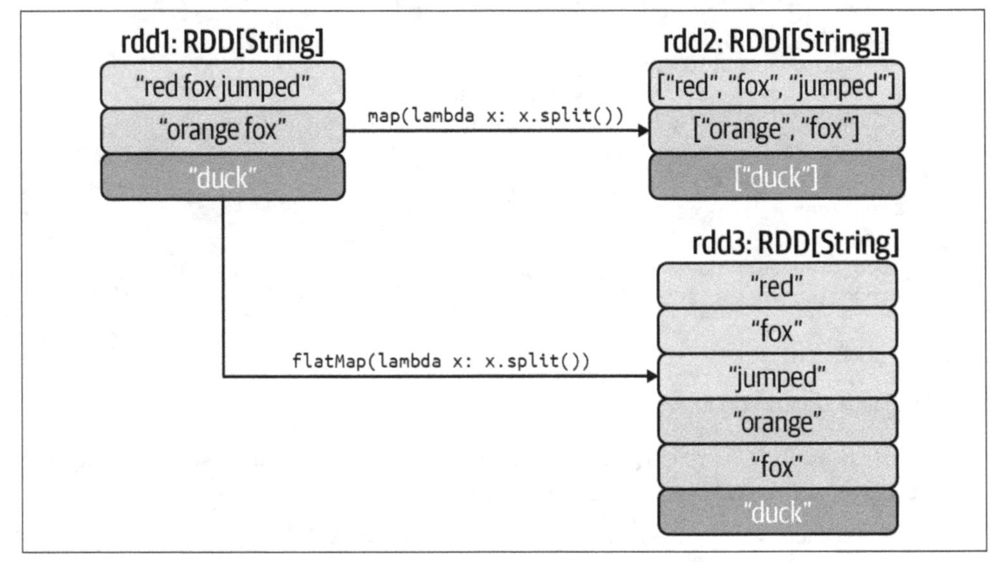

Figure 3-9. The difference between `map()` and `flatMap()`

Apply `flatMap()` to a DataFrame

The `RDD.flatMap()` is a one-to-many transformation: it takes one element of source RDD and transforms it into many (0, 1, 2, 3, or more) target elements. PySpark's DataFame does not have `flatMap()` transformation, however, DataFrame has the function `pyspark.sql.functions.explode(col)`, which is used to flatten the column. The `explode(column)` returns a new row for each element in the given `column` (expressed as a list or dictionary) and uses the default column name `col` for elements in the array and key and value for elements in the dictionary unless specified otherwise.

Below is a complete example, which shows how to use the `explode()` function as an equivalent to `RDD.flatMap()` transformation.

Let's first create a DataFrame, in which one column is a list (to be exploded by the `explode()` function).

```
some_data = [
    ('alex', ['Java','Scala', 'Python']),
    ('jane', ['Cobol','Snobol']),
```

```
    ('bob', ['C++',]),
    ('ted', []),
    ('max', [])
]

>>> df = spark.createDataFrame(
    data=some_data, schema = ['name', 'known_languages'])

>>> df.show(truncate=False)
+----+---------------------+
|name| known_languages     |
+----+---------------------+
|alex| [Java, Scala, Python]|
|jane| [Cobol, Snobol]     |
|bob | [C++]               |
|ted | []                  |
|max | []                  |
+----+---------------------+
```

Next, we will flatten the known_languages column:

```
>>> exploded = df.select(df.name,
    explode(df.known_languages).alias('language'))
>>> exploded.show(truncate=False)
+----+--------+
|name|language|
+----+--------+
|alex|  Java  |
|alex|  Scala |
|alex|  Python|
|jane|  Cobol |
|jane|  Snobol|
|bob |  C++   |
+----+--------+
```

As you can see, when exploding a column, if a column is an empty list, it's dropped from the exploded result (tex and max are dropped since they have associated empty lists).

Next, we'll look at exploding multiple columns for a given DataFrame. Note that only one generator is allowed per select clause: this means you can not explode two columns at the same time (but you can explode them iteratively one-by-one). The following example shows how to explode two columns:

```
>>> some_data = [
...     ('alex', ['Java','Scala', 'Python'], ['MS', 'PHD']),
...     ('jane', ['Cobol','Snobol'], ['BS', 'MS']),
...     ('bob', ['C++'], ['BS', 'MS', 'PHD']),
...     ('ted', [], ['BS', 'MS']),
...     ('max', ['FORTRAN'], []),
...     ('dan', [], [])
... ]
```

```
>>>
>>> df = spark.createDataFrame(data=some_data,
   schema = ['name', 'languages', 'education'])
>>> df.show(truncate=False)
+----+--------------------+------------+
|name|languages           |education   |
+----+--------------------+------------+
|alex|[Java, Scala, Python]|[MS, PHD]   |
|jane|[Cobol, Snobol]     |[BS, MS]    |
|bob |[C++]               |[BS, MS, PHD]|
|ted |[]                  |[BS, MS]    |
|max |[FORTRAN]           |[]          |
|dan |[]                  |[]          |
+----+--------------------+------------+
```

Next we explode the `languages` column, which is an array:

```
>>> exploded_1 = df.select(df.name,
   explode(df.languages).alias('language'), df.education)
>>> exploded_1.show(truncate=False)
+----+--------+------------+
|name|language|education   |
+----+--------+------------+
|alex|Java    |[MS, PHD]   |
|alex|Scala   |[MS, PHD]   |
|alex|Python  |[MS, PHD]   |
|jane|Cobol   |[BS, MS]    |
|jane|Snobol  |[BS, MS]    |
|bob |C++     |[BS, MS, PHD]|
|max |FORTRAN |[]          |
+----+--------+------------+
```

Note that the names `ted` and `dan` were dropped since the exploded column value was an empty list.

Next, we explode the `education` column:

```
>>> exploded_2 = exploded_1.select(exploded_1.name, exploded_1.language,
   explode(exploded_1.education).alias('degree'))
>>> exploded_2.show(truncate=False)
+----+--------+------+
|name|language|degree|
+----+--------+------+
|alex|Java    |    MS|
|alex|Java    |   PHD|
|alex|Scala   |    MS|
|alex|Scala   |   PHD|
|alex|Python  |    MS|
|alex|Python  |   PHD|
|jane|Cobol   |    BS|
|jane|Cobol   |    MS|
|jane|Snobol  |    BS|
|jane|Snobol  |    MS|
```

```
|bob |C++     |    BS|
|bob |C++     |    MS|
|bob |C++     |   PHD|
+----+--------+------+
```

Note that the name max is dropped since the exploded column value was an empty list.

Next we'll look at a transformation that is specific to RDDs whose elements are (key, value) pairs.

The mapValues() Transformation

The `mapValues()` transformation is only applicable for pair RDDs (`RDD[(K, V)]`, where `K` is the key and `V` is the value). It operates on the value only (`V`), leaving the key unchanged, unlike the `map()` transformation, which operates on the entire RDD element.

Informally, given the source RDD `RDD[(K, V)]` and the function `f: V -> T`, we may say that `rdd.mapValues(f)` is equivalent to the following `map()`:

```
# source rdd: RDD[(K, V)]
# target result: RDD[(K, T)]
result = rdd.map( lambda (k, v): (k, f(v)) )
```

The `mapValues()` transformation is defined as:

```
pyspark.RDD.mapValues (Python method)
mapValues(f)

f: V --> U ❶
mapValues: RDD[(K, V)] --> RDD[(K, f(V))]
```

❶ The function `f()` can transform the data type `V` to any desired data type `T`. `V` and `T` can be the same or different.

The `mapValues()` transformation passes each value in the pair RDD through a `map()` function without changing the keys; this also retains the original RDD's partitioning (the changes are done in place and the structure and number of partitions are not changed).

The following is an example of a `mapValues()` transformation:

```
>>> pairs = [
    ("A", []), ("Z", [40]),
    ("C", [10, 20, 30]), ("D", [60, 70])
  ]
>>> rdd = spark.sparkContext.parallelize(pairs) ❶
>>> rdd.collect()
[('A', []), ('Z', [40]), ('C', [10, 20, 30]), ('D', [60, 70])]
```

```
>>>
>>> def f(x):
>>>     if len(x) == 0: return 0
>>>     else: return len(x)+1
>>>
>>> rdd2 = rdd.mapValues(f) ❷
>>> rdd2.collect()
[('A', 0), ('Z', 2), ('C', 4), ('D', 3)]
```

❶ `rdd` is an `RDD[(String, [Integer])]`.

❷ `rdd2` is an `RDD[(String, Integer)]`.

`mapValues()` is a 1-to-1 transformation, as illustrated by Figure 3-10.

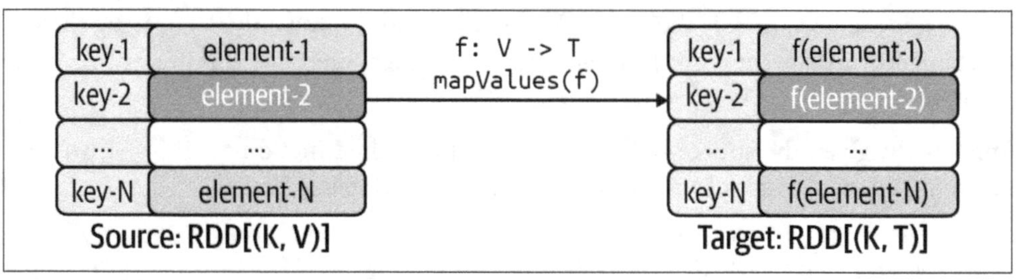

Figure 3-10. The `mapValues()` transformation

The flatMapValues() Transformation

The `flatMapValues()` transformation is a combination of `flatMap()` and `mapValues()`. It's similar to `mapValues()`, but `flatMapValues()` runs the `flatMap()` function on the values of `RDD[(K, V)]` (an RDD of (key, value) pairs) instead of the `map()` function. It does this without changing the keys, retaining the original RDD's partitioning. Here's an example:

```
>>> rdd = spark.sparkContext.parallelize([
  ('S', []), ❶
  ('Z', [7]),
  ('A', [1, 2, 3]),
  ('B',[4, 5])
]) ❷

>>># function is applied to entire
>>># value, and then result is flattened
>>> rdd2 = rdd.flatMapValues(lambda v: [i*3 for i in v]) ❸
>>> rdd2.collect()
[('Z', 21),
 ('A', 3), ('A', 6), ('A', 9),
 ('B', 12), ('B', 15)]
```

❶ This element will be dropped since the value is empty.

❷ `rdd` is an `RDD[(String, [Integer])]`.

❸ `rdd2` is an `RDD[(String, Integer)]`; note that the key `S` is dropped since its value was an empty list

Here's another example:

```
>>> rdd = spark.sparkContext.parallelize([
  ("A", ["x", "y", "z"]),
  ("B", ["p", "r"]),
  ("C", ["q"]),
  ("D", [])
]) ❶

>>> def f(x): return x
>>> rdd2 = rdd.flatMapValues(f) ❷
>>> rdd2.collect()
[
 ('A', 'x'), ('A', 'y'), ('A', 'z'),
 ('B', 'p'), ('B', 'r'),
 ('C', 'q')
]
```

❶ `rdd` is an `RDD[(String, [String])]`.

❷ `rdd2` is an `RDD[(String, String)]`.

Again, if the value for a key is empty (`[]`), then no output value is generated (the key is dropped as well). Therefore, no element is generated for the `D` key.

Next we'll look at the `mapPartitions()` transformation, which, in my opinion, is the most important of Spark's mapper transformations.

The mapPartitions() Transformation

`mapPartitions()` is a powerful distributed mapper transformation that processes a single partition (instead of an element) at a time. It implements the summarization design pattern, summarizing each partition of a source RDD into a single element of the target RDD. The goal of this transformation is to process one partition at a time (although, many partitions can be processed independently and concurrently), iterate through all of the partition's elements, and summarize the result in a compact data structure such as a dictionary, list of elements, tuples, or list of tuples.

The `mapPartitions()` transformation has the following signature:

```
mapPartitions(f, preservesPartitioning=False)
# Returns a new RDD by applying a function, f(), to each partition
# of this RDD. If source RDD has N partitions, then your function
# will be called N times, independently and concurrently.
```

Let's say that your source RDD has *N* partitions. The `mapPartitions()` transformation maps a single partition of the source RDD into your desired data type, `T` (for example, this could be a single value, a tuple, a list, or a dictionary). Therefore, the target RDD will be an `RDD[T]`, of length *N*. This is an ideal transformation when you want to reduce (or aggregate) each partition comprised of a set of source RDD elements into a condensed data structure of type `T`: it maps a single partition into a single element of the target RDD.

A high-level overview is presented in Figure 3-11.

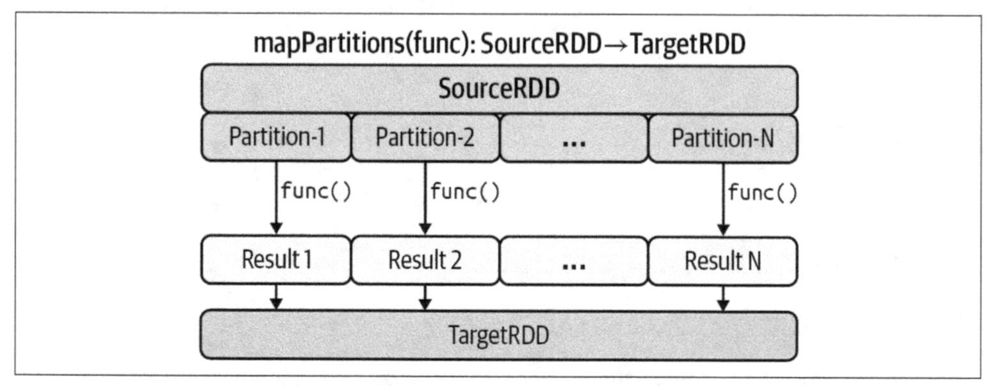

Figure 3-11. The `mapPartition()` transformation

To help you understand the logic of the `mapPartitions()` transformation, I'll present a simple, concrete example. Suppose you have a source `RDD[Integer]` with 100,000,000,000 elements and your RDD is partitioned into 10,000 chunks or partitions. So, each partition will have about 10,000,000 elements. If you have enough cluster resources to run 10,000 mappers in parallel, then each mapper will receive a partition. Since you will be processing one partition at time, you have the chance to filter elements and summarize each partition into a single desired data structure (such as a tuple, list, or dictionary).

Let's say that you want to find the `(minimum, maximum, count)` for the source RDD of numbers. Each mapper will find a local `(minimum, maximum, count)` per partition, and then eventually, you can find the final `(minimum, maximum, count)` for all of the partitions. Here, the target data type is a triplet:

```
T = (int, int, int) = (minimum, maximum, count)
```

`mapPartitions()` is an ideal transformation when you want to map each partition into small amount of condensed or reduced information. You can filter out undesired elements of the source RDD and then summarize the remaining elements in your data structure of choice.

Let's walk through the main flow of the `mapPartitions()` transformation:

1. First, define a function that accepts a single partition of the source RDD (an `RDD[Integer]`) and returns a data type `T`, where:

   ```
   T = (int, int, int) = (minimum, maximum, count)
   ```

   Let *N* be the number of partitions for your source RDD. Given a partition `p` (where `p` in `{1, 2, ..., N}`), `mapPartitions()` will compute ($minimum_p$, $maximum_p$, $count_p$) per partition `p`:

   ```
   def find_min_max_count(single_partition):
     # find (minimum, maximum, count) by iterating single_partition
     return [(minimum, maximum, count)]
   #end-def
   ```

2. Next, apply the `mapPartitions()` transformation:

   ```
   # source RDD: source_rdd = RDD[Integer]
   # target RDD: min_max_count_rdd = RDD(int, int, int)
   min_max_count_rdd = source_rdd.mapPartitions(find_min_max_count)
   min_max_count_list = min_max_count_rdd.collect()
   print(min_max_count_list)
   [
    (min1, max1, count1),
    (min2, max2, count2),
    ...
    (minN, maxN, countN)
   ]
   ```

3. Finally, we need to collect the content of `min_max_count_rdd` and find the final `(minimum, maximum, count)`:

   ```
   # minimum = min(min1, min2, ..., minN)
   minimum = min(min_max_count_list)[0]
   # maximum = max(max1, max2, ..., maxN)
   maximum = max(min_max_count_list)[1]
   # count = (count1+count2+...+countN)
   count = sum(min_max_count_list)[2]
   ```

We can define our function as follows. Note that by using a Boolean flag, `first_time`, we avoid making any assumptions about range of numeric values:

```
def find_min_max_count(single_partition_iterator):
        first_time = True
        for n in single_partition_iterator:
```

```
        if (first_time):
            minimum = n;
            maximum = n;
            count = 1
            first_time = True
        else:
            maximum = max(n, maximum)
            minimum = min(n, minimum)
            count += 1
    #end-for
    return [(minimum, maximum, count)]
#end-def
```

Next, let's create an `RDD[Integer]` and then apply the `mapPartitions()` transformation:

```
integers = [1, 2, 3, 1, 2, 3, 70, 4, 3, 2, 1]
# spark : SparkSession
source_rdd = spark.sparkContext.parallelize(integers)
# source RDD: source_rdd = RDD[Integer]
# target RDD: min_max_count_rdd = RDD(int, int, int)
min_max_count_rdd = source_rdd.mapPartitions(find_min_max_count)

min_max_count_list = min_max_count_rdd.collect() ❶
# compute the final values:
minimum = min(min_max_count_list)[0]
maximum = max(min_max_count_list)[1]
count = sum(min_max_count_list)[2]
```

 The `collect()` is scalable here, because the number of partitions will be in the thousands and not the millions.

In summary, if you have a large amount of data that you want to reduce to a smaller amount of information (a summarization task), the `mapPartitions()` transformation is a possible option. For example, it's very useful for finding the minimum and maximum or top 10 values in your dataset. The `mapPartitions()` transformation:

- Implements the summarization design pattern, combining all the source RDD elements in a single partition into a single, compact element of the target RDD (such as a dictionary, tuple, or list of objects or tuples).
- Can be used as an alternative to `map()` and `foreach()`, but is called once per partition instead of for each element in an RD.
- Enables the programmer to do initialization on a per-partition rather than per-element basis.

Next, I'll discuss a very important topic: how to handle and process an empty partition when using the `mapPartitions()` transformation.

Handling Empty Partitions

In our previous solution, we used the `mapPartitions(func)` transformation, which separates input data into many partitions and then applies the function `func()` (provided by the programmer) to each partition in parallel. But what if one or more of these partitions are empty? In this case, there will be no data (no elements in that partition) to iterate. We need to write our custom function `func()` (the partition handler) in such a way that it will handle empty partitions properly and gracefully. We cannot just ignore them.

Empty partitions may occur for various reasons. If there is an exception while the Spark partitioner is partitioning the data (for example, due to corrupted records after a network failure mid-transfer), then some partitions might be empty. Another reason might be that the partitioner does not have enough data to put any into a given partition. Regardless of why these partitions exist, we need to handle them proactively.

To illustrate the concept of an empty partition, I'll first define a function, `debug_partition()`, to show the contents of each partition:

```
def debug_partition(iterator):
    #print("type(iterator)=", type(iterator))
    print("elements = ", list(elements))
#end-def
```

Remember that displaying or debugging the content of a partition can be costly and should be avoided by all means in production environments. I have included `print` statements for teaching and debugging purposes only.

Now let's create an RDD and partition it in a way that will force the creation of empty partitions. We do this by setting the number of partitions higher than the number of RDD elements:

```
>>> sc
<SparkContext master=local[*] appName=PySparkShell>
>>> numbers = [1, 2, 3, 4, 5]
>>> rdd = sc.parallelize(numbers, 7) ❶
>>> rdd.collect()
[1, 2, 3, 4, 5]
>>> rdd.getNumPartitions()
7
```

❶ Force the creation of empty partitions.

We can examine each partition using the `debug_partition()` function:

```
>>> rdd.foreachPartition(debug_partition)
elements =  [4]
elements =  [3]
elements =  [2]
elements =  [] ❶
elements =  [] ❶
elements =  [5]
elements =  [1]
```

❶ An empty partition

From this test program we can observe the following:

- A partition can be empty (with no RDD elements). Your custom function must handle empty partitions proactively and gracefully—that is, it must return a proper value. Empty partitions cannot be just ignored.
- The `iterator` data type (which represents a single partition and is passed as a parameter to `mapPartitions()`) is `itertools.chain`. `itertools.chain` is an iterator that returns elements from the first iterable until it is exhausted, then proceeds to the next iterable, until all of the iterables are exhausted. It's used for treating consecutive sequences as a single sequence.

Now the question is, how do we handle an empty partition in PySpark? The following pattern can be used to handle an empty partition. The basic idea is to use Python's `try-except` combination, where the `try` block lets you test a block of code for errors and the `except` block lets you handle the error:

```
# This is the template function
# to handle a single partition.
#
# source RDD: RDD[T]
#
# parameter: iterator

def func(iterator): ❶
    print("type(iterator)=", type(iterator))
    #   ('type(iterator)=', <type 'itertools.chain'>)

    try:
        first_element = next(iterator) ❷
        # if you are here it means that
        # the partition is NOT empty;
        # iterate/process the partition
        # and return a proper result

    except StopIteration: ❸
        # if you are here it means that this
```

```
        # partition is empty; now, you need
        # to handle it and return a proper result
#end-def
```

 `iterator` represents a single partition of elements of type `T`.

❷ Try to get the first element (as `first_element`, of type `T`) for a given partition. If this fails (throws an exception), then control will go to the `except` (exception happened) block.

❸ You will be here when a given partition is empty. You cannot just ignore empty partitions, you must handle the error and return a proper value.

Handling Empty Partitions

Typically, for empty partitions you should return some special value that can be filtered out easily by the `filter()` transformation. For example, for the DNA base count problem, you might return a `null` value (instead of an actual dictionary) and then filter the `null` values after the completion of the `mapPartitions()` transformation.

To handle an empty partition when looking for the `(min, max, count)`, we will rewrite the partition handler function as follows:

```
def find_min_max_count_revised(single_partition_iterator):
    try:
        first_element = next(single_partition_iterator)
        # if you are here it means that
        # the partition is NOT empty;
        # process the partition and return a proper result
                minimum = first_element;
                maximum = first_element;
                count = 1

            for n in single_partition_iterator:
                        maximum = max(n, maximum)
                        minimum = min(n, minimum)
                        count += 1
            #end-for
            return [(minimum, maximum, count)]
    except StopIteration:
        # if you are here it means that this
        # partition is empty; now, you need
        # to handle it gracefully and return
        # a proper result
        # return a value that we can filter out later ❶
            return [None]
#end-def
```

❶ We return [None] so that we can filter it out.

The following code shows how to filter out empty partitions:

```
integers = [1, 2, 3, 1, 2, 3, 70, 4, 3, 2, 1]
# spark: SparkSession
source_rdd = spark.sparkContext.parallelize(integers, 4)
# source RDD: source_rdd = RDD[Integer]
# target RDD: min_max_count_rdd = RDD(int, int, int)
min_max_count_rdd = source_rdd.mapPartitions(find_min_max_count_revised)

# filter out fake values returned from empty partitions
min_max_count_rdd_filtered = min_max_count_rdd.filter(lambda x: x is not None) ❶

# compute the final triplet (minimum, maximum, count)
final_triplet = min_max_count_rdd_filtered.reduce(
  lambda x, y: (min(x[0], y[0]), max(x[1], y[1]), x[2]+y[2]))
print(final_triplet)
(1, 70, 11)
```

❶ Drop the result of empty partitions.

Benefits and Drawbacks

Spark's mapPartitions() is an efficient transformation with numerous benefits, summarized here:

Low processing overhead
: The mapper function is applied once per RDD partition rather than per RDD element, which limits the number of function calls to the number of partitions rather than the number of elements. Note that for some transformations, such as map() and flatMap(), the overhead of invoking a function for each element in all the partitions can be substantial.

Efficient local aggregation
: Since mapPartitions() works on the partition level, it gives the user the opportunity to perform filtering and aggregation at that level. This local aggregation greatly reduces the amount of shuffled data. With mapPartitions(), we are reducing a partition into a small, contained data structure. Reducing the amount of sorting and shuffling results in greater efficiency and reliability of reduce operations.

Avoidance of explicit filtering step
: This transformation enables us to squeeze in the filter() step during iteration of a partition (which may be comprised of thousands or millions of elements), effectively combining a map()/flatMap() operation with a filter() operation. As you iterate partition elements, you can drop the ones you don't need, then

map and aggregate the remaining elements into your desired data type (such as a list, tuple, dictionary, or custom data type). You can even apply multiple filters at the same time. This results in greater efficiency, as you avoid the overhead of setting up and managing multiple data transformation steps.

Avoidance of repetitive heavy initialization
With `mapPartitions()` you may use broadcast variables (shared among all cluster nodes) to initialize the data structures required for aggregation of partition elements. If you need to do heavyweight initialization, then you will not pay a heavy price, since the number of initializations is limited to the number of partitions. When using narrow transformations like `map()` and `flatMap()`, the creation of such data structures can be very inefficient due to repetitive initialization and de-initialization. With `mapPartitions()`, the initialization is performed only once (at the beginning of a function) for all the data records residing in a given partition. An example of heavy initialization could be the initialization of a database (relational or HBase) connection to read/update/insert a record.

There are also a few potential drawbacks to using the `mapPartitions()` transformation:

- Since we are applying a function to the whole partition, debugging might be harder than with other mapper transformations.
- Proper partitioning of data for `mapPartitions()` is critical. You want to maximize the cluster utilization for this kind of transformation; the number of partitions should be greater than the number of available mappers/executors so that there will not be any idle mappers/executors.

DataFrames and mapPartitions() Transformation

Given a DataFrame, you can easily summarize your data with a SQL transformation:

```
# step-1: create your desired DataFrame
df = <a-dataframe-with-some-columns>

# step-2: register your Dataframe as a table
df.registerTempTable("my_table")

# step-3: apply summarization by a SQL transformation
df2 = spark.sql("select min(col1), max(col1), ... from my_table")
```

Spark's DataFrame does not have a direct support for mapPartitions(), but it is very easy to apply equivalent of `mapPartitions()` to a DataFrame. The following example finds the minimum price for a group of items:

```
>>> tuples3 = [
  ('clothing', 'shirt', 20), ('clothing', 'tshirt', 10), ('clothing', 'pants', 30),
  ('fruit', 'banana', 3), ('fruit', 'apple', 4), ('fruit', 'orange', 5),
  ('veggie', 'carrot', 7),  ('veggie', 'tomato', 8), ('veggie', 'potato', 9)]
>>>
>>> df = spark.createDataFrame(tuples3, ["group_id", "item", "price"])
>>> df.show(truncate=False)
+--------+------+-----+
|group_id|item  |price|
+--------+------+-----+
|clothing|shirt |20   |
|clothing|tshirt|10   |
|clothing|pants |30   |
|fruit   |banana|3    |
|fruit   |apple |4    |
|fruit   |orange|5    |
|veggie  |carrot|7    |
|veggie  |tomato|8    |
|veggie  |potato|9    |
+--------+------+-----+

# Find minimum price for all items
>>> df.agg({'price': 'min'}).show()
+----------+
|min(price)|
+----------+
|         3|
+----------+

# Find minimum price for each group of items
>>> df.groupby('group_id').agg({'price': 'min'}).show()
+--------+----------+
|group_id|min(price)|
+--------+----------+
|clothing|        10|
|   fruit|         3|
|  veggie|         7|
+--------+----------+
```

You may apply multiple aggregation functions to a DataFrame:

```
>>> import pyspark.sql.functions as F

>>> df.groupby('group_id')
      .agg(F.min("price").alias("minimum"), F.max("price").alias("maximum"))
      .show()
+--------+-------+-------+
|group_id|minimum|maximum|
+--------+-------+-------+
```

```
|clothing|      10|      30|
|   fruit|       3|       5|
|  veggie|       7|       9|
+--------+------+-------+
```

PySpark's DataFrame data abstraction does not directly support `mapPartitions()` transformation, but if you wish to use it, you may convert your DataFrame into an RDD (by applying `DataFrame.rdd`) and then apply `mapPartitions()` transformation to an RDD:

```
# SparkSession available as 'spark'.
>>> tuples3 = [ ('alex', 440, 'PHD'), ('jane', 420, 'PHD'),
...             ('bob', 280, 'MS'), ('betty', 200, 'MS')]
>>>
>>> df = spark.createDataFrame(tuples3, ["name", "amount", "education"])
>>> df.show()
+-----+------+---------+
| name|amount|education|
+-----+------+---------+
| alex|   440|      PHD|
| jane|   420|      PHD|
|  bob|   280|       MS|
|betty|   200|       MS|
+-----+------+---------+

>>> df
DataFrame[name: string, amount: bigint, education: string]
>>>
>>> my_rdd = df.rdd
>>> my_rdd.collect()
[Row(name='alex', amount=440, education='PHD'),
Row(name='jane', amount=420, education='PHD'),
Row(name='bob', amount=280, education='MS'),
Row(name='betty', amount=200, education='MS')]
```

We may now apply `mapPartitions()` to `my_rdd`:

```
def my_custom_function(partition): ❶
    ... initialize your data structures
    for single_row in partition:
       ...
    #end-for
    return <summary-of-single-partition>
#end-def

result = my_rdd.mapPartitions(my_custom_function)
```

❶ Note that when iterating `partition`, each element (`single_row`) will be a `Row` object.

Summary

To recap:

- Spark offers many simple and powerful transformations (such as `map()`, `flatMap()`, `filter()`, and `mapPartitions()`) that you can use to convert one form of data into another. Spark transformations enable us to perform ETL operations in a simple way.
- If your data requires you to map one element (such as a `String`) into another element (such as a tuple, (key, value pair, or list), you can use the `map()` or `flatMap()` transformation.
- When you want to summarize a lot of data into a small amount of meaningful information (the summarization design pattern), `mapPartitions()` is a good choice.
- The `mapPartitions()` transformation allows you to do heavy initialization (for example, setting up a database connection) once for each partition instead of for every RDD element. This can help the performance of your data analysis when you are dealing with heavyweight initialization on large datasets.
- Some Spark transformations have differences in performance, so you need to select the transformations you use in a way that suits both your data and your performance needs. For example, for summarizing data, `mapPartitions()` will usually perform and scale better than `map()`.

The next chapter will focus on reductions in Spark.

CHAPTER 4
Reductions in Spark

This chapter focuses on reduction transformations on RDDs in Spark. In particular, we'll work with RDDs of (key, value) pairs, which are a common data abstraction required for many operations in Spark. Some initial ETL operations may be required to get your data into a (key, value) form, but with pair RDDs you may perform any desired aggregation over a set of values.

Spark supports several powerful reduction transformations and actions. The most important reduction transformations are:

- `reduceByKey()`
- `combineByKey()`
- `groupByKey()`
- `aggregateByKey()`

All of the `*ByKey()` transformations accept a source `RDD[(K, V)]` and create a target `RDD[(K, C)]` (for some transformations, such as `reduceByKey()`, `V` and `C` are the same). The function of these transformations is to reduce all the values of a given key (for all unique keys), by finding, for example:

- The average of all values
- The sum and count of all values
- The mode and median of all values
- The standard deviation of all values

Reduction Transformation Selection

As with mapper transformations, it's important to select the right tool for the job. For some reduction operations (such as finding the median), the reducer needs access to all the values at the same time. For others, such as finding the sum or count of all values, it doesn't. If you want to find the median of values per key, then `groupByKey()` will be a good choice, but this transformation does not do well if a key has lots of values (which might cause an OOM problem). On the other hand, if you want to find the sum or count of all values, then `reduceByKey()` might be a good choice: it merges the values for each key using an associative and commutative reduce function.

This chapter will show you how to use the most important Spark reduction transformations, through simple working PySpark examples. We will focus on the transformations most commonly used in Spark applications. I'll also discuss the general concept of reduction, and monoids as a design principle for efficient reduction algorithms. We'll start by looking at how to create pair RDDs, which are required by Spark's reduction transformations.

Source Code

Complete programs for this chapter available in the book's GitHub repository (*https://oreil.ly/CH3X2*).

Creating Pair RDDs

Given a set of keys and their associated values, a reduction transformation reduces the values of each key using an algorithm (sum of value, median of values, etc.). The reduction transformations presented in this chapter thus work on (key, value) pairs, which means that the RDD elements must conform to this format. There are several ways to create pair RDDs in Spark. For example, you can also use `parallelize()` on collections (such as lists of tuples and dictionaries), as shown here:

```
>>> key_value = [('A', 2), ('A', 4), ('B', 5), ('B', 7)]
>>> pair_rdd = spark.sparkContext.parallelize(key_value)
>>> pair_rdd.collect() ❶
[('A', 2), ('A', 4), ('B', 5), ('B', 7)]
>>> pair_rdd.count()
4
>>> hashmap = pair_rdd.collectAsMap()
>>> hashmap
{'A': 4, 'B': 7}
```

❶ `pair_rdd` has two keys, `{'A', 'B'}`.

Next, suppose you have weather-related data and you want to create pairs of `(city_id, temperature)`. You can do this using the `map()` transformation. Assume that your input has the following format:

```
<city_id><,><latitude><,><longitude><,><temperature>
```

First, define a function to create the desired (key, value) pairs:

```
def create_key_value(rec):
  tokens = rec.split(",")
  city_id = tokens[0]
  temperature = tokens[3]
  return (city_id, temperature) ❶
```

 The key is `city_id` and the value is `temperature`.

Then use `map()` to create your pair RDD:

```
input_path = <your-temperature-data-path>
rdd = spark.sparkContext.textFile(input_path)
pair_rdd = rdd.map(create_key_value)
# or you can write this using a lambda expression as:
# pair_rdd = rdd.map(lambda rec: create_key_value(rec))
```

The are many other ways to create (key, value) pair RDDs: `reduceByKey()`, for example, accepts a source `RDD[(K, V)]` and produces a target `RDD[(K, V)]`, and `combineByKey()` accepts a source `RDD[(K, V)]` and produces a target `RDD[(K, C)]`.

Reduction Transformations

Typically, a reduction transformation reduces the data size from a large batch of values (such as list of numbers) to a smaller one. Examples of reductions include:

- Finding the sum and average of all values
- Finding the mean, mode, and median of all values
- Calculating the mean and standard deviation of all values
- Finding the `(min, max, count)` of all values
- Finding the top 10 of all values

In a nutshell, a reduction transformation roughly corresponds to the fold operation (also called reduce, accumulate, or aggregate) in functional programming. The transformation is either applied to all data elements (such as when finding the sum of all elements) or to all elements per key (such as when finding the sum of all elements per key).

A simple addition reduction over a set of numbers `{47, 11, 42, 13}` for a single partition is illustrated in Figure 4-1.

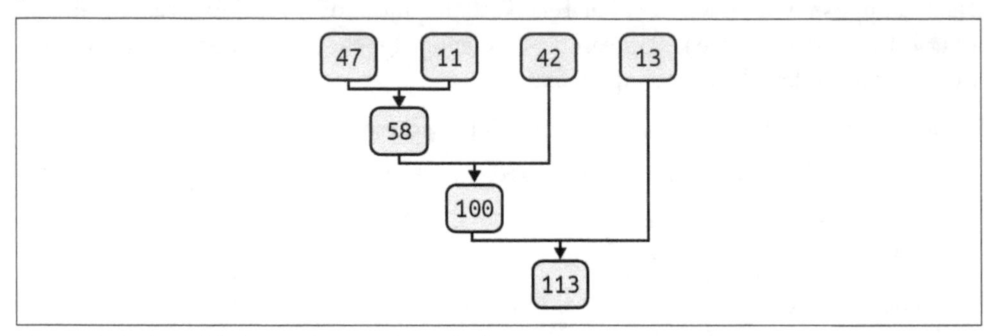

Figure 4-1. An addition reduction in a single partition

Figure 4-2 shows a reduction that sums the elements of two partitions. The final reduced values for Partition-1 and Partition-2 are `21` and `18`. Each partition performs local reductions and finally, the results from the two partitions are reduced.

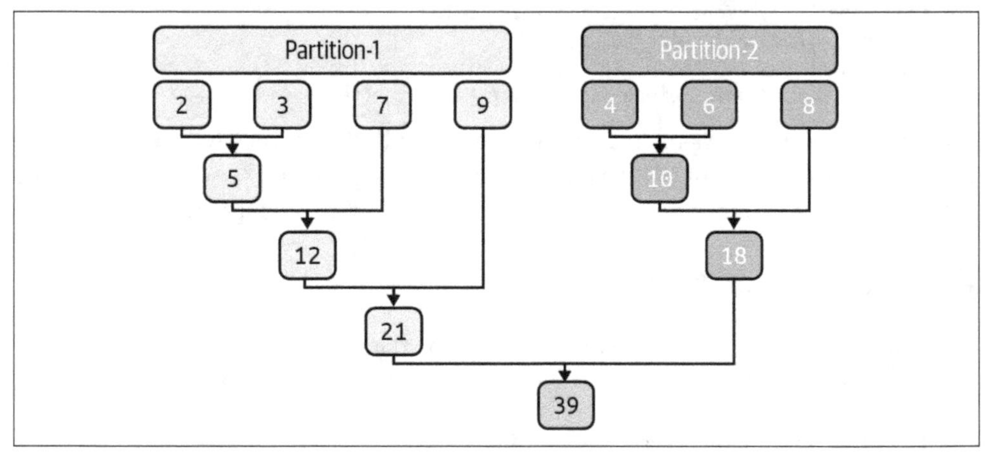

Figure 4-2. An addition reduction over two partitions

The reducer is a core concept in functional programming, used to transform a set of objects (such as numbers, strings, or lists) into a single value (such as the sum of numbers or concatenation of string objects). Spark and the MapReduce paradigm use this concept to aggregate a set of values into a single value per key. Consider the following (key, value) pairs, where the key is a `String` and the value is a list of `Integers`:

```
(key1, [1, 2, 3])
(key2, [40, 50, 60, 70, 80])
(key3, [8])
```

The simplest reducer will be an addition function over a set of values per key. After we apply this function, the result will be:

```
(key1, 6)
(key2, 300)
(key3, 8)
```

Or you may reduce each (key, value) to (key, pair) where the pair is `(sum-of-values, count-of-values)`:

```
(key1, (6, 3))
(key2, (300, 5))
(key3, (8, 1))
```

Reducers are designed to operate concurrently and independently, meaning that there is no synchronization between reducers. The more resources a Spark cluster has, the faster reductions can be done. In the worst possible case, if we have only one reducer, then reduction will work as a queue operation. In general, a cluster will offer many reducers (depending on resource availability) for the reduction transformation.

In MapReduce and distributed algorithms, reduction is a required operation in solving a problem. In the MapReduce programming paradigm, the programmer defines a mapper and a reducer with the following `map()` and `reduce()` signatures (note that [] denotes an iterable):

`map()`
    $(K_1, V_1) \rightarrow [(K_2, V_2)]$

`reduce()`
    $(K_2, [V_2]) \rightarrow [(K_3, V_3)]$

The `map()` function maps a (key_1, $value_1$) pair into a set of (key_2, $value_2$) pairs. After all the map operations are completed, the sort and shuffle is done automatically (this functionality is provided by the MapReduce paradigm, not implemented by the programmer). The MapReduce sort and shuffle phase is very similar to Spark's `groupByKey()` transformation.

The `reduce()` function reduces a (key_2, [$value_2$]) pair into a set of (key_3, $value_3$) pairs. The convention is used to denote a list of objects (or an iterable list of objects). Therefore, we can say that a reduction transformation takes a list of values and reduces it to a tangible result (such as the sum of values, average of values, or your desired data structure).

Spark's Reductions

Spark provides a rich set of easy-to-use reduction transformations. As stated at the beginning of this chapter, our focus will be on reductions of pair RDDs. Therefore, we will assume that each RDD has a set of keys and for each key (such as K) we have a set of values:

```
{ (K, V1), (K, V2), ..., (K, Vn) }
```

Table 4-1 lists the reduction transformations available in Spark.

Table 4-1. Spark's reduction transformations

Transformation	Description
aggregateByKey()	Aggregates the values of each key using the given combine functions and a neutral "zero value"
combineByKey()	Generic function to combine the elements for each key using a custom set of aggregation functions
countByKey()	Counts the number of elements for each key, and returns the result to the master as a dictionary
foldByKey()	Merges the values for each key using an associative function and a neutral "zero value"
groupByKey()	Groups the values for each key in the RDD into a single sequence
reduceByKey()	Merges the values for each key using an associative and commutative reduce function
sampleByKey()	Returns a subset of this RDD sampled by key, using variable sampling rates for different keys as specified by fractions
sortByKey()	Sorts the RDD by key, so that each partition contains a sorted range of the elements in ascending order

These transformation functions all act on (key, value) pairs represented by RDDs. In this chapter, we will look only at reductions of data over a set of given unique keys. For example, given the following (key, value) pairs for the key K:

```
{ (K, V1), (K, V2), ..., (K, Vn) }
```

we are assuming that K has a list of n (> 0) values:

```
[ V1, V2, ..., Vn ]
```

To keep it simple, the goal of reduction is to generate the following pair (or set of pairs):

```
(K, R)
```

where:

```
f(V1, V2, ..., Vn) -> R
```

The function `f()` is called a *reducer* or *reduction* function. Spark's reduction transformations apply this function over a list of values to find the reduced value, `R`. Note that Spark does not impose any ordering among the values ($[V_1, V_2, ..., V_n]$) to be reduced.

This chapter will include practical examples of solutions demonstrating the use of the most common of Spark's reduction transformations: `reduceByKey()`, `groupByKey()`, `aggregateByKey()`, and `combineByKey()`. To get you started, let's look at a very simple example of the `groupByKey()` transformation. As the example in Figure 4-3 shows, it works similarly to the SQL `GROUP BY` statement. In this example, we have four keys, `{A, B, C, P}`, and their associated values are grouped as a list of integers. The source RDD is an `RDD[(String, Integer)]`, where each element is a pair of `(String, Integer)`. The target RDD is an `RDD[(String, [Integer])]`, where each element is a pair of `(String, [Integer])`; the value is an iterable list of integers.

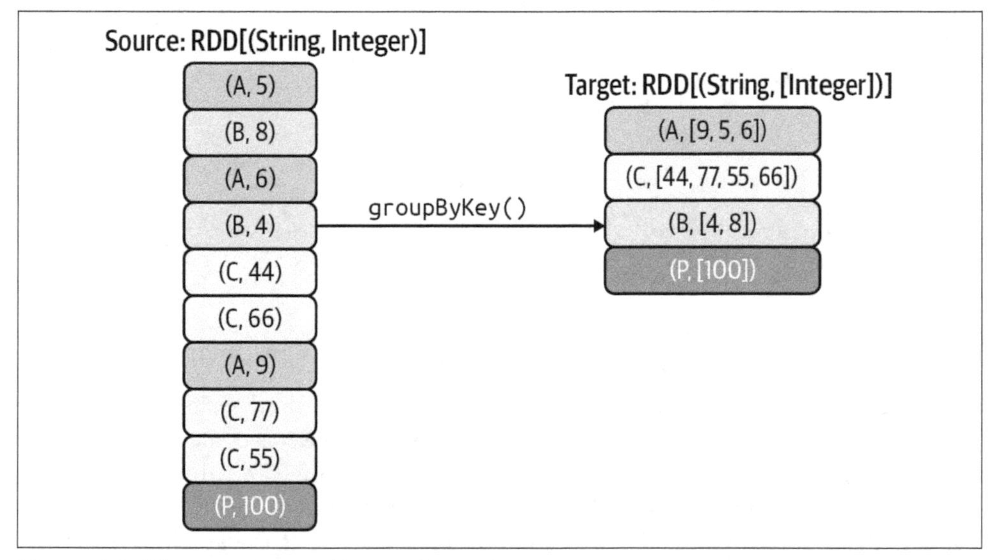

Figure 4-3. The `groupByKey()` transformation

By default, Spark reductions do not sort the reduced values. For example, in Figure 4-3, the reduced value for key `B` could be `[4, 8]` or `[8, 4]`. If desired, you may sort the values before the final reduction. If your reduction algorithm requires sorting, you must sort the values explicitly.

Now that you have a general understanding of how reducers work, let's move on to a practical example that demonstrates how different Spark reduction transformations can be used to solve a data problem.

Simple Warmup Example

Suppose we have a list of pairs (K, V), where K (the key) is a String and V (the value) is an Integer:

```
[
 ('alex', 2), ('alex', 4), ('alex', 8),
 ('jane', 3), ('jane', 7),
 ('rafa', 1), ('rafa', 3), ('rafa', 5), ('rafa', 6),
 ('clint', 9)
]
```

In this example, we have four unique keys:

```
{ 'alex', 'jane', 'rafa', 'clint' }
```

Suppose we want to combine (sum) the values per key. The result of this reduction will be:

```
[
 ('alex', 14),
 ('jane', 10),
 ('rafa', 15),
 ('clint', 9)
]
```

where:

```
key: alex =>    14 = 2+4+8
key: jane =>    10 = 3+7
key: rafa =>    15 = 1+3+5+6
key: clint =>    9 (single value, no operation is done)
```

There are many ways to add these numbers to get the desired result. How did we arrive at these reduced (key, value) pairs? For this example, we could use any of the common Spark transformations. Aggregating or combining the values per key is a type of reduction—in the classic MapReduce paradigm, this is called a *reduce by key* (or simply *reduce*) function. The MapReduce framework calls the application's (user-defined) reduce function once for each unique key. The function iterates through the values that are associated with that key and produces zero or more outputs as (key, value) pairs, solving the problem of combining the elements of each unique key into a single value. (Note that in some applications, the result might be more than a single value.)

Here I present four different solutions using Spark's transformations. For all solutions, we will use the following Python data and key_value_pairs RDD:

```
>>> data = ❶
[
 ('alex', 2), ('alex', 4), ('alex', 8),
 ('jane', 3), ('jane', 7),
 ('rafa', 1), ('rafa', 3), ('rafa', 5), ('rafa', 6),
 ('clint', 9)
]
>>> key_value_pairs = spark.SparkContext.parallelize(data) ❷
>>> key_value_pairs.collect()
[
 ('alex', 2), ('alex', 4), ('alex', 8),
 ('jane', 3), ('jane', 7),
 ('rafa', 1), ('rafa', 3), ('rafa', 5), ('rafa', 6),
 ('clint', 9)
]
```

 `data` is a Python collection—a list of (key, value) pairs.

❷ `key_value_pairs` is an `RDD[(String, Integer)]`.

Solving with reduceByKey()

Summing the values for a given key is pretty straightforward: add the first two values, then the next one, and keep going. Spark's `reduceByKey()` transformation merges the values for each key using an associative and commutative reduce function. Combiners (optimized mini-reducers) are used in all cluster nodes before merging the values per partition.

For the `reduceByKey()` transformation, the source RDD is an `RDD[(K, V)]` and the target RDD is an `RDD[(K, V)]`. Note that source and target data types of the RDD values (`V`) are the same. This is a limitation of `reduceByKey()`, which can be avoided by using `combineByKey()` or `aggregateByKey()`).

We can apply the `reduceByKey()` transformation using a lambda expression (anonymous function):

```
# a is (an accumulated) value for key=K
# b is a value for key=K
sum_per_key = key_value_pairs.reduceByKey(lambda a, b: a+b)
sum_per_key.collect()
[('jane', 10), ('rafa', 15), ('alex', 14), ('clint', 9)]
```

Alternatively, we can use a defined function, such as add:

```
from operator import add
sum_per_key = key_value_pairs.reduceByKey(add)
sum_per_key.collect()
[('jane', 10), ('rafa', 15), ('alex', 14), ('clint', 9)]
```

Adding values per key by reduceByKey() is an optimized solution, since aggregation happens at the partition level before the final aggregation of all the partitions.

Solving with groupByKey()

We can also solve this problem by using the groupByKey() transformation, but this solution will not perform as well because it involves moving lots of data to the reducer nodes (you'll learn more about why this is the case when we discuss the shuffle step later in this chapter).

With the reduceByKey() transformation, the source RDD is an RDD[(K, V)] and the target RDD is an RDD[(K, [V])]. Note that the source and target data types are not the same: the value data type for the source RDD is V, while for the target RDD it is [V] (an iterable/list of Vs).

The following example demonstrates the use of groupByKey() with a lambda expression to sum the values per key:

```
sum_per_key = key_value_pairs
                .grouByKey() ❶
                .mapValues(lambda values: sum(values)) ❷
sum_per_key.collect()
[('jane', 10), ('rafa', 15), ('alex', 14), ('clint', 9)]
```

❶ Group values per key (similar to SQL's GROUP BY). Now each key will have a set of Integer values; for example, the three pairs {('alex', 2), ('alex', 4), ('alex', 8)} will be reduced to a single pair, ('alex', [2, 4, 8]).

❷ Add values per key using Python's sum() function.

Solving with aggregateByKey()

In simplest form, the aggregateByKey() transformation is defined as:

```
aggregateByKey(zero_value, seq_func, comb_func)

source RDD: RDD[(K, V)]
target RDD: RDD[(K, C))
```

It aggregates the values of each key from the source RDD into a target RDD, using the given combine functions and a neutral "zero value" (the initial value used for each partition). This function can return a different result type (C) than the type of the values in the source RDD (V), though in this example both are Integer data types. Thus, we need one operation for merging values within a single partition (merging values of type V into a value of type C) and one operation for merging values between partitions (merging values of type C from multiple partitions). To avoid unnecessary memory allocation, both of these functions are allowed to modify and return their first argument instead of creating a new C.

The following example demonstrates the use of the aggregateByKey() transformation:

```
# zero_value -> C
# seq_func: (C, V) -> C
# comb_func: (C, C) -> C

>>> sum_per_key = key_value_pairs.aggregateByKey(
... 0, ❶
... (lambda C, V: C+V), ❷
... (lambda C1, C2: C1+C2) ❸
... )
>>> sum_per_key.collect()
[('jane', 10), ('rafa', 15), ('alex', 14), ('clint', 9)]
```

❶ The zero_value applied on each partition is 0.

❷ seq_func is used on a single partition.

❸ comb_func is used to combine the values of partitions.

Solving with combineByKey()

The combineByKey() transformation is the most general and powerful of Spark's reduction transformations. In its simplest form, it is defined as:

```
combineByKey(create_combiner, merge_value, merge_combiners)

source RDD: RDD[(K, V)]
target RDD: RDD[(K, C))
```

Like aggregateByKey(), the combineByKey() transformation turns a source RDD[(K, V)] into a target RDD[(K, C)]. Again, V and C can be different data types (this is part of the power of combineByKey()—for example, V can be a String or Integer, while C can be a list, tuple, or dictionary), but for this example both are Integer data types.

The combineByKey() interface allows us to customize the reduction and combining behavior as well as the data type. Thus, to use this transformation we have to provide three functions:

`create_combiner`
: This function turns a single `V` into a `C` (e.g., creating a one-element list). It is used within a single partition to initialize a `C`.

`merge_value`
: This function merges a `V` into a `C` (e.g., adding it to the end of a list). This is used within a single partition to aggregate values into a `C`.

`merge_combiners`
: This function combines two `C`s into a single `C` (e.g., merging the lists). This is used in merging values from two partitions.

Our solution with `combineByKey()` looks like this:

```
>>> sum_per_key = key_value_pairs.combineByKey(
...             (lambda v: v), ❶
...             (lambda C,v: C+v), ❷
...             (lambda C1,C2: C1+C2) ❸
... )
>>> sum_per_key.collect()
[('jane', 10), ('rafa', 15), ('alex', 14), ('clint', 9)]
```

❶ `create_combiner` creates the initial values in each partition.

❷ `merge_value` merges the values in a partition.

❸ `merge_combiners` merges the values from the different partitions into the final result.

To give you a better idea of the power of the `combineByKey()` transformation, let's look at another example. Suppose we want to find the mean of values per key. To solve this, we can create a combined data type (`C`) as `(sum, count)`, which will hold the sums of values and their associated counts:

```
# C = combined type as (sum, count)
>>> sum_count_per_key = key_value_pairs.combineByKey(
...             (lambda v: (v, 1)),
...             (lambda C,v: (C[0]+v, C[1]+1),
...             (lambda C1,C2: (C1[0]+C2[0], C1[1]+C2[1]))
... )
>>> mean_per_key = sum_count_per_key.mapValues(lambda C: C[0]/C[1])
```

Given three partitions named `{P1, P2, P3}`, Figure 4-4 shows how to create a combiner (data type `C`), how to merge a value into a combiner, and finally how to merge two combiners.

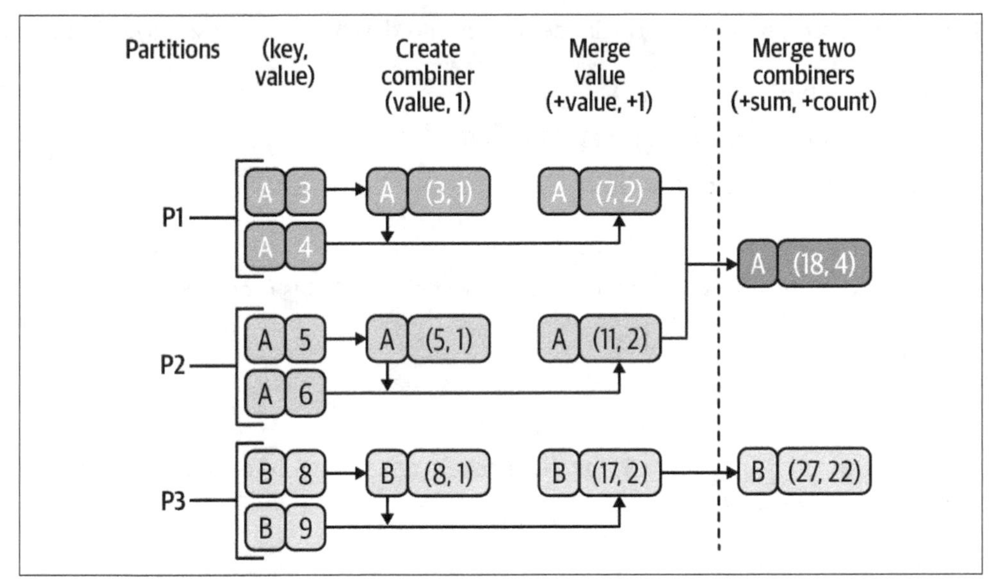

Figure 4-4. `combineByKey()` transformation example

Next, I will discuss the concept of monoids, which will help you to understand how combiners function in reduction transformations.

What Is a Monoid?

Monoids are a useful design principle for writing efficient MapReduce algorithms.[1] If you don't understand monoids, you might write reducer algorithms that do not produce semantically correct results. If your reducer is a monoid, then you can be sure that it will produce correct output in a distributed environment.

Since Spark's reductions execute on a partition-by-partition basis (i.e., your reducer function is distributed rather than being a sequential function), to get the proper output you need to make sure that your reducer function is semantically correct. We'll look at some examples of using monoids shortly, but first let's examine the underlying mathematical concept.

In algebra, a monoid is an algebraic structure with a single associative binary operation and an identity element (also called a zero element).

1 For further details, see "Monoidify! Monoids as a Design Principle for Efficient MapReduce Algorithms" (*https://oreil.ly/XOYg8*) by Jimmy Lin.

For our purposes, we can informally define a monoid as `M = (T, f, Zero)`, where:

- `T` is a data type.
- `f()` is a binary operation: `f: (T, T) -> T`.
- `Zero` is an instance of `T`.

`Zero` is an identity (neutral) element of type `T`; this is not necessarily the number zero.

If `a`, `b`, `c`, and `Zero` are of type `T`, for the triple `(T, f, Zero)` to be a monoid the following properties must hold:

- Binary operation

  ```
  f: (T, T) -> T
  ```

- Neutral element

  ```
  for all a in T:

  f(Zero, a) = a
  f(a, Zero) = a
  ```

- Associativity

  ```
  for all a, b, c in T:

  f(f(a, b), c) = f(a, f(b, c))
  ```

Not every binary operation is a monoid. For example, the `mean()` function over a set of integers is not an associative function and therefore is not a monoid, as the following proof shows:

```
mean(10, mean(30, 50)) != mean(mean(10, 30), 50)

where

   mean(10, mean(30, 50))
      = mean (10, 40)
      = 25

   mean(mean(10, 30), 50)
      = mean (20, 50)
      = 35

   25 != 35
```

What does this mean? Given an `RDD[(String, Integer)]`, we might be tempted to write the following transformation to find an average per key:

```
# rdd: RDD[(String, Integer)]
# WRONG REDUCTION to find average by key
avg_by_key = rdd.reduceByKey(lambda x, y: (x+y)/2)
```

But this will not produce the correct results, because the average of averages is not an average—in other words, the mean/average function used here is not a monoid. Suppose that this `rdd` has three elements: `{("A", 1), ("A", 2), ("A", 3)}`; `{("A", 1), ("A", 2)}` are in partition 1 and `{("A", 3)}` is in partition 2. Using the preceding solution will result in aggregated values of `("A", 1.5)` for partition 1 and `("A", 3.0)` for partition 2. Combining the results for the two partitions will then give us a final average of (1.5 + 3.0) / 2 = 2.25, which is not the correct result (the average of the three values is 2.0). If your reducer is a monoid, it is guaranteed to behave properly and produce correct results.

Monoid and Non-Monoid Examples

To help you understand and recognize monoids, let's look at some monoid and non-monoid examples. The following are examples of monoids:

- Integers with addition:

```
((a + b ) + c) = (a + (b + c))
0 + n = n
n + 0 = n
The zero element for addition is the number 0.
```

- Integers with multiplication:

```
((a * b) * c) = (a * (b * c))
1 * n = n
n * 1 = n
The zero element for multiplication is the number 1.
```

- Strings with concatenation:

```
(a + (b + c)) = ((a + b) + c)
"" + s = s
s + "" = s
The zero element for concatenation is an empty string of size 0.
```

- Lists with concatenation:

```
List(a, b) + List(c, d) = List(a,b,c,d)
```

- Sets with their union:

```
Set(1,2,3) + Set(2,4,5)
   = Set(1,2,3,2,4,5)
   = Set(1,2,3,4,5)
```

```
S + {} = S
{} + S = S
The zero element is an empty set {}.
```

And here are some non-monoid examples:

- Integers with mean function:

  ```
  mean(mean(a,b),c) != mean(a, mean(b,c))
  ```

- Integers with subtraction:

  ```
  ((a - b) -c) != (a - (b - c))
  ```

- Integers with division:

  ```
  ((a / b) / c) != (a / (b / c))
  ```

- Integers with mode function:

  ```
  mode(mode(a, b), c) != mode(a, mode(b, c))
  ```

- Integers with median function:

  ```
  median(median(a, b), c) != median(a, median(b, c))
  ```

In some cases, it is possible to convert a non-monoid into a monoid. For example, with a simple change to our data structures we can find the correct mean of a set of numbers. However, there is no algorithm to convert a non-monoid structure to a monoid automatically.

Writing distributed algorithms in Spark is much different from writing sequential algorithms on a single server, because the algorithms operate in parallel on partitioned data. Therefore, when writing a reducer, you need to make sure that your reduction function is a monoid. Now that you understand this important concept, let's move on to some practical examples.

The Movie Problem

The goal of this first example is to present a basic problem and then provide solutions using different Spark reduction transformations by means of PySpark. For all reduction transformations, I have carefully selected the data types such that they form a monoid.

The movie problem can be stated as follows: given a set of users, movies, and ratings, (in the range 1 to 5), we want to find the average rating of all movies by a user. So, if the user with `userID=100`) has rated four movies:

```
(100, "Lion King", 4.0)
(100, "Crash", 3.0)
```

```
(100, "Dead Man Walking", 3.5)
(100, "The Godfather", 4.5)
```

we want to generate the following output:

```
(100, 3.75)
```

where:

```
3.75 = mean(4.0, 3.0, 3.5, 4.5)
     = (4.0 + 3.0 + 3.5 + 4.5) / 4
     = 15.0 / 4
```

For this example, note that the `reduceByKey()` transformation over a set of ratings will not always produce the correct output, since the average (or mean) is not an algebraic monoid over a set of float/integer numbers. In other words, as discussed in the previous section, the mean of means is not equal to the mean of all input numbers. Here is a simple proof. Suppose we want to find the mean of six values (the numbers 1–6), stored in a single partition. We can do this with the `mean()` function as follows:

```
mean(1, 2, 3, 4, 5, 6)
   = (1 + 2 + 3 + 4 + 5 + 6) / 6
   = 21 / 6
   = 3.5 [correct result]
```

Now, let's make `mean()` function as a distributed function. Suppose the values are stored on three partitions:

```
Partition-1: (1, 2, 3)
Partition-2: (4, 5)
Partition-3: (6)
```

First, we compute the mean of each partition:

```
mean(1, 2, 3, 4, 5, 6)
  =  mean (
            mean(Partition-1),
            mean(Partition-2),
            mean(Partition-3)
           )

mean(Partition-1)
  = mean(1, 2, 3)
  = mean( mean(1,2), 3)
  = mean( (1+2)/2, 3)
  = mean(1.5, 3)
  = (1.5+3)/2
  = 2.25

mean(Partition-2)
  = mean(4,5)
  = (4+5)/2
  = 4.5
```

```
mean(Partition-3)
  = mean(6)
  = 6
```

Then we find the mean of these values. Once all partitions are processed, therefore, we get:

```
mean(1, 2, 3, 4, 5, 6)
  =  mean (
            mean(Partition-1),
            mean(Partition-2),
            mean(Partition-3)
           )
  = mean(2.25, 4.5, 6)
  = mean(mean(2.25, 4.5), 6)
  = mean((2.25 + 4.5)/2, 6)
  = mean(3.375, 6)
  = (3.375 + 6)/2
  = 9.375 / 2
  = 4.6875  [incorrect result]
```

To avoid this problem, we can use a monoid data structure (which supports associativity and commutativity) such as a pair of `(sum, count)`, where `sum` is the total sum of all numbers we have seen so far (per partition) and `count` is the number of ratings we have seen so far. If we define our `mean()` function as:

```
mean(pair(sum, count)) = sum / count
```

we get:

```
mean(1,2,3,4,5,6)
  = mean(mean(1,2,3), mean(4,5), mean(6))
  = mean(pair(1+2+3, 1+1+1), pair(4+5, 1+1), pair(6,1))
  = mean(pair(6, 3), pair(9, 2), pair(6,1))
  = mean(mean(pair(6, 3), pair(9, 2)), pair(6,1))
  = mean(pair(6+9, 3+2), pair(6,1))
  = mean(pair(15, 5), pair(6,1))
  = mean(pair(15+6, 5+1))
  = mean(pair(21, 6))
  = 21 / 6 = 3.5 [correct result]
```

As this example shows, by using a monoid we can achieve associativity. Therefore, you may apply the `reduceByKey()` transformation when your function `f()` is commutative and associative:

```
# a = (sum1, count1)
# b = (sum2, count2)
# f(a, b) = a + b
#         = (sum1+sum2, count1+count2)
#
reduceByKey(lambda a, b: f(a, b))
```

For example, the addition (+) operation is commutative and associative, but the mean/average function does not satisfy these properties.

As we saw in Chapter 1, a commutative function ensures that the result is independent of the order of elements in the RDD being aggregated:

```
f(A, B) = f(B, A)
```

An associative function ensures that the order in which elements are grouped during the aggregation does not affect the final result:

```
f(f(A, B), C) = f(A, f(B, C))
```

Input Dataset to Analyze

The sample data we'll use for this problem is a dataset from MovieLens (*https://oreil.ly/KOyq4*). For simplicity, I will assume that you have downloaded and unzipped the files into a */tmp/movielens/* directory. Note that there is no requirement to put the files at the suggested location; you may place your files in your preferred directory and update your input paths accordingly.

The full MovieLens dataset (*ml-latest.zip*) is 265 MB. If you want to use a smaller dataset to run, test, and debug the programs listed here, you can instead download the small MovieLens dataset (*https://oreil.ly/hAfIQ*), a 1 MB file consisting of 100,000 ratings and 3,600 tag applications applied to 9,000 movies by 600 users.

All ratings are contained in the file *ratings.csv*. Each line of this file after the header row represents one rating of one movie by one user, and has the following format:

```
<userId><,><movieId><,><rating><,><timestamp>
```

In this file:

- The lines are ordered first by `userId`, then, for each user, by `movieId`.
- Ratings are made on a 5-star scale, with half-star increments (0.5 stars to 5.0 stars).
- Timestamps represent seconds since midnight Coordinated Universal Time (UTC) of January 1, 1970 (this field is ignored in our analysis).

After unzipping the downloaded file, you should have the following files:

```
$ ls -l /tmp/movielens/
      8,305  README.txt
    725,770  links.csv
  1,729,811  movies.csv
```

```
620,204,630  ratings.csv
 21,094,823  tags.csv
```

First, check the number of records (the number of records you see might be different based on when you downloaded the file):

```
$ wc -l /tmp/movielens/ratings.csv
22,884,378 /tmp/movielens/ratings.csv
```

Next, take a look at the first few records:

```
$ head -6 /tmp/movielens/ratings.csv
userId,movieId,rating,timestamp
1,169,2.5,1204927694
1,2471,3.0,1204927438
1,48516,5.0,1204927435
2,2571,3.5,1436165433
2,109487,4.0,1436165496
```

Since we are using RDDs, we do not need the metadata associated with the data. Therefore, we can remove the first line (the header line) from the *ratings.csv* file:

```
$ tail -n +2 ratings.csv > ratings.csv.no.header
$ wc -l ratings.csv ratings.csv.no.header
22,884,378 ratings.csv
22,884,377 ratings.csv.no.header
```

Now that we've acquired our sample data, we can work through a few solutions to this problem. The first solution will use `aggregateByKey()`, but before we get to that I'll present the logic behind this transformation.

The aggregateByKey() Transformation

Spark's `aggregateByKey()` transformation initializes each key on each partition with the zero value, which is an initial combined data type (`C`); this is a neutral value, typically `(0, 0)` if the combined data type is `(sum, count)`. This zero value is merged with the first value in the partition to create a new `C`, which is then merged with the second value. This process continues until we've merged all the values for that key. Finally, if the same key exists in multiple partitions, these values are combined together to produce the final `C`.

Figures 4-5 and 4-6 show how `aggregateByKey()` works with different zero values. The zero value is applied per key, per partition. This means that if a key *X* is in *N* partitions, the zero value is applied *N* times (each of these *N* partitions will be initialized to the zero value for key *X*). Therefore, it's important to select this value carefully.

Figure 4-5 demonstrates how `aggregateByKey()` works with `zero-value=(0, 0)`.

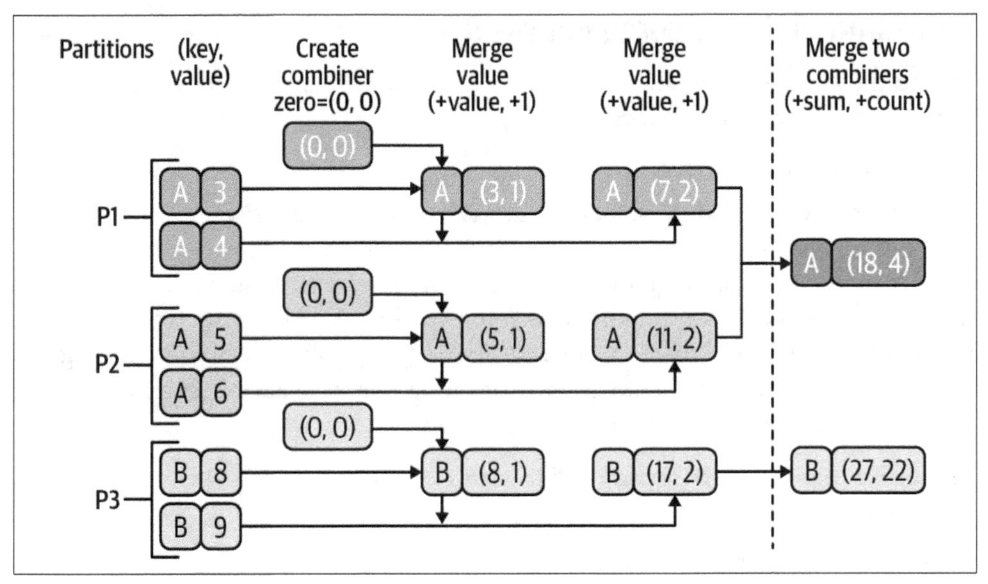

Figure 4-5. `aggregateByKey()` with `zero-value=(0, 0)`

Typically, you would use (0, 0) but Figure 4-6 demonstrates how the same transformation works with a zero value of (10, 20).

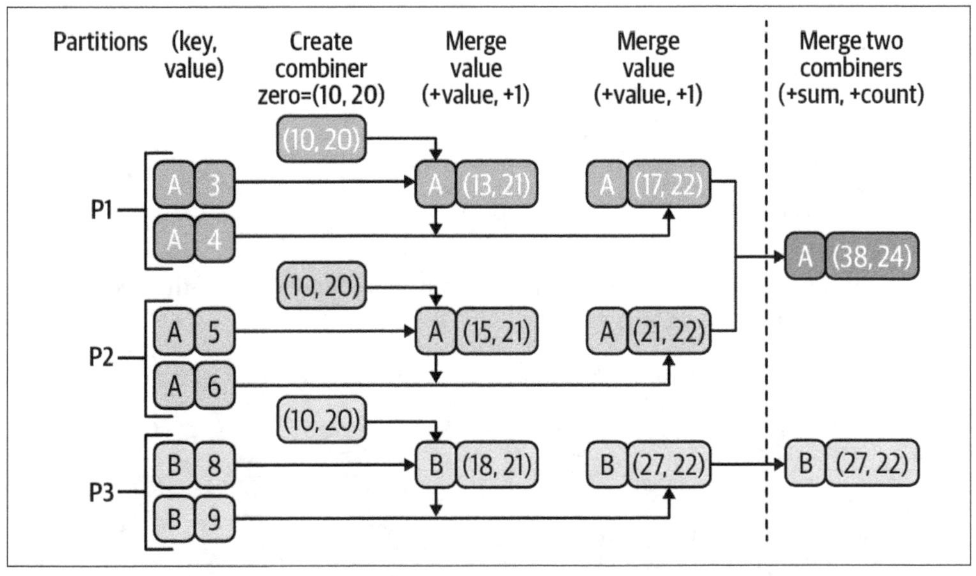

Figure 4-6. `aggregateByKey()` with `zero-value=(10, 20)`

First Solution Using aggregateByKey()

To find the average rating for each user, the first step is to map each record into (key, value) pairs of the form:

```
(userID-as-key, rating-as-value)
```

The simplest way to add up values per key is to use the `reduceByKey()` transformation, but we can't use `reduceByKey()` to find the average rating per user because, as we've seen, the mean/average function is not a monoid over a set of ratings (as float numbers). To make this a monoid operation, we use a pair data structure (a tuple of two elements) to hold a pair of values, `(sum, count)`, where `sum` is the aggregated sum of ratings and `count` is the number of ratings we have added (summed) so far, and we use the `aggregateByKey()` transformation.

Let's prove that the pair structure `(sum, count)` with an addition operator over a set of numbers is a monoid.

If we use `(0.0, 0)` as our zero element, it is neutral:

```
f(A, Zero) = A
f(Zero, A) = A

A = (sum, count)

f(A, Zero)
  = (sum+0.0, count+0)
  = (sum, count)
  = A

f(Zero, A)
  = (0.0+sum, 0+count)
  = (sum, count)
  = A
```

The operation is commutative (that is, the result is independent of the order of the elements in the RDD being aggregated):

```
f(A, B) = f(B, A)

A = (sum1, count1)
B = (sum2, count2)

f(A, B)
  = (sum1+sum2, count1+count2)
  = (sum2+sum1, count2+count1)
  = f(B, A)
```

It is also associative (the order in which elements are aggregated does not affect the final result):

```
f(f(A, B), C) = f(A, f(B, C))

A = (sum1, count1)
B = (sum2, count2)
C = (sum3, count3)

f(f(A, B), C)
  = f((sum1+sum2, count1+count2), (sum3, count3))
  = (sum1+sum2+sum3, count1+count2+count3)
  = (sum1+(sum2+sum3), count1+(count2+count3))
  = f(A, f(B, C))
```

To make things simple, we'll define a very basic Python function, `create_pair()`, which accepts a record of movie rating data and returns a pair of `(userID, rating)`:

```
# Define a function that accepts a CSV record
# and returns a pair of (userID, rating)
# Parameters: rating_record (as CSV String)
# rating_record = "userID,movieID,rating,timestamp"
def create_pair(rating_record):
        tokens = rating_record.split(",")
        userID = tokens[0]
        rating = float(tokens[2])
        return (userID, rating)
#end-def
```

Next, we test the function:

```
key_value_1 = create_pair("3,2394,4.0,920586920")
print key_value_1
('3', 4.0)

key_value_2 = create_pair("1,169,2.5,1204927694")
print key_value_2
('1', 2.5)
```

Here is a PySpark solution using `aggregateByKey()` and our `create_pair()` function. The combined type (`C`) to denote values for the `aggregateByKey()` operation is a pair of `(sum-of-ratings, count-of-ratings)`.

```
# spark: an instance of SparkSession
ratings_path = "/tmp/movielens/ratings.csv.no.header"
rdd = spark.sparkContext.textFile(ratings_path)
# load user-defined Python function
ratings = rdd.map(lambda rec : create_pair(rec)) ❶
ratings.count()
#
# C = (C[0], C[1]) = (sum-of-ratings, count-of-ratings)
# zero_value -> C = (0.0, 0)
# seq_func: (C, V) -> C
# comb_func: (C, C) -> C
sum_count = ratings.aggregateByKey( ❷
    (0.0, 0), ❸
```

```
        (lambda C, V: (C[0]+V, C[1]+1)), ❹
        (lambda C1, C2: (C1[0]+C2[0], C1[1]+C2[1])) ❺
    )
```

 The source RDD, `ratings`, is an `RDD[(String, Float)]` where the key is a `userID` and the value is a `rating`.

❷ The target RDD, `sum_count`, is an `RDD[(String, (Float, Integer))]` where the key is a `userID` and the value is a pair `(sum-of-ratings, count-of-ratings)`.

❸ `C` is initialized to this value in each partition.

❹ This is used to combine values within a single partition.

❺ This is used to combine the results from different partitions.

Let's break down what's happening here. First, we the `aggregateByKey()` function and create a result set "template" with the initial values. We're starting the data out as `(0.0, 0)`, so the initial sum of ratings is `0.0` and the initial count of records is `0`. For each row of data, we're going to do some adding. `C` is the new template, so `C[0]` is referring to our "sum" element (`sum-of-ratings`), while `C[1]` is the "count" element (`count-of-ratings`). Finally, we combine the values from the different partitions. To do this, we simply add the `C1` values to the `C2` values based on the template we made.

The data in the `sum_count` RDD will end up looking like the following:

```
sum_count
  = [(userID, (sum-of-ratings, count-of-ratings)), ...]
  = RDD[(String, (Float, Integer))]

[
  (100, (40.0, 10)),
  (200, (51.0, 13)),
  (300, (340.0, 90)),
  ...
]
```

This tells us that user `100` has rated 10 movies and the sum of all their ratings was 40.0; user `200` has rated 13 movies and the sum of their ratings was 51.0

Now, to get the actual average rating per user, we need to use the `mapValues()` transformation and divide the first entry (`sum-of-ratings`) by the second entry (`count-of-ratings`):

```
# x =  (sum-of-ratings, count-of-ratings)
# x[0] = sum-of-ratings
# x[1] = count-of-ratings
# avg = sum-of-ratings / count-of-ratings
average_rating = sum_count.mapValues(lambda x: (x[0]/x[1])) ❶
```

❶ `average_rating` is an `RDD[(String, Float)]` where the key is a `userID` and the value is an `average-rating`.

The contents of this RDD are as follows, giving us the result we're looking for:

```
average_rating
[
  (100, 4.00),
  (200, 3.92),
  (300, 3.77),
  ...
]
```

Second Solution Using aggregateByKey()

Here, I'll present another solution using the `aggregateByKey()` transformation. Note that to save space, I have trimmed the output generated by the PySpark shell.

The first step is to read the data and create (key, value) pairs, where the key is a `userID` and the value is a `rating`:

```
# ./bin/pyspark
SparkSession available as 'spark'.
>>># create_pair() returns a pair (userID, rating)
>>># rating_record = "userID,movieID,rating,timestamp"
>>> def create_pair(rating_record):
...     tokens = rating_record.split(",")
...     return (tokens[0], float(tokens[2]))
...
>>> key_value_test = create_pair("3,2394,4.0,920586920")
>>> print key_value_test
('3', 4.0)
>>> ratings_path = "/tmp/movielens/ratings.csv.no.header"
>>> rdd = spark.sparkContext.textFile(ratings_path)
>>> rdd.count()
22884377
>>> ratings = rdd.map(lambda rec : create_pair(rec))
>>> ratings.count()
22884377
>>> ratings.take(3)
[(u'1', 2.5), (u'1', 3.0), (u'1', 5.0)]
```

Once we've created the (key, value) pairs, we can apply the `aggregateByKey()` transformation to sum up the ratings. The initial value of `(0.0, 0)` is used for each partition, where `0.0` is the sum of the ratings and `0` is the number of ratings:

```
>>># C is a combined data structure, (sum, count)
>>> sum_count = ratings.aggregateByKey( ❶
...     (0.0, 0), ❷
...     (lambda C, V: (C[0]+V, C[1]+1)), ❸
...     (lambda C1, C2: (C1[0]+C2[0], C1[1]+C2[1]))) ❹
```

```
>>> sum_count.count()
247753

>>> sum_count.take(3)
[
 (u'145757', (148.0, 50)),
 (u'244330', (36.0, 17)),
 (u'180162', (1882.0, 489))
]
```

❶ The target RDD is an `RDD[(String, (Float, Integer))]`.

❷ `C` is initialized to `(0.0, 0)` in each partition.

❸ This lambda expression adds a single value of `V` to `C` (used in a single partition).

❹ This lambda expression combines the values across partitions (adds two `C`s to create a single `C`).

We could use Python functions instead of lambda expressions. To do this, we would need to write the following functions:

```
# C = (sum, count)
# V is a single value of type Float
def seq_func(C, V):
    return (C[0]+V, C[1]+1)
#end-def

# C1 = (sum1, count1)
# C2 = (sum2, count2)
def comb_func(C1, C2):
    return (C1[0]+C2[0], C1[1]+C2[1])
#end-def
```

Now, we can compute `sum_count` using the defined functions:

```
sum_count = ratings.aggregateByKey(
    (0.0, 0),
    seq_func,
    comb_func
)
```

The previous step created RDD elements of the following type:

```
(userID, (sum-of-ratings, number-of-ratings))
```

Next, we do the final calculation to find the average rating per user:

```
>>># x refers to a pair of (sum-of-ratings, number-of-ratings)
>>># where
>>>#      x[0] denotes sum-of-ratings
>>>#      x[1] denotes number-of-ratings
```

```
>>>
>>> average_rating = sum_count.mapValues(lambda x:(x[0]/x[1]))
>>> average_rating.count()
247753

>>> average_rating.take(3)
[
 (u'145757', 2.96),
 (u'244330', 2.1176470588235294),
 (u'180162', 3.8486707566462166)
]
```

Next, I'll present a solution to the movies problem using `groupByKey()`.

Complete PySpark Solution Using groupByKey()

For a given set of `(K, V)` pairs, `groupByKey()` has the following signature:

```
groupByKey(numPartitions=None, partitionFunc=<function portable_hash>)
groupByKey : RDD[(K, V)] --> RDD[(K, [V])]
```

If the source RDD is an `RDD[(K, V)]`, the `groupByKey()` transformation groups the values for each key (`K`) in the RDD into a single sequence as a list/iterable of `V`s. It then hash-partitions the resulting RDD with the existing partitioner/parallelism level. The ordering of elements within each group is not guaranteed, and may even differ each time the resulting RDD is evaluated.

You can customize both the number of partitions (`numPartitions`) and partitioning function (`partitionFunc`).

Be Careful with groupByKey()

The `groupByKey()` operation can be very expensive. If you are grouping a large number of values in order to perform an aggregation (such as a sum or average, or a statistical function) over each key, using `combineByKey()`, `aggregateByKey()`, or `reduceByKey()` will provide much better scalability and performance. Also note that the `groupByKey()` transformation assumes that the data for a key will fit in memory. If you have more data for a given key than will fit in memory, then you might get an OOM error.

When possible, you should avoid using `groupByKey()`. While both the `groupByKey()` and `reduceByKey()` transformations can produce the correct result, `reduceByKey()` works much better (i.e., scales out better) on a large dataset. That's because Spark knows it can combine output with a common key on each partition before shuffling the data.

Other alternatives that may be preferable to groupByKey() include:

combineByKey()
: This can be used when you are combining elements but your return type may differ from your input value type.

foldByKey()
: This merges the values for each key using an associative function and a neutral zero value.

Here, I present a complete solution using the groupByKey() transformation.

The first step is to read the data and create (key, value) pairs, where the key is a userID and the value is a rating:

```
>>># spark: SparkSession
>>> def create_pair(rating_record):
...     tokens = rating_record.split(",")
...     return (tokens[0], float(tokens[2]))
...
>>> key_value_test = create_pair("3,2394,4.0,920586920")
>>> print key_value_test
('3', 4.0)

>>> ratings_path = "/tmp/movielens/ratings.csv.no.header"
>>> rdd = spark.sparkContext.textFile(ratings_path)
>>> rdd.count()
22884377
>>> ratings = rdd.map(lambda rec : create_pair(rec)) ❶
>>> ratings.count()
22884377
>>> ratings.take(3)
[
 (u'1', 2.5),
 (u'1', 3.0),
 (u'1', 5.0)
]
```

 ratings is an RDD[(String, Float)]

Once we've created the (key, value) pairs, we can apply the groupByKey() transformation to group all ratings for a user. This step creates (userID, [R_1, ..., R_n]) pairs, where R_1, ..., R_n are all of the ratings for a unique userID.

As you will notice, the groupByKey() transformation works exactly like SQL's GROUP BY. It groups values of the same key as an iterable of values:

```
>>> ratings_grouped = ratings.groupByKey() ❶
>>> ratings_grouped.count()
247753
```

```
>>> ratings_grouped.take(3)
[
 (u'145757', <ResultIterable object at 0x111e42e50>), ❷
 (u'244330', <ResultIterable object at 0x111e42dd0>),
 (u'180162', <ResultIterable object at 0x111e42e10>)
]
>>> ratings_grouped.mapValues(lambda x: list(x)).take(3) ❸
[
 (u'145757', [2.0, 3.5, ..., 3.5, 1.0]),
 (u'244330', [3.5, 1.5, ..., 4.0, 2.0]),
 (u'180162', [5.0, 4.0, ..., 4.0, 5.0])
]
```

❶ `ratings_grouped` is an `RDD[(String, [Float])]` where the key is a `userID` and the value is a list of `ratings`.

❷ The full name of `ResultIterable` is `pyspark.resultiterable.ResultIterable`.

❸ For debugging, convert the `ResultIterable` object to a list of `Integers`.

To find the average rating per user, we sum up all the ratings for each `userID` and then calculate the averages:

```
>>># x refers to all ratings for a user as [R1, ..., Rn]
>>># x: ResultIterable object
>>> average_rating = ratings_grouped.mapValues(lambda x: sum(x)/len(x)) ❶
>>> average_rating.count()
247753
>>> average_rating.take(3)
[
 (u'145757', 2.96),
 (u'244330', 2.12),
 (u'180162', 3.85)
]
```

❶ `average_rating` is an `RDD[(String, Float)]` where the key is `userID` and the value is `average-rating`.

Complete PySpark Solution Using reduceByKey()

In its simplest form, `reduceByKey()` has the following signature (the source and target data types, `V`, must be the same):

```
reduceByKey(func, numPartitions=None, partitionFunc)
reduceByKey: RDD[(K, V)] --> RDD[(K, V)]
```

`reduceByKey()` transformation merges the values for each key using an associative and commutative reduce function. This will also perform the merging locally on each mapper before sending the results to a reducer, similarly to a combiner in

MapReduce. The output will be partitioned with numPartitions partitions, or the default parallelism level if numPartitions is not specified. The default partitioner is HashPartitioner.

Since we want to find the average rating for all movies rated by a user, and we know that the mean of means is not a mean (the mean function is not a monoid), we need to add up all the ratings for each user and keep track of the number of movies they've rated. Then, (sum_of_ratings, number_of_ratings) is a monoid over an addition function, but at the end we need to perform one more mapValues() transformation to find the actual average rating by dividing sum_of_ratings by number_of_ratings. The complete solution using reduceByKey() is given here. Note that reduceByKey() is more efficient and scalable than a groupByKey() transformation, since merging and combining are done locally before sending data for the final reduction.

Step 1: Read data and create pairs

The first step is to read the data and create (key, value) pairs, where the key is a userID and the value is a pair of (rating, 1). To use reduceByKey() for finding averages, we need to find the (sum_of_ratings, number_of_ratings). We start by reading the input data and creating an RDD[String]:

```
>>># spark: SparkSession
>>> ratings_path = "/tmp/movielens/ratings.csv.no.header"
>>># rdd: RDD[String]
>>> rdd = spark.sparkContext.textFile(ratings_path)
>>> rdd.take(3)
[
 u'1,169,2.5,1204927694',
 u'1,2471,3.0,1204927438',
 u'1,48516,5.0,1204927435'
]
```

Then we transform the RDD[String] into an RDD[(String, (Float, Integer))]:

```
>>> def create_combined_pair(rating_record):
...     tokens = rating_record.split(",")
...     userID = tokens[0]
...     rating = float(tokens[2])
...     return (userID, (rating, 1))
...
>>># ratings: RDD[(String, (Float, Integer))]
>>> ratings = rdd.map(lambda rec : create_combined_pair(rec)) ❶
>>> ratings.count()
22884377
>>> ratings.take(3)
[
 (u'1', (2.5, 1)),
 (u'1', (3.0, 1)),
```

```
 (u'1', (5.0, 1))
]
```

❶ Create the pair RDD.

Step 2: Use reduceByKey() to sum up ratings

Once we've created the `(userID, (rating, 1))` pairs we can apply the `reduceByKey()` transformation to sum up all the ratings and the number of ratings for a given user. The output of this step will be tuples of `(userID, (sum_of_ratings, number_of_ratings))`:

```
>>># x refers to (rating1, frequency1)
>>># y refers to (rating2, frequency2)
>>># x = (x[0] = rating1, x[1] = frequency1)
>>># y = (y[0] = rating2, y[1] = frequency2)
>>># x + y = (rating1+rating2, frequency1+frequency2)
>>># ratings is the source RDD ❶
>>> sum_and_count = ratings.reduceByKey(lambda x, y: (x[0]+y[0],x[1]+y[1])) ❷
>>> sum_and_count.count()
247753
>>> sum_and_count.take(3)
[
 (u'145757', (148.0, 50)),
 (u'244330', (36.0, 17)),
 (u'180162', (1882.0, 489))
]
```

❶ The source RDD (`ratings`) is an `RDD[(String, (Float, Integer))]`.

❷ The target RDD (`sum_and_count`) is an `RDD[(String, (Float, Integer))]`. Notice that the data types for the source and target are the same.

Step 3: Find average rating

Divide `sum_of_ratings` by `number_of_ratings` to find the average rating per user:

```
>>># x refers to (sum_of_ratings, number_of_ratings)
>>># x = (x[0] = sum_of_ratings, x[1] = number_of_ratings)
>>># avg = sum_of_ratings / number_of_ratings = x[0] / x[1]
>>> avgRating = sum_and_count.mapValues(lambda x : x[0] / x[1])
>>> avgRating.take(3)
[
 (u'145757', 2.96),
 (u'244330', 2.1176470588235294),
 (u'180162', 3.8486707566462166)
]
```

Complete PySpark Solution Using combineByKey()

`combineByKey()` is a more general and extended version of `reduceByKey()` where the result type can be different than the type of the values being aggregated. This is a limitation of `reduceByKey()`; it means that, given the following:

```
# let rdd represent (key, value) pairs
# where value is of type T
rdd2 = rdd.reduceByKey(lambda x, y: func(x,y))
```

`func(x,y)` must create a value of type `T`.

The `combineByKey()` transformation is an optimization that aggregates values for a given key before sending aggregated partition values to the designated reducer. This aggregation is performed in each partition, and then the values from all the partitions are merged into a single value. Thus, like with `reduceByKey()`, each partition outputs at most one value for each key to send over the network, which speeds up the shuffle step. However, unlike with `reduceByKey()`, the type of the combined (result) value does not have to match the type of the original value.

For a given set of `(K, V)` pairs, `combineByKey()` has the following signature (this transformation has many different versions; this is the simplest form):

```
combineByKey(create_combiner, merge_value, merge_combiners)
combineByKey : RDD[(K, V)] --> RDD[(K, C)]

V and C can be different data types.
```

This is a generic function to combine the elements for each key using a custom set of aggregation functions. It converts an `RDD[(K, V)]` into a result of type `RDD[(K, C)]`, where `C` is a combined type. It can be a simple data type such as `Integer` or `String`, or it can be a composite data structure such as a (key, value) pair, a triplet `(x, y, z)`, or whatever else you desire. This flexibility, makes `combineByKey()` a very powerful reducer.

As discussed earlier in this chapter, given a source RDD `RDD[(K, V)]`, we have to provide three basic functions:

```
create_combiner: (V) -> C
merge_value: (C, V) -> C
merge_combiners: (C, C) -> C
```

To avoid memory allocation, both `merge_value` and `merge_combiners` are allowed to modify and return their first argument instead of creating a new `C` (this avoids creating new objects, which can be costly if you have a lot of data).

In addition, users can control (by providing additional parameters) the partitioning of the output RDD, the serializer that is used for the shuffle, and whether to perform map-side aggregation (i.e., if a mapper can produce multiple items with the same key). The `combineByKey()` transformation thus provides quite a bit of flexibility, but it is a little more complex to use than some of the other reduction transformations.

Let's see how we can use `combineByKey()` to solve the movie problem.

Step 1: Read data and create pairs

As in the previous solutions, the first step is to read the data and create (key, value) pairs where the key is a `userID` and the value is a `rating`:

```
>>># spark: SparkSession
>>># create and return a pair of (userID, rating)
>>> def create_pair(rating_record):
...     tokens = rating_record.split(",")
...     return (tokens[0], float(tokens[2]))
...
>>> key_value_test = create_pair("3,2394,4.0,920586920")
>>> print key_value_test
('3', 4.0)

>>> ratings_path = "/tmp/movielens/ratings.csv.no.header"
>>> rdd = spark.sparkContext.textFile(ratings_path) ❶
>>> rdd.count()
22884377
>>> ratings = rdd.map(lambda rec : create_pair(rec)) ❷
>>> ratings.count()
22884377
>>> ratings.take(3)
[
 (u'1', 2.5),
 (u'1', 3.0),
 (u'1', 5.0)
]
```

❶ `rdd` is an `RDD[String]`.

❷ `ratings` is an `RDD[(String, Float)]`.

Step 2: Use combineByKey() to sum up ratings

Once we've created the `(userID, rating)` pairs , we can apply the `combineByKey()` transformation to sum up all the ratings and the number of ratings for each user. The output of this step will be `(userID, (sum_of_ratings, number_of_ratings))` pairs:

```
>>># v is a rating from (userID, rating)
>>># C represents (sum_of_ratings, number_of_ratings)
>>># C[0] denotes sum_of_ratings
```

```
>>># C[1] denotes number_of_ratings
>>># ratings: source RDD ❶
>>> sum_count = ratings.combineByKey( ❷
          (lambda v: (v, 1)), ❸
          (lambda C,v: (C[0]+v, C[1]+1)), ❹
          (lambda C1,C2: (C1[0]+C2[0], C1[1]+C2[1])) ❺
    )
>>> sum_count.count()
247753
>>> sum_count.take(3)
[
 (u'145757', (148.0, 50)),
 (u'244330', (36.0, 17)),
 (u'180162', (1882.0, 489))
]
```

❶ The source RDD is an `RDD[(String, Float)]`.

❷ The target RDD is an `RDD[(String, (Float, Integer))]`.

❸ This turns a `V` (a single value) into a `C` as `(V, 1)`.

❹ This merges a `V` (rating) into a `C` as `(sum, count)`.

❺ This combines two `Cs` into a single `C`.

Step 3: Find average rating

Divide `sum_of_ratings` by `number_of_ratings` to find the average rating per user:

```
>>># x = (sum_of_ratings, number_of_ratings)
>>># x[0] = sum_of_ratings
>>># x[1] = number_of_ratings
>>># avg = sum_of_ratings / number_of_ratings
>>> average_rating = sum_count.mapValues(lambda x:(x[0] / x[1]))
>>> average_rating.take(3)
[
 (u'145757', 2.96),
 (u'244330', 2.1176470588235294),
 (u'180162', 3.8486707566462166)
]
```

Next, we'll examine the shuffle step in Spark's reduction transformations.

The Shuffle Step in Reductions

Once all the mappers have finished emitting (key, value) pairs, MapReduce's magic happens: the sort and shuffle step. This step groups (sorts) the output of the map phase by keys and sends the results to the reducer(s). From an efficiency and scalability point of view, it's different for different transformations.

The idea of sorting by keys should be familiar by now, so here I'll focus on the shuffle. In a nutshell, shuffling is the process of redistributing data across partitions. It may or may not cause data to be moved across JVM processes, or even over the wire (between executors on separate servers).

I'll explain the concept of shuffling with an example. Imagine that you have a 100-node Spark cluster. Each node has records containing data on the frequency of URL visits, and you want to calculate the total frequency per URL. As you know by now, you can achieve this by reading the data and creating (key, value) pairs, where the key is a `URL` and the value is a `frequency`, then summing up the frequencies for each URL. But if the data is spread across the cluster, how can you sum up the values for the same key stored on different servers? The only way to do this is to get all the values for the same key onto the same server; then you can sum them up easily. This process is called shuffling.

There are many transformations (such as `reduceByKey()` and `join()`) that require shuffling of data across the cluster, but it can be an expensive operation. Shuffling data for `groupByKey()` is different from shuffling `reduceByKey()` data, and this difference affects the performance of each transformation. Therefore, it is very important to properly select and use reduction transformations.

Consider the following PySpark solution to a simple word count problem:

```
# spark: SparkSession
# We use 5 partitions for textFile(), flatMap(), and map()
# We use 3 partitions for the reduceByKey() reduction
rdd = spark.sparkContext.textFile("input.txt", 5)\
   .flatMap(lambda line: line.split(" "))\
   .map(lambda word: (word, 1))\
   .reduceByKey(lambda a, b: a + b, 3)\ ❶
   .collect()
```

❶ 3 is the number of partitions.

Since we directed the reduceByKey() transformation to create three partitions, the resulting RDD will be partitioned into three chunks, as depicted in Figure 4-7. The RDD operations are compiled into a directed acyclic graph of RDD objects, where each RDD maintains a pointer to the parent(s) it depends on. As this figure shows, at shuffle boundaries the DAG is partitioned into *stages* (Stage 1, Stage 2, etc.) that are executed in order.

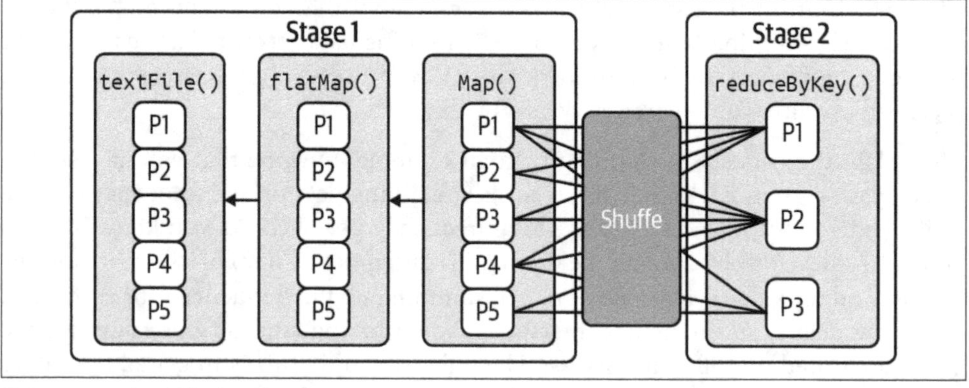

Figure 4-7. Spark's shuffle concept

Since shuffling involves copying data across executors and servers, this is a complex and costly operation. Let's take a closer look at how it works for two Spark reduction transformations, groupByKey() and reduceByKey(). This will help illustrate the importance of choosing the appropriate reduction.

Shuffle Step for groupByKey()

The groupByKey() shuffle step is pretty straightforward. It does not merge the values for each key; instead, the shuffle happens directly. This means a large volume of data gets sent to each partition, because there's no reduction in the initial data values. The merging of values for each key happens after the shuffle step. With groupByKey(), a lot of data needs to be stored on final worker nodes (reducers), which means you may run into OOM errors if there's lots of data per key. Figure 4-8 illustrates the process. Note that after groupByKey(), you need to call mapValues() to generate your final desired output.

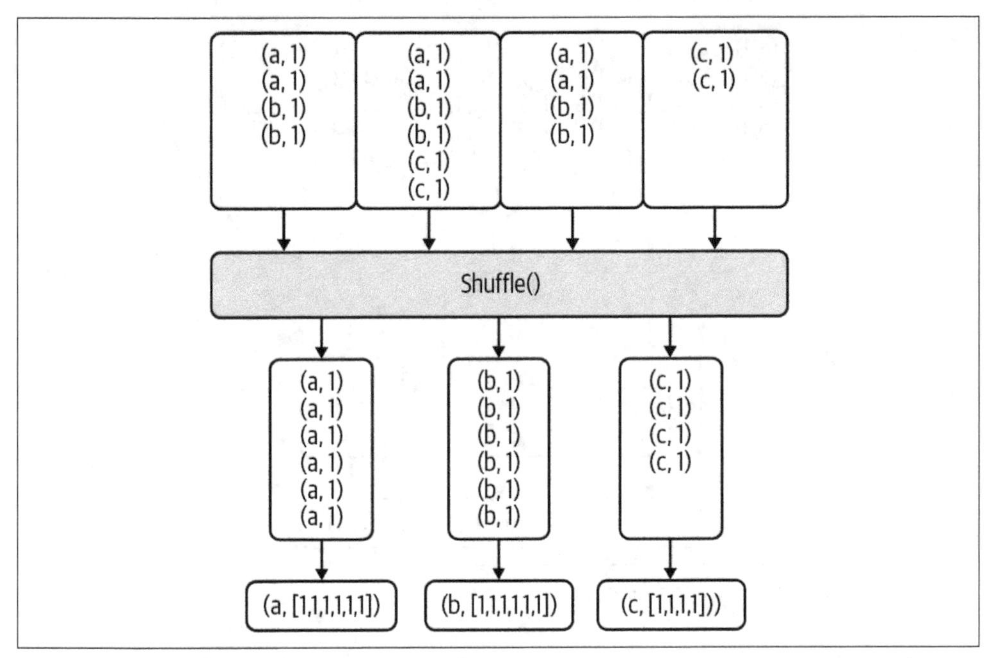

Figure 4-8. Shuffle step for `groupByKey()`

Because `groupByKey()` does not merge or combine values, it's an expensive operation that requires moving large amounts of data over the network.

Shuffle Step for reduceByKey()

With `reduceByKey()`, the data in each partition is combined so that there is at most one value for each key in each partition. Then the shuffle happens, and this data is sent over the network to the reducers, as illustrated in Figure 4-9. Note that with `reduceByKey()`, you do not need need to call `mapValues()` to generate your final desired output. In general, it's equivalent to using `groupByKey()` and `mapValues()`, but because of the reduction in the amount of data sent over the network it is a much more efficient and performant solution.

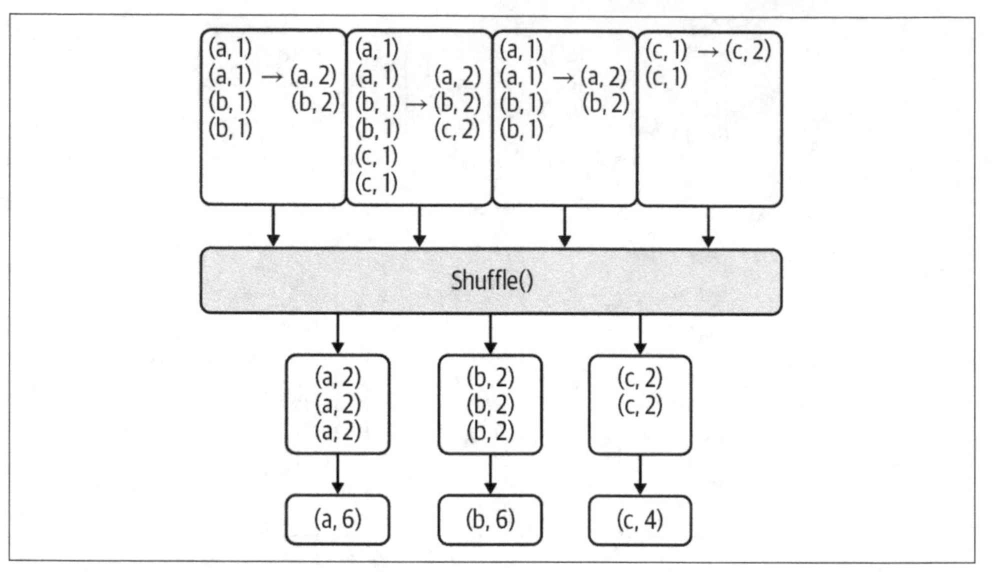

Figure 4-9. Shuffle step for `reduceByKey()`

Summary

This chapter introduced Spark's reduction transformations and presented multiple solutions to a real-world data problem with the most commonly used of these transformations: `reduceByKey()`, `aggregateByKey()`, `combineByKey()`, and `groupByKey()`. As you've seen, there are many ways to solve the same data problem, but they do not all have the same performance.

Table 4-2 summarizes the types of transformations performed by these four reduction transformations (note that `V` and `C` can be different data types).

Table 4-2. Comparison of Spark reductions

Reduction	Source RDD	Target RDD
`reduceByKey()`	`RDD[(K, V)]`	`RDD[(K, V)]`
`groupByKey()`	`RDD[(K, V)]`	`RDD[(K, [V])]`
`aggregateByKey()`	`RDD[(K, V)]`	`RDD[(K, C)]`
`combineByKey()`	`RDD[(K, V)]`	`RDD[(K, C)]`

We learned that some of the reduction transformations (such as `reduceByKey()` and `combineByKey()`) are preferable over `groupByKey()`, due to the shuffle step for `groupByKey()` being more expensive. When possible, you should `reduceByKey()` instead of `groupByKey()`, or use `combineByKey()` when you are combining elements but your return type differs from your input value type. Overall, for large volumes of data, `reduceByKey()` and `combineByKey()` will perform and scale out better than `groupByKey()`.

The `aggregateByKey()` transformation is more suitable for aggregations by key that involve computations, such as finding the sum, average, variance, etc. The important consideration here is that the extra computation spent for map-side combining can reduce the amount of data sent out to other worker nodes and the driver.

In the next chapter we'll move on to cover partitioning data.

PART II

Working with Data

CHAPTER 5
Partitioning Data

Partitioning is defined as "the act of dividing; separation by the creation of a boundary that divides or keeps apart." Data partitioning is used in tools like Spark, Amazon Athena, and Google BigQuery to improve query execution performance. To scale out big data solutions, data is divided into partitions that can be managed, accessed, and executed separately and in parallel.

As discussed in previous chapters of this book, Spark splits data into smaller chunks, called *partitions*, and then processes these partitions in a parallel fashion (many partitions can be processed concurrently) using executors on the worker nodes. For example, if your input has 100 billion records, then Spark might split it into 10,000 partitions, where each partition will have about 10 million elements:

- Total records: 100,000,000,000
- Number of partitions: 10,000
- Number of elements per partition: 10,000,000
- Maximum possible parallelism: 10,000

By default, Spark implements hash-based partitioning with a `HashPartitioner`, which uses Java's `Object.hashCode()` function.

Partitioning data can improve manageability and scalability, reduce contention, and optimize performance. Suppose you have hourly temperature data for cities in all the countries in the world (7 continents and 195 countries), and the goal is to query and analyze data for a given continent, country, or or set of countries. If you do not partition your data accordingly, for each query you'll have to load, read, and apply your mapper and reducer to the entire dataset to get the result you're looking for. This is not very efficient, since for most queries you only actually need a subset of the data. A much faster approach is to just load the data that you need.

Data partitioning in Spark is primarily done for the purpose of parallelism to allow tasks to execute independently, but in query tools such as Amazon Athena and Google BigQuery, its purpose is to allow you to analyze a slice of the data rather than the whole dataset. PySpark make it very easy to physically partition DataFrames by column name so that these tools can perform queries efficiently.

> **Source Code**
>
> Complete programs for this chapter are available in the book's GitHub repository (*https://oreil.ly/swJwW*).

Introduction to Partitions

By partitioning your data, you can restrict the amount of data scanned by each query, thus improving performance and reducing cost. For example, Amazon Athena, which leverages Spark and Hive for partitioning, lets you partition your data by any key (BigQuery provides the same functionality). Therefore, for our earlier example of weather data, you can just select and use specific folders for your query rather than using the entire data set for all countries.

If your data is represented in a table, such as a Spark DataFrame, partitioning is a way of dividing that table into related parts based on the values of particular columns. Partitioning can be based on one or more columns (these columns are called partition keys). The values in these partitioned columns are used to determine which partition each row should be stored in. Using partitions makes it easy to execute queries on slices of the data rather than loading the entire dataset for analysis. For example, genomics data records include a total of 25 chromosomes, which are labeled as `{chr1, chr2, ..., chr22, chrX, chrY, chrMT}`. Since in most genomics analyses, you do not mix chromosomes, it makes sense to partition this data by chromosome ID. This can reduce the analysis time by enabling you to load just the data for the desired chromosome.

Partitions in Spark

Suppose you're using a distributed storage system like HDFS or Amazon S3, where your data is distributed among many cluster nodes. How do your Spark partitions work? As your physical data is distributed in partitions across the physical cluster, Spark treats each partition as a high-level logical data abstraction (RDD or

DataFrame) in memory (and on disk if there is not sufficient memory), as illustrated in Figure 5-1. The Spark cluster will optimize partition access and will read the partition closest to it in the network, observing data locality.

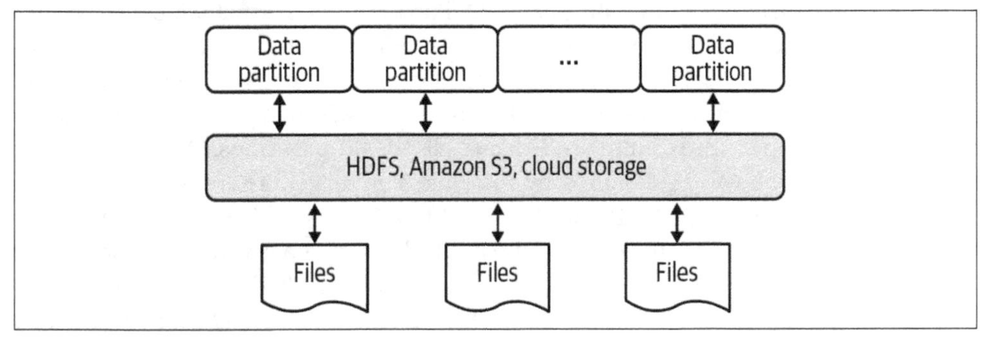

Figure 5-1. Logical model of partitioning in Spark

In Spark, the main purpose of partitioning data is to achieve maximum parallelism, by having executors on cluster nodes execute many tasks at the same time. Spark executors are launched at the start of a Spark application in coordination with the Spark cluster manager. They are worker node processes responsible for running individual tasks in a given Spark job/application. Breaking up data into partitions allows executors to process those partitions in parallel and independently, with each executor assigned its own data partition to work on (see Figure 5-2). No synchronization is required.

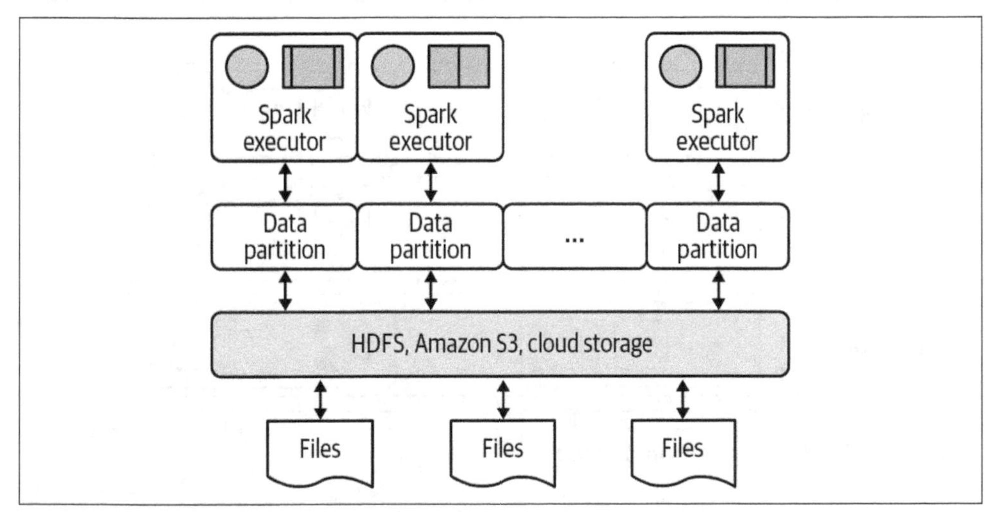

Figure 5-2. Spark partitioning in action

To understand how partitions enable us to achieve maximum performance and throughput in Spark, imagine that we have an RDD of 10 billion elements with 10,000 partitions (each partition will have about 1 million elements) and we want to execute a `map()` transformation on this RDD. Further imagine that we have a cluster of 51 nodes (1 master and 50 worker nodes), where the master acts as a cluster manager and has no executors, and each worker node can execute 5 mapper functions at the same time. This means that at any time 5 × 50 = 250 mappers are executing in parallel and independently, until we exhaust all 10,000 partitions. As each mapper finishes, a new one will be assigned by the cluster manager. Therefore, on average, each worker node will handle 10,000 / 250 = 40 partitions. This scenario guaranties that all worker nodes are utilized, which should be your goal when partitioning to achieve maximum optimization. In this scenario, if there had been 100 partitions (instead of 10,000), then each partition would have had about 100 million elements and only 100 / 5 = 20 worker nodes would have been utilized. The remaining 30 worker nodes might be idle (underutilization indicates a waste of resources).

Figure 5-3 shows how Spark executors process partitions.

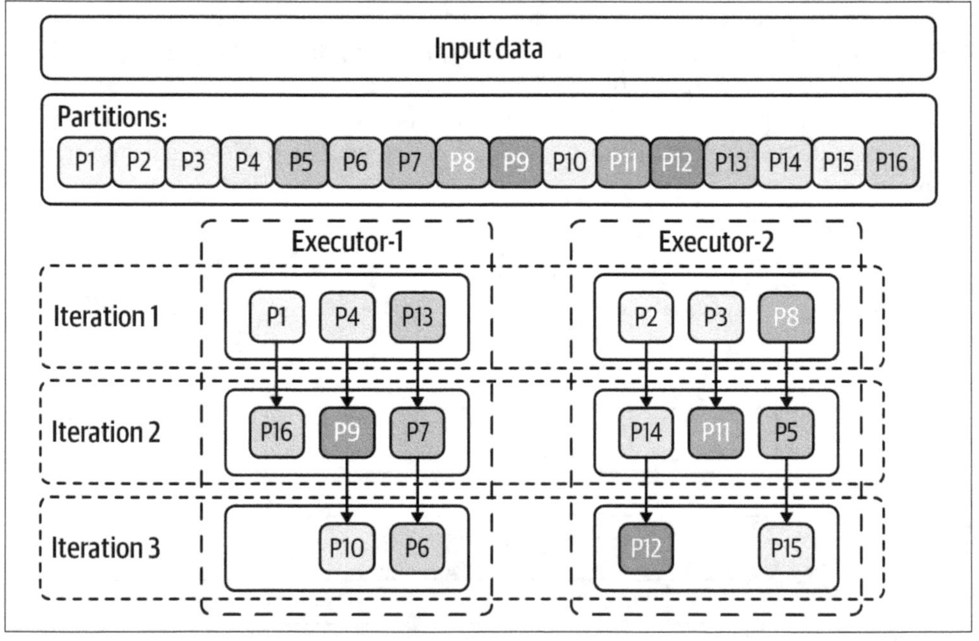

Figure 5-3. Example of partitioning data in Spark

In this figure, the input data is partitioned into 16 chunks. Given two executors, `Executor-1` and `Executor-2`, that can each process at most three partitions at a time, three iterations are required to process (such as through a mapper transformation) all of the partitions.

Another reason for partitioning in Spark is that the datasets are often so large that they cannot be stored in a single node. As the earlier example showed, how the partitioning is done is important, as it determines how the cluster's hardware resources are utillized when executing any job. The optimal partitioning should maximize utilization of hardware resources by maximizing parallelism for data transformations.

The following factors affect data partitioning choices:

Available resources
: The number of cores on which a task can run

External data sources
: Size of local collections, input filesystem used (such as HDFS, S3, etc.)

Transformations used to derive RDDs and DataFrames
: Rules affecting the use of partitions when an RDD/DataFrame is derived from another RDD/DataFrame

Let's see how partitioning works in a Spark computing environment. When Spark reads a datafile into an RDD (or DataFrame), it automatically partitions that RDD into multiple smaller chunks, regardless of the RDD's size. Then, when we apply a transformation (such as `map()`, `reduceByKey()`, etc.) on an RDD, the transformation is applied to each of its partitions. Spark spawns a single task per partition, which will run inside the executor's JVM (each worker can process one task at a time). Each stage contains as many tasks as there are partitions of the RDD and will perform the transformations requested in that stage on all of the partitions in parallel. This process is illustrated by Figure 5-4.

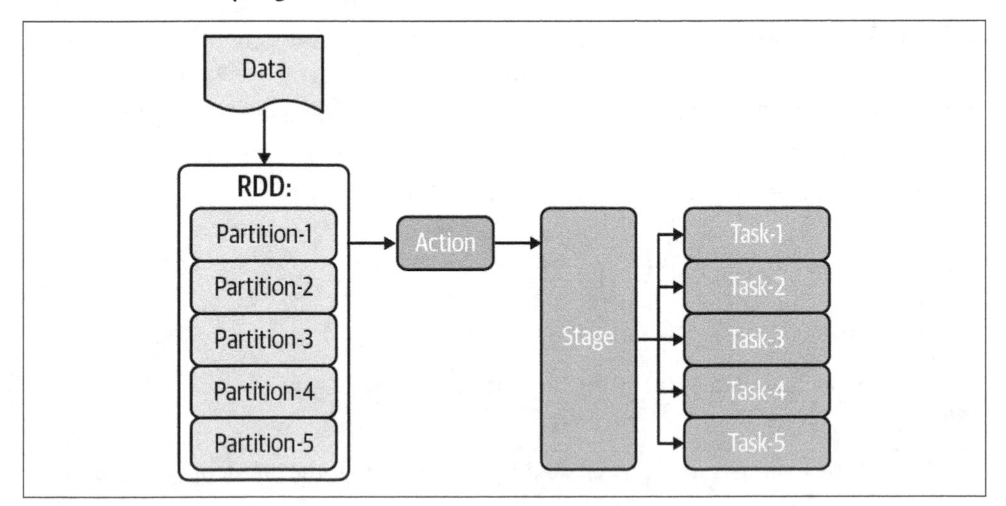

Figure 5-4. Operating on partitioned data in Spark

Partitions in Spark do not span multiple machines. This means that each partition is sent to a single worker machine, and tuples in the same partition are guaranteed to be on the same machine.

Just as proper partitioning can improve the performance of your data analysis, improper partitioning can harm performance of your data analysis. For example, suppose you have a Spark cluster with 501 nodes (1 master and 500 worker nodes). For an RDD with 10 billion elements the proper number of partitions would be over 500 (say, 1,000), to ensure that all cluster nodes are utilized at the same time. If you had 100 partitions and each worker could accept at most 2 tasks, then most of your worker nodes (about 400 of them) would be idle and useless. The more fully you utilize the worker nodes, the faster your query will run.

Next, we'll dig more deeply into how partitioning is done in Spark.

Managing Partitions

Spark has both a default and a custom partitioner. That means when you create an RDD, you can let Spark set the number of partitions, or you can set it explicitly. The number of partitions in the default case depends on the data source, the cluster size, and the available resources. Most of the time, the default partitioning will work just fine, but if you are an experienced Spark programmer, you may prefer to set the number of partitions explicitly using the `RDD.repartition`, `RDD.coalesce()`, or `DataFrame.coalesce()` function.

Spark offers several functions to manage partitioning. You can use `RDD.repartition(numPartitions)` to return a new RDD that has exactly `numPartitions` partitions. This function can increase or decrease the level of parallelism in the RDD, as the following example shows:

```
>>> rdd = sc.parallelize([1,2,3,4,5,6,7,8,9,10], 3)
>>> rdd.getNumPartitions()
3
>>> sorted(rdd.glom().collect()) ❶
[[1, 2, 3], [4, 5, 6], [7, 8, 9, 10]]
>>> len(rdd.repartition(2).glom().collect())
2
>>> len(rdd.repartition(5).glom().collect())
5
```

❶ `RDD.glom()` returns an RDD created by coalescing all the elements in each partition into a list.

Internally, the `RDD.repartition()` function uses a shuffle to redistribute the data. If you are decreasing the number of partitions in the RDD, consider using `RDD.coalesce()` instead, which can avoid performing a shuffle. `RDD.coalesce(numPartitions, shuffle=False)` returns a new RDD that is reduced into `numPartitions` partitions (you don't need to provide the second parameter, as by default the shuffle is avoided). This concept is demonstrated by the following example:

```
>>> nums = [1, 2, 3, 4, 5, 6, 7, 8, 9, 10]
>>> sc.parallelize(nums, 3).glom().collect()
[[1, 2, 3], [4, 5, 6], [7, 8, 9, 10]]
>>> sc.parallelize(nums, 3).coalesce(2).glom().collect()
[[1, 2, 3], [4, 5, 6, 7, 8, 9, 10]]
```

Default Partitioning

The default partitioning of an RDD or DataFrame happens when the programmer does not set the number of partitions explicitly. In this case, the number of partitions depends on the data and resources available in the cluster.

Default Number of Partitions

For production environments, most of the time, the default partitioner will work well. It ensures that all cluster nodes are utilized and that no cluster nodes/executors are idle.

When you create an RDD or a DataFrame, there is an option for setting the number of partitions. For example, when creating an RDD from a Python collection, you may set the number of partitions using the following API (where `numSlices` represents the number of partitions, or slices, to create):

```
SparkContext.parallelize(collection, numSlices=None)
```

Similarly, when you use `textfile()` to read a text file from a filesystem (such as HDFS or S3) and return it as an `RDD[String]`, you can set the `minPartitions` parameter:

```
SparkContext.textFile(name, minPartitions=None, use_unicode=True)
```

In both cases, if you do not set the optional parameter, Spark will set it to the default number of partitions (based on data size and available resources in the cluster). Here, I'll demonstrate creating an RDD from a collection without setting the number of partitions. First, I'll introduce a simple debugger function to display the elements of each partition:

```
>>> def debug(iterator):
...     print("elements=", list(elements))
```

I can then create an RDD and use this to display the contents of the partitions:

```
>>> numbers = [1, 2, 3, 4, 5, 6, 7, 8, 9, 10, 11, 12]
>>> rdd = sc.parallelize(numbers)
>>> num_partitions = rdd.getNumPartitions()
>>> num_partitions
8
>>> rdd.foreachPartition(debug)
elements= [1]
elements= [11, 12]
elements= [4]
elements= [2, 3]
elements= [10]
elements= [8, 9]
elements= [7]
elements= [5, 6]
```

Note that this function is intended for testing and teaching purposes only and should not be used in a production environment, where each partition may contain millions of elements.

Explicit Partitioning

As mentioned in the previous section, the programmer can also explicitly set the number of partitions when creating an RDD.

Setting the Number of Partitions

Before you set the number of partitions explicitly in a production environment, you need to understand your data and your cluster. Make sure that no cluster nodes/executors are idle.

Here, I create an RDD from the same collection but specify the number of partitions at the time of creation:

```
>>> numbers = [1, 2, 3, 4, 5, 6, 7, 8, 9, 10, 11, 12]
>>> rdd = sc.parallelize(numbers, 3) ❶
>>> rdd.getNumPartitions()
3
```

 The number of partitions is 3.

Next, let's debug the created RDD and view the contents of the partitions:

```
>>> rdd.foreachPartition(debug)
elements= [5, 6, 7, 8]
elements= [1, 2, 3, 4]
elements= [9, 10, 11, 12]
```

We can then apply the `mapPartitions()` transformation on this RDD:

```
>>> def adder(iterator):
...     yield sum(iterator)
...
>>> rdd.mapPartitions(adder).collect()
[10, 26, 42]
```

Physical Partitioning for SQL Queries

In this section, our focus is on the physical partitioning of data rather than RDD and DataFrame partitioning. Physical partitioning is a technique to improve the performance of queries on data utilized by query tools like Hive, Amazon Athena, and Google BigQuery. Athena and BigQuery are serverless services for querying data using SQL. Given a SQL query, proper physical data partitioning at the field level enablles us to read, scan, and query one or more slices of a dataset rather than reading and analyzing the whole dataset, greatly improving query performance. Spark also allows us to implement physical data partitioning on disk, as you'll see in the next section.

Partitioning data by specific fields (which are used in SQL's `WHERE` clause) plays a crucial role when querying data with Athena or BigQuery. By limiting the volume of data scanned, it dramatically speeds up query execution and reducing costs, since cost is based on the amount of data scanned.

Consider our earlier example of temperature data for cities around the world. By looking at the data, you can see that each continent has a list of countries, and each country has a set of cities. If you are going to query this data by continent, country, and city, then it makes a lot of sense to partition your data by these three fields: `(continent, country, city)`. The simple partitioning solution will be to create one folder per continent, then partition each continent by country, and finally partition each country by city. Then, instead of scanning the entire directory structure under *<root-dir>/*, the following query:

```
SELECT <some-fields-from-my_table>
    FROM my_table
       WHERE continent = 'north_america'
         AND country = 'usa'
         AND city = 'Cupertino'
```

will only scale this:

```
<root-dir>/continent=north_america/country=usa/city=Cupertino
```

As this example shows, partitioning can enable us to scan a very limited portion of our data, rather than the whole dataset. For example, if you have a query that involves the United States, you'll only need to scan one folder rather than scanning all 195 folders. In big data analysis, partitioning data by directories is very effective since we do not have an indexing mechanism like with relational tables. In fact, you can think of partitioning as a very simple indexing mechanism. Partitioning allows you to limit the amount of data scanned by each query, thus improving performance and reducing costs.

Let's look at another example. Given a world temperature dataset, you could create this partitioned table as follows in Amazon Athena:

```
CREATE EXTERNAL TABLE world_temperature(
 day_month_year DATE,
 temperature DOUBLE
)
PARTITIONED BY (
  continent STRING, ❶
  country STRING, ❷
  city STRING    ❸
)
STORED AS PARQUET
LOCATION s3://<bucket-name>/dev/world_temperature/
tblproperties ("parquet.compress"="SNAPPY");
```

❶ First partition by `continent`.

❷ Then partition by `country`.

❸ Finally, partition by `city`.

If you then query this table and specify a partition in the `WHERE` clause, Amazon Athena will scan the data only from that partition.

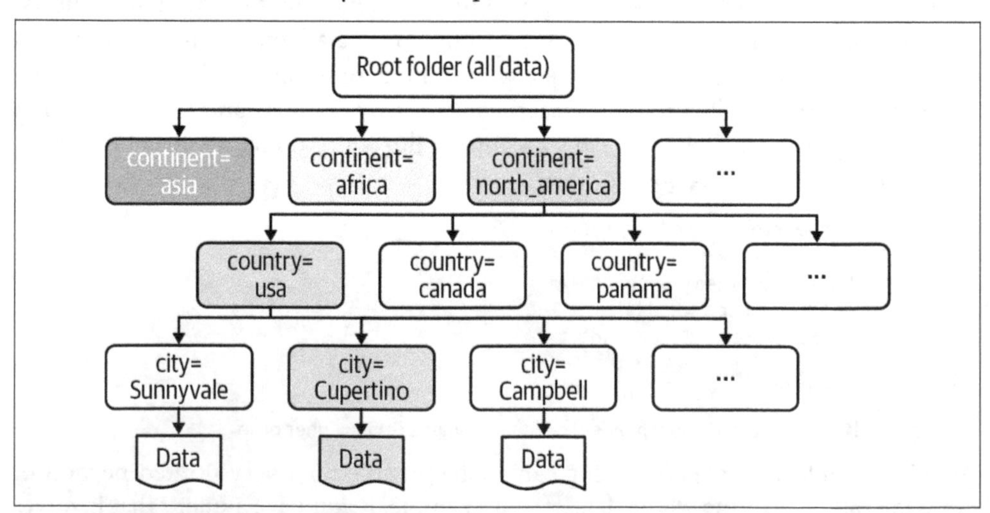

Figure 5-5. Querying partitioned data

Note that if you were qoing to query this data by `year`, `month`, and `day`, you could partition the same data into another form, where the partition fields are `year`, `month`, and `day`. In this case your schema will change to the following:

```
CREATE EXTERNAL TABLE world_temperature_by_date(
  day_month_year DATE,
  continent STRING,
  country STRING,
  city STRING,
  temperature DOUBLE
)
PARTITIONED BY (
  year INTEGER,  ❶
  month INTEGER, ❷
  day, INTEGER   ❸
)
STORED AS PARQUET
LOCATION s3://<bucket-name>/dev/world_temperature_by_date/
tblproperties ("parquet.compress"="SNAPPY");
```

❶ First partition by `year`.

❷ Then partition by `month`.

❸ Finally, partition by `day`.

With this new schema, you can issue SQL queries like this one:

```
SELECT <some-fields>
    FROM world_temperature_by_date
       WHERE year = 2020
         AND month = 8
         AND day = 16
```

As this example illustrates, to partition your data effectively you need to understand the queries that you will execute against your table (i.e., your data expressed as a table).

As another example, suppose you have customer data, where each record has the following format:

```
<customer_id><,><date><,><transaction_id><,><item><,><transaction_value>
<date>=DAY/MONTH/YEAR>
```

Further, assume that your goal is to analyze data by a given year, or by a combination of year and month. Partitioning the data is a good idea, as it will allow you to limit the amount of data scanned by selecting specific folders (by year or by year and month). Figure 5-6 shows what this might look like.

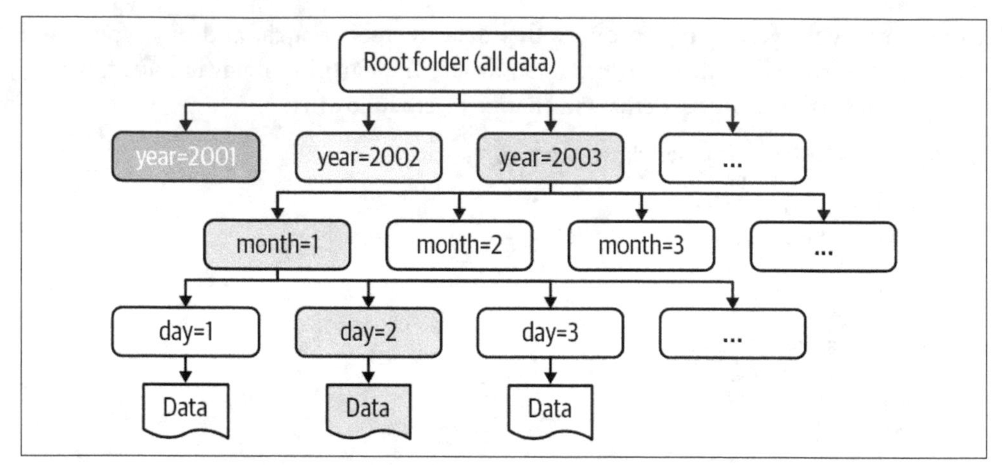

Figure 5-6. Querying data partitioned by year/month/day

Now, lets dig into how to partition data in Spark.

Physical Partitioning of Data in Spark

Spark offers a simple DataFrame API for physical partitioning of your data. Let `df` denote a DataFrame for our example data, with records of the form:

```
<customer_id><,><date><,><transaction_id><,><amount>
<date> = <day></><month></><year>
```

We can physically partition our data using the `DataFrameWriter.partitionBy()` method, either into a text format (row-based) or a binary format such as Parquet (column-based). The following subsections show how.

Partition as Text Format

The following code snippet shows how to partition data (represented as a DataFrame) by year and month into a text format. First, we create a DataFrame with four columns:

```
# df: a DataFrame with four columns:
#   <customer_id>
#   <date> (as DAY/MONTH/YEAR)
#   <transaction_id>
#   <amount>
df = spark.read.option("inferSchema", "true")\
          .csv(input_path)\
          .toDF('customer_id', 'date', 'transaction_id', 'amount')
```

Next, we add two new columns (year and month):

```
df2 = df.withColumn("year", get_year(df.date))\ ❶
        .withColumn("month", get_month(df.date)) ❷
```

❶ Add a year column.

❷ Add a month column.

Finally, we partition by year and month and then write and save our DataFrame:

```
df2.write ❶
  .partitionBy("year", "month")\ ❷
  .text(output_path) ❸
```

❶ Get a DataFrameWriter object.

❷ Partition the data by the desired columns.

❸ Save each partition in a text file.

A complete solution for partitioning data is available in the book's GitHub repository, in the file *partition_data_as_text_by_year_month.py*. A sample run with detailed output is also provided, in the file *partition_data_as_text_by_year_month.log*.

Partition as Parquet Format

Partitioning data into Parquet format (*http://parquet.apache.org*) has a few advantages: data aggregation can be done faster than with text data since Parquet stores data in columnar format, and Parquet stores metadata as well. The process is the same, except instead of using the text() function of the DataFrameWriter class, you use the parquet() function:

```
# partition data
df2.write.partitionBy('year', 'month')\
  .parquet(output_path)
```

If desired, you may partition your data by other columnar formats too, such as ORC (*http://orc.apache.org*) or CarbonData (*http://carbondata.apache.org*). If you want to just create a single partitioned file per partition, you can repartition the data before partitioning. Spark's repartition(numPartitions, *cols) function returns a new DataFrame partitioned by the given partitioning expressions. The resulting DataFrame is hash-partitioned. For example, this creates a single output file per partition ('year', 'month'):

```
# partition data
df2.repartition('year', 'month')\
  .write.partitionBy('year', 'month')\
  .parquet(output_path)
```

We can view the physical partitioning of data by examining the output path:

```
$ ls -lR /tmp/output
-rw-r--r--  ...    0 Feb 11 21:04 _SUCCESS
drwxr-xr-x  ...  192 Feb 11 21:04 year=2018
drwxr-xr-x  ...  160 Feb 11 21:04 year=2019
/tmp/output/year=2018:
drwxr-xr-x  ...  128 Feb 11 21:04 month=10
drwxr-xr-x  ...  128 Feb 11 21:04 month=12
drwxr-xr-x  ...  128 Feb 11 21:04 month=3
drwxr-xr-x  ...  128 Feb 11 21:04 month=9
/tmp/output/year=2018/month=10:
-rw-r--r--  ...  1239 Feb 11 21:04 part-00000...snappy.parquet
/tmp/output/year=2018/month=12:
total 8
-rw-r--r--  ...  1372 Feb 11 21:04 part-00000...snappy.parquet
...
```

How to Query Partitioned Data

To optimize query performance, you should include the physically partitioned column(s) in your SQL `WHERE` clauses. For example, if you have partitioned your data by `("year", "month", "day")`, then the following will be optimized queries:

```
-- Query data for year = 2012
   SELECT <some-columns>
      FROM <table-name>
         WHERE year = 2012

-- Query data for year = 2012 and month = 7
   SELECT <some-columns>
      FROM <table-name>
         WHERE year = 2012
           AND month = 7
```

The `WHERE` clause will guide the query engine to analyze slices of the data rather than the whole dataset, which is what it will do if you query non-partitioned columns. Let's take a look at an example using Amazon Athena.

Amazon Athena Example

To access and query your data in Athena using SQL, you need to implement the following simple steps:

1. Consider the types of queries you will issue, then partition your data accordingly. For example, if you're working with genome data and your SQL queries will look like this:

```
SELECT *
   FROM genome_table
      WHERE chromosome = 'chr7' AND ....
```

Then you should partition your data by the `chromosome` column. Load your data into a DataFrame (which includes a `chromosome` column), then partition it by chromosome and save it in S3 in Parquet format:

```
# create a DataFrame
df = <dataframe-includes-chromosome-column>

# define your output location
s3_output_path = 's3://genomics_bucket01:/samples/'

# partition data by chromosome column
# and save it as Parquet format
df.repartition("chromosome")\
  .write.mode("append")\
  .partitionBy("chromosome")\
  .parquet(s3_output_path)
```

2. Next, define your schema, specifying the same S3 location you defined in the previous step:

```
CREATE EXTERNAL TABLE `genome_table`(
  `sample_barcode` string,
  `allelecount` int,
  ...
)
PARTITIONED BY (
  `chromosome`
)
STORED AS PARQUET
LOCATION 's3://genomics_bucket01:/samples/'
tblproperties ("parquet.compress"="SNAPPY");
```

Note that the `chromosome` column is a data field defined in the `PARTITIONED BY` section.

3. Now that your schema is ready, you can execute/run it (this will create metadata used by Amazon Athena).

4. Load your partitions:

```
MSCK REPAIR TABLE genome_table;
```

5. Once your partitions are ready, you can start executing SQL queries like this one:

```
SELECT sum(allelecount)
   FROM genome_table
       WHERE chromosome = 'chr7';
```

Since you've partitioned your data by the `chromosome` column, only one directory, `chromosome=chr7`, will be read/scanned for this SQL query.

Summary

Partitioning in Spark is the process of splitting data (expressed as an RDD or DataFrame) into multiple partitions on which you can execute transformations in parallel, allowing for faster completion of data analysis tasks. You can also write partitioned data into multiple subdirectories in a filesystem for faster reads by downstream systems. To recap:

- Physical data partitioning involves partitioning data (expressed as an RDD or DataFrame) by data fields/columns into smaller pieces (chunks) in order to manage and access the data at a more fine-grained level.
- Data partitioning enables us to reduce the cost of storing a large amount of data as well as speeding up the processing of big datasets.
- When using serverless services such as Amazon Athena and Google BigQuery you need to partition your data by fields/columns, mainly used in the `WHERE` clause of SQL queries. It's important to understand the kinds of queries you'll be making and partition the data accordingly.
- In a nutshell, data partitioning gives us the following advantages:
  - It improves query performance and manageability. For a given query, you just analyze the relevant slice(s) of data based on the query clause.
  - It reduces the cost of querying the data, which is based on the amount of data scanned.
  - It simplifies common ETL tasks, as you can browse and view data based on the partitions.
  - It makes ad hoc querying easier and faster, since you can analyze slices of the data instead of the whole dataset.
  - It enables us to simulate partial indexing of relational database tables.

Next, we'll look at graph algorithms.

CHAPTER 6

Graph Algorithms

So far we've mainly been focusing on record data, which is typically stored in flat files or relational databases and can be represented as a matrix (a set of rows with named columns). Now we'll turn our attention to graph-based data, which depicts the relationships between two or more data points. A common example is social network data: for example, if "Alex" is a "friend" of "Jane" and "Jane" is a "friend" of "Bob," these relationships form a graph. Airline/flight data is another common example of graph data; we'll explore both of these (and others) in this chapter.

Data structures are specific ways of organizing and storing data in computers so that it can be used effectively. In addition to linear data structures like the ones we've primarily been working with in the previous chapters (arrays, lists, tuples, etc.), these include nonlinear structures such as trees, hash maps, and graphs.

This chapter introduces GraphFrames, a powerful external package for Spark that provides APIs for representing directed and undirected graphs, querying and analyzing graphs, and running algorithms on graphs. We'll start by exploring graphs and what they are used for, then look at how to use the GraphFrames API in PySpark to build and query graphs. We'll dig into a few of the algorithms GraphFrames supports, such as finding triangles and motif finding, then walk through some practical, real-world applications.

Source Code

Complete programs for this chapter are available in the book's GitHub repository (*https://oreil.ly/YXJzd*).

Introduction to Graphs

Graphs are nonlinear data structures used to visually illustrate relationships in data. Informally, a graph is a pair `(V, E)`, where:

- `V` is a set of nodes, called vertices.
- `E` is a collection of pairs of vertices, called edges.
- `V` (vertices) and `E` (edges) are positions and store elements.

In general, each node is identified by a unique identifier and a set of associated attributes. An edge is identified by two node identifiers (the source and target nodes) and a set of associated attributes. A path represents a sequence of edges between two vertices. For example, in the case of an airline network:

- A vertex represents an airport and stores the three-letter airport code and other vital information (city, state, etc.).
- An edge represents a flight route between two airports and stores the mileage of the route.

An edge can be *directed* or *undirected*, as shown in Figure 6-1. A directed edge consists of an ordered pair of vertices `(u, v)`, where the first vertex (`u`) is the source and the second vertex (`v`) is the destination. An undirected edge consists of an unordered pair of vertices `(u, v)`.

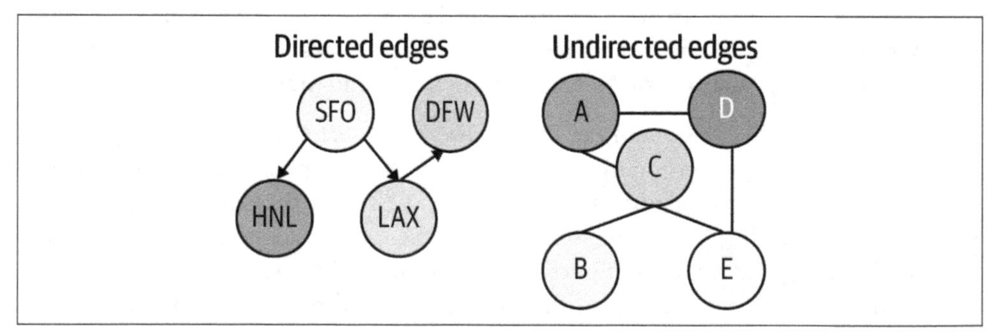

Figure 6-1. Directed and undirected edges

Similarly, a graph can be either directed (composed of directed edges) or undirected (composed of undirected edges). Figure 6-2 shows an example of a directed graph. it represents a small set of airports as vertices (identified by the airport codes, such as SJC, LAX, etc.) and shows the relationships between originating airports and flight destinations with edges.

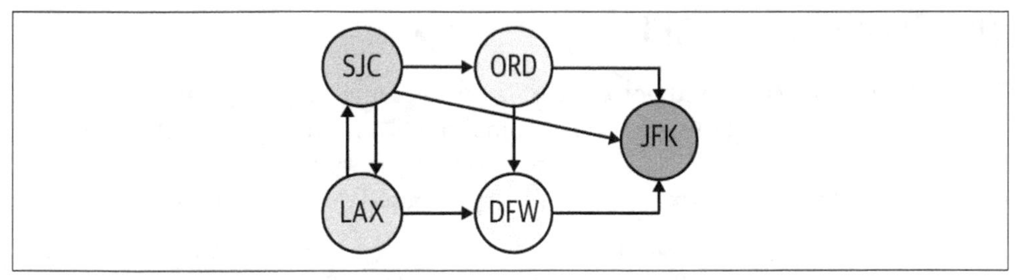

Figure 6-2. Directed graph example

Figure 6-3 shows an undirected graph with six nodes, labeled as `{A, B, C, D, E, F}`, connected with edges. In this example, the nodes might represent cities and edges might represent the distances between the cities. As you can see, in an undirected graph all the edges are bidirectional.

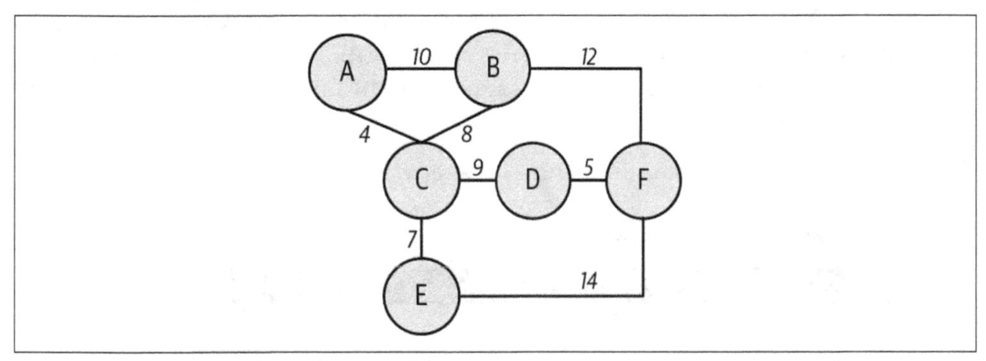

Figure 6-3. Undirected graph example

To convert a directed graph to an undirected graph, you add an additional edge for every directed edge. That is, if there is a directed edge as `(u, v)`, then you add an edge as `(v, u)`.

Certain types of data are particularly well suited to being expressed using graphs. For instance, in network analysis, data is usually modeled as a graph or set of graphs. Graphs and matrices are commonly used to represent and analyze information about patterns of ties among social actors (users, friends, followers) and objects (such as products, stories, genes, etc.). We'll look at some real-world examples of how graphs can be used to solve data problems later in this chapter, but first, let's dive into the GraphFrames API.

The GraphFrames API

Spark offers two distinct and powerful APIs for implementing graph algorithms such as PageRank, shortest paths, connected components, and triangle counting: GraphX and GraphFrames. GraphX is a core component of Spark based on RDDs, while GraphFrames (an open source external library) is based on DataFrames.

We'll be concentrating on GraphFrames, as at the time of writing GraphX (a general-purpose graph processing library optimized for fast distributed computing) only has APIs for Scala and Java, not Python. GraphFrames provides high-level APIs in all three languages, so we can use it in PySpark and optionally interface with selected GraphX functions under the covers.

In addition to the functionality of GraphX, GraphFrames offers extended functionality taking advantage of Spark's DataFrames. It provides the scalability and high performance of DataFrames and a unified API for graph processing. GraphFrames gives us powerful tools for running graph queries and algorithms; among other benefits, it simplifies interactive graph queries and supports motif finding, also known as graph pattern matching.

Table 6-1 summarizes the key differences between the two libraries.

Table 6-1. GraphFrames versus GraphX

Feature	GraphFrames	GraphX
Based on	DataFrames	RDDs
Supported languages	Scala, Java, Python	Scala, Java
Use cases	Algorithms and queries	Algorithms
Vertex/edge attributes	Any number of DataFrame columns	Any vertex (VD) or edge (ED) type
Return types	GraphFrame or DataFrame	Graph<VD,ED> or RDD
Supports motif finding	Yes	No direct support

The main class in the GraphFrames library is `graphframes.GraphFrame`, which builds a graph using the GraphFrames API. The `GraphFrame` class is defined as:

```
class GraphFrame {
  def vertices: DataFrame ❶
  def edges: DataFrame ❷
  def find(pattern: String): DataFrame ❸
  def degrees(): DataFrame ❹
  def pageRank(): GraphFrame ❺
  def connectedComponents(): GraphFrame ❻
  ...
}
```

❶ `vertices` is a DataFrame.

❷ edges is a DataFrame.

❸ Searches for structural patterns in a graph (motif finding).

❹ Returns the degree of each vertex in the graph as a DataFrame.

❺ Runs the PageRank algorithm on the graph.

❻ Computes the connected components of the graph.

How to Use GraphFrames

Let's dive in and use the GraphFrames API to build some graphs. Since GraphFrames is an external package (not a main component of the Spark API), to use it in the PySpark shell we have to explicitly make it available. The first step is to download and install it. GraphFrames is a collaborative effort by UC Berkeley, MIT, and Databricks. You can find the latest distribution of the GraphFrames package on Spark Packages (*https://oreil.ly/w3neM*), and the documentation is available on GitHub (*https://oreil.ly/T1ZBY*).

You can use the `--packages` argument in the PySpark shell to download the GraphFrames package and any dependencies automatically. Here, I've specified a particular version of the package (`0.8.2-spark3.2-s_2.12`). To use a different version, just change the last part of the `--packages` argument. From the OS command prompt, you can import the library with the following commands (note that the output here has been trimmed):

```
export SPARK_HOME=/Users/mparsian/spark-3.2.0
export GF="graphframes:graphframes:0.8.2-spark3.2-s_2.12"
$SPARK_HOME/bin/pyspark --packages $GF
...
graphframes#graphframes added as a dependency
found graphframes#graphframes;0.8.2-spark3.2-s_2.12 in spark-packages
...
Spark context available as 'sc'
SparkSession available as 'spark'.

>>> from graphframes import GraphFrame
```

If the import succeeds, you're ready to start using the GraphFrames API. The following example shows how to create a `GraphFrame`, query it, and run the PageRank algorithm on the graph. We'll go into more detail on PageRank in Chapter 8; for now, you just need to know that it's an algorithm used to rank pages in web search results.

In the GraphFrames API, a graph is represented as an instance of `GraphFrame(v, e)`, where `v` represents the vertices (as a DataFrame) and `e` represents the edges (as a DataFrame). Consider the simple graph in Figure 6-4.

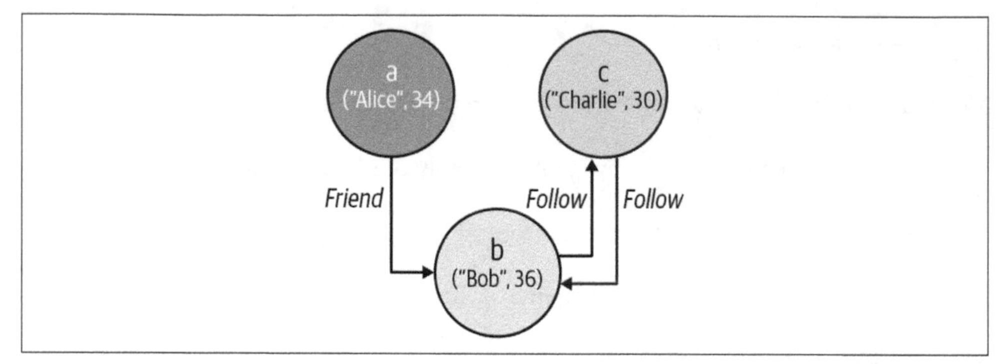

Figure 6-4. A simple graph

In the following steps, we will build this graph using the GraphFrames API and apply some simple graph queries and algorithms to it.

1. Create a vertex DataFrame with unique ID column, `id`. The `id` column is required by the GraphFrames API; it uniquely identifies all the vertices for the graph to be built. You can include additional columns too, depending on the node attributes. Here, we create `vertices` as a DataFrame with three columns (`DataFrame["id", "name", "age"]`):

```
>>># spark is an instance of SparkSession
>>> vertices = [("a", "Alice", 34), \
                ("b", "Bob", 36), \
                ("c", "Charlie", 30)] ❶
>>> column_names = ["id", "name", "age"]
>>> v = spark.createDataFrame(vertices, column_names) ❷
>>> v.show()
+---+-------+---+
| id|   name|age|
+---+-------+---+
|  a|  Alice| 34|
|  b|    Bob| 36|
|  c|Charlie| 30|
+---+-------+---+
```

❶ A Python collection representing vertices.

❷ `v` represents vertices as a DataFrame.

2. Create an edge DataFrame with `src` and `dst` columns. In addition to these required columns, which represent the source and destination vertex IDs, you can include additional attributes as required. We want to store information on the types of relationships between nodes in our graph, so we'll include a

relationship column. Here, we create edges as a DataFrame with three columns (DataFrame["src", "dst", "relationship"]:

```
>>> edges = [("a", "b", "friend"), \
             ("b", "c", "follow"), \
             ("c", "b", "follow")] ❶
>>> column_names = ["src", "dst", "relationship"]
>>> e = sqlContext.createDataFrame(edges, column_names) ❷
>>> e.show()
+---+---+------------+
|src|dst|relationship|
+---+---+------------+
|  a|  b|      friend|
|  b|  c|      follow|
|  c|  b|      follow|
+---+---+------------+
```

❶ A Python collection representing edges.

❷ e represents edges as a DataFrame.

3. The next step is to create our graph. With the GraphFrames API, a graph is built as an instance of GraphFrame, which is a pair of vertices (as v) and edges (as e):

```
>>> from graphframes import GraphFrame ❶
>>> graph = GraphFrame(v, e) ❷
>>> graph ❸
GraphFrame(v:[id: string, name: string ... 1 more field],
           e:[src: string, dst: string ... 1 more field])
```

❶ Import the required class GraphFrame.

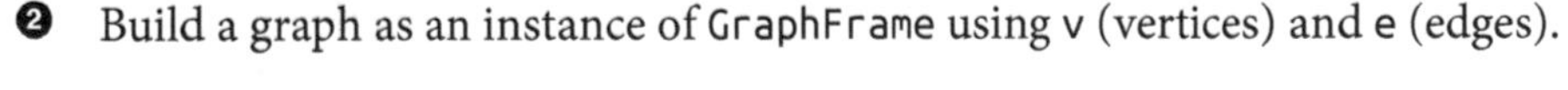

❷ Build a graph as an instance of GraphFrame using v (vertices) and e (edges).

❸ Inspect the built graph.

4. Once the graph is built, we can start issuing queries and applying algorithms. For example, we can issue the following query to get the "in-degree" of each vertex in the graph (that is, the number of edges that terminate in that vertex):

```
>>> graph.inDegrees.show()
+---+--------+
| id|inDegree|
+---+--------+
|  c|       1|
|  b|       2|
+---+--------+
```

The result is a DataFrame with two columns: `id` (the ID of the vertex) and `inDegree`, which stores the in-degree of the vertex as an integer. Note that vertices with no incoming edges are not returned in the result.

5. Next, let's count the number of "follow" connections in the graph:

```
>>> graph.edges.filter("relationship = 'follow'").count()
2
```

6. Finally, we can run the PageRank algorithm on the graph and show the results:

```
>>> pageranks = graph.pageRank(resetProbability=0.01, maxIter=20) ❶
>>> pageranks.vertices.select("id", "pagerank").show() ❷
+---+------------------+
| id|          pagerank|
+---+------------------+
|  b|1.0905890109440908|
|  a|              0.01|
|  c|1.8994109890559092|
+---+------------------+
```

❶ Run the PageRank algorithm on the given graph for 20 iterations.

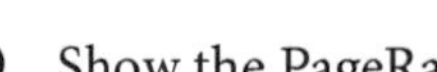

❷ Show the PageRank values for each node of the given graph.

GraphFrames Functions and Attributes

As the previous example suggests, GraphFrames functions (also known as graph operations, or GraphOps) give you access to a lot of details about your graphs. As well as various graph algorithm implementations (which we'll examine in more detail in the next section), the API exposes attributes that enable you to easily get information about the graph's vertices, edges, and degrees (`degrees`, `inDegrees`, and `outDegrees`).

For example, if `graph` is an instance of `GraphFrame` you can get the vertices and edges as DataFrames as follows:

```
vertices_as_dataframes = graph.vertices ❶
edges_as_dataframes = graph.edges ❷
```

❶ The `Graphframe.vertices` attribute returns the graph's vertices as a DataFrame.

❷ The `Graphframe.edges` attribute returns the graph's edges as a DataFrame.

A complete list of the available attributes and functions can be found in the API documentation (*https://oreil.ly/6JMVO*), but note that not all of those functions can be used with DataFrames. If you know how to work with DataFrames, you can also apply `sort()`, `groupBy()`, and `filter()` operations on the output of these functions to get more information, as we did to count the number of "follow" connections in our example graph (you'll learn more about working with DataFrames in the following chapters).

GraphFrames Algorithms

The GraphFrames API provides a set of algorithms for tasks such as finding a particular pattern or subgraph (also known as a "motif") in the graph, which is usually an expensive operation. Since Spark uses MapReduce and distributed algorithms it can run these operations relatively quickly, but they are still time-consuming processes. In addition to motif finding (with `find()`), the supported algorithms include:

- Motif finding
- Breadth-first search (BFS)
- Connected components
- Strongly connected components
- Label propagation
- PageRank
- Shortest path
- Triangle count

Let's dig in to a few of these algorithms in more detail.

Finding Triangles

This section provides efficient solutions to find, count, and list all triangles for a given graph or set of graphs using the GraphFrames API. Before we look at an example, we need to define a triad and a triangle. Let `T = (a, b, c)` be a set of three distinct nodes in a graph identified by `G`. Then `T` is a triad if two of those nodes are connected (`{(a, b), (a, c)}`) and it is a triangle if all three nodes are connected (`{(a, b), (a, c), (b, c)}`).

In graph analysis, there are three important metrics:

1. Global clustering coefficient
2. Transitivity ratio, defined as $T = 3 \times m / n$, where m is the number of triangles in the graph and n is the number of connected triads of vertices
3. Local clustering coefficient

Triangle counting (counting the number of triangles for each node in a graph) is a common task in social network analysis, where it's used to detect and measure the cohesiveness of communities. It's also often used in the computation of network indices like clustering coefficients (*https://oreil.ly/iTkRj*). An efficient algorithm is needed for this task, as in some cases the graphs can have hundreds of millions of nodes (e.g., users in a social network) and edges (the relationships between these users).

Triangle Counting with MapReduce

Chapter 16 of my book *Data Algorithms* (O'Reilly) provides two MapReduce solutions that find, count, and list all triangles for a given graph or set of graphs. Solutions are provided in Java, MapReduce, and Spark.

The GraphFrames package provides a convenient method, `GraphFrame.triangleCount()`, that computes the number of triangles passing through each vertex. Let's walk through an example that shows how to build a graph from nodes and edges and then find the number of triangles passing through each node.

Step 1: Build a graph

First, we'll define the vertices:

```
>>># SparkSession available as 'spark'.
>>># Display the vertex and edge DataFrames
>>> vertices = [('a', 'Alice',34), \
                ('b', 'Bob', 36), \
                ('c', 'Charlie',30), \
                ('d', 'David',29), \
                ('e', 'Esther',32), \
                ('f', 'Fanny',36), \
                ('g', 'Gabby',60)]
```

Next, we define the edges between nodes:

```
>>> edges = [('a', 'b', 'friend'),
             ('b', 'c', 'follow'), \
             ('c', 'b', 'follow'), \
             ('f', 'c', 'follow'), \
             ('e', 'f', 'follow'), \
             ('e', 'd', 'friend'), \
             ('d', 'a', 'friend'), \
             ('a', 'e', 'friend')]
```

Once we have vertices and edges, we can build a graph:

```
>>> v = spark.createDataFrame(vertices, ["id", "name", "age"]) ❶
>>> e = spark.createDataFrame(edges, ["src", "dst", "relationship"]) ❷
>>> from graphframes import GraphFrame
>>> graph = GraphFrame(v, e) ❸
```

❶ The `id` column is required for a vertex DataFrame.

❷ The `src` and `dst` columns are required for an edge DataFrame.

❸ The graph is built as a `GraphFrame` object.

Now let's examine the graph and its vertices and edges:

```
>>> graph
GraphFrame(v:[id: string, name: string ... 1 more field],
           e:[src: string, dst: string ... 1 more field])

>>> graph.vertices.show()
+---+-------+---+
| id|   name|age|
+---+-------+---+
|  a|  Alice| 34|
|  b|    Bob| 36|
|  c|Charlie| 30|
|  d|  David| 29|
|  e| Esther| 32|
|  f|  Fanny| 36|
|  g|  Gabby| 60|
+---+-------+---+

>>> graph.edges.show()
+---+---+------------+
|src|dst|relationship|
+---+---+------------+
|  a|  b|      friend|
|  b|  c|      follow|
|  c|  b|      follow|
|  f|  c|      follow|
|  e|  f|      follow|
|  e|  d|      friend|
|  d|  a|      friend|
|  a|  e|      friend|
+---+---+------------+
```

Step 2: Count triangles

Next, we'll use the `GraphFrame.triangleCount()` method to count the number of triangles passing through each vertex in this graph:

```
>>> results = g.triangleCount()
>>> results.show()
+-----+---+-------+---+
|count| id|   name|age|
+-----+---+-------+---+
|    0|  g|  Gabby| 60|
|    0|  f|  Fanny| 36|
|    1|  e| Esther| 32|
|    1|  d|  David| 29|
|    0|  c|Charlie| 30|
```

```
|    0|  b|     Bob| 36|
|    1|  a|   Alice| 34|
+-----+---+-------+---+
```

To show only the vertex IDs and the number of triangles passing through each vertex, we can write:

```
>>> results.select("id", "count").show()
+---+-----+
| id|count|
+---+-----+
|  g|    0|
|  f|    0|
|  e|    1|
|  d|    1|
|  c|    0|
|  b|    0|
|  a|    1|
+---+-----+
```

The results suggest that there are three triangles in our graph. However, these are all really the same triangle, with different roots:

```
Triangle rooted by e:  e -> d -> a -> e
Triangle rooted by d:  d -> a -> e -> d
Triangle rooted by a:  a -> e -> d -> a
```

In the next section, I will show you how to use the GraphFrames API's motif finding algorithm to drop duplicate triangles.

Motif Finding

Motifs in graphs are patterns of interactions between vertices, such as triangles and other subgraphs. For example, since Twitter data is not bidirectional (if Alex follows Bob, there's no guarantee that Bob will follow Alex), we can use motif finding to find all bidirectional user relationships. Motif finding enables us to execute queries to discover a variety of structural patterns in graphs, and the GraphFrames API provides strong support for this.

GraphFrames uses a simple domain-specific language (DSL) for expressing structural queries. For example, the following query:

```
graph.find("(a)-[e1]->(b); (b)-[e2]->(a)")
```

will search for pairs of vertices `{a, b}` connected by edges in both directions (bidirectional relationships). It will return a DataFrame of all such structures in the graph, with columns for each of the named elements (vertices or edges) in the motif. In this case, the returned columns will be "`a, b, e1, e2`" (where `e1` represents an edge from `a` to `b` and `e2` represents an edge from `b` to `a`).

In the GraphFrames framework, the DSL for expressing structural patterns is defined as follows:

- The basic unit of a pattern is an edge. An edge connects one node to another one; for example, `"(a)-[e]->(b)"` expresses an edge `e` from vertex `a` to vertex `b`. Note that vertices are denoted by parentheses (`(a)` and `(b)`), while edges are denoted by square brackets (`[e]`).
- A pattern is expressed as a union of edges. Edge patterns can be joined with semicolons (`;`). For example, the motif `"(a)-[e1]->(b); (b)-[e2]->(c)"` specifies two edges (`e1` and `e2`), from `a` to `b` and `b` to `c`.
- Within a pattern, names can be assigned to vertices and edges. For example, `"(a)-[e]->(b)"` has three named elements: vertices `{a, b}` and an edge `e`. These names serve two purposes:
  - The names can identify common elements among edges. For example, `"(a)-[e1]->(b); (b)-[e2]->(c)"` specifies that the same vertex `b` is the destination of edge `e1` and the source of edge `e2`.
  - The names are used as column names in the resulting DataFrame. For example, if a motif contains named vertex `a`, then the resulting DataFrame will contain a column `a` which is a `StructType` with subfields equivalent to the schema (columns) of `GraphFrame.vertices`. Similarly, an edge `e` in a motif will produce a column `e` in the resulting DataFrame with subfields equivalent to the schema (columns) of `GraphFrame.edges`.
- It is acceptable to omit names for vertices or edges in motifs when they are not needed. For example, the motif `"(a)-[]->(b)"` expresses an edge between vertices `a` and `b` but does not assign a name to the edge. There will be no column for the anonymous edge in the resulting DataFrame. Similarly, the motif `"(a)-[e]->()"` indicates an out-edge of vertex `a` but does not name the destination vertex, and `"()-[e]->(b)"` indicates an in-edge of vertex `b` but does not name the source vertex.
- An edge can be negated by using an exclamation point (`!`) to indicate that the edge should not be present in the graph. For example, the motif `(a)-[]->(b); !(b)-[]->(a)` finds edges from `a` to `b` for which there is no edge from `b` to `a` ("a" follows "b", but "b" does not follow "a").

Triangle counting with motifs

The motif finding algorithm in the GraphFrames API enables us to find structural patterns (such as triangles) in a graph easily by defining a motif. For example, if `"{a, b, c}"` denotes three nodes in a graph, then we can define a motif for a triangle as:

```
a -> b -> c -> a
```

This definition includes three vertices (a, b, and c) such that:

```
a is connected to b (as an edge a -> b)
b is connected to c (as an edge b -> c)
c is connected to a (as an edge c -> a)
```

You can also build more complex relationships involving edges and vertices using motifs.

```
(a)-[e]->(b)
```

Creating Undirected Graphs

It is important to note that the GraphFrames API represents all graphs as directed (see Figure 6-5).

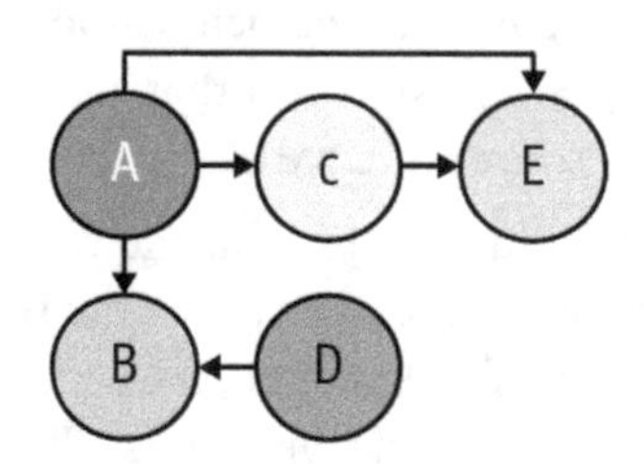

Figure 6-5. Directed graph example

By definition, a directed graph is a graph with a set of vertices that are connected together, where all the edges are directed from one vertex to another. But for some applications, it is desirable to work with undirected graphs—for example, Facebook users form an undirected graph since relationships between nodes are bidirectional. How do we convert a directed graph into an undirected graph? The solution is straightforward: given a directed graph, for every edge `[a -> b]` create another edge `[b -> a]` and then make the edges distinct so that there will not be duplicates. You'll see how to do this soon.

To help you understand the concept of motif finding, let's look at another example. Given a `GraphFrame` object `g`, we will walk through a few trials to find the optimal way of identifying triangles. Assume that our graph is undirected: if we have an edge `[a -> b]`, then we will have another edge as `[b -> a]`.

Trial 1. Our first approach will be to find a triangle as "`a -> b -> c -> a`":

```
>>> triangles = g.find("(a)-[e1]->(b);
                        (b)-[e2]->(c);
                        (c)-[e3]->(a)")
>>> triangles.show()
```

```
+-----+------+-----+------+-----+------+
|    a|    e1|    b|    e2|    c|    e3|
+-----+------+-----+------+-----+------+
|[1,1]|[1,2,]|[2,2]|[2,4,]|[4,4]|[4,1,]|
|[2,2]|[2,1,]|[1,1]|[1,4,]|[4,4]|[4,2,]|
|[1,1]|[1,4,]|[4,4]|[4,2,]|[2,2]|[2,1,]|
|[4,4]|[4,1,]|[1,1]|[1,2,]|[2,2]|[2,4,]|
|[2,2]|[2,4,]|[4,4]|[4,3,]|[3,3]|[3,2,]|
|[2,2]|[2,4,]|[4,4]|[4,1,]|[1,1]|[1,2,]|
|[4,4]|[4,2,]|[2,2]|[2,3,]|[3,3]|[3,4,]|
|[4,4]|[4,2,]|[2,2]|[2,1,]|[1,1]|[1,4,]|
|[2,2]|[2,3,]|[3,3]|[3,4,]|[4,4]|[4,2,]|
|[3,3]|[3,2,]|[2,2]|[2,4,]|[4,4]|[4,3,]|
|[3,3]|[3,4,]|[4,4]|[4,2,]|[2,2]|[2,3,]|
|[4,4]|[4,3,]|[3,3]|[3,2,]|[2,2]|[2,4,]|
|[5,5]|[5,6,]|[6,6]|[6,7,]|[7,7]|[7,5,]|
|[6,6]|[6,5,]|[5,5]|[5,7,]|[7,7]|[7,6,]|
|[5,5]|[5,7,]|[7,7]|[7,6,]|[6,6]|[6,5,]|
|[7,7]|[7,5,]|[5,5]|[5,6,]|[6,6]|[6,7,]|
|[6,6]|[6,7,]|[7,7]|[7,5,]|[5,5]|[5,6,]|
|[7,7]|[7,6,]|[6,6]|[6,5,]|[5,5]|[5,7,]|
+-----+------+-----+------+-----+------+
```

This trial finds triangles, but there is problem with duplicated output (since our graph is undirected).

Trial 2. Let's try again, this time adding a filter to remove duplicate triangles. This filter ensures that `e1.src` and `e1.dst` are not the same:

```
>>> triangles = g.find("(a)-[e1]->(b);
                        (b)-[e2]->(c);
                        (c)-[e3]->(a)")
                 .filter("e1.src < e1.dst")
>>> triangles.show()
+-----+------+-----+------+-----+------+
|    a|    e1|    b|    e2|    c|    e3|
+-----+------+-----+------+-----+------+
|[1,1]|[1,2,]|[2,2]|[2,4,]|[4,4]|[4,1,]|
|[1,1]|[1,4,]|[4,4]|[4,2,]|[2,2]|[2,1,]|
|[2,2]|[2,4,]|[4,4]|[4,3,]|[3,3]|[3,2,]|
|[2,2]|[2,4,]|[4,4]|[4,1,]|[1,1]|[1,2,]|
|[2,2]|[2,3,]|[3,3]|[3,4,]|[4,4]|[4,2,]|
|[3,3]|[3,4,]|[4,4]|[4,2,]|[2,2]|[2,3,]|
|[5,5]|[5,6,]|[6,6]|[6,7,]|[7,7]|[7,5,]|
|[5,5]|[5,7,]|[7,7]|[7,6,]|[6,6]|[6,5,]|
|[6,6]|[6,7,]|[7,7]|[7,5,]|[5,5]|[5,6,]|
+-----+------+-----+------+-----+------+
```

This is better, but we still have some duplicates in our results.

Trial 3. In our final trial, we'll add another filter that will enable us to uniquely identify all triangles without duplicates:

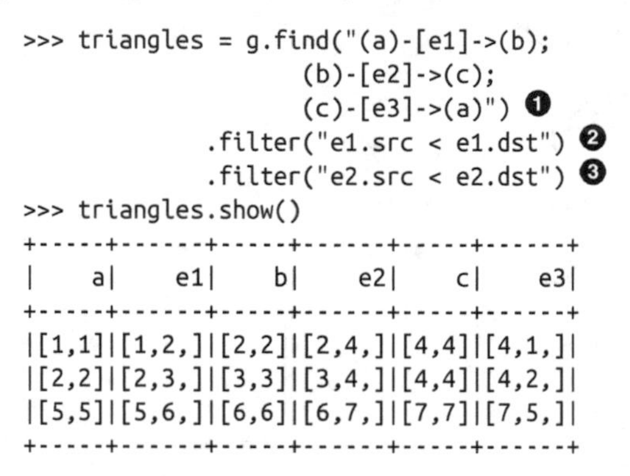

```
>>> triangles = g.find("(a)-[e1]->(b);
                        (b)-[e2]->(c);
                        (c)-[e3]->(a)") ❶
                 .filter("e1.src < e1.dst") ❷
                 .filter("e2.src < e2.dst") ❸
>>> triangles.show()
+-----+------+-----+------+-----+------+
|    a|    e1|    b|    e2|    c|    e3|
+-----+------+-----+------+-----+------+
|[1,1]|[1,2,]|[2,2]|[2,4,]|[4,4]|[4,1,]|
|[2,2]|[2,3,]|[3,3]|[3,4,]|[4,4]|[4,2,]|
|[5,5]|[5,6,]|[6,6]|[6,7,]|[7,7]|[7,5,]|
+-----+------+-----+------+-----+------+
```

❶ Find triangles {`a -> b -> c -> a`}.

❷ Make sure that `e1.src` and `e1.dst` are not the same.

❸ Make sure that `e2.src` and `e2.dst` are not the same.

Finding unique triangles with motifs

In this section I'll show you how to build a `GraphFrame` from a set of vertices and edges, and then find the unique triangles in the graph.

Input. The required components for building a graph (using GraphFrames) are vertices and edges. Assume that our vertices and edges are defined in two files:

- *sample_graph_vertices.txt*
- *sample_graph_edges.txt*

Let's examine these input files:

```
$ head -4 sample_graph_vertices.txt
vertex_id
0
1
2

$ head -4 sample_graph_edges.txt
edge_weight,from_id,to_id
0,5,15
1,18,8
2,6,1
```

To comply with the GraphFrames API, we'll perform the following cleanup and filtering tasks:

1. Rename `vertex_id` to `id`.
2. Drop the column `edge_weight`.
3. Rename `from_id` to `src`.
4. Rename `to_id` to `dst`.

Output. The expected output will be unique triangles from the built graph. Note that given three vertices `{a, b, c}` of a triangle, it can be represented in any of the following six ways:

```
a -> b -> c -> a
a -> c -> b -> a
b -> a -> c -> b
b -> c -> a -> b
c -> a -> b -> c
c -> b -> a -> c
```

The goal is to output only one of these representations.

Algorithm. The complete PySpark solution is presented as *unique_triangles_finder.py*. Using the GraphFrames motif finding algorithm and DataFrames, the solution is pretty simple:

1. Create a DataFrame for vertices: `vertices_df`.
2. Create a DataFrame for edges: `edges_df`.
3. Build a graph as a `GraphFrame`.
4. Apply a motif which is a triangle pattern.
5. Filter out duplicate triangles.

Building `vertices_df` is straightforward. In building `edges_df`, to make sure that our graph is undirected, if there is a connection from a `src` vertex to a `dst` vertex, then we add an extra edge from `dst` to `src`. This way we will be able to find all the triangles.

We'll start by finding all the triangles, including potential duplicates:

```
>>> graph = GraphFrame(vertices_df, edges_df)
>>># find all triangles, which might have duplicates
>>> motifs = graph.find("(a)-[]->(b);
                         (b)-[]->(c);
                         (c)-[]->(a)")
>>> print("motifs.count()=", motifs.count())
42
```

Next, we'll use the DataFrame's powerful filtering mechanism to remove duplicate triangles, keeping only one representation of a triangle `{a, b, c}` where `a > b > c`:

```
>>> unique_triangles = motifs[(motifs.a > motifs.b) &
                              (motifs.b > motifs.c)] ❶
>>> unique_triangles.count()
7
>>> unique_triangles.show(truncate=False)
+----+----+----+
|a   |b   |c   |
+----+----+----+
|[42]|[32]|[30]|
|[5] |[31]|[15]|
|[8] |[22]|[18]|
|[8] |[22]|[17]|
|[7] |[39]|[28]|
|[52]|[51]|[50]|
|[73]|[72]|[71]|
+----+----+----+
```

❶ Remove duplicate triangles.

Note that `motifs.count()` returned 42 (since a triangle can be represented in six different ways, as shown earlier) and `unique_triangles.count()` returns 7 ($6 \times 7 = 42$)

Other motif finding examples

The combination of GraphFrames and DataFrames is a very powerful tool for solving graph-related problems and beyond. I've demonstrated how to use motifs to find triangles, but there are many other applications. We'll look at a few of them here.

Finding bidirectional vertices. Using motifs, you can build more complex relationships involving a graph's edges and vertices. The following example finds the pairs of vertices with edges in both directions between them. The result is a DataFrame in which the column names are motif keys. Let `graph` be an instance of a `GraphFrame`. Then, finding bidirectional vertices can be expressed as:

```
# search for pairs of vertices with edges
# in both directions between them
bidirectional = graph.find("(a)-[e1]->(b);
                            (b)-[e2]->(a)") ❶
```

❶ `bidirectional` will have columns `a`, `e1`, `b`, and `e2`.

Since the result is a DataFrame, more complex queries can build on top of the motif. For instance, we can find all the reciprocal relationships in which one person is older than 30 as follows:

```
older_than_30 = bidirectional.filter("b.age > 30 or a.age > 30")
```

Finding subgraphs. A subgraph is a graph whose vertices and edges are subsets of another graph. You can build subgraphs by filtering on a subset of edges and vertices. For example, we can construct a subgraph containing only relationships where the follower is younger than the user being followed:

```
# graph is an instance of GraphFrame
paths = graph.find("(a)-[e]->(b)")\
  .filter("e.relationship = 'follow'")\
  .filter("a.age < b.age")

# The `paths` variable contains the vertex
# information, which we can extract:
selected_edges = paths.select("e.src", "e.dst", "e.relationship")

# Construct the subgraph
sample_subgraph = GraphFrame(g.vertices, selected_edges)
```

Friend recommendation. Another common task in social networks that is made easy by the GraphFrames motif finding algorithm is making friend recommendations. For example, to recommend whom users might like to follow, we might search for triplets of users `(A, B, C)` where "`A` follows `B`" and "`B` follows `C`," but "`A` does not follow `C`." This can be expressed as:

```
# g is an instance of GraphFrame
# Motif: "A -> B", "B -> C", but not "A -> C"
results = g.find("(A)-[]->(B);
                  (B)-[]->(C);
                  !(A)-[]->(C)")

# Filter out loops (with DataFrame operation)
results_filtered = results.filter("A.id != C.id")

# Select recommendations for A to follow C
recommendations = results_filtered.select("A", "C")
```

Product recommendations. As a final example, we'll look at product recommendations. Consider a case where a customer who bought product `p` also purchased two other products, `a` and `b`. This relationship is depicted in Figure 6-6.

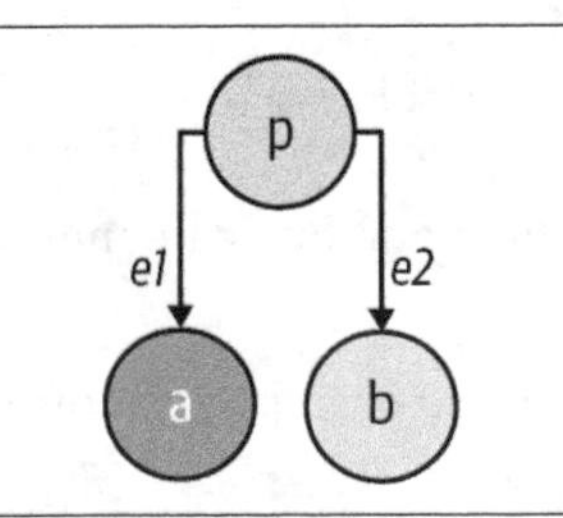

Figure 6-6. Relationship between purchased products

There are two separate edges, from product p to a and b. Therefore, this motif can be expressed as:

```
graph = GraphFrame(vertices, edges)
motifs = graph.find("(p)-[e1]->(a);
                     (p)-[e2]->(b)")
              .filter("(a != b)")
```

We can also apply filters to the result of motif finding. For example, here we specify the value of the vertex p as 1200 (denoting the product with that id):

```
motifs.filter("p.id == 1200").show()
```

The following example shows how to find strong relationships between two products (i.e., products that are often purchased together). In this example, we specify edges from p to a and a to b, and another one from b to a. This pattern typically represents the case in which when a customer buys a product p, they may also buy a and then go on to buy b. This can be indicative of some prioritization of the items being purchased (see Figure 6-7).

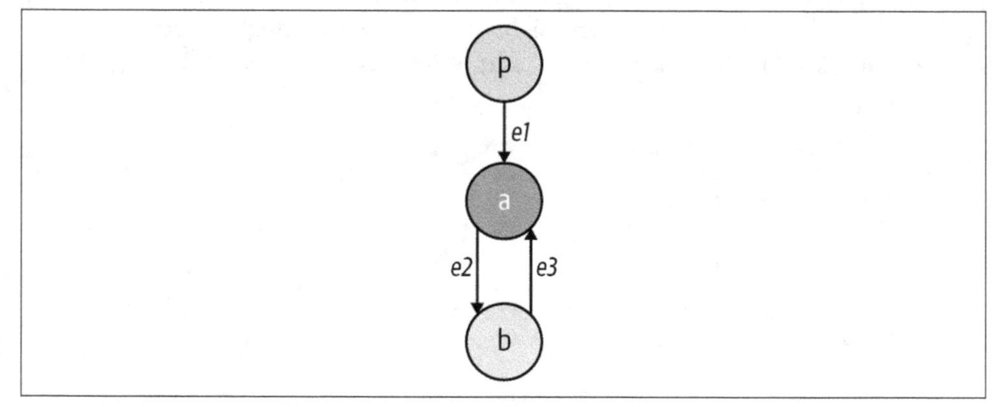

Figure 6-7. Product relationships

The motif for finding products with this type of relationship can be expressed as:

```
graph = GraphFrame(vertices, edges)
strong_motifs = graph.find("(p)-[]->(a);
                            (a)-[]->(b);
                            (b)-[]->(a)")
strong_motifs.show()
```

Recall that in motif definition the notation [e] denotes an edge labeled as e, while [] denotes an edge without a name.

Next, we'll dive into some real-world examples of how GraphFrames can be used.

Other Graph Algorithms

Once you've created a `GraphFrame`, there are many interesting out-of-the-box analytics that you can perform on it. The options range from simple degree algorithms, for tasks such as:

- Finding the in-degree of each vertex with `graph.inDegrees().show()`
- Finding the out-degree of each vertex with `graph.outDegrees().show()`
- Finding the degree of each vertex (the total number of connections, in and out) with `graph.degrees().show()`

to more complex algorithms for tasks like:

- Counting the number of triangles with `graph.triangleCount().run().select("id", "count").show()`
- Running static label propagation to detect communities with `graph.labelPropagation().maxIter(10).run().show()`
- Running the PageRank algorithm on the graph:

```
graph.pageRank()
 .maxIter(0).resetProbability(0.15)
 .run()
 .vertices()
 .show()
```

- Running the shortest paths algorithm with a set of landmarks with:

```
graph.shortestPaths()
 .landmarks(getLandmarks())
 .run()
 .show()
```

Real-World Applications

The purpose of this section is to present some real-world applications using the motif finding feature of the GraphFrames API.

Gene Analysis

Let's start by walking through an example of how to use GraphFrames along with motifs for gene analysis. A gene is a unit of heredity that is transferred from a parent to its offspring and is held to determine some characteristic of the offspring. Gene relationships have been analyzed for Down syndrome with labeled transition graphs (*https://oreil.ly/mc3Ip*) based on gene interaction data (directed graphs where vertices represent genes and an edge represents a relationship between genes). For example, three vertices (XAB2, ERCC8, and POLR2A, denoting three genes) and two edges (denoting the interactions between them) can be represented by the following raw data:

```
XAB2,ERCC8,Reconstituted Complex
XAB2,POLR2A,Affinity Capture-Western
```

One important analysis is to find motifs between specific vertices, which can help detect conditions like Down syndrome or Alzheimer's disease. Examples include the Hedgehog signaling pathway (HSP), illustrated in Figure 6-8, and the gene regulatory network shown in Figure 6-9.

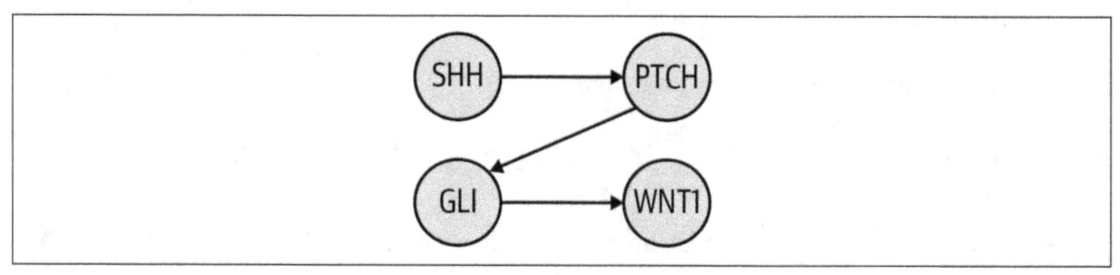

Figure 6-8. The Hedgehog signaling pathway relationship

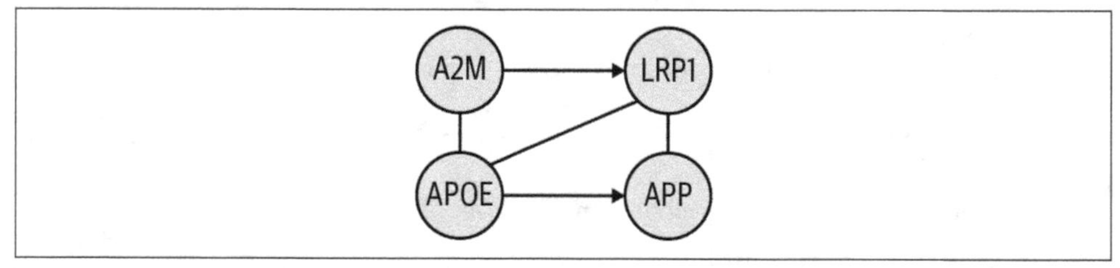

Figure 6-9. Gene regulatory network linked to Alzheimer's disease

These patterns and relationships can be easily detected by the GraphFrames API's motif finding feature. We can also find the most important genes using the PageRank algorithm, or find gene communities by running label propagation algorithm for many iterations.

Let's walk through building the graph. The input has the following format:

```
<source-gene><,><destination-gene><,><type-of-relationship>
```

Here are a few examples of what the input records look like:

```
BRCA1,BRCA1,Biochemical Activity
SET,TREX1,Co-purification
SET,TREX1,Reconstituted Complex
PLAGL1,EP300,Reconstituted Complex
```

Since we have input only for edges, we will derive the vertices from the edges.

Motif finding for genes

Earlier, I showed two structural patterns. To express the HSP as a motif, we would write:

```
hsp = graph.find(
          "(shh)-[e1]->(ptch); " +
          "(ptch)-[e2]->(gli); " +
          "(gli)-[e3]->(wnt1)")
         .filter("shh.id = 'SHH'")
         .filter("ptch.id = 'PTCH'")
         .filter("gli.id = 'GLI'")
         .filter("wnt1.id = 'WNT1'")
```

This is very powerful and straightforward: search for three nodes connected to each other, and further restrict them to specific nodes.

Social Recommendations

Recommendation systems are popular these days in applications like social networks (such as Twitter and Facebook) and shopping sites (such as Amazon). In this section, based on the blog post "Using Graphframes for Social Recommendation" (*https://oreil.ly/SDNka*) by Hamed Firooz, I'll show you how to build a simple social recommendation system using Spark's GraphFrames package.

Let's assume that we have two types of objects: users and tables, which contain messages sent between users. These objects will be represented as vertices in a graph), and the relationships between them will be represented as edges. Users can follow each other, and this is a one-way connection (unlike the "friend" relationship on Facebook, which is bidirectional). Tables contain two types of data: public and private. A user can choose to either "follow" a table, which gives them access to public messages, or be a "member" of table, which gives them access to all messages and also the ability to send messages to other members and followers of the table.

We'll base our analysis on the sample graph in Figure 6-10, which shows data for six users and three tables.

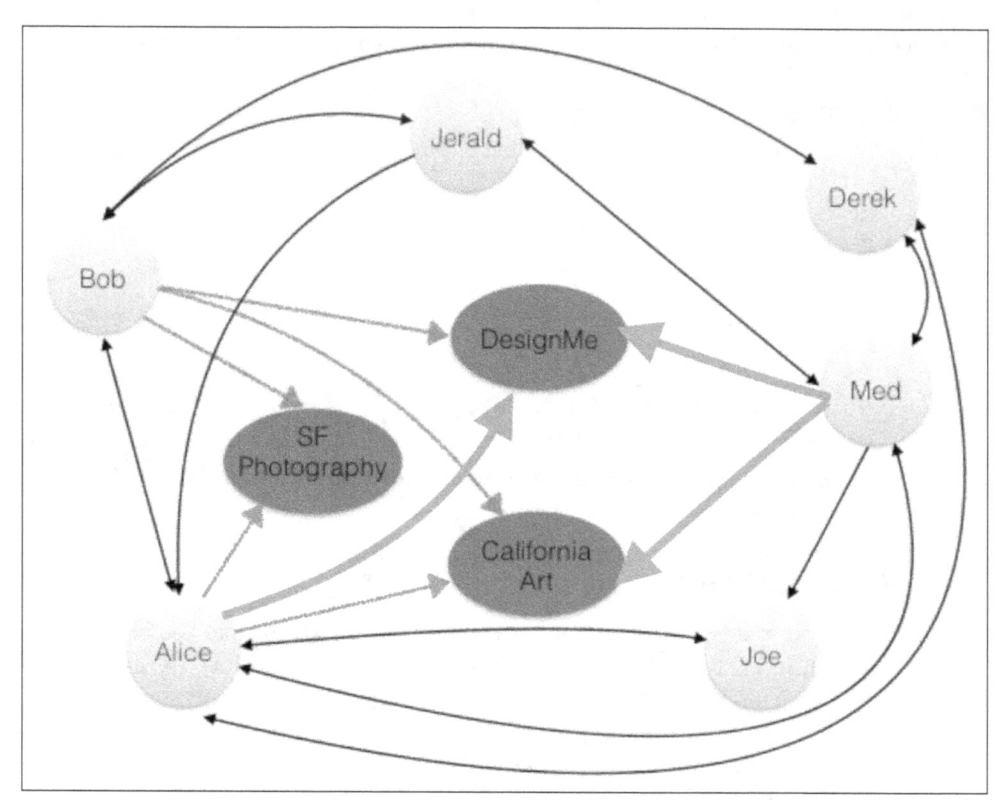

Figure 6-10. Sample social graph (Source: "Using Graphframes for Social Recommendation" (https://oreil.ly/SDNka))

Given this graph, suppose we want to recommend that person B follow person A if the following four conditions are satisfied:

1. A and B are not connected. A does not follow B, and B does not follow A.
2. A and B have at least four nodes in common. This means they each are connected to at least four nodes.
3. At least two of those four nodes are tables.
4. A is a member of those two tables.

We can express this using the GraphFrames motif finding algorithm as follows (recall from "Motif Finding" on page 172 that the `!` character indicates negation; i.e., that the edge should not be present in the graph):

Remember that GraphFrame motif finding uses a domain-specific language (DSL) for expressing structural pattern and queries. For example, the following motif finds the triangles by using the `find()` function:

```
graph.find("(a)-[e1]->(b);
           (b)-[e2]->(c);
           (c)-[e3]->(a)")
```

will search for triangles as pairs of vertices "a, b, and c" such that:

```
{ (a, b), (b, c), (c, a) }
```

It will return a DataFrame of all such structures in the graph, with columns for each of the named elements (vertices or edges) in the motif. In this case, the returned columns will be "a, b, c, e1, e2, e3". To express negation in motif finding, the exclamation ("!") character is used; an edge can be negated to indicate that the edge should not be present in the graph. For example, the following motif:

```
"(a)-[]->(b); !(b)-[]->(a)"
```

finds edges from "a to b" for which there is no edge from "b to a".

Our social recommendation can be achieved by GraphFrames "motif finding":

```
one_hub_connection = graph.find(
    "(a)-[ac1]->(c1); (b)-[bc1]->(c1); " +
    "(a)-[ac2]->(c2); (b)-[bc2]->(c2); " +
    "(a)-[ac3]->(c3); (b)-[bc3]->(c3); " +
    "(a)-[ac4]->(c4); (b)-[bc4]->(c4); " +
    "!(a)-[]->(b); !(b)-[]->(a)") ❶
           .filter("c1.type = 'table'") ❷
           .filter("c2.type = 'table'")
           .filter("a.id != b.id") ❸
           .filter("c1.id != c2.id") ❹
           .filter("c2.id != c3.id")
           .filter("c3.id != c4.id")

recommendations = one_hub_connection
                    .select("a", "b")
                    .distinct()
recommendations.show()
recommendations.printSchema()
```

❶ Make sure a and b are not connected.

❷ Make sure that at least two of those four nodes to which both a and b are connected are of type 'table'.

❸ Make sure a is not the same as b.

❹ Make sure the four nodes are not the same.

The output will be:

```
+--------------+--------------+
|             a|             b|
+--------------+--------------+
|[3,Med,person]|[1,Bob,person]|
|[1,Bob,person]|[3,Med,person]|
+--------------+--------------+

root
|-- a: struct (nullable = false)
|    |-- id: string (nullable = false)
|    |-- name: string (nullable = false)
|    |-- type: string (nullable = false)
|-- b: struct (nullable = false)
|    |-- id: string (nullable = false)
|    |-- name: string (nullable = false)
|    |-- type: string (nullable = false)
```

This is a good example of the power of motif finding in GraphFrames. We are interested in finding two nodes `{a, b}`, which are both connected to four other nodes `{c1, c2, c3, c4}`. This is expressed as:

```
(a)-[ac1]->(c1);
(b)-[bc1]->(c1);
(a)-[ac2]->(c2);
(b)-[bc2]->(c2);
(a)-[ac3]->(c3);
(b)-[bc3]->(c3);
(a)-[ac4]->(c4);
(b)-[bc4]->(c4);
```

The motif expresses the following rules:

- `a` and `b` are not connected to each other. This is expressed as:

  ```
  !(a)-[]->(b);
  !(b)-[]->(a)
  ```

- At least two of those four nodes are tables. This is expressed using two filters:

  ```
  filter("c1.type = 'table'")
  filter("c2.type = 'table'")
  ```

- `a` and `b` are not the same user. This is expressed as:

  ```
  filter("a.id != b.id")
  ```

- `a` and `b` are connected to four unique nodes. This is expressed as:

  ```
  .filter("c1.id != c2.id")
  .filter("c2.id != c3.id")
  .filter("c3.id != c4.id")
  ```

Finally, since there are many ways to traverse the graph for a given motif, we want to make sure that we eliminate the duplicate entries. We can do this as follows:

```
recommendation = one_hub_connection
    .select("a", "b")
    .distinct()
```

Facebook Circles

In this section we will use motif finding to analyze Facebook relationships.

Input

For input, we'll use data from the Stanford Network Analysis Project (SNAP) (*https://oreil.ly/j9ZJA*) consisting of "circles" (or "friends lists") from Facebook. The data was collected from survey participants using a Facebook app and has been anonymized. The dataset includes node features (profiles), circles, and ego networks.

Let's take at a look at the downloaded data:

```
$ wc -l  stanford_fb_edges.csv  stanford_fb_vertices.csv
   88,235  stanford_fb_edges.csv
    4,039  stanford_fb_vertices.csv
```

This tells us that we have 4,039 vertices and 88,235 edges. Next, we'll examine the first few lines of each file. As you can see, these files have headers that we can use as column names when we create our DataFrames (I've renamed the columns to follow the GraphFrames guidelines):

```
$ head -5 stanford_fb_edges.csv
src,dst
0,1
0,2
0,3
0,4

$ head -5 stanford_fb_vertices.csv
id,birthday,hometown_id,work_employer_id,education_school_id,education_year_id
1098,None,None,None,None,None
1142,None,None,None,None,None
1304,None,None,None,None,None
1593,None,None,None,None,None
```

Building the graph

Since we have vertices and edges as CSV files with headers, our first step is to build DataFrames for these. We'll start with the vertices DataFrame:

```
>>> vertices_path = 'file:///tmp/stanford_fb_vertices.csv'
>>> vertices = spark ❶
        .read ❷
```

```
            .format("csv") ❸
            .option("header", "true") ❹
            .option("inferSchema", "true") ❺
            .load(vertices_path) ❻

>>> vertices.count()
4039

>>> vertices.printSchema()
root
 |-- id: integer (nullable = true)
 |-- birthday: string (nullable = true)
 |-- hometown_id: string (nullable = true)
 |-- work_employer_id: string (nullable = true)
 |-- education_school_id: string (nullable = true)
 |-- education_year_id: string (nullable = true)

>>> vertices.show(3, truncate=False)
+----+--------+--------+-----------+----------+---------+
|id  |birthday|hometown|work_      |education_|education|
|    |        |_id     |employer_id|school_id |_year_id |
+----+--------+--------+-----------+----------+---------+
|1098|None    |None    |None       |None      |None     |
|1142|None    |None    |None       |None      |None     |
|1917|None    |None    |None       |None      |72       |
+----+--------+--------+-----------+----------+---------+
```

❶ `spark` is an instance of `SparkSession`.

❷ Return a `DataFrameReader` to read the input file.

❸ Specify the type of file to be read.

❹ Indicate that the input CSV file has a header.

❺ Infer the DataFrame schema from the input file; this option requires one extra pass over the data and is `false` by default.

❻ Provide the path for the CSV file.

Then build and inspect our `edges` DataFrame:

```
>>> edges_path = 'file:///tmp/stanford_fb_edges.csv'
>>> edges = spark ❶
            .read ❷
            .format("csv") ❸
            .option("header","true") ❹
            .option("inferSchema", "true") ❺
            .load(edges_path) ❻
```

```
>>> edges.count()
88234

>>> edges.printSchema()
root
 |-- src: integer (nullable = true)
 |-- dst: integer (nullable = true)

>>> edges.show(4, truncate=False)
+---+---+
|src|dst|
+---+-- +
|0  |1  |
|0  |2  |
|0  |3  |
|0  |4  |
+---+---+
```

❶ spark is an instance of SparkSession.

❷ Return a DataFrameReader to read the input file.

❸ Specify the type of file to be read.

❹ Indicate that the input CSV file has a header.

❺ Infer the DataFrame schema from the input file.

❻ Provide the path for the CSV file.

Once we have our two DataFrames, we can create the GraphFrame object:

```
>>> from graphframes import GraphFrame
>>> graph = GraphFrame(vertices, edges)
>>> graph
GraphFrame(v:[id: int, birthday: string ... 4 more fields],
e:[src: int, dst: int])
>>> graph.triplets.show(3, truncate=False)
+----------------------------------+-------+----------------------------------+
|src                               |edge   |dst                               |
+----------------------------------+-------+----------------------------------+
|[0, None, None, None, None, None]|[0, 1] |[1, None, None, None, None, None] |
|[0, None, None, None, None, None]|[0, 2] |[2, None, None, None, None, None] |
|[0, None, None, None, None, None]|[0, 3] |[3, 7, None, None, None, None]    |
+----------------------------------+-------+----------------------------------+
```

Motif finding

Now that we've built our graph, we can do some analysis. First, we'll find all connected vertices with the same birthday:

```
same_birthday = graph.find("(a)-[]->(b)")
                     .filter("a.birthday = b.birthday")
print "count: %d" % same_birthday.count()
selected = same_birthday.select("a.id", "b.id", "b.birthday")
```

Next, we'll count the number of triangles passing through each vertex in this graph:

```
>>> triangle_counts = graph.triangleCount()
>>> triangle_counts.show(5, truncate=False)
+-----+---+--------+-----------+----------------+----------+---------+
|count|id |birthday|hometown_id|work_employer_id|education |education|
|     |   |        |           |                |_school_id|_year_id |
+-----+---+--------+-----------+----------------+----------+---------+
|80   |148|None    |None       |None            |None      |None     |
|361  |463|None    |None       |None            |None      |None     |
|312  |471|None    |None       |None            |52        |None     |
|399  |496|None    |None       |None            |52        |None     |
|38   |833|None    |None       |None            |None      |None     |
+-----+---+--------+-----------+----------------+----------+---------+
```

The following graph query finds "friends of friends" who are not connected to each other, but who graduated the same year from the same school:

```
>>> from pyspark.sql.functions import col

>>> friends_of_friends = graph.find("(a)-[]->(b);
                                     (b)-[]->(c);
                                     !(a)-[]->(c)") \
       .filter("a.education_school_id = c.education_school_id")
       .filter("a.education_year_id = c.education_year_id")

>>> filtered = friends_of_friends
       .filter("a.id != c.id") \
       .select(col("a.id").alias("source"), "a.education_school_id", \
           "a.education_year_id", col("c.id").alias("target"), \
           "c.education_school_id", "c.education_year_id")

>>> filtered.show(5)
+------+----------+---------+------+----------+---------+
|source|education |education|target|education |education|
|source|_school_id|_year_id |      |_school_id|_year_id |
+------+----------+---------+------+----------+---------+
|     3|      None|     None|   246|      None|     None|
|     3|      None|     None|    79|      None|     None|
|     3|      None|     None|   290|      None|     None|
|     5|      None|     None|   302|      None|     None|
|     9|      None|     None|   265|      None|     None|
+------+----------+---------+------+----------+---------+
```

Finally, we run the PageRank algorithm on our graph:

```
>>> page_rank =
     graph.pageRank(resetProbability=0.15, tol=0.01)
          .vertices
          .sort('pagerank', ascending=False)

>>> page_rank.select("id", "pagerank")
             .show(5, truncate=False)
+----+------------------+
|id  |pagerank          |
+----+------------------+
|1911|37.59716511250488 |
|3434|37.555460465662755|
|2655|36.34549422981058 |
|1902|35.816887526732344|
|1888|27.459048061380063|
+----+------------------+
```

Connected Components

Given millions of DNA samples and data on the genomic relationships between each pair of samples, how do you find connected families? Given social networks (such as Facebook or Twitter), how do you identify connected communities? To solve these kinds of problems, you can use the connected components algorithm.

The goal of this algorithm is to identify independent, disconnected subgraphs. Before I present the algorithm itself, let's define the concept of connected components. Let `G` be a graph defined as a set of vertices `V` and a set of edges `E`, where each edge is a pair of vertices:

```
G = (V, E)
```

A path from `x` in `V` to `y` in `V` can then be described by a sequence of vertices:

$$x = u_0, u_1, u_2, ..., u_n = y$$

where we have an edge from u_i to $u_{\{i+1\}}$ for each `0 <= i <= n-1`. Note that vertices can repeat, allowing the path to cross or fold onto itself. Now, we can define a connected component. We say that a graph `G` is connected if there is a path between every pair of vertices. So, we can say that a connected component of a graph is a sub-graph in which any two vertices are connected to each other by paths, and which is connected to no additional vertices in the supergraph. The smallest connected component can be a single vertex, which does not connect to any other vertex. For example, the graph in Figure 6-11 has three connected components.

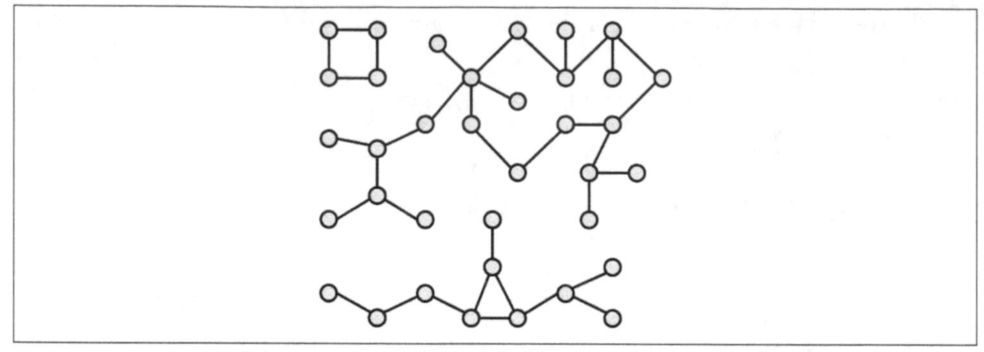

Figure 6-11. Connected components example

Finding and identifying connected components is at the heart of many graph applications. For example, consider the problem of identifying family clusters in a set of DNA samples. We can represent each DNA sample by a vertex and add an edge between each pair of samples that are deemed "connected" (parent–offspring, sibling, second-degree relative, third-degree relative, etc.). The connected components of this graph correspond to different family groups.

Given a graph, how do we identify its connected components? The algorithm involves a breadth-first or depth-first search that begins at some vertex `v` and traverses outward node by node until it finds the entire connected component containing `v`. To find all the connected components of a graph, we loop through its vertices, starting a new search whenever the loop reaches a vertex not already included in a previously found connected component.

Connected components in Spark

The connected components algorithm labels each connected component of the graph with the ID of its lowest-numbered vertex. To use this algorithm, we first build a graph as an instance of `GraphFrame` as usual, then call the `connectedComponents()` method to compute the connected components of the graph. This method has the following signature:

```
connectedComponents(
    algorithm='graphframes',
    checkpointInterval=2,
    broadcastThreshold=1000000
)

Parameters:
   algorithm - connected components algorithm
      to use  (default: "graphframes"); supported
      algorithms are "graphframes" and "graphx".

   checkpointInterval - checkpoint interval in
```

```
        terms of number of iterations (default: 2)

      broadcastThreshold - broadcast threshold
        in propagating component assignments
        (default: 1000000)

   Returns:
      DataFrame with new vertices column "component"
```

Its use looks something like the following:

```
vertices = <DataFrame-representing-vertices>
edges = <DataFrame-representing-edges>

graph = GraphFrame(vertices, edges)
connected_components = graph.connectedComponents()
connected_components.explain(extended=True)

connected_components
        .groupBy('component')
        .count()
        .orderBy('count', ascending=False)
        .show()

connected_components.select("id", "component")
                    .orderBy("component")
                    .show()
```

Analyzing Flight Data

The purpose of this section is to show how to build and execute graph queries. The example provided here is inspired by the blog post "Analyzing Flight Delays with Apache Spark GraphFrames and MapR Database" (*https://oreil.ly/nI3CD*) by Carol McDonald, which provides a solution for flight data analysis in Scala using GraphFrames. The presented solution is an equivalent solution in PySpark.

Input

The data for vertices (airports) and edges (flights) is provided in JSON format. We will read these datafiles and create two DataFrames for vertices and edges. Then we'll use these to create a graph represented as an instance of GraphFrame.

Vertices. The data for vertices is provided in the file *airports.json* (*https://oreil.ly/WrNCf*). Let's review the first two records of this file:

```
{"id":"ORD","City":"Chicago","State":"IL","Country":"USA"}
{"id":"LGA","City":"New York","State":"NY","Country":"USA"}
```

Edges. The data for edges (flight data) is provided as a JSON file *flightdata2018.json* (*https://oreil.ly/VTJlj*). The first record looks like this:

```
{
"id":"ATL_BOS_2018-01-01_DL_104",
"fldate":"2018-01-01",
"month":1,
"dofW":1,
"carrier":"DL",
"src":"ATL",
"dst":"BOS",
"crsdephour":9,
"crsdeptime":850,
"depdelay":0.0,
"crsarrtime":1116,
"arrdelay":0.0,
"crselapsedtime":146.0,
"dist":946.0
}
```

Building the graph

To build a graph as an instance of `GraphFrame`, we have to create two DataFrames. We'll start by building the vertex DataFrame, from the file *airports.json*:

```
>>> airports_path = '/book/code/chap06/airports.json'
>>> vertices = spark.read.json(airports_path)
>>> vertices.show(3)
+------------+-------+-----+---+
|        City|Country|State| id|
+------------+-------+-----+---+
|     Chicago|    USA|   IL|ORD|
|    New York|    USA|   NY|LGA|
|      Boston|    USA|   MA|BOS|
+------------+-------+-----+---+

>>> vertices.count()
13
```

Then we'll build the edge DataFrame from *flightdata2018.json*:

```
>>> flights_path = '/book/code/chap06/flightdata2018.json'
>>> edges = spark.read.json(flights_path)
>>> edges.select("src", "dst", "dist", "depdelay")
     .show(3)
+---+---+-----+--------+
|src|dst| dist|depdelay|
+---+---+-----+--------+
|ATL|BOS|946.0|     0.0|
|ATL|BOS|946.0|     8.0|
|ATL|BOS|946.0|     9.0|
+---+---+-----+--------+
```

```
>>> edges.count()
282628
```

We can now build our graph using these two DataFrames:

```
>>> from graphframes import GraphFrame
>>> graph = GraphFrame(vertices, edges)
>>> graph
GraphFrame(
v:[id: string, City: string ... 2 more fields],
e:[src: string, dst: string ... 12 more fields]
)
>>> graph.vertices.count()
13
>>> graph.edges.count()
282628
```

Flight analysis

Now that we have created a graph, we can execute queries on it. For example, now we can query the `GraphFrame` to answer the following questions:

- How many airports are there?

  ```
  >>> num_of_airports = graph.vertices.count()
  >>> num_of_airports
  13
  ```

- How many flights are there?

  ```
  >>> num_of_flights = graph.edges.count()
  >>> num_of_flights
  282628
  ```

- Which flight routes have the longest distance?

  ```
  >>> from pyspark.sql.functions import col
  >>> graph.edges
       .groupBy("src", "dst")
       .max("dist")
       .sort(col("max(dist)").desc())
       .show(4)
  +---+---+---------+
  |src|dst|max(dist)|
  +---+---+---------+
  |MIA|SEA|   2724.0|
  |SEA|MIA|   2724.0|
  |BOS|SFO|   2704.0|
  |SFO|BOS|   2704.0|
  +---+---+---------+
  ```

- Which flight routes have the highest average delays?

```
>>> graph.edges
     .groupBy("src", "dst")
     .avg("depdelay")
     .sort(col("avg(depdelay)").desc())
     .show(5)
+---+---+-----------------+
|src|dst|    avg(depdelay)|
+---+---+-----------------+
|ATL|EWR|25.520159946684437|
|DEN|EWR|25.232164449818622|
|MIA|SFO|24.785953177257525|
|MIA|EWR|22.464104423495286|
|IAH|EWR| 22.38344914718888|
+---+---+-----------------+
```

- Which flight departure hours have the highest average delays?

```
>>> graph.edges
      .groupBy("crsdephour")
      .avg("depdelay")
      .sort(col("avg(depdelay)").desc())
      .show(5)
+----------+-----------------+
|crsdephour|    avg(depdelay)|
+----------+-----------------+
|        19|22.915831356645498|
|        20|22.187089292616932|
|        18|22.183962000558815|
|        17|20.553385253108907|
|        21| 19.89884280327656|
+----------+-----------------+
```

- What are the longest delays for flights that are greater than 1,500 miles in distance? Note that the output here has been trimmed to fit the page.

```
>>> graph.edges
      .filter("dist > 1500")
      .orderBy(col("depdelay").desc())
      .show(3)
+-------+--------+------+----+---+----------+---------+-----+---+
|carrier|depdelay|  dist|dofW|dst|    fldate|       id|month|src|
+-------+--------+------+----+---+----------+---------+-----+---+
|     AA|  1345.0|1562.0|   4|DFW|2018-06-28|BOS_DFW...|    6|BOS|
|     AA|  1283.0|2342.0|   1|MIA|2018-07-09|LAX_MIA...|    7|LAX|
|     AA|  1242.0|2611.0|   3|LAX|2018-03-28|BOS_LAX...|    3|BOS|
+-------+--------+------+----+---+----------+---------+-----+---+
```

- What is the average delay for delayed flights departing from Atlanta (ATL)?

```
>>> graph.edges
     .filter("src = 'ATL' and depdelay > 1")
     .groupBy("src", "dst")
     .avg("depdelay")
     .sort(col("avg(depdelay)").desc())
     .show(3)
+---+---+-----------------+
|src|dst|    avg(depdelay)|
+---+---+-----------------+
|ATL|EWR|  58.1085801063022|
|ATL|ORD| 46.42393736017897|
|ATL|DFW|39.454460966542754|
+---+---+-----------------+
```

Viewing the Execution Plan

To view Spark's logical and physical plans for DataFrame execution, you can use `DataFrame.explain()`:

```
explain(extended=False)

Description:
     Prints the (logical and physical) plans
     to the console for debugging purpose.

     For extended plan view, set extended=True
```

For example, for the previous query, you could view the execution plan as follows:

```
graph.edges
     .filter("src = 'ATL' and depdelay > 1")
     .groupBy("src", "dst")
     .avg("depdelay")
     .sort(col("avg(depdelay)").desc())
     .explain()
```

Note that you should always filter your RDD/DataFrame before applying an expensive transformation. This will drop nonrequired elements/rows from the RDD/DataFrame and hence improve the performance for future transformations, by reducing the amount of data passed between transformations.

- What are the worst departure hours for delayed flights departing from Atlanta?

```
>>> graph.edges
     .filter("src = 'ATL' and depdelay > 1")
     .groupBy("crsdephour")
     .avg("depdelay")
     .sort(col("avg(depdelay)").desc())
```

```
    .show(4)
+----------+-----------------+
|crsdephour|     avg(depdelay)|
+----------+-----------------+
|        23|52.833333333333336|
|        18| 51.57142857142857|
|        19| 48.93338815789474|
|        17|48.383354350567465|
+----------+-----------------+
```

- What are the four most frequent flight routes in the dataset?

```
>>> flight_route_count = graph.edges
     .groupBy("src", "dst")
     .count()
     .orderBy(col("count").desc())
     .show(4)
+---+---+-----+
|src|dst|count|
+---+---+-----+
|LGA|ORD| 4442|
|ORD|LGA| 4426|
|LAX|SFO| 4406|
|SFO|LAX| 4354|
+---+---+-----+
```

To find this information, we get the count of flights for all possible flight routes and sort them in descending order. We'll use the resulting DataFrame later, to find flight routes with no direct connection.

- Which airports have the most incoming and outgoing flights?

```
>>> graph.degrees
     .orderBy(col("degree").desc())
     .show(3)
+---+------+
| id|degree|
+---+------+
|ORD| 64386|
|ATL| 60382|
|LAX| 53733|
+---+------+
```

To answer this question we use the GraphFrames `degrees` operation, which returns the count of all edges (incoming and outgoing) of each vertex in the graph.

- What are the most important airports, according to the PageRank algorithm?

```
# Run PageRank until convergence to tolerance "tol"
>>> ranks = graph.pageRank(resetProbability=0.15, tol=0.01)
>>> ranks
GraphFrame(
v:[id: string, City: string ... 3 more fields],
e:[src: string, dst: string ... 13 more fields]
)
>>> ranks.vertices.orderBy(col("pagerank").desc()).show(3)
+------------+-------+-----+---+------------------+
|        City|Country|State| id|          pagerank|
+------------+-------+-----+---+------------------+
|     Chicago|    USA|   IL|ORD|1.4151923966632058|
|     Atlanta|    USA|   GA|ATL|1.3342533126163776|
| Los Angeles|    USA|   CA|LAX| 1.197905124144182|
+------------+-------+-----+---+------------------+
```

The PageRank algorithm provided by the GraphFrames API is based on Google's PageRank. It's an iterative algorithm that measures the importance of each vertex in a graph by determining which vertices have the most connections to other vertices (i.e., the most edges). This output indicates that the city of Chicago's airport is the most important (since it has the highest PageRank score) of all the airports examined.

You can also run the PageRank algorithm for a fixed number of iterations, rather than using the tolerance level for convergence, as shown here:

```
# Run PageRank for a fixed number of iterations
results = graph.pageRank(resetProbability=0.15, maxIter=10)
```

For more details on using the PageRank algorithm, refer to Chapter 8.

Next we'll consider a slightly more complicated query: what are the flight routes with no direct connection? To answer this question, we will use the GraphFrames API's motif finding algorithm. First we'll create a subgraph from the `flight_route_count` DataFrame that we created earlier, which gives us a subgraph with all the possible flight routes. Then we'll do a `find()` to search for flights from `a` to `b` and `b` to `c` where there is no flight from `a` to `c`. Finally we'll use a DataFrame filter to remove duplicates. This example shows how graph queries can be easily combined with DataFrame operations like `filter()`.

Using our flight_route_count DataFrame, we can use the following pattern to search for flights from a to b and b to c where there is no direct flight from a to c:

```
>>> sub_graph = GraphFrame(graph.vertices, flight_route_count)
>>> sub_graph
GraphFrame(
v:[id: string, City: string ... 2 more fields],
e:[src: string, dst: string ... 1 more field]
)
>>> results = sub_graph.find(
                        "(a)-[]->(b);
                        (b)-[]->(c);
                        !(a)-[]->(c)"
                     )
                  .filter("c.id != a.id")
```

This produces the following results:

```
>>> results.show(5)
+--------------------+--------------------+--------------------+
|                   a|                   b|                   c|
+--------------------+--------------------+--------------------+
|[New York, USA, N...|[Denver, USA, CO,...|[San Francisco, U...|
|[Los Angeles, USA...|[Miami, USA, FL, ...|[New York, USA, N...|
|[New York, USA, N...|[Denver, USA, CO,...|[Newark, USA, NJ,...|
|[New York, USA, N...|[Miami, USA, FL, ...|[Newark, USA, NJ,...|
|[Newark, USA, NJ,...|[Atlanta, USA, GA...|[New York, USA, N...|
+--------------------+--------------------+--------------------+
```

Suppose we want to find which cities do not offer direct flights to one particular airport. To answer this question, we can use the shortest path algorithm to compute the shortest paths from each vertex (airport) to one or more "landmark" vertices (airports). Here we search for the shortest path from each airport to LGA. The results (distances greater than 1) show that there are no direct flights from IAH, CLT, LAX, DEN, or DFW to LGA:

```
>>> results = graph.shortestPaths(landmarks=["LGA"])
>>> results.show(5)
+-------------+-------+-----+---+----------+
|         City|Country|State| id| distances|
+-------------+-------+-----+---+----------+
|      Houston|    USA|   TX|IAH|[LGA -> 1]|
|    Charlotte|    USA|   NC|CLT|[LGA -> 1]|
|  Los Angeles|    USA|   CA|LAX|[LGA -> 2]|
|       Denver|    USA|   CO|DEN|[LGA -> 1]|
|       Dallas|    USA|   TX|DFW|[LGA -> 1]|
+-------------+-------+-----+---+----------+
```

Now suppose we want to find out if there are any direct flights between two specific airports. The breadth-first search (BFS) algorithm finds the shortest path from a beginning vertex to an end vertex. The beginning and end vertices are specified as DataFrame expressions, and maxPathLength sets a limit on the length of the paths between them. Here, we see that there are no direct flights between LAX and LGA, although there are connecting flights (note that the output has been truncated to fit the page):

```
# bfs() signature:
# bfs(fromExpr, toExpr, edgeFilter=None, maxPathLength=10)
# Returns a DataFrame with one row for each shortest
# path between matching vertices.
>>> paths = graph.bfs("id = 'LAX'", "id = 'LGA'", maxPathLength=1)
>>> paths.show()
+----+-------+-----+---+
|City|Country|State| id|
+----+-------+-----+---+
+----+-------+-----+---+

>>> paths = graph.bfs("id = 'LAX'", "id = 'LGA'", maxPathLength=2)
>>> paths.show(4)
+--------+----------------+-------+----------------+---------+
|    from|              e0|     v1|              e1|       to|
+--------+----------------+-------+----------------+---------+
|[Los Ang|[0.0, UA, 1333, 8|[Houston|[0.0, UA, 1655, 1|[New York|
|[Los Ang|[0.0, UA, 1333, 8|[Houston|[22.0, UA, 2233, |[New York|
|[Los Ang|[0.0, UA, 1333, 8|[Houston|[6.0, UA, 1912, 1|[New York|
|[Los Ang|[0.0, UA, 1333, 8|[Houston|[0.0, UA, 2321, 1|[New York|
+--------+----------------+-------+----------------+---------+
```

We can also use motif finding to identify connecting flights between two airports. Here, we'll use a motif query to search for the pattern of `a` to `c` through `b`, then apply a DataFrame filter on the results for `a = LAX` and `c = LGA`. The results show some flights from LAX to LGA connecting through IAH:

```
>>> graph.find("(a)-[ab]->(b);
                (b)-[bc]->(c)"
              ).filter("a.id = 'LAX'")
               .filter("c.id = 'LGA'")
               .limit(4)
               .select("a", "b", "c")
               .show()
+-------------------+------------------+-------------------+
|                  a|                 b|                  c|
+-------------------+------------------+-------------------+
|[Los Angeles, USA...|[Houston, USA, TX...|[New York, USA, N...|
|[Los Angeles, USA...|[Houston, USA, TX...|[New York, USA, N...|
|[Los Angeles, USA...|[Houston, USA, TX...|[New York, USA, N...|
|[Los Angeles, USA...|[Houston, USA, TX...|[New York, USA, N...|
+-------------------+------------------+-------------------+
```

By combining motif finding with DataFrame operations we could narrow these results down even further, for example to exclude flights with an arrival time before the initial departure flight time, and/or to identify flights with a specific carrier.

Summary

To recap:

- Spark provides two graph libraries, GraphX (based on RDDs) and GraphFrames (based on DataFrames). GraphX is Spark's internal API for graphs and graph-parallel computation and is available only for Java and Scala. GraphFrames is an external package for Spark that provides high-level APIs in Python, Scala, and Java. It is available in PySpark, whereas GraphX is not.
- GraphFrames provide:
  - Python, Java, and Scala APIs
  - Expressive graph queries by using "motif finding"
  - Query plan optimizers from Spark SQL
  - Graph algorithms

Next, we'll cover how Spark interacts with outside data sources.

CHAPTER 7

Interacting with External Data Sources

In Spark, in order to run any algorithm you need to read input data from a data source, then apply your algorithm in the form of a set of PySpark transformations and actions (expressed as a DAG), and finally write your desired output to a target data source. So, to write algorithms that perform well, it's important to understand reading and writing from and to external data sources.

In the previous chapters, we have explored interacting with the built-in data sources (RDDs and DataFrames) in Spark. In this chapter, we will focus on how Spark interfaces with external data sources.

> **Source Code**
>
> Complete programs for this chapter are available in the book's GitHub repository (*https://oreil.ly/xyh68*).

As Figure 7-1 shows, Spark can read data from a huge range of external storage systems like the Linux filesystem, Amazon S3, HDFS, Hive tables, and relational databases (such as Oracle, MySQL, or PostgreSQL) through its data source interface. This chapter will show you how to read data in and then convert it into RDDs or DataFrames for further processing. I'll also show you how Spark's data can be written back to external storage systems like files, Amazon S3, and JDBC-compliant databases.

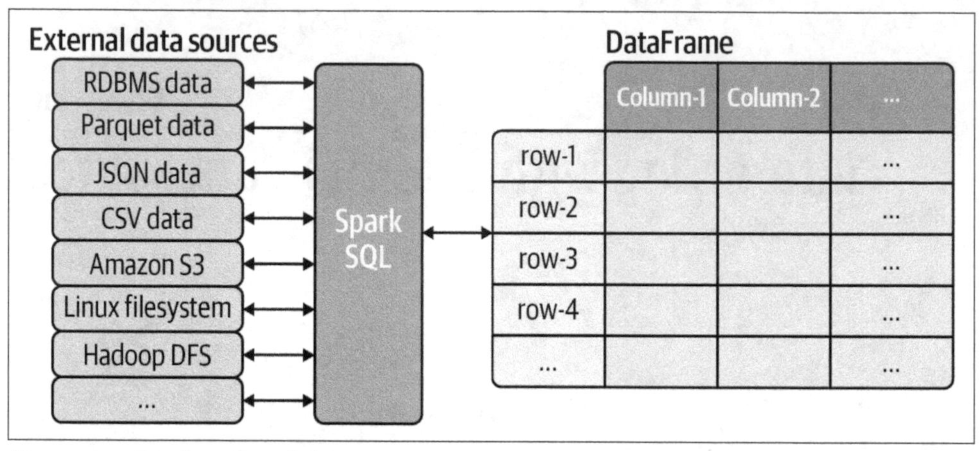

Figure 7-1. Spark external data sources

Relational Databases

Let's start with relational databases. A relational database is a collection of data items organized as a set of formally described tables (created using the SQL `CREATE TABLE` statement) from which data can be accessed or reassembled in many different ways without the tables themselves needing to be reorganized. Open source relational databases (such as MySQL and PostgreSQL) are currently the predominant choice for storing data like social media network records, financial records, medical records, personal information, and manufacturing data. There are also many well-known and widely used licensed proprietary relational databases, such as MS SQL Server and Oracle.

Informally, a relational database table has a set of rows and named columns, as shown in Figure 7-2. Each row in a table can have its own unique key (called a primary key). Rows in a table can be linked to rows in other tables by adding a column for the unique key of the linked row (such columns are known as foreign keys).

	id: INTEGER	Name: STRING	Age: INTEGER	Salary: DOUBLE
row-1	99000100	alex	28	54500.50
row-2	99000200	jane	42	68500.80
row-3	99000300	joe	48	44900.20
row-4	99000400	rafael	31	126000.00
...	...	...	...	...

Figure 7-2. A relational database table example

PySpark provides two classes for reading data from and writing data to relational databases, as well as to other external data sources. These two classes are defined as:

`class pyspark.sql.DataFrameReader(spark)`
: This is the interface used to read data into a DataFrame from an external storage system (filesystem, key/value store, etc.). Use `spark.read()` to access this.

`class pyspark.sql.DataFrameWriter(df)`
: This is the interface used to write a DataFrame to an external storage system. Use `DataFrame.write()` to access this.

Reading from a Database

PySpark enables us to read in data from a relational database table and create a new DataFrame from it. You can read a table from any JDBC-compliant database, using the `pyspark.sql.DataFrameReader.load()` Python method. The `load()` method is defined as:

```
load(path=None, format=None, schema=None, **options)
t :class`DataFrame`.

Parameters:
     path - optional string or a list of string
            for file-system backed data sources.
   format - optional string for format of the data
            source. Default to 'parquet'.
   schema - optional pyspark.sql.types.StructType for
            the input schema or a DDL-formatted string
            (for example `col-1 INT, col-2 DOUBLE`).
  options - all other string options
```

In order to read in data from a JDBC-compliant database table, you need to specify `format("jdbc")`. You can then pass in table attributes and connection parameters (such as the JDBC URL and your database credentials) as `options(<key>, <value>)` pairs.

To read data from and write it to a JDBC-compliant relational database, you will need access to the database server and sufficient privileges.

Step 1. Create a database table

In this step, we'll connect to a MySQL database server and create a table called `dept` with seven rows. We execute the `mysql` client program to enter into the MySQL client shell (if you have installed a MySQL database on your MacBook, for example, the MySQL client will be available at */usr/local/bin/mysql*):

```
$ mysql -uroot -p ❶
Enter password: <your-root-password> ❷
Welcome to the MySQL monitor.  Commands end with ; or \g.
Server version: 5.7.18 MySQL Community Server (GPL)

mysql> show databases; ❸
+--------------------+
| Database           | ❹
+--------------------+
| information_schema |
| mysql              | ❺
| performance_schema |
+--------------------+
3 rows in set (0.00 sec)
```

❶ Invoke the MySQL shell client.

❷ Enter a valid password for the `root` user.

❸ List the databases available in the MySQL database server.

❹ These three databases are created by the MySQL database server.

❺ The `mysql` database manages users, groups, and privileges.

Next, we'll create and select a database:

```
mysql> create database metadb; ❶
mysql> use metadb; ❷
Database changed
mysql>
mysql> show tables; ❸
Empty set (0.00 sec)
```

❶ Create a new database called `metadb`.

❷ Make `metadb` your current default database.

❸ Show the tables in the metadb database (since it is a new database, there will be no tables in it).

Then we'll create a new table called dept inside the metadb database:

```
mysql> create table dept ( ❶
    ->   dept_number int,
    ->   dept_name  varchar(128),
    ->   dept_location varchar(128),
    ->   manager varchar(128)
    -> );

mysql> show tables; ❷
+-----------------+
| Tables_in_metadb |
+-----------------+
| dept            |
+-----------------+

mysql> desc dept; ❸
+---------------+--------------+------+-----+---------+-------+
| Field         | Type         | Null | Key | Default | Extra |
+---------------+--------------+------+-----+---------+-------+
| dept_number   | int(11)      | YES  |     | NULL    |       |
| dept_name     | varchar(128) | YES  |     | NULL    |       |
| dept_location | varchar(128) | YES  |     | NULL    |       |
| manager       | varchar(128) | YES  |     | NULL    |       |
+---------------+--------------+------+-----+---------+-------+
```

❶ This is the table definition for dept, which has four columns.

❷ List the tables in the metadb database.

❸ Describe the schema for dept table.

Finally, we insert the following seven rows into the dept table, using the INSERT statement:

```
mysql> INSERT INTO dept
  -> (dept_number,  dept_name,  dept_location, manager)
  -> VALUES
  ->  (10, 'ACCOUNTING', 'NEW YORK, NY', 'alex'),
  ->  (20, 'RESEARCH',   'DALLAS, TX', 'alex'),
  ->  (30, 'SALES',      'CHICAGO, IL', 'jane'),
  ->  (40, 'OPERATIONS', 'BOSTON, MA', 'jane'),
  ->  (50, 'MARKETING', 'Sunnyvale, CA', 'jane'),
  ->  (60, 'SOFTWARE', 'Stanford, CA', 'jane'),
  ->  (70, 'HARDWARE', 'BOSTON, MA', 'sophia');
```

We can examine the contents of the dept table to make sure that it has these seven rows:

```
mysql> select * from dept;
+-------------+------------+---------------+---------+
| dept_number | dept_name  | dept_location | manager |
+-------------+------------+---------------+---------+
|          10 | ACCOUNTING | NEW YORK, NY  | alex    |
|          20 | RESEARCH   | DALLAS, TX    | alex    |
|          30 | SALES      | CHICAGO, IL   | jane    |
|          40 | OPERATIONS | BOSTON, MA    | jane    |
|          50 | MARKETING  | Sunnyvale, CA | jane    |
|          60 | SOFTWARE   | Stanford, CA  | jane    |
|          70 | HARDWARE   | BOSTON, MA    | sophia  |
+-------------+------------+---------------+---------+
7 rows in set (0.00 sec)
```

At this point, we are sure that there is a `metadb` database on the database server, which has a `dept` table with seven records.

Step 2: Read the database table into a DataFrame

Once you have a JDBC-compliant table (such as `dept`), then you can use the `pyspark.sql.DataFrameReader` class's methods (a combination of `option()` and `load()`) to read the contents of the table and create a new DataFrame. To perform this read, you need a JAR file, which is a MySQL JDBC driver (you may download this JAR file from the MySQL website (*https://dev.mysql.com/downloads*)). You can put the JAR file containing the MySQL driver class wherever you like; I'll place it in:

```
.../code/jars/mysql-connector-java-5.1.42.jar
```

MySQL offers standard database driver connectivity (see Connector/J (*https://oreil.ly/WwK6k*) for details) for using MySQL with applications and tools that are compatible with industry standards ODBC and JDBC. Any system that works with ODBC or JDBC can use MySQL.

Next, we enter the PySpark shell by passing the JAR file to the `$SPARK_HOME/bin/pyspark` program:

```
export JAR=/book/code/jars/mysql-connector-java-5.1.42.jar ❶
$SPARK_HOME/bin/pyspark --jars $JAR ❷

SparkSession available as ``'spark'``.
>>> spark  ❸
<pyspark.sql.session.SparkSession object at 0x10a5f2a50>
>>>
```

❶ This is the driver class JAR for MySQL.

❷ Start the PySpark shell, loading the MySQL driver class JAR.

❸ Make sure the SparkSession is available.

Now we can use the SparkSession to read a relational table and create a new DataFrame:

```
dataframe_mysql = spark \ ❶
   .read \ ❷
   .format("jdbc") \ ❸
   .option("url", "jdbc:mysql://localhost/metadb") \ ❹
   .option("driver", "com.mysql.jdbc.Driver") \ ❺
   .option("dbtable", "dept") \ ❻
   .option("user", "root") \ ❼
   .option("password", "mp22_pass") \ ❽
   .load() ❾
```

❶ spark is an instance of SparkSession

❷ Returns a DataFrameReader that can be used to read data in as a DataFrame

❸ Indicates that you are reading JDBC-compliant data

❹ The database URL

❺ The JDBC driver (loaded from the JAR file)

❻ The database table name

❼ The database username

❽ The database password

❾ Loads data from a JDBC data source and returns it as a DataFrame

Let's take a look at the newly created DataFrame:

```
>>> dataframe_mysql.count() ❶
7
>>> dataframe_mysql.show() ❷
+-----------+----------+------------+-------+
|dept_number| dept_name|dept_location|manager|
+-----------+----------+------------+-------+
|         10|ACCOUNTING| NEW YORK, NY|   alex|
|         20|  RESEARCH|   DALLAS, TX|   alex|
|         30|     SALES|  CHICAGO, IL|   jane|
|         40|OPERATIONS|   BOSTON, MA|   jane|
|         50| MARKETING|Sunnyvale, CA|   jane|
|         60|  SOFTWARE| Stanford, CA|   jane|
|         70|  HARDWARE|   BOSTON, MA| sophia|
+-----------+----------+------------+-------+
```

❶ Count the number of rows in the DataFrame.

❷ Print the first 20 rows to the console.

We can also examine its schema:

```
>>> dataframe_mysql.printSchema ❶
<bound method DataFrame.printSchema of
DataFrame[
            dept_number: int,
            dept_name: string,
            dept_location: string,
            manager: string
           ]
```

❶ Print out the schema in tree format.

Step 3: Query the DataFrame

PySpark offers many ways to access a DataFrame. In addition to various SQL-like methods (such as `select(<columns>)`, `groupBy(<columns>)`, `min()`, `max()`, etc.), it allows you to execute fully fledged SQL queries on your DataFrame by first registering it as a "table" and then issuing queries against that registered table. We will discuss DataFrame table registration shortly. First, we will execute some SQL-like queries using DataFrame methods.

Here, we select all rows for two columns, `dept_number` and `manager`:

```
>>> dataframe_mysql.select("dept_number", "manager") ❶
               .show() ❷
+-----------+-------+
|dept_number|manager|
+-----------+-------+
|         10|   alex|
|         20|   alex|
|         30|   jane|
|         40|   jane|
|         50|   jane|
|         60|   jane|
|         70| sophia|
+-----------+-------+
```

❶ Select the `dept_number` and `manager` columns from the DataFrame.

❷ Display the selection result.

Next, we group all rows by `manager` and then find the minimum `dept_number`:

```
>>> dataframe_mysql.select("dept_number", "manager")
                   .groupBy("manager")
                   .min("dept_number")
```

```
                     .collect()
[
 Row(manager=u'jane', min(dept_number)=30),
 Row(manager=u'sophia', min(dept_number)=70),
 Row(manager=u'alex', min(dept_number)=10)
]
```

Here we group all rows by `manager` and then find the frequencies of the grouped data:

```
>>> dataframe_mysql.select("dept_number", "manager")
                   .groupBy("manager")
                   .count()
                   .show()
+--------+-------+
|manager | count |
+--------+-------+
| jane   |  4    |
| sophia |  1    |
| alex   |  2    |
+--------+-------+
```

And here we do the same but additionally order the output by the `manager` column:

```
>>> dataframe_mysql.select("dept_number", "manager")
                   .groupBy("manager")
                   .count()
                   .orderBy("manager")
                   .show()
+--------+-------+
|manager | count |
+--------+-------+
| alex   |  2    |
| jane   |  4    |
| sophia |  1    |
+--------+-------+
```

To execute fully fledged SQL queries against a DataFrame, first you have to register your DataFrame as a table:

```
DataFrame.registerTempTable(<your-desired-table-name>)
```

You can then execute regular SQL queries on it, as if it were a relational database table:

```
>>> dataframe_mysql.registerTempTable("mydept") ❶
>>> spark.sql("select * from mydept where dept_number > 30") ❷
         .show() ❸
+-----------+----------+-------------+-------+
|dept_number| dept_name|dept_location|manager|
+-----------+----------+-------------+-------+
|         40|OPERATIONS|   BOSTON, MA|   jane|
|         50| MARKETING|Sunnyvale, CA|   jane|
|         60|  SOFTWARE| Stanford, CA|   jane|
```

```
|         70|  HARDWARE|   BOSTON, MA| sophia|
+-----------+----------+-------------+-------+
```

❶ Register this DataFrame as a temporary table using the given name.

❷ You can now issue a SQL query against your registered table.

❸ This prints the first 20 rows to the console.

This query uses the "like" pattern matching for the dept_location column:

```
>>> spark.sql("select * from mydept where dept_location like '%CA'")
        .show()
+-----------+---------+-------------+-------+
|dept_number| dept_name|dept_location|manager|
+-----------+---------+-------------+-------+
|         50| MARKETING|Sunnyvale, CA|   jane|
|         60|  SOFTWARE| Stanford, CA|   jane|
+-----------+---------+-------------+-------+
>>>
```

And here we use GROUP BY:

```
>>> spark.sql("select manager, count(*) as count from mydept group by manager")
  .show()
+-------+-----+
|manager|count|
+-------+-----+
|   jane|    4|
| sophia|    1|
|   alex|    2|
+-------+-----+
```

Writing a DataFrame to a Database

We can write or save a Spark DataFrame to an external data source, such as a relational database table, using the DataFrameWriter.save() method. Let's walk through an example.

First, we'll create a list of triplets (<name>, <age>, <salary>) as a local Python collection:

```
>>> triplets = [ ("alex", 60, 18000),
...              ("adel", 40, 45000),
...              ("adel", 50, 77000),
...              ("jane", 40, 52000),
...              ("jane", 60, 81000),
...              ("alex", 50, 62000),
...              ("mary", 50, 92000),
...              ("mary", 60, 63000),
...              ("mary", 40, 55000),
...              ("mary", 40, 55000)
...            ]
```

Then we'll convert this into a Spark DataFrame with the SparkSession.createDataFrame() method:

```
>>> tripletsDF = spark.createDataFrame( ❶
...                     triplets, ❷
...                     ['name', 'age', 'salary'] ❸
...              )
```

```
>>> tripletsDF.show() ❹
+----+---+------+
|name|age|salary|
+----+---+------+
|alex| 60| 18000|
|adel| 40| 45000|
|adel| 50| 77000|
|jane| 40| 52000|
|jane| 60| 81000|
|alex| 50| 62000|
|mary| 50| 92000|
|mary| 60| 63000|
|mary| 40| 55000|
|mary| 40| 55000|
+----+---+------+
```

 Create a new DataFrame.

 Convert triplets into a DataFrame.

❸ Impose a schema on the created DataFrame.

❹ Display the contents of the newly created DataFrame.

Now, we can convert the DataFrame into a relational table called `triplets`:

```
tripletsDF
  .write ❶
  .format("jdbc") ❷
  .option("driver", "com.mysql.jdbc.Driver") ❸
  .mode("overwrite") ❹
  .option("url", "jdbc:mysql://localhost/metadb") ❺
  .option("dbtable", "triplets") ❻
  .option("user", "root") ❼
  .option("password", "mp22_pass") ❽
  .save() ❾
```

❶ Returns a `DataFrameWriter` that can be used to write to an external device

❷ Indicates that you are writing to a JDBC-compliant database

❸ The JDBC driver (loaded from the JAR file)

❹ Overwrites the table if it already exists

❺ The database URL

❻ The target database table name

❼ The database username

❽ The database password

❾ Saves the DataFrame data as a database table

When writing the contents of a DataFrame to an external device, you can choose desired mode. The Spark JDBC writer supports the following modes:

`append`
: Append the contents of this DataFrame to any existing data.

`overwrite`
: Overwrite any existing data.

`ignore`
: Silently ignore this operation if data already exists.

`error` *(default case)*
: Throw an exception if data already exists.

Here, we verify that the `triplets` table was created in the `metadb` database on the MySQL database server under the `'metadb'` database:

```
$ mysql -uroot -p ❶
Enter password:  <password> ❷
Welcome to the MySQL Server version: 5.7.18

mysql> use metadb; ❸
Database changed

mysql> desc triplets; ❹
+--------+------------+------+-----+--------+-------+
| Field  | Type       | Null | Key | Default | Extra |
+--------+------------+------+-----+--------+-------+
| name   | text       | YES  |     | NULL    |       |
| age    | bigint(20) | YES  |     | NULL    |       |
| salary | bigint(20) | YES  |     | NULL    |       |
+--------+------------+------+-----+--------+-------+

mysql> select * from triplets; ❺
+------+-----+--------+
| name | age | salary |
+------+-----+--------+
| jane |  40 |  52000 |
| adel |  50 |  77000 |
| jane |  60 |  81000 |
| alex |  50 |  62000 |
| mary |  40 |  55000 |
| mary |  40 |  55000 |
| adel |  40 |  45000 |
```

```
| mary |   60 |  63000 |
| alex |   60 |  18000 |
| mary |   50 |  92000 |
+------+------+--------+
10 rows in set (0.00 sec)
```

1. Start the MySQL client shell.
2. Enter the password for the `root` user.
3. Select the desired database.
4. Make sure that the `triplets` table was created.
5. Display the content of the `triplets` tables.

Next, we read the `triplets` table back from the MySQL relational database to make sure that the table is readable:

```
>>> tripletsDF_mysql =
      spark (1)
       .read (2)
       .format("jdbc") (3)
       .option("url", "jdbc:mysql://localhost/metadb") (4)
       .option("driver", "com.mysql.jdbc.Driver") (5)
       .option("dbtable", "triplets") (6)
       .option("user", "root") (7)
       .option("password", "mp22_pass") (8)
       .load() (9)

>>> tripletsDF_mysql.show() (10)
+----+---+------+
|name|age|salary|
+----+---+------+
|jane| 40| 52000|
|adel| 50| 77000|
|jane| 60| 81000|
|alex| 50| 62000|
|mary| 40| 55000|
|mary| 40| 55000|
|adel| 40| 45000|
|mary| 60| 63000|
|alex| 60| 18000|
|mary| 50| 92000|
+----+---+------+
```

1. An instance of `SparkSession`
2. Returns a `DataFrameReader` that can be used to read data in as a DataFrame

❸ Indicates that you are reading JDBC-compliant data

❹ The database URL

❺ The JDBC driver (loaded from the JAR file)

❻ The database table to be read

❼ The database username

❽ The database password

❾ Loads data from a JDBC data source and returns it as a DataFrame

❿ Shows the contents of the newly created DataFrame

Finally, we'll execute some SQL queries on the newly created DataFrame.

The following query finds the minimum and maximum of the `salary` column:

```
>>> tripletsDF_mysql.registerTempTable("mytriplets") ❶
>>> spark.sql("select min(salary), max(salary) from mytriplets") ❷
        .show() ❸
+-----------+-----------+
|min(salary)|max(salary)|
+-----------+-----------+
|      18000|      92000|
+-----------+-----------+
```

❶ Register this DataFrame as a temporary table using the name `mytriplets`.

❷ Execute the SQL statement and create a new DataFrame.

❸ Display the result of the SQL statement.

Here, we aggregate the `age` column by using SQL's `GROUP BY`:

```
>>> spark.sql("select age, count(*) from mytriplets group by age").show()
+---+--------+
|age|count(1)|
+---+--------+
| 50|       3|
| 60|       3|
| 40|       4|
+---+--------+
```

Next, we sort the result of the previous SQL query:

```
>>> spark.sql("select age, count(*) from mytriplets group by age order by age")
  .show()
```

```
+---+--------+
|age|count(1)|
+---+--------+
| 40|       4|
| 50|       3|
| 60|       3|
+---+--------+
```

Reading Text Files

Spark allows us to read text files and create DataFrames from them. Consider the following text file:

```
$ cat people.txt
Alex,30,Tennis
Betty,40,Swimming
Dave,20,Walking
Jeff,77,Baseball
```

Let's first create an RDD[Row] (where each element is a Row object):

```
>>> from pyspark.sql import Row

>>> def create_row(rec):
        p = rec.split(",")
        return Row(name=p[0], age=int(p[1]), hobby=p[2])
>>> #end-def
>>> input_path = "people.txt"
>>> # Load a text file and convert each line to a Row
>>> records = spark.sparkContext.textFile(input_path) ❶
>>> records.collect()
[
 u'Alex,30,Tennis',
 u'Betty,40,Swimming',
 u'Dave,20,Walking',
 u'Jeff,77,Baseball'
]
>>> people = records.map(create_row) ❷
>>> people.collect()
[
 Row(age=30, hobby=u'Tennis', name=u'Alex'),
 Row(age=40, hobby=u'Swimming', name=u'Betty'),
 Row(age=20, hobby=u'Walking', name=u'Dave'),
 Row(age=77, hobby=u'Baseball', name=u'Jeff')
]
```

❶ records is an RDD[String].

❷ people is an RDD[Row].

Now that we have people as an RDD[Row], it is straightforward to create a DataFrame:

```
>>> people_df = spark.createDataFrame(people) ❶
>>> people_df.show()
+---+--------+-----+
|age|   hobby| name|
+---+--------+-----+
| 30|  Tennis| Alex|
| 40|Swimming|Betty|
| 20| Walking| Dave|
| 77|Baseball| Jeff|
+---+--------+-----+
>>> people_df.printSchema() ❷
root
 |-- age: long (nullable = true)
 |-- hobby: string (nullable = true)
 |-- name: string (nullable = true)
```

❶ people_df is a DataFrame[Row].

❷ Display the schema of the created DataFrame.

Next, we'll use a SQL query to manipulate the created DataFrame:

```
>>> people_df.registerTempTable("people_table") ❶
>>> spark.sql("select * from people_table").show() ❷
+---+--------+-----+
|age|   hobby| name|
+---+--------+-----+
| 30|  Tennis| Alex|
| 40|Swimming|Betty|
| 20| Walking| Dave|
| 77|Baseball| Jeff|
+---+--------+-----+

>>> spark.sql("select * from people_table where age > 35").show() ❸
+---+--------+-----+
|age|   hobby| name|
+---+--------+-----+
| 40|Swimming|Betty|
| 77|Baseball| Jeff|
+---+--------+-----+
```

❶ Register the people_df DataFrame as a temporary table using the name people_table.

❷ spark.sql(*sql-query*) creates a new DataFrame.

❸ spark.sql(*sql-query*) creates a new DataFrame.

We can save our DataFrame as a text file with DataFrame.write().

Reading and Writing CSV Files

A comma-separated values file is a text file that allows data to be saved in a table-structured format. The following is a simple example of a CSV file with a header row (metadata containing the names of the columns, separated by commas), called *cats.with.header.csv*:

```
$ cat cats.with.header.csv
#name,age,gender,weight ❶
cuttie,2,female,6 ❷
mono,3,male,9 ❸
fuzzy,1,female,4 ❹
```

❶ Header record starts with #, describes columns

 First record

❸ Second record

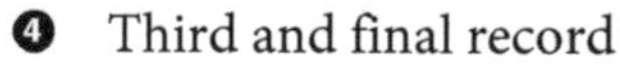

❹ Third and final record

The following is a simple example of a CSV file without a header, called *cats.no.header.csv*:

```
$ cat cats.no.header.csv
cuttie,2,female,6
mono,3,male,9
fuzzy,1,female,4
```

In the next section, we'll use these two files to demonstrate how Spark reads CSV files.

Reading CSV Files

Spark offers many methods to load CSV files into a DataFrame. I'll show you a few of them here.

In this example, using the PySpark shell, we read a CSV file with a header and load it as a DataFrame:

```
# spark : pyspark.sql.session.SparkSession object
input_path = '/pyspark_book/code/chap08/cats.with.header.csv'
cats = spark ❶
         .read ❷
         .format("csv") ❸
         .option("header", "true") ❹
         .option("inferSchema", "true") ❺
         .load(input_path) ❻
```

❶ Create a new DataFrame as cats using a SparkSession.

❷ Return a DataFrameReader that can be used to read data in as a DataFrame.

❸ Specify that the input data source format is CSV.

❹ Indicate that the input CSV file has a header (note that the header is not part of the actual data).

❺ Infer the DataFrame schema from the input file.

❻ Provide the path for the CSV file.

We can now display the contents of the newly created DataFrame and its inferred schema:

```
>>> cats.show() ❶
+------+---+------+------+
|  name|age|gender|weight|
+------+---+------+------+
|cuttie|  2|female|     6|
|  mono|  3|  male|     9|
| fuzzy|  1|female|     4|
+------+---+------+------+

>>> cats.printSchema ❷
<bound method DataFrame.printSchema of DataFrame
[
 name: string,
 age: int,
 gender: string,
 weight: int
]>
>>> cats.count() ❸
3
```

❶ Display the contents of the DataFrame.

❷ Display the schema of the DataFrame.

❸ Display the size of the DataFrame.

Now I'll show you how to read a CSV file without a header and create a new DataFrame from it:

```
input_path = '/pyspark_book/code/chap08/cats.no.header.csv'
cats2 = spark ❶
            .read ❷
            .format("csv") ❸
```

```
                  .option("header","false") ❹
                  .option("inferSchema", "true") ❺
                  .load(input_path) ❻
```

❶ Create a new DataFrame as `cats` using a `SparkSession`.

❷ Return a `DataFrameReader` that can be used to read data in as a DataFrame.

❸ Specify that the input data source format is CSV.

❹ Indicate that the input CSV file has no header.

❺ Infer the DataFrame schema from the input file.

❻ Provide the path for the CSV file.

Let's inspect the contents of the newly created DataFrame and its inferred schema:

```
>>> cats2.show()
+------+---+------+---+
|   _c0|_c1|   _c2|_c3| ❶
+------+---+------+---+
|cuttie|  2|female|  6|
|  mono|  3|  male|  9|
| fuzzy|  1|female|  4|
+------+---+------+---+
```

❶ Default column names

Next, we'll define a schema with four columns:

```
>>> from pyspark.sql.types import StructType
>>> from pyspark.sql.types import StructField
>>> from pyspark.sql.types import StringType
>>> from pyspark.sql.types import IntegerType
>>>
>>> catsSchema = StructType([
... StructField("name", StringType(), True),
... StructField("age", IntegerType(), True),
... StructField("gender", StringType(), True),
... StructField("weight", IntegerType(), True)
... ])
```

Here's what happens if we use the defined schema to read in the same CSV file and create a DataFrame from it:

```
>>> input_path = '/book/code/chap07/cats.no.header.csv'
>>> cats3 = spark
   .read
   .format("csv")
   .option("header","false")
```

```
    .option("inferSchema", "true")
    .load(input_path, schema = catsSchema)
>>> cats3.show()
+------+---+------+------+
|  name|age|gender|weight| ❶
+------+---+------+------+
|cuttie|  2|female|     6|
|  mono|  3|  male|     9|
| fuzzy|  1|female|     4|
+------+---+------+------+

>>> cats.count()
3
```

❶ Explicit column names

We can apply this predefined schema to any headerless CSV file:

```
>>> cats4 = spark
    .read ❶
     .csv("file:///tmp/cats.no.header.csv", ❷
          schema = catsSchema, ❸
          header = "false") ❹
>>> cats4.show()
+------+---+------+------+
|  name|age|gender|weight| ❺
+------+---+------+------+
|cuttie|  2|female|     6|
|  mono|  3|  male|     9|
| fuzzy|  1|female|     4|
+------+---+------+------+

>>> cats4.printSchema
<bound method DataFrame.printSchema of DataFrame
[
 name: string,
 age: int,
 gender: string,
 weight: int
]>
>>> cats4.count()
3
```

❶ Return a `DataFrameReader` that can be used to read data in as a DataFrame.

❷ Read a CSV file.

❸ Use the given schema for the CSV file.

❹ Indicate that the CSV file has no header.

❺ Explicit column names are used.

Writing CSV Files

There are several ways that you can create CSV files from DataFrames in Spark. The easiest option is to use the `.csv()` method of the `DataFrameWriter` class, accessed through `DataFrame.write()`. This method is defined as follows (note that this is just a small subset of the available parameters):

```
csv(path, mode=None, compression=None, sep=None, ...)
Saves the content of the DataFrame in CSV format
at the specified path.

Parameters:
  path - the path in any Hadoop supported file system.
  mode - specifies the behavior of the save operation when data already exists.
         "append":  Append contents of this DataFrame to existing data.
         "overwrite": Overwrite existing data.
         "ignore": Silently ignore this operation if data already exists.
         "error": Throw an exception if data already exists.
  compression - compression codec to use when saving to file.
  sep - sets a single character as a separator for each field and value.
         If None is set, it uses the default value.
```

Let's use this method to save our `cats4` DataFrame as a CSV file:

```
>>> cats4.show()
+------+---+------+------+
|  name|age|gender|weight|
+------+---+------+------+
|cuttie|  2|female|     6|
|  mono|  3|  male|     9|
| fuzzy|  1|female|     4|
+------+---+------+------+

>>> cats4.write.csv("file:///tmp/cats4", sep = ';')
```

Then examine the saved file(s):

```
$ ls -l /tmp/cats4
total 8
-rw-r--r--  ...   0 Apr 12 16:46 _SUCCESS
-rw-r--r--  ...  49 Apr 12 16:46 part-00000-...-c000.csv

$ cat /tmp/cats4/part*
cuttie;2;female;6
mono;3;male;9
fuzzy;1;female;4
```

Note that in the output of the `ls` (list) command, we see two types of files:

- A zero-sized *SUCCESS* file, which indicates that the `write` operation was successful.
- One or more files whose names begin with *part-*, which represent the output from a single partition.

Note also that there's no header data in the saved file.

Let's try that again, this time specifying that we want a header row:

```
>>> cats4.write.csv("file:///tmp/cats48",
                    sep = ';',
                    header = 'true')

$ ls -l /tmp/cats48
total 8
-rw-r--r--  ...   0 Apr 12 16:49 _SUCCESS
-rw-r--r--  ...  72 Apr 12 16:49 part-00000-...-c000.csv

$ cat /tmp/cats48/part*
name;age;gender;weight ❶
cuttie;2;female;6
mono;3;male;9
fuzzy;1;female;4
```

❶ The header from our DataFrame

Reading and Writing JSON Files

JavaScript Object Notation is a lightweight, text-based data interchange format that is easy for humans to read and write. A JSON object is composed of a set of (key, value) pairs enclosed in curly braces, like this:

```
{
  "first_name" : "John", ❶
  "last_name" : "Smith",
  "age" : 23,
  "gender" : "Male",
  "cars": [ "Ford", "BMW", "Fiat" ] ❷
}
```

❶ A simple (key, value) pair

❷ An array value

Reading JSON Files

JSON data can read with the `DataFrameReader.json()` method, which can take a set of parameters such as the path and schema. Consider the following JSON file:

```
$ cat $SPARK_HOME/examples/src/main/resources/employees.json
{"name":"Michael", "salary":3000}
{"name":"Andy", "salary":4500}
{"name":"Justin", "salary":3500}
{"name":"Berta", "salary":4000}
```

We can read this file and convert it to a DataFrame as follows:

```
>>> data_path = 'examples/src/main/resources/employees.json'
>>> df = spark.read.json(data_path)
>>> df.show()
+-------+------+
|   name|salary|
+-------+------+
|Michael|  3000|
|   Andy|  4500|
| Justin|  3500|
|  Berta|  4000|
+-------+------+

>>> df.printSchema
<bound method DataFrame.printSchema of DataFrame
[
 name: string,
 salary: bigint
]>
>>> df.count()
4
```

You can also use the `load()` method and pass it one or more JSON files:

```
>>> data_path = 'examples/src/main/resources/employees.json'
>>> df2 = spark.read.format('json')
           .load([data_path,  data_path]) ❶
>>> df2.show()
+-------+------+
|   name|salary|
+-------+------+
|Michael|  3000|
|   Andy|  4500|
| Justin|  3500|
|  Berta|  4000|
|Michael|  3000| ❷
|   Andy|  4500|
| Justin|  3500|
|  Berta|  4000|
+-------+------+
```

```
>>> df2.printSchema
<bound method DataFrame.printSchema of DataFrame
[
 name: string,
 salary: bigint
]>
>>> df2.count()
8
```

 Note that `data_path` is loaded twice.

❷ The file's contents are therefore included twice in the resulting DataFrame. You can also use this method to create a DataFrame from several input files.

Writing JSON Files

To write a DataFrame as a `json` object, we can use `DataFrameWriter.json()` method. The method accepts a set of parameters and saves the contents of the DataFrame in JSON format:

```
json(
     path,
     mode=None,
     compression=None,
     dateFormat=None,
     timestampFormat=None
)

Parameters:
  path - the path in any Hadoop supported file system
  mode - specifies the behavior of the save operation when data already exists.
         Possible values are: "append", "overwrite", "ignore", "error"
  compression - compression codec to use when saving to file.
  dateFormat - sets the string that indicates a date format.
  timestampFormat - sets the string that indicates a timestamp format.
```

Let's first create a DataFrame:

```
>>> data = [("name", "alex"), ("gender", "male"), ("state", "CA")]
>>> df = spark.createDataFrame(data, ['key', 'value'])
>>> df.show()
+------+-----+
|   key|value|
+------+-----+
|  name| alex|
|gender| male|
| state|   CA|
+------+-----+
```

Next, write it to an output path as JSON:

```
>>> df.write.json('/tmp/data')
```

```
$ ls -l /tmp/data
total 24
-rw-r--r-- ...   0 Apr  2 01:15 _SUCCESS
-rw-r--r-- ...   0 Apr  2 01:15 part-00000-....-c000.json
-rw-r--r-- ...   0 Apr  2 01:15 part-00001-....-c000.json
...
-rw-r--r-- ...  29 Apr  2 01:15 part-00007-....-c000.json
```

Note that we have eight filenames that begin with *part-*: this means that our DataFrame was represented by eight partitions.

Let's take a look at these files:

```
$ cat /tmp/data/part*
{"key":"name","value":"alex"}
{"key":"gender","value":"male"}
{"key":"state","value":"CA"}
```

If you want to create a single file output, then you may put your `DataFrame` into a single partition before writing it out:

```
>>> df.repartition(1).write.json('/tmp/data') ❶
```

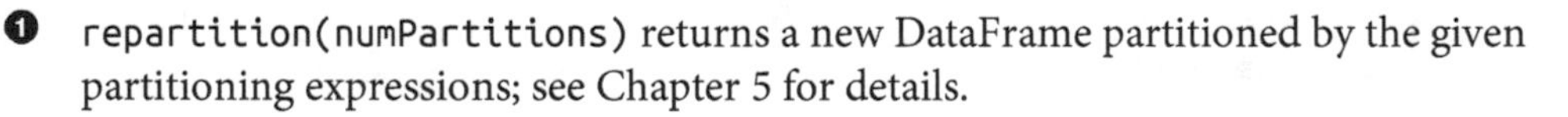

❶ `repartition(numPartitions)` returns a new DataFrame partitioned by the given partitioning expressions; see Chapter 5 for details.

Reading from and Writing to Amazon S3

Amazon Simple Storage Service (S3) is a service offered by Amazon Web Services (AWS) that provides object storage through a web services interface. S3 objects are treated as web objects—that is, they are accessed via internet protocols using a URL identifier. Every S3 object has a unique URL, in this format:

```
http://s3.<region>.amazonaws.com/<bucket>/<key>
```

For example:

```
http://s3.us-east-1.amazonaws.com/project-dev/dna/sample123.vcf
```

where: `project-dev` is the bucket name and `dna/sample123.vcf` is a key.

S3 objects can also be accessed through the following URI schemas:

`s3n`
: Uses the S3 Native FileSystem, a native filesystem for reading and writing regular files on S3.

`s3a`
: Uses the S3A Filesystem, a successor to the native filesystem. Designed to be a switch-in replacement for `s3n`, this filesystem binding supports larger files and promises higher performance.

`s3`
: Uses the S3 Block FileSystem, a block-based filesystem backed by S3. Files are stored as blocks, just like they are in HDFS.

The difference between `s3` and `s3n`/`s3a` is that `s3` is a block-based overlay on top of Amazon S3, while `s3n`/`s3a` are not (they are object-based). The difference between `s3n` and `s3a` is that `s3n` supports objects up to 5 GB in size, while `s3a` supports objects up to 5 TB in size and has better performance (both features are because it uses multi-part upload).

For example, using the `s3` URI schema, we can access the *sample72.vcf* file as:

```
s3://project-dev/dna/sample72.vcf
```

In general, to access any services from AWS, you have to be authenticated. There are many ways to do this. One method is to export your access key and secret key from the command line:

```
export AWS_ACCESS_KEY_ID="AKIAI74O5KPLUQGVOJWQ"
export AWS_SECRET_ACCESS_KEY="LmuKE7afdasdfxK2vj1nfA0Bp"
```

Another option is to set your credentials using the `SparkContext` object:

```
# spark: SparkSession
sc = spark.sparkContext
# set access key
sc._jsc.hadoopConfiguration()
   .set("fs.s3.awsAccessKeyId", "AKIAI74O5KPLUQGVOJWQ")
# set secret key
sc._jsc.hadoopConfiguration()
  .set("fs.s3.awsSecretAccessKey", "LmuKE7afdasdfxK2vj1nfA0Bp")
```

Reading from Amazon S3

You'll need to use the `s3`, `s3n`, or `s3a` (for bigger S3 objects) URI schema for reading objects from S3.

If `spark` is an instance of `SparkSession`, then you may use the following to load a text file (an Amazon S3 object) and return a DataFrame (denoted as the variable `df`) with a single string column named `value`:

```
s3_object_path = "s3n://bucket-name/object-path"
df = spark.read.text(s3_object_path)
```

The following example shows how to read an S3 object. First we use the boto3 library (boto3 is the AWS SDK for Python, which allows Python developers to write software that makes use of Amazon services like S3 and EC2) to verify that the object exists, and then we read it using PySpark.

In the following code, we check for the existence of the s3://caselog-dev/tmp/csv_file_10_rows.csv:

```
>>> import boto3
>>> s3 = boto3.resource('s3')
>>> bucket = 'caselog-dev'
>>> key = 'tmp/csv_file_10_rows.csv'
>>> obj = s3.Object(bucket, key)
>>> obj
s3.Object(bucket_name='caselog-dev', key='tmp/csv_file_10_rows.csv')
>>> obj.get()['Body'].read().decode('utf-8')
u'0,a,0.0\n1,b,1.1\n2,c,2.2\n3,d,\n4,,4.4\n,f,5.5\n,,\n7,h,7.7\n8,i,8.8\n9,j,9.9'
```

Then, we load the object and create a new DataFrame[String]:

```
>>> s3_object_path = "s3n://caselog-dev/tmp/csv_file_10_rows.csv" ❶
>>> df = spark.read.text(s3_object_path) ❷
>>> df.show() ❸
+-------+
|  value|
+-------+
|0,a,0.0|
|1,b,1.1|
|2,c,2.2|
|   3,d,|
| 4,,4.4|
| ,f,5.5|
|     ,,|
|7,h,7.7|
|8,i,8.8|
|9,j,9.9|
+-------+

>>> df.printSchema  ❹
<bound method DataFrame.printSchema of DataFrame[value: string]>
```

❶ Define your S3 object path.

❷ Use SparkSession (as spark) to load the S3 object and create a DataFrame.

❸ Show the contents of the newly created DataFrame.

❹ Display the schema for the newly created DataFrame.

Writing to Amazon S3

Once you've created your DataFrame:

```
>>># spark: SparkSession
>>> pairs_data = [("alex", 4), ("alex", 8),
                  ("rafa", 3), ("rafa", 6)]
>>> df = spark.createDataFrame(pairs_data, ['name', 'number'])
```

you may examine the contents and its associated schema:

```
>>> df.show()
+----+------+
|name|number|
+----+------+
|alex|     4|
|alex|     8|
|rafa|     3|
|rafa|     6|
+----+------+

>>> df.printSchema
<bound method DataFrame.printSchema of DataFrame
[
 name: string,
 number: bigint
]>
```

Next, save the data to the Amazon S3 filesystem:

```
>>> df
     .write
     .format("csv")
     .mode("overwrite")
     .save("s3n://caselog-dev/output/pairs")
```

You will see that the following files are created:

```
https://s3.amazonaws.com/caselog-dev/output/pairs/_SUCCESS
https://s3.amazonaws.com/caselog-dev/output/pairs/part-00000-...-c000.csv
https://s3.amazonaws.com/caselog-dev/output/pairs/part-00001-...-c000.csv
```

Now let's read it back:

```
>>># Read S3 object as text
>>> s3_object_path = "s3n://caselog-dev/output/pairs"
>>> df = spark.read.text(s3_object_path)
>>> df.show()
+------+
| value|
+------+
|alex,4|
|alex,8|
|rafa,3|
|rafa,6|
```

```
+------+

>>> df.printSchema
<bound method DataFrame.printSchema of DataFrame[value: string]>
```

We can also read the S3 object as CSV:

```
>>> df2 = spark.read.format("csv").load(s3_object_path)
>>> df2.show()
+----+---+
| _c0|_c1| ❶
+----+---+
|alex|  4|
|alex|  8|
|rafa|  3|
|rafa|  6|
+----+---+
```

❶ Default column names

Reading and Writing Hadoop Files

Hadoop (*http://hadoop.apache.org*) is an open source MapReduce programming framework that supports the processing and storage of extremely large datasets in a distributed computing environment. It's designed to scale up from single servers to thousands of machines. The Hadoop project, sponsored by the Apache Software Foundation (*http://apache.org*) (ASF), includes these modules:

Hadoop Common
: The common utilities that support the other Hadoop modules.

Hadoop Distributed File System (HDFS)
: A distributed filesystem that provides high-throughput access to application data. HDFS allows for the distributed processing of large datasets across clusters of computers using MapReduce programming models.

Hadoop YARN
: A framework for job scheduling and cluster resource management.

Hadoop MapReduce
: A YARN-based system for parallel processing of large datasets.

In this section, I'll show you how to read files from HDFS and create RDDs and DataFrames and how to write RDDs and DataFrames into HDFS. To follow along, you'll need access to a Hadoop cluster.

Reading Hadoop Text Files

To illustrate the complete process of reading a file from HDFS, first we'll create a text file in HDFS, then we'll use PySpark to read it in as a DataFrame as well as an RDD.

Let *name_age_salary.csv* be a text file in a Linux filesystem (this file can be created with any text editor—note that `$` is the Linux operating system prompt):

```
$ export input_path = "/book/code/chap07/name_age_salary.csv"
$ cat $input_path
alex,60,18000
adel,40,45000
adel,50,77000
jane,40,52000
jane,60,81000
alex,50,62000
mary,50,92000
mary,60,63000
mary,40,55000
mary,40,55000
```

Create a */test* directory in HDFS using the **`$HADOOP_HOME/bin/hdfs`** command:

```
$ hdfs dfs -mkdir /test
```

Then I copy *name_age_salary.csv* to the *hdfs:///test/* directory:

```
$ hdfs dfs -put $input_path /test/
$ hdfs dfs -ls /test/
-rw-r--r--   1 ...  140 ... /test/name_age_salary.csv
```

And I examine the contents of the file:

```
$ hdfs dfs -cat /test/name_age_salary.csv
alex,60,18000
adel,40,45000
adel,50,77000
jane,40,52000
jane,60,81000
alex,50,62000
mary,50,92000
mary,60,63000
mary,40,55000
mary,40,55000
```

Now that we have created a file in HDFS, we will read it and create a DataFrame and an RDD from its contents.

First, we read the HDFS file and create a DataFrame with default column names (`_c0, _c1, _c2`). The general format for an HDFS URI is:

```
hdfs://<server>:<port>/<directories>/<filename>
```

where *<server>* is the hostname of the NameNode and *<port>* is the NameNode's port number.

In this example I use a Hadoop instance installed on my MacBook; the NameNode is `localhost` and the port number is `9000`:

```
>>> uri = 'hdfs://localhost:9000/test/name_age_salary.csv'
>>> df = spark.read.csv(uri)
>>> df.show()
+----+---+-----+
| _c0|_c1|  _c2| ❶
+----+---+-----+
|alex| 60|18000|
|adel| 40|45000|
|adel| 50|77000|
|jane| 40|52000|
|jane| 60|81000|
|alex| 50|62000|
|mary| 50|92000|
|mary| 60|63000|
|mary| 40|55000|
|mary| 40|55000|
+----+---+-----+
```

❶ Default column names

Let's examine the schema for the newly created DataFrame:

```
>>> df.printSchema
<bound method DataFrame.printSchema of DataFrame
[
 _c0: string,
 _c1: string,
 _c2: string
]>
```

If you want to impose your own explicit schema (column names and data types) on a DataFrame, then you may do so as follows:

```
>>> from pyspark.sql.types import StructType
>>> from pyspark.sql.types import StructField
>>> from pyspark.sql.types import StringType
>>> from pyspark.sql.types import IntegerType
>>>
>>> empSchema = StructType([ ❶
    StructField("name", StringType(), True),
    StructField("age", IntegerType(), True),
    StructField("salary", StringType(), True)
    ])
>>>
>>> uri = 'hdfs://localhost:9000/test/name_age_salary.csv'
>>> df2 = spark.read.csv(uri, schema = empSchema) ❷
```

```
>>> df2.show()
+----+---+------+
|name|age|salary| ❸
+----+---+------+
|alex| 60| 18000|
|adel| 40| 45000|
|adel| 50| 77000|
|jane| 40| 52000|
|jane| 60| 81000|
|alex| 50| 62000|
|mary| 50| 92000|
|mary| 60| 63000|
|mary| 40| 55000|
|mary| 40| 55000|
+----+---+------+

>>> df2.printSchema
<bound method DataFrame.printSchema of DataFrame
[
 name: string,
 age: int,
 salary: string
]>
```

❶ Explicit schema definition

❷ Enforce an explicit schema

❸ Explicit column names

You can also read in an HDFS file and create an `RDD[String]` from it:

```
>>> rdd = spark.sparkContext.textFile(uri)

>>> rdd.collect()
[
 u'alex,60,18000',
 u'adel,40,45000',
 u'adel,50,77000',
 u'jane,40,52000',
 u'jane,60,81000',
 u'alex,50,62000',
 u'mary,50,92000',
 u'mary,60,63000',
 u'mary,40,55000',
 u'mary,40,55000'
]
```

Writing Hadoop Text Files

PySpark's API enables us to save our RDDs and DataFrames into HDFS as files. First let's look at how to save an RDD into an HDFS file:

```
>>> pairs = [('alex', 2), ('alex', 3),
             ('jane', 5), ('jane', 6)]
>>> rdd = spark.sparkContext.parallelize(pairs)
>>> rdd.collect()
[('alex', 2), ('alex', 3), ('jane', 5), ('jane', 6)]
>>> rdd.count()
4
>>> rdd.saveAsTextFile("hdfs://localhost:9000/test/pairs")
```

The `RDD.saveAsTextFile(path)` method writes the elements of the dataset as a text file (or set of text files) into a given directory in the local filesystem, HDFS, or any other Hadoop-supported filesystem. Spark will call the `toString()` method on each element to convert it to a line of text in the file.

Next, let's examine what is created in HDFS (the output here is formatted to fit the page):

```
$ hdfs dfs -ls hdfs://localhost:9000/test/pairs
Found 9 items
-rw-r--r-- ...  0 ... hdfs://localhost:9000/test/pairs/_SUCCESS
-rw-r--r-- ...  0 ... hdfs://localhost:9000/test/pairs/part-00000
-rw-r--r-- ... 12 ... hdfs://localhost:9000/test/pairs/part-00001
...
-rw-r--r-- ... 12 ... hdfs://localhost:9000/test/pairs/part-00007

$ hdfs dfs -cat hdfs://localhost:9000/test/pairs/part*
(alex, 2)
(alex, 3)
(jane, 5)
(jane, 6)
```

The reason we got eight *part-** files is because the source RDD had eight partitions:

```
>>> rdd.getNumPartitions()
8
```

If you want to create a single *part-** file, then you should create a single RDD partition:

```
>>> rdd_single = spark.sparkContext.parallelize(pairs, 1)
>>> rdd_single.collect()
[('alex', 2), ('alex', 3), ('jane', 5), ('jane', 6)]
>>> rdd_single.getNumPartitions()
1
>>> rdd_single.saveAsTextFile("hdfs://localhost:9000/test/pairs_single")
```

Let's examine what is created in the HDFS row:

```
$ hdfs dfs -ls hdfs://localhost:9000/test/pairs_single
Found 2 items
-rw-r--r--  0  hdfs://localhost:9000/test/pairs_single/_SUCCESS
-rw-r--r-- 48  hdfs://localhost:9000/test/pairs_single/part-00000

$ hdfs dfs -cat hdfs://localhost:9000/test/pairs_single/part-00000
(alex, 2)
(alex, 3)
(jane, 5)
(jane, 6)
```

We can save a DataFrame into HDFS by using a `DataFrameWriter`:

```
>>> pairs = [('alex', 2), ('alex', 3),
             ('jane', 5), ('jane', 6)]
>>>
>>> pairsDF = spark.createDataFrame(pairs)
>>> pairsDF.show()
+----+---+
|  _1| _2|
+----+---+
|alex|  2|
|alex|  3|
|jane|  5|
|jane|  6|
+----+---+

>>> pairsDF.write.csv("hdfs://localhost:9000/test/pairs_df")
```

Here's what's created in the HDFS:

```
$ hdfs dfs -ls hdfs://localhost:9000/test/pairs_df
Found 9 items
-rw-... 0 hdfs://localhost:9000/test/pairs_df/_SUCCESS
-rw-... 0 hdfs://localhost:9000/test/pairs_df/part-00000-...-c000.csv
...
-rw-... 7 hdfs://localhost:9000/test/pairs_df/part-00007-...-c000.csv

$ hdfs dfs -cat hdfs://localhost:9000/test/pairs_df/part*
alex,2
alex,3
jane,5
jane,6
```

You may save your DataFrames into HDFS in different data formats. For example, to save a DataFrame in Parquet format, you can use the following template:

```
# df is an existing DataFrame object.
# format options are 'csv', 'parquet', 'json'
df.write.save(
   '/target/path/',
   format='parquet',
   mode='append'
)
```

Reading and Writing HDFS SequenceFiles

Hadoop offers to persist any file types, including `SequenceFiles` in HDFS. `SequenceFiles` are flat files consisting of binary (key, value) pairs. Hadoop defines a `SequenceFile` class as `org.apache.hadoop.io.SequenceFile`. `SequenceFile` provides `SequenceFile.Writer`, `SequenceFile.Reader`, and `SequenceFile.Sorter` classes for writing, reading, and sorting, respectively. `SequenceFile` is the standard binary serialization format for Hadoop. It stores records of `Writable` (key, value) pairs, and supports splitting and compression. `SequenceFiles` are commonly used for intermediate data storage in MapReduce pipelines, since they are more efficient than text files.

Reading HDFS SequenceFiles

Spark supports reading `SequenceFiles` using the `SparkContext.sequenceFile()` method. For example, to read a `SequenceFile` with `Text` keys and `DoubleWritable` values in Python, we would do the following:

```
# spark: an instance of SparkSession
rdd = spark.sparkContext.sequenceFile(path)
```

Note that unlike with Java or Scala, we do not pass the data types of (key, value) pairs to the Spark API; Spark automatically converts Hadoop's `Text` to `String` and `DoubleWritable` to `Double`.

Writing HDFS SequenceFiles

PySpark's `RDD.saveAsSequenceFile()` method allows users to save an RDD of (key, value) pairs as a `SequenceFile`. For example, we can create an RDD from a Python collection and save it as a `SequenceFile` as follows:

```
# spark: an instance of SparkSession
pairs = [('key1', 10.0), ('key2', 20.0),
         ('key3', 30.0), ('key4', 40.0)]
rdd = spark.sparkContext.parallelize(pairs)
rdd.saveAsSequenceFile('/tmp/sequencefile/')
```

We can then read the newly created `SequenceFile` and convert it to an RDD of (key, value) pairs:

```
# spark: an instance of SparkSession
rdd2 = spark.sparkContext.sequenceFile('/tmp/sequencefile/')
rdd2.collect()
[(u'key1', 10.0),
 (u'key2', 20.0),
 (u'key3', 30.0),
 (u'key4', 40.0)
]
```

Reading and Writing Parquet Files

Parquet (*https://parquet.apache.org*) is a columnar data format supported by many data processing systems. It's self-describing (metadata is included), language-independent, and ideal for fast analytics.

Spark SQL provides support for both reading and writing Parquet files while automatically preserving the schema of the original data. When writing Parquet files, all columns are automatically converted to be nullable for compatibility reasons.

Figure 7-3 illustrates a logical table and its associated row and column layouts.

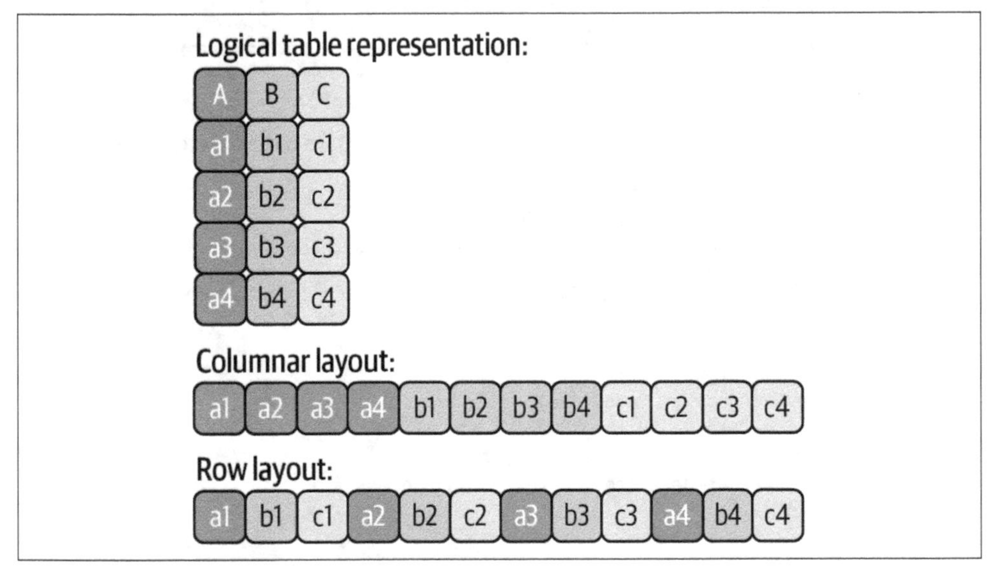

Figure 7-3. Logical table with row layout and column

Writing Parquet Files

In this section, I'll show you how to use the PySpark API to read a JSON file into a DataFrame and then save it as a Parquet file. Suppose we have the following JSON file:

```
$ cat examples/src/main/resources/employees.json
{"name":"Michael", "salary":3000}
{"name":"Andy", "salary":4500}
{"name":"Justin", "salary":3500}
{"name":"Berta", "salary":4000}
```

Using `DataFrameReader`, we read the JSON file into a DataFrame object as `peopleDF`:

```
>>> input_path = "examples/src/main/resources/employees.json"
>>> peopleDF = spark.read.json(input_path)
>>> peopleDF.show()
```

```
+-------+------+
|   name|salary|
+-------+------+
|Michael|  3000|
|   Andy|  4500|
| Justin|  3500|
|  Berta|  4000|
+-------+------+

>>> peopleDF.printSchema()
root
 |-- name: string (nullable = true)
 |-- salary: long (nullable = true)
```

We can then save this as a Parquet file, maintaining the schema information:

```
>>> peopleDF.write.parquet("file:///tmp/people.parquet")
```

You can inspect the contents of the directory to view the generated Parquet file:

```
$ ls -l /tmp/people.parquet/
-rw-r--r-- ...   0 Apr 30 15:06 _SUCCESS
-rw-r--r-- ... 634 Apr 30 15:06 part-00000-...-c000.snappy.parquet
```

For testing and debugging purposes, you may create Parquet files from Python collections:

```
>>> tuples =  [("alex", "Math", 97),
               ("jane", "Econ", 82),
               ("jane", "Math", 99)]
>>> column_names = ["name", "subject", "grade"]
>>> df = spark.createDataFrame(tuples, column_names) ❶
>>> df.show()
+----+-------+-----+
|name|subject|grade|
+----+-------+-----+
|alex|   Math|   97|
|jane|   Econ|   82|
|jane|   Math|   99|
+----+-------+-----+

>>> df.write.parquet("file:///tmp/parquet") ❷
```

 Convert your Python collection into a DataFrame.

❷ Save your DataFrame as a set of Parquet files.

Again, you can inspect the directory to view the created Parquet files:

```
$ ls -1 /tmp/parquet
_SUCCESS
part-00000-...-c000.snappy.parquet
part-00002-...-c000.snappy.parquet
```

```
part-00005-...-c000.snappy.parquet
part-00007-...-c000.snappy.parquet
```

Reading Parquet Files

In this section, using PySpark, we'll read in the Parquet file we just created. Note that Parquet files are self-describing, so the schema is preserved. The result of loading a Parquet file is a DataFrame:

```
>>> input_path = "file:///tmp/people.parquet"
>>> parquetFile = spark.read.parquet(input_path)
>>> parquetFile.show()
+-------+------+
|   name|salary|
+-------+------+
|Michael|  3000|
|   Andy|  4500|
| Justin|  3500|
|  Berta|  4000|
+-------+------+

>>> parquetFile.printSchema()
root
 |-- name: string (nullable = true)
 |-- salary: long (nullable = true)
```

Parquet files can also be used to create a temporary view and then used in SQL statements:

```
>>> parquetFile.createOrReplaceTempView("parquet_table") ❶
>>> query = "SELECT name, salary FROM parquet_table WHERE salary > 3800"
>>> filtered = spark.sql(query)
>>> filtered.show()
+-----+------+
| name|salary|
+-----+------+
| Andy|  4500|
|Berta|  4000|
+-----+------+
```

❶ `parquet_table` acts as a relational table.

Parquet supports collection data types, including an array type. The following example reads a Parquet file that uses arrays:

```
>>> parquet_file = "examples/src/main/resources/users.parquet"
>>> usersDF = spark.read.parquet(parquet_file)
>>> users.show()
+------+--------------+----------------+
|  name|favorite_color|favorite_numbers|
+------+--------------+----------------+
|Alyssa|          null|  [3, 9, 15, 20]|
```

```
|   Ben|             red|                []|
+------+----------------+------------------+

>>> usersDF.printSchema()
root
 |-- name: string (nullable = true)
 |-- favorite_color: string (nullable = true)
 |-- favorite_numbers: array (nullable = true)
 |    |-- element: integer (containsNull = true)
```

Reading and Writing Avro Files

Apache Avro (*https://avro.apache.org*) is a language-neutral data serialization system. It stores the data definition in JSON format, making it easy to read and interpret, while the data itself is stored in a compact, efficient binary format. Avro files include markers that can be used to split large datasets into subsets suitable for MapReduce processing. Avro is a very fast serialization format.

Reading Avro Files

Using PySpark, we can read an Avro file and create an associated DataFrame as follows:

```
$ pyspark --packages org.apache.spark:spark-avro_2.11:2.4.0 ❶
SparkSession available as spark.

>>> path = "/book/code/chap08/twitter.avro"
>>> df = spark.read.format("avro").load(path) ❷
>>> df.show(truncate=False)
+----------+-----------------------------------+----------+
|username  |tweet                              |timestamp |
+----------+-----------------------------------+----------+
|miguno    |Rock: Nerf paper, scissors is fine.|1366150681|
|BlizzardCS|Works as intended.  Terran is IMBA.|1366154481|
+----------+-----------------------------------+----------+
```

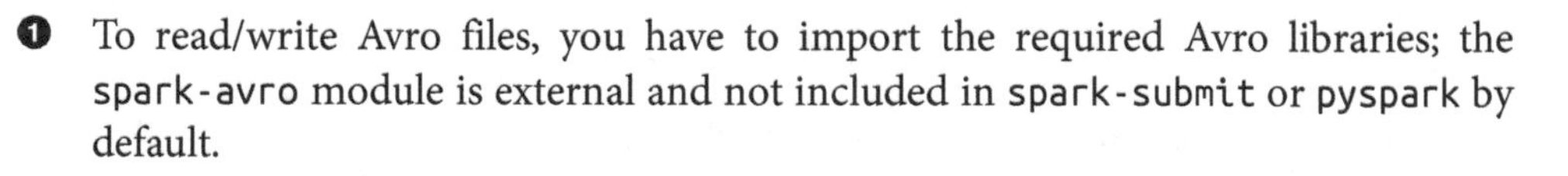

❶ To read/write Avro files, you have to import the required Avro libraries; the `spark-avro` module is external and not included in `spark-submit` or `pyspark` by default.

❷ Read an Avro file and create a DataFrame.

Writing Avro Files

It's just as easy to create an Avro file from a DataFrame. Here, we'll use the DataFrame created in the previous section), saving it as an Avro file and then reading it back in as a DataFrame:

```
$ pyspark --packages org.apache.spark:spark-avro_2.11:2.4.0 ❶
SparkSession available as spark.

>>># df : DataFrame (created in previous section)
>>> output_path = "/tmp/avro/mytweets.avro"
>>> df.select("username", "tweet")
      .write.format("avro")
      .save(output_path) ❷
>>> df2 = spark.read.format("avro").load(outputPath) ❸
>>> df2.show(truncate=False)
+----------+-----------------------------------+
|username  |tweet                              |
+----------+-----------------------------------+
|miguno    |Rock: Nerf paper, scissors is fine.|
|BlizzardCS|Works as intended.  Terran is IMBA.|
+----------+-----------------------------------+
```

❶ Import the required Avro libraries.

❷ Create an Avro file.

❸ Create a DataFrame from the new Avro file.

Reading from and Writing to MS SQL Server

MS SQL Server (*https://oreil.ly/2JckS*) is a relational database management system from Microsoft, designed and built to manage and store information as records in relational tables.

Writing to MS SQL Server

The following example shows how to write a DataFrame (`df`) into a new SQL Server table:

```
# define database URL
server_name = "jdbc:sqlserver://{SERVER_ADDRESS}"
database_name = "my_database_name"
url = server_name + ";" + "databaseName=" + database_name + ";"
# define table name and username/password
table_name = "my_table_name"
username = "my_username"
password = "my_password"

try:
  df.write \
    .format("com.microsoft.sqlserver.jdbc.spark") \ ❶
    .mode("overwrite") \ ❷
    .option("url", url) \
    .option("dbtable", table_name) \
    .option("user", username) \
```

```
        .option("password", password) \
        .save()
except ValueError as error :
    print("Connector write failed", error)
```

 The JAR file containing this class must be in your CLASSPATH.

❷ The `overwrite` mode first drops the table if it already exists in the database by default.

To append your DataFrame rows to an existing table, you just need to replace `mode("overwrite")` with `mode("append")`.

Note that Spark's MS SQL connector by default uses the `READ_COMMITTED` isolation level when performing a bulk insert into the database. If you wish to override the isolation level, use this `mssqlIsolationLevel` option as shown here:

```
    .option("mssqlIsolationLevel", "READ_UNCOMMITTED")
```

Reading from MS SQL Server

To read from an existing SQL Server table, you can use the following code snippet as a template:

```
jdbc_df = spark.read \
        .format("com.microsoft.sqlserver.jdbc.spark") \
        .option("url", url) \
        .option("dbtable", table_name) \
        .option("user", username) \
        .option("password", password)\
        .load()
```

Reading Image Files

Spark 2.4.0.+ enables us to read binary data which can be useful in many machine learning applications (such as face recognition and logistic regression). Spark can load image files from a directory into a DataFrame, transforming compressed images (*.jpg*, *.png*, etc.) into raw image representations via `ImageIO` in the Java library. The loaded *DataFrame* has one `StructType` column, `"image"`, containing image data stored as an image schema.

Creating a DataFrame from Images

Suppose we have the following images in a directory:

```
$ ls -l chap07/images
-rw-r--r--@ ...  27295 Feb  3 10:55 cat1.jpg
-rw-r--r--@ ...  35914 Feb  3 10:55 cat2.jpg
-rw-r--r--@ ...  26354 Feb  3 10:55 cat3.jpg
```

```
-rw-r--r--@ ...  30432 Feb  3 10:55 cat4.jpg
-rw-r--r--@ ...   6641 Feb  3 10:53 duck1.jpg
-rw-r--r--@ ...  11621 Feb  3 10:54 duck2.jpg
-rw-r--r--@ ...     13 Feb  3 10:55 not-image.txt ❶
```

❶ Not an image

We can load all the images into a DataFrame and ignore any files that are not images as follows:

```
>>> images_path = '/book/code/chap07/images'
>>> df = spark.read
            .format("image") ❶
            .option("dropInvalid", "true") ❷
            .load(images_path) ❸
>>> df.count()
6
```

 The `format` has to be `"image"`.

❷ Drop/ignore non-image files.

❸ Load images and create a DataFrame.

Let's examine the DataFrame's schema:

```
>>> df.printSchema()
root
 |-- image: struct (nullable = true)
 |    |-- origin: string (nullable = true) ❶
 |    |-- height: integer (nullable = true) ❷
 |    |-- width: integer (nullable = true) ❸
 |    |-- nChannels: integer (nullable = true) ❹
 |    |-- mode: integer (nullable = true) ❺
 |    |-- data: binary (nullable = true) ❻
```

❶ File path of the image

❷ Height of the image

❸ Width of the image

❹ Number of image channels

❺ OpenCV-compatible type

❻ Image bytes

Now, let's examine some of the columns in the created image DataFrame:

```
>>> df.select("image.origin", "image.width", "image.height")
      .show(truncate=False)
+-----------------------+-----+------+
|origin                 |width|height|
+-----------------------+-----+------+
|file:///book/.../cat2.jpg |300  |311   |
|file:///book/.../cat4.jpg |199  |313   |
|file:///book/.../cat1.jpg |300  |200   |
|file:///book/.../cat3.jpg |300  |296   |
|file:///book/.../duck2.jpg|275  |183   |
|file:///book/.../duck1.jpg|227  |222   |
+-----------------------+-----+------+
```

Summary

To recap:

- Reading and writing data is an integral part of data algorithms. Data sources should be carefully selected based on project and data requirements.
- The Spark DataSource API provides a pluggable mechanism for accessing structured data though Spark SQL. Data sources can be more than just simple pipes that convert data and pull it into Spark.
- Spark SQL supports reading data from existing relational database tables, Apache Hive tables, columnar storage formats like Parquet and ORC, and row-based storage formats like Avro. Spark provides a simple API to integrate with all JDBC-compliant relational databases, Amazon S3, HDFS, and more. You can also easily read data from and save it to external data sources such as text, CSV, and JSON files.

CHAPTER 8
Ranking Algorithms

This chapter introduces the following two ranking algorithms and presents their associated implementations in PySpark:

Rank product
: This algorithm finds the ranks of items (such as genes) among all items. It was originally developed for the detection of differentially expressed genes in replicated microarray experiments, but has since achieved widespread acceptance and is now used more broadly, including in machine learning. Spark does not provide an API for the rank product, so I will present a custom solution.

PageRank
: PageRank is an iterative algorithm for measuring the importance of nodes in a given graph. This algorithm is used heavily by search engines (such as Google) to find the importance of each web page (document) relative to all web pages (a set of documents). In a nutshell, given a set of web pages, the PageRank algorithm calculates a quality ranking for each page. The Spark API offers multiple solutions for the PageRank algorithm. I'll present one of those, using the GraphFrames API, as well as two custom solutions.

Source Code

Complete programs for this chapter are available in the book's GitHub repository (*https://oreil.ly/UDBX4*).

Rank Product

The rank product is an algorithm commonly used in the field of bioinformatics, also known as computational biology. It was originally developed as a biologically motivated test for the detection of differentially expressed genes in replicated micro-array experiments. As well as expression profiling, it can be used to combine ranked lists in other application domains, such as for statistical meta-analysis and general feature selection. In bioinformatics and machine learning, the rank product has emerged as a simple and intuitive yet powerful ranking method.

The algorithm does not use any statistics (such as mean or variance), but rather scores items (such as genes) on the basis of their ranks in multiple comparisons. It's particularly useful if you have very few replicates (in the context of gene analysis), or if you want to analyze how well the results from two studies agree.

The rank product algorithm is based on the assumption that under the null hypothesis, given that the order of all items is random, the probability (p) of finding a specific item among the top r of n items in a list is:

$$p = \frac{r}{n}$$

Multiplying these probabilities leads to the definition of the rank product:

$$RP = \left(\Pi_i \frac{r_i}{n_i}\right)$$

where r_i is the rank of the item in the ith list and n_i is the total number of items in the ith list. The smaller the RP value is, the smaller the probability is that the observed placement of the item at the top of the lists is due to chance. The rank product is equivalent to calculating the geometric mean rank; replacing the product by the sum leads to a statistic (average rank) that is slightly more sensitive to outlier data and puts a higher premium on consistency between the ranks in various lists.

Is this a big data problem? Consider 100 studies, each with 1,000,000 assays and each assay with 60,000 records. This translates to 100 × 1,000,000 × 60,000 = 6,000,000,000,000 records, which is definitely big data.

Calculation of the Rank Product

Given n genes and k replicates, let $e_{g,i}$ be the fold change and $r_{g,i}$ the rank of gene g in the ith replicate.

Compute the rank product (RP) via the geometric mean:

$$RP(g) = \left(\Pi_{i=1}^{k} r_{g,i}\right)^{1/k}$$

or

$$RP(g) = \sqrt[k]{\left(\Pi_{i=1}^{k} r_{g,i}\right)}$$

Formalizing Rank Product

To help you understand the rank product algorithm, I will provide a concrete example. Let `{A1, ..., Ak}` be datasets of (key, value) pairs, where the keys are unique per dataset. For example, a key might be an item, a user, or a gene, and a value might be the number of items sold, the number of friends of that user, or a gene value such as fold change or test expression. Ranks are assigned (typically based on the sorted values of the datasets), and the rank product of `{A1, ..., Ak}` is computed based on the ranks `ri` for key `i` across all datasets.

Let's work through a very simple example using three datasets, A_1, A_2, A_3. Suppose dataset A_1 is composed of the following (key, value) pairs:

```
A1 = { (K1, 30), (K2, 60), (K3, 10), (K4, 80) }
```

If we assign the ranks based on the descending sorted values of the keys, we get:

```
Rank(A1) = { (K1, 3), (K2, 2), (K3, 4), (K4, 1) }
```

since `80 > 60 > 30 > 10`. Note that 1 is the highest rank (assigned to the largest value). We then do the same for dataset A_2, which has the following contents:

```
A2 = { (K1, 90), (K2, 70), (K3, 40), (K4, 50) }
```

This gives us:

```
Rank(A2) = { (K1, 1), (K2, 2), (K3, 4), (K4, 3) }
```

since `90 > 70 > 50 > 40`. Finally, dataset A_3 looks like this:

```
A3 = { (K1, 4), (K2, 8) }
```

In this case assigning the ranks gives us:

```
Rank(A3) = { (K1, 2), (K2, 1) }
```

since 8 > 4. The rank product of $\{A_1, A_2, A_3\}$ is then expressed as:

$$\left(K_1, \sqrt[3]{3 \times 1 \times 2}\right),$$

$$\left(K_2, \sqrt[3]{2 \times 2 \times 1}\right),$$

$$\left(K_3, \sqrt[2]{4 \times 4}\right),$$

$$\left(K_4, \sqrt[2]{1 \times 3}\right)$$

Rank Product Example

Now let's walk through a real-world example of using rank product:

- Let $S = \{S_1, S_2, ..., S_k\}$ be a set of k studies, where $k > 0$ and each study represents a micro-array experiment.
- Let S_i $(i=1, 2, ..., k)$ be a study, which has an arbitrary number of assays identified by $\{A_{i1}, A_{i2}, ...\}$.
- Let each assay (which can be represented as a text file) be a set of an arbitrary number of records in the following format:

  ```
  <gene_id><,><gene_value_as_double_data_type>
  ```

- Let gene_id be in $\{g_1, g_2, ..., g_n\}$ (we have n genes).

To find the rank product of all studies, first we find the mean of values per gene per study, then for each study we sort the genes by value and assign each one a rank. For example, suppose our first study has three assays with the values shown in Table 8-1.

Table 8-1. Gene values for study 1

Assay 1	Assay 2	Assay 3
g1,1.0	g1,2.0	g1,12.0
g2,3.0	g2,5.0	null
g3,4.0	null	g3,2.0
g4,1.0	g4,3.0	g4,15.0

The first step is to find the mean of values for each gene (per study). This gives us:

```
g1, 5.0
g2, 4.0
g3, 2.0
g4, 8.0
```

Sorting by value will generate the following results:

```
g4, 8.0
g1, 5.0
g2, 4.0
g3, 2.0
```

Next, we assign each gene a rank for that study, based on the sorted values. In this case, the result will be as follows (where the last column is the rank):

```
g4, 8.0, 1
g1, 5.0, 2
g2, 4.0, 3
g3, 2.0, 4
```

We repeat this process for all the studies to find the rank product (RP) for each gene per study. If:

$$S_1 = \{(g_1, r_{11}), (g_2, r_{12}), \ldots\}$$

$$S_2 = \{(g_1, r_{21}), (g_2, r_{22}), \ldots\}$$

$$\ldots$$

$$S_k = \{(g_1, r_{k1}), (g_2, r_{k2}), \ldots\}$$

Then, the rank product of gene g_j can be expressed as:

$$RP(g_j) = \left(\Pi_{i=1}^{k} r_{i,j}\right)^{1/k}$$

or:

$$RP(g_j) = \sqrt[k]{\left(\Pi_{i=1}^{k} r_{i,j}\right)}$$

Now, let's dig into a solution using PySpark.

PySpark Solution

As mentioned previously, Spark does not provide an API for the rank product algorithm, so I've developed my own solution.

A webcast presenting my solution for rank product using the Java API for Spark is available on the O'Reilly website (*https://oreil.ly/clYwx*), and the associated Java Spark code is available on GitHub (*https://oreil.ly/pPmOX*).

The PySpark solution presented here will accept `K` input paths (continuing with the previous example, we'll say that each path represents a study, which may have any number of assay files). At a high level, these are the steps we'll use to find the rank product of each gene that appears in these studies:

1. Find the mean value per gene per study (in some situations you may prefer to apply other functions to find the median). We'll use COPA scores as our values.[1]
2. Sort the genes by value per study and then assign rank values (rank values will be `{1, 2, ..., N}` where `1` is assigned to the highest value and *N* is assigned to the lowest).
3. Finally, compute the rank product per gene for all studies. This can be accomplished by grouping all ranks by key.

To implement the final step, we may use `RDD.groupByKey()` or `RDD.combineByKey()`. Both solutions are available on GitHub (*https://oreil.ly/SFfH3*), labeled as *rank_product_using_groupbykey.py* and *rank_product_using_combinebykey.py*.

Note that the PySpark solution using `combineByKey()` is more efficient than the `groupByKey()` solution. As discussed in Chapter 4, this is because `combineByKey()` intermediate values are reduced (or combined) by local workers before being sent for the final reduction, whereas with `groupByKey()` there is no local reduction; all values are sent to one location for further processing. I will only present the solution with `combineByKey()` in detail here.

Input data format

Each assay (which can be represented as a text file) is a set of an arbitrary number of records in the following format:

```
<gene_id><,><gene_value_as_double_data_type>
```

where `gene_id` is a key which has an associated value of type `Double`.

For demonstration purposes, where `K=3` (number of studies), I will use the following sample input:

1 Cancer Outlier Profile Analysis (COPA) is an outlier detection method used in gene analysis. Genes are grouped into mutually exclusive gene pairs, and ranked according to the number of tumor samples in which either of them is an outlier.

```
$ cat /tmp/rankproduct/input/rp1.txt
K_1,30.0
K_2,60.0
K_3,10.0
K_4,80.0

$ cat /tmp/rankproduct/input/rp2.txt
K_1,90.0
K_2,70.0
K_3,40.0
K_4,50.0

$ cat /tmp/rankproduct/input/rp3.txt
K_1,4.0
K_2,8.0
```

Output data format

We will generate output in the following format:

```
<gene_id><,><R><,><N>
```

where *<R>* is the rank product among all the input datasets and *<N>* is the number of values participating in computing the rank product.

Rank product solution using combineByKey()

The complete solution is presented in the program *rank_product_using_combineby-key.py*. It requires the following input/output parameters:

```
# define input/output parameters:
#    sys.argv[1] = output path
#    sys.argv[2] = number of studies (K)
#    sys.argv[3] =   input path for study 1
#    sys.argv[4] =   input path for study 2
#    ...
#    sys.argv[K+2] = input path for study K
```

To implement a PySpark solution to the rank product problem using the `combineByKey()` transformation I used the following driver program, which calls several Python functions:

```
# Create an instance of SparkSession
spark = SparkSession.builder.getOrCreate()

# Handle input parameters
output_path = sys.argv[1]

# K = number of studies to process
K = int(sys.argv[2])

# Define studies_input_path
studies_input_path = [sys.argv[i+3] for i in range(K)]
```

```
# Step 1: Compute the mean per gene per study
means = [compute_mean(studies_input_path[i]) for i in range(K)]

# Step 2: Compute the rank of each gene per study
ranks = [assign_rank(means[i]) for i in range(K)]

# Step 3: Calculate the rank product for each gene
# rank_products: RDD[(gene_id, (ranked_product, N))]
rank_products = compute_rank_products(ranks)

# Step 4: Save the result
rank_products.saveAsTextFile(output_path)
```

Let's take a closer look at the three main steps.

Step 1: Compute the mean per gene per study. To find the rank product of our dataset, we first need to find the mean value of each gene per study. This is accomplished with the `compute_mean()` function. To calculate the mean of values per key (`gene_id`) using the `combineByKey()` transformation, we can create a combined data type as `(Double, Integer)` which denotes `(sum-of-values, count-of-values)`. Finally, to find the means, we divide `sum-of-values` by `count-of-values`:

```
# Compute mean per gene for a single study = set of assays
# @param input_Path set of assay paths separated by ","
# @RETURN RDD[(String, Double)]
def compute_mean(input_path):
   # genes as string records: RDD[String]
   raw_genes = spark.sparkContext.textFile(input_path)

   # create RDD[(String, Double)]=RDD[(gene_id, test_expression)]
   genes = raw_genes.map(create_pair)

   # create RDD[(gene_id, (sum, count))]
   genes_combined = genes.combineByKey(
       lambda v: (v, 1), # createCombiner
       lambda C, v: (C[0]+v, C[1]+1), # addAndCount
       lambda C, D: (C[0]+D[0], C[1]+D[1]) # mergeCombiners
   )

   # now compute the mean per gene
   genes_mean = genes_combined.mapValues(lambda p: float(p[0])/float(p[1]))
   return genes_mean
#end-def
```

Step 2: Compute the rank of each gene per study. To compute the rank of each `gene_id`, we perform the following three substeps: . Sort values based on absolute value of COPA scores. To sort by COPA score, we will swap the keys with the values and then sort by key. . Assign a rank from 1 (for the gene with the highest COPA score) to *n* (for the gene with the lowest COPA score). . Calculate the rank for each `gene_id` using `Math.power(`R_1 `*` R_2 `* ... *` R_n`, 1/n)`.

This entire step is accomplished by the `assign_rank()` function. Ranks are assigned by using `RDD.zipWithIndex()`, which zips this RDD with its element indices (these indices will be the ranks). Spark indices start from 0, so we add 1 when computing the rank product:

```
# @param rdd : RDD[(String, Double)]: (gene_id, mean)
# @returns: RDD[(String, Long)]: (gene_id, rank)
def assign_rank(rdd):
    # Swap key and value (will be used for sorting by key)
    # Convert value to abs(value)
    swapped_rdd = rdd.map(lambda v: (abs(v[1]), v[0]))

    # Sort COPA scores in descending order. We need 1 partition so
    # that we can zip numbers into this RDD with zipWithIndex().
    # If we do not use 1 partition, then indexes will be meaningless.
    # sorted_rdd : RDD[(Double,String)]
    sorted_rdd = swapped_rdd.sortByKey(False, 1)

    # Use zipWithIndex(). Zip values will be 0, 1, 2, ...
    # but for ranking we need 1, 2, 3, .... Therefore,
    # we will add 1 when calculating the rank product.
    # indexed:  RDD[((Double,String), Long)]
    indexed = sorted_rdd.zipWithIndex()

    # add 1 to index to start with 1 rather than 0
    # ranked:  RDD[(String, Long)]
    ranked = indexed.map(lambda v: (v[0][1], v[1]+1))
    return ranked
#end-def
```

Step 3: Calculate the rank product for each gene. Finally, we call `compute_rank_products()` to calculate the rank product for each gene, which combines all the ranks into one RDD and then calculates the rank product for each gene using the `combineByKey()` transformation:

```
# return RDD[(String, (Double, Integer))] = (gene_id, (ranked_product, N))
# where N is the number of elements for computing the rank product
# @param ranks: array of RDD[(String, Long)]
def compute_rank_products(ranks):
        # combine all ranks into one
        union_rdd = spark.sparkContext.union(ranks)

        # next, find unique keys with their associated COPA scores
        # we need 3 basic function to be able to use combinebyKey()
        # combined_by_gene: RDD[(String, (Double, Integer))]
        combined_by_gene = union_rdd.combineByKey(
             lambda v: (v, 1), # createCombiner as C
             lambda C, v: (C[0]*v, C[1]+1), # multiplyAndCount
```

```
                lambda C, D: (C[0]*D[0], C[1]+D[1]) # mergeCombiners
                    )

        # next calculate rank products and the number of elements
        rank_products = combined_by_gene.mapValues(
            lambda v : (pow(float(v[0]), float(v[1])), v[1])
        )

        return rank_products
#end-def
```

Let's go through a sample run using `combineByKey()`:

```
INPUT1=/tmp/rankproduct/input/rp1.txt
INPUT2=/tmp/rankproduct/input/rp2.txt
INPUT3=/tmp/rankproduct/input/rp3.txt
OUTPUT=/tmp/rankproduct/output
PROG=rank_product_using_combinebykey.py
./bin/spark-submit $PROG $OUTPUT 3 $INPUT1 $INPUT2 $INPUT3

output_path=/tmp/rankproduct/output
K=3
studies_input_path ['/tmp/rankproduct/input/rp1.txt',
'/tmp/rankproduct/input/rp2.txt',
'/tmp/rankproduct/input/rp3.txt']
input_path /tmp/rankproduct/input/rp1.txt
raw_genes ['K_1,30.0', 'K_2,60.0', 'K_3,10.0', 'K_4,80.0']
genes [('K_1', 30.0), ('K_2', 60.0), ('K_3', 10.0), ('K_4', 80.0)]
genes_combined [('K_2', (60.0, 1)), ('K_3', (10.0, 1)),
                ('K_1', (30.0, 1)), ('K_4', (80.0, 1))]
input_path /tmp/rankproduct/input/rp2.txt
raw_genes ['K_1,90.0', 'K_2,70.0', 'K_3,40.0', 'K_4,50.0']
genes [('K_1', 90.0), ('K_2', 70.0), ('K_3', 40.0), ('K_4', 50.0)]
genes_combined [('K_2', (70.0, 1)), ('K_3', (40.0, 1)),
                ('K_1', (90.0, 1)), ('K_4', (50.0, 1))]
input_path /tmp/rankproduct/input/rp3.txt
raw_genes ['K_1,4.0', 'K_2,8.0']
genes [('K_1', 4.0), ('K_2', 8.0)]
genes_combined [('K_2', (8.0, 1)), ('K_1', (4.0, 1))]
sorted_rdd [(80.0, 'K_4'), (60.0, 'K_2'), (30.0, 'K_1'), (10.0, 'K_3')]
indexed [((80.0, 'K_4'), 0), ((60.0, 'K_2'), 1),
         ((30.0, 'K_1'), 2), ((10.0, 'K_3'), 3)]
ranked [('K_4', 1), ('K_2', 2), ('K_1', 3), ('K_3', 4)]
sorted_rdd [(90.0, 'K_1'), (70.0, 'K_2'), (50.0, 'K_4'), (40.0, 'K_3')]
indexed [((90.0, 'K_1'), 0), ((70.0, 'K_2'), 1),
         ((50.0, 'K_4'), 2), ((40.0, 'K_3'), 3)]
ranked [('K_1', 1), ('K_2', 2), ('K_4', 3), ('K_3', 4)]
sorted_rdd [(8.0, 'K_2'), (4.0, 'K_1')]
indexed [((8.0, 'K_2'), 0), ((4.0, 'K_1'), 1)]
ranked [('K_2', 1), ('K_1', 2)]
```

Here is the final output per key:

```
$ cat /rankproduct/output/part*
(K_2,(1.5874010519681994, 3))
(K_1,(1.8171205928321397, 3))
(K_4,(1.7320508075688772, 2))
(K_3,(4.0, 2))
```

Rank product solution using groupByKey()

A rank product solution using the `groupByKey()` transformation instead of `combineByKey()` is available on GitHub, as *rank_product_using_groupbykey.py*. Overall, the `combineByKey()` solution is more scalable because of how the shuffle step is implemented by these two transformations: `combineByKey()` uses combiners as much as possible, but `groupByKey()` takes all the values to a single place and then applies the required algorithms.

PageRank

In this section we'll turn our attention to another ranking algorithm: PageRank. This algorithm made Google stand out from other search engines, and it is still an essential part of how search engines know what pages a user is likely to want to see, as it allows them to determine a page's relevance or importance with respect to others. Extensions of the PageRank algorithm have also been used to fight against spam.

For details on how PageRank works under the hood (or at least, how it used to), see the article "Understanding Google Page Rank" (*https://oreil.ly/9DDEn*) by Ian Rogers.

The PageRank algorithm measures the importance of each node in a graph (such as the web pages on the internet), assuming an edge from node `u` to node `v` represents an endorsement of `v`'s importance by `u`. The main premise is that a node is important if other important nodes point to it. For example, if a Twitter user is followed by many other users—particularly users who themselves have large numbers of followers—then that user will be ranked highly. Any web designer who wants to improve their site's search engine ranking should take the time to fully understand how PageRank really works. (Note that PageRank is purely a link analysis algorithm and says nothing about the language, content, or size of a page.)

Figure 8-1 illustrates the concept of PageRank using a simple graph representing a set of linked documents.

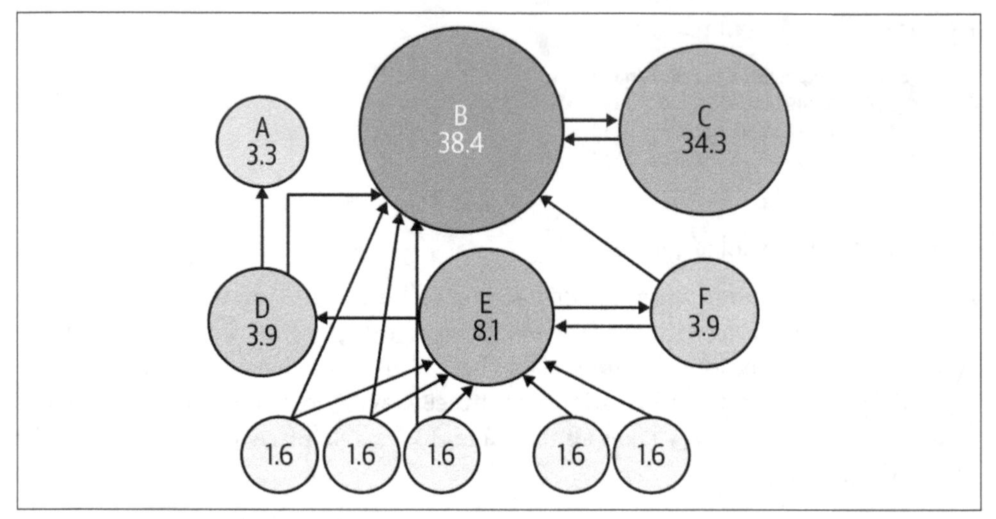

Figure 8-1. PageRank example

Notice that page C has a higher PageRank than page E, even though there are fewer links to C; this is because the one link to C comes from a very important page (page B) and hence is of high value. Without damping, all web surfers would eventually end up on pages B or C (since they have the highest PageRank scores), and all other pages would have PageRank scores close to zero.

The PageRank algorithm is an iterative and converging algorithm. It begins at step one with some initial PageRank (as a `Double` data type) assigned to all pages, and the algorithm is then applied iteratively until it arrives at a steady state called the convergence point. This is the point at which a PageRank has been distributed to all pages, and a subsequent iteration of the algorithm will produce little or no further change in the distribution (you can specify the threshold for this).

Let's take a look at how the algorithm is defined. Here, we'll assume page A is pointed to (cited) by pages $\{T_1, \ldots, T_n\}$. The PageRank (*PR*) of page `A` is then given as follows:

$$PR(A) = (1 - d) + d \times \left[\frac{PR(T_1)}{L(T_1)} + \ldots + \frac{PR(T_n)}{L(T_n)} \right]$$

where d is a damping factor that can be set between 0 and 1 (the usual value is 0.85), $PR(T_i)$ is the PageRank of page T_i that links to page A, and $L(T_i)$ is the number of outbound links on page T_i. Note that the PageRanks form a probability distribution over web pages, so the sum of all web pages' PageRanks will be 1.

Why is a damping factor added? PageRank is based on the random surfer model. Essentially, the damping factor is a decay factor. It represents the chance that a user will stop clicking links and request another random page (e.g., by directly typing in a new URL rather than following a link on the current page). A damping factor of 0.85 indicates that we assume there is about a 15% chance that a typical user won't follow any links on the page and instead will navigate to a new random URL.

Given a graph of web pages with incoming and outgoing links, the PageRank algorithm can tell us the importance or relevance of each node. The PageRank of each page depends on the PageRanks of the pages pointing to it. In short, PageRank is a "vote," by all the other pages on the web, about how important a page is.

PageRank's Iterative Computation

Given a set of N web pages, PageRank can be computed either iteratively or algebraically. The iterative method can be defined as follows:

1. At `(t = 0)`, an initial probability distribution is assumed, usually:

$$PR(p_i, 0) = \frac{1}{N}$$

2. At each time step, the computation, as detailed above, yields:

$$PR(p_i, t+1) = \frac{1-d}{N} + d \sum_{p_j \in B_{p_i}} \frac{PR(p_j, t)}{L(p_j)}$$

It is believed that Google (and other search engines) recalculates PageRank scores each time it crawls the web and rebuilds its search index. As the number of documents in the collection increases, the accuracy of the initial approximation of PageRank decreases for all documents. Therefore, the PageRank algorithm ranks websites by the number and quality of incoming links. The quality of an incoming link is defined as a function of the PageRank of the site that provides the link.

Please note that this is an extremely simplified description of the original PageRank algorithm. Google (and others who use similar PageRank algorithms) take many other factors, such as keyword density, traffic, domain age, etc., into consideration for calculating the PageRank of a web page.

Next, I'll show you how the PageRank is calculated. Suppose we have the following simple graph:

```
$ cat simple_graph.txt
A B
B A
A D
D A
```

Setting `d = 0.85`, we can write:

```
PR(A) = (1-d) + d (PR(B)/L(B) + PR(D)/L(D))
PR(B) = (1-d) + d (PR(A)/L(A))
PR(D) = (1-d) + d (PR(A)/L(A))
```

where:

```
L(A) = 2
L(B) = 1
L(D) = 1
```

To calculate these `PR()` iteratively, we need to initialize `PR(A)`, `PR(B)`, `PR(D)`. We'll initialize all of them to `1.0`, then iteratively calculate `PR(A)`, `PR(B)`, `PR(D)` until these values do not change (i.e., converge). The results are shown in Table 8-2.

Table 8-2. PageRank iterations with initial value of 1.00

Iteration	PR(A)	PR(B)	PR(D)
0	1.0000	1.0000	1.0000
1	1.8500	0.9362	0.9362
...	...	...	...
99	1.4595	0.7703	0.7703
100	1.4595	0.7703	0.7703

Note that no matter what you use as the initial value, the PageRank algorithm converges and you get the desired results. Table 8-3 shows the results with an initialization value of 40.00.

Table 8-3. PageRank iterations with initial value of 40.00

Iteration	PR(A)	PR(B)	PR(D)
0	40.0000	40.0000	40.0000
1	68.1500	29.1138	29.1137
...	...	...	...
99	1.4595	0.7703	0.7703
100	1.4595	0.7703	0.7703

In both cases, the results are the same after 100 iterations:

```
PR(A) = 1.4595
PR(B) = 0.7703
PR(D) = 0.7703
```

As you saw in Chapter 6, Spark provides APIs for implementing the PageRank algorithm through the GraphX and GraphFrames libraries. To help you understand how the algorithm works, here I'll present a couple of custom PageRank solutions in PySpark.

Custom PageRank in PySpark Using RDDs

I'll start by providing a simple custom solution using PySpark. The complete program and sample input data are available in the book's GitHub repository, in the files *pagerank.py* and *pagerank_data.txt*.

This solution uses Spark RDDs to implement the PageRank algorithm. It does not use GraphX or GraphFrames, but I'll present a GraphFrames example later.

Input data format

Let's assume that our input has the following syntax:

```
<source-URL-ID><,><neighbor-URL-ID>
```

Output data format

The goal of the PageRank algorithm is to generate output of the form:

```
<URL-ID> <page-rank-value>
```

The result will look something like this, if the algorithm is run for 15 iterations:

```
$ spark-submit pagerank.py pagerank_data.txt 15
1 has rank: 0.86013842528.
3 has rank: 0.33174213968.
2 has rank: 0.33174213968.
5 has rank: 0.473769824736.
4 has rank: 0.33174213968.
```

PySpark Solution

Our custom solution involves the following steps:

1. Read the input path and the number of iterations:

   ```
   input_path = sys.argv[1]
   num_of_iterations = int(sys.argv[2])
   ```

2. Create an instance of `SparkSession`:

   ```
   spark = SparkSession.builder.getOrCreate()
   ```

3. Create an RDD[String] from the input path:

```
records = spark.sparkContext.textFile(input_path)
```

4. Load all the URLs from the input file and initialize their neighbors:

```
def create_pair(record_of_urls):
    # record_of_urls = "<source-URL><,><neighbor-URL>"
    tokens = record_of_urls.split(",")
    source_URL = tokens[0]
    neighbor_URL = tokens[1]
    return (source_URL, neighbor_URL)
#end-def

links = records.map(lambda rec: create_pair(rec)) ❶
               .distinct() ❷
               .groupByKey() ❸
               .cache() ❹
```

 Create a pair of (source_URL, neighbor_URL).

❷ Make sure there are no duplicate pairs.

❸ Find all neighbor URLs.

❹ Cache the result, because it will be used many times in the iteration.

5. Transform URL neighbors into ranks of 1.0:

```
ranks = links.map(lambda url_neighbors: (url_neighbors[0], 1.0)) ❶
```

❶ ranks is an RDD[(String, Float)].

6. Calculate and update the URL ranks iteratively. To perform this step, we need two basic functions:

```
def recalculate_rank(rank):
    new_rank = (rank * 0.85) + 0.15
    return new_rank
#end-def

def compute_contributions(urls_rank):
    # calculates URL contributions
    # to the ranks of other URLs
    urls = urls_rank[1][0]
    rank = urls_rank[1][1]

    num_urls = len(urls)
    for url in urls:
        yield (url, rank / num_urls)
#end-def
```

Now, let's perform the iterations:

```
for iteration in range(num_of_iterations):
    # calculates URL contributions
    # to the ranks of other URLs
    contributions = links
       .join(ranks) ❶
       .flatMap(compute_contributions)

    # recalculates URL ranks based
    # on neighbor contributions
    ranks = contributions.reduceByKey(lambda x,y : x+y)
                         .mapValues(recalculate_rank)
#end-for
```

 Note that `links.join(ranks)` will create elements of the form `[(URL_ID, (ResultIterable, <rank-as-float>)), ...]`.

7. Collect the PageRank values for all the URLs and dump them to the console:

```
for (link, rank) in ranks.collect():
    print("%s has rank: %s." % (link, rank))
```

Sample output

Sample output is provided for 20 iterations. You can observe the convergence of the PageRank algorithm in the higher iterations (iteration numbers 16 to 20):

```
iteration/node   1      2      3      4      5
0              1.00   1.00   1.00   1.00   null
1              2.27   0.36   0.36   0.36   0.79
2              0.92   0.63   0.63   0.63   0.79
...
19             0.86   0.33   0.33   0.33   0.47
20             0.85   0.33   0.33   0.33   0.47
```

Custom PageRank in PySpark Using an Adjacency Matrix

This section presents another custom solution for the PageRank algorithm, using an adjacency matrix as input. An adjacency matrix is a matrix used to represent a finite graph. The elements of the matrix indicate whether or not pairs of nodes are adjacent in the graph. For example, if node `A` links to three other nodes (say, `B`, `C`, and `D`), that is presented as an adjacency matrix row like this:

```
A B C D
```

Suppose we have the graph shown in Figure 8-2.

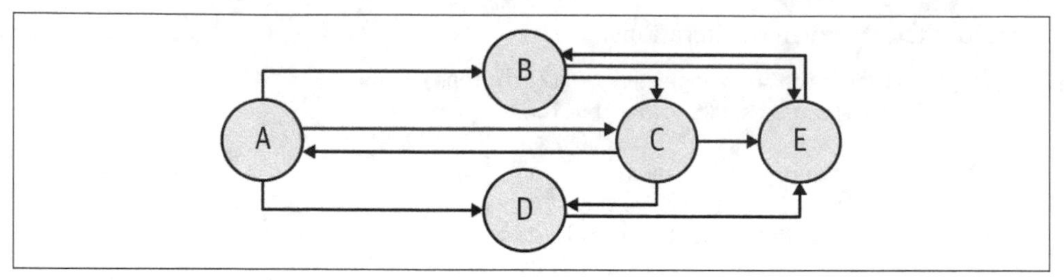

Figure 8-2. A simple directed graph with five nodes

The adjacency matrix for this graph looks like this (where the first item in each row is the source node and the other items are target nodes):

```
A B C D
B C E
C A D E
D E
E B
```

A visual inspection of the graph or the matrix suggests that `E` is an important node, since it's referenced by many other nodes. Therefore, we expect that the PageRank value of node `E` will be higher than that of the other nodes.

This solution again uses Spark RDDs to implement the PageRank algorithm and does not use GraphX or GraphFrames. The complete program and sample input data are available in the book's GitHub repository, in the files *pagerank_2.py* and *pagerank_data_2.txt*.

Input data format

Let's assume that our input has the following syntax, where `S` is a single space:

```
<source-node><S><target-node-1><S><target-node-2><S>...

where S is a single space
```

Output data format

The goal of the PageRank algorithm is to generate output of the form:

```
<node> <page-rank-value>
```

PySpark solution

Our second PySpark solution consists of three main steps:

1. Mapping: For each node `i`, calculate the value to assign to each outlink (rank / number of neighbors) and propagate it to the adjacent nodes.

2. Reducing: For each node `i`, sum the upcoming votes/values and update the rank (R_i).
3. Iteration: Repeat until the values converge (stable or within a defined margin).

The complete PySpark solution is presented here. First, we import the required libraries and read the input parameters:

```
from __future__ import print_function
import sys
from pyspark.sql import SparkSession

# Define your input path
input_path = sys.argv[1]
print("input_path: ", input_path)
# input_path:  pagerank_data_2.txt

# Define number of iterations
ITERATIONS = int(sys.argv[2])
print("ITERATIONS: ", ITERATIONS)
# ITERATIONS:  40
```

Next, we read the matrix and create pairs of `(K, V)`, where `K` is the source node and `V` is a list of target nodes:

```
# Create an instance of SparkSession
spark = SparkSession.builder.getOrCreate()

# Read adjacency list and create RDD[String]
matrix = spark.sparkContext.textFile(input_path)
print("matrix=", matrix.collect())
# matrix= ['A B C D', 'B C E', 'C A D E', 'D E', 'E B']
# x = "A B C"
# returns (A, [B, C])
def create_pair(x):
  tokens = x.split(" ")
  # tokens[0]: source node
  # tokens[1:]: target nodes (links from the source node)
  return (tokens[0], tokens[1:])
#end-def

# create links from source node to target nodes
links = matrix.map(create_pair)
print("links=", links.collect())
# links= [('A', ['B', 'C', 'D']),
#         ('B', ['C', 'E']),
#         ('C', ['A', 'D', 'E']),
#         ('D', ['E']),
#         ('E', ['B'])]
```

We count the nodes and initialize the rank of each to `1.0`:

```
# Find node count
N = links.count()
print("node count N=", N)
# node count N=5

# Create and initialize the ranks
ranks = links.map(lambda node: (node[0], 1.0/N))
print("ranks=", ranks.collect())
# ranks= [('A', 0.2), ('B', 0.2), ('C', 0.2), ('D', 0.2), ('E', 0.2)]
```

Then we implement the three steps of the PageRank algorithm:

```
for i in range(ITERATIONS):
  # Join graph info with rank info, propagate rank scores
  # to all neighbors (rank/(number of neighbors),
  # and add up ranks from all incoming edges
  ranks = links.join(ranks)\
    .flatMap(lambda x : [(i, float(x[1][1])/len(x[1][0])) for i in x[1][0]])\
    .reduceByKey(lambda x,y: x+y)
  print(ranks.sortByKey().collect())
```

Partial output is given here:

```
[('A', 0.0667), ('B', 0.2667), ('C', 0.1667), ('D', 0.1334), ('E', 0.3667)]
[('A', 0.0556), ('B', 0.3889), ('C', 0.1556), ('D', 0.0778), ('E', 0.3223)]
...
[('A', 0.0638), ('B', 0.3404), ('C', 0.1915), ('D', 0.0851), ('E', 0.3191)]
[('A', 0.0638), ('B', 0.3404), ('C', 0.1915), ('D', 0.0851), ('E', 0.3191)]
```

The PageRank algorithm indicates that node `E` is the most important node, since its page rank (`0.3191`) is the highest. We also observe that, since the PageRanks form a probability distribution, the sum of the values for all the nodes will be 1:

```
PR(A) + PR(B) + PR(C) + PR(D) + PR(E) =
0.0638 + 0.3404 + 0.1915 + 0.0851 + 0.3191 =
0.9999
```

To wrap up this section, I'll quickly run through an example using GraphFrames.

PageRank with GraphFrames

The following example in PySpark shows how to find the PageRank of a graph using the GraphFrames package introduced in Chapter 6. There are at least two ways to calculate the page rank of a given graph:

Tolerance

Specify the tolerance allowed at convergence (note that a smaller tolerance results in greater accuracy of the PageRank results):

```
# build graph as a GraphFrame instance
graph = GraphFrame(vertices, edges)
#
# NOTE: You cannot specify maxIter()
# and tol() at the same time.
# damping factor = 1 - 0.15 = 0.85
# tol = the tolerance allowed at convergence
# (smaller => more accurate)
# pagerank is computed as a GraphFrame:
pagerank = graph
             .pageRank()
             .resetProbability(0.15)
             .tol(0.0001)
             .run()
```

Maximum iterations

Specify the maximum number of iterations for which the algorithm can run (more iterations results in greater accuracy):

```
# build graph as a GraphFrame instance
graph = GraphFrame(vertices, edges)
# NOTE: You cannot specify maxIter()
# and tol() at the same time.
# damping factor = 1 - 0.15 = 0.85
# maxIter = the max. number of iterations
# (higher => more accurate)
# pagerank is computed as a GraphFrame:
pagerank = graph
            .pageRank()
            .resetProbability(0.15)
            .maxIter(30)
            .run()
```

Summary

To recap:

- We covered two ranking algorithms, rank product (mostly used in gene analysis) and PageRank (primarily used in search engine algorithms).
- Spark does not provide an API for the rank product, but I presented a custom PySpark solution.
- Spark is capable of handling record-level algorithms as well as graph algorithms —two custom PySpark implementations of PageRank were presented, in addition to the use of the GraphFrames API.

In the following chapters, we'll turn our attention to some practical fundamental data design patterns.

PART III
Data Design Patterns

CHAPTER 9

Classic Data Design Patterns

This chapter discusses some of the most fundamental and classic data design patterns used in the vast majority of big data solutions. Even though these are simple design patterns, they are useful in solving many common data problems, and I've used many of them in examples in this book. In this chapter, I will present PySpark implementations of the following design patterns:

1. Input-Map-Output
2. Input-Filter-Output
3. Input-Map-Reduce-Output
4. Input-Multiple-Maps-Reduce-Output
5. Input-Map-Combiner-Reduce-Output
6. Input-MapPartitions-Reduce-Output
7. Input-Inverted-Index-Pattern-Output

Source Code

Complete programs for this chapter are available in the book's GitHub repository (*https://oreil.ly/WG0Hr*).

Before we get started, however, I'd like to address the question of what I mean by "design patterns." In computer science and software engineering, given a commonly occurring problem, a design pattern is a reusable solution to that problem. It's a template or best practice for how to solve a problem, not a finished design that can be transformed directly into code. The patterns presented in this chapter will equip you to handle a wide range of data analysis tasks.

The data design patterns discussed in this chapter are basic patterns. You can create your own, depending on your requirements. For additional examples, see "MapReduce: Simplified Data Processing on Large Clusters" (*https://oreil.ly/jS7MV*) by Jeffrey Dean and Sanjay Ghemawat.

MapReduce Versus Spark

MapReduce is a programming paradigm that enables massive parallel and distributed scalability across hundreds or thousands of servers in a Hadoop cluster. A typical MapReduce job consists of a driver and three functions: `map()`, `reduce()`, and `combine()` as an optional local reducer. The `map()` function provides functionality equivalent to Spark's `map()`, `flatMap()`, and `filter()`, while the `reduce()` function provides functionality equivalent to Spark's `reduceByKey()` and `groupByKey()`. However, as we've seen, Spark's implementation is not limited to these functions. It can be thought of as a superset of MapReduce, offering higher-level data abstractions (RDDs and DataFrames) and a very rich API for solving data problems. The implementations of data design patterns presented here use PySpark rather than the MapReduce paradigm.

Input-Map-Output

Input-Map-Output is the simplest design pattern for data analysis: as illustrated in Figure 9-1, you read the input from a set of files, then apply a series of functions to each record, and finally produce the desired output. There is no restriction on what a mapper can create from its input: it can create a set of new records or (key, value) pairs.

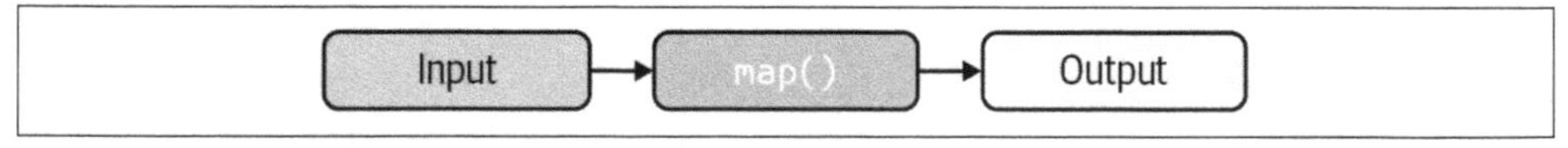

Figure 9-1. The Input-Map-Output design pattern

No reduction is involved, but sometimes the map phase is used to clean and reformat data. This a very common design pattern used to change the format of input data and generate output data, which can be used by other mappers and reducers.

RDD Solution

Sometimes the map phase is used to clean and reformat data before generating (key, value) pairs to be consumed by reducers.

Consider a scenario where the input records have a gender field that can contain values such as:

- Female representation: `"0", "f", "F", "Female", "female"`
- Male representation: `"1", "m", "M", "Male", "male"`

and you want to normalize the gender field as `{"female", "male", "unknown"}`. Let's assume that each record has the following format:

```
<user_id><,><gender><,><address>
```

The following function can facilitate the `map()` transformation and will create a triplet of `(user_id, normalized_gender, address)` per input record:

```
# rec: an input record
def normalize_gender(rec):
  tokens = rec.split(",")
  user_id = tokens[0]
  gender = tokens[1].lower()
  if gender in ('0', 'f', 'female'):
    normalized_gender = "female"
  elif gender in ('1', 'm', 'male'):
    normalized_gender = "male"
  else:
    normalized_gender = "unknown"

  return (user_id, normalized_gender, tokens[2])
#end-def
```

Given a source `rdd` as an `RDD[String]`, then your mapper transformation will be as follows:

```
# source rdd : RDD[String]
# target rdd_mapped : RDD[(String, String, String)]
# RDD.map() is a 1-to-1 transformation
rdd_mapped = rdd.map(normalize_gender)
```

Another scenario might be analyzing movie rating records of the form `<user_id><,><movie_id><,><rating>`, where your goal is to create a (key, value) pair of `(<movie_id>, (<user_id>, <rating>)` per record. Further assume that all ratings will be converted to integer numbers. You can use the following mapper function for this:

```
# rec: <user_id><,><movie_id><,><rating>
def create_pair(rec):
  tokens = rec.split(",")
```

```
    user_id = tokens[0]
    movie_id = tokens[1]
    rating = int(tokens[2])

    return (movie_id, (user_id, rating))
  #end-def
```

What if you want to map a single input record/element into multiple target elements, dropping (filtering out) records/elements where appropriate? To map a single record into multiple target elements, Spark offers the `flatMap()` transformation for this; it works on a single element (like `map()`) and produces multiple target elements. So, if your input is `RDD[V]` and you want to map each `V` into a set of elements of type `T`, you can do this with `flatMap()` as follows:

```
# source_rdd: RDD[V]
# target_rdd: RDD[T]
target_rdd = source_rdd.flatMap(custom_map_function)

# v an element of source_rdd
def custom_map_function(v):
  # t iterable<T>
  t = <use-v-to-create-an-iterable-of-T-data-type-elements>
  return t
#end-def
```

For example, if for input record `v` you create `t = [t1, t2, t3]`, then `v` will be mapped to three elements of the `target_rdd` as `t1`, `t2`, and `t3`. If `t=[]`—an empty list—then no element will be created in the `target_rdd`: `v` is filtered out.

As this example suggests, if you want to map and filter at the same time, mapping some records and filtering others, you can implement this with `flatMap()` as well. For example, suppose you have records in the following format:

```
<word1><,><word2><;><word1><,><word2><;>...<word1><,><word2>
```

Your goal is to keep only the records consisting of two words, separated by a comma (that is, bigrams); you want to drop (filter out) all the other records.

Consider this source RDD:

```
records = ['w1,w2;w3,w4', 'w9', 'w5,w6;w7,w8;w10,w11']
rdd = spark.sparkContext.parallelize(records)
```

Now, `rdd` has three elements. You would like to keep `'w1,w2'`, `'w3,w4'`, `'w5,w6'`, `'w7,w8'`, and `'w10,w11'` but drop `'w9'` (since this is not a bigram). The following PySpark snippet shows how to achieve this:

```
# map and filter
def map_and_filter(rec):
  if ";" in rec:
    bigrams = rec.split(";")
    result = []
```

```
    for bigram in bigrams:
      words = bigram.split(",")
      if len(words) == 2: result.append(bigram)
    return result
  else:
    # no semicolon in rec
    words = rec.split(",")
    if len(words) == 2: return [rec]
    else: return []
#end-def

# map and filter with flatMap()
mapped_and_filtered = rdd.flatMap(map_and_filter)
mapped_and_filtered.collect()
['w1,w2', 'w3,w4', 'w5,w6', 'w7,w8', 'w10,w11']
```

As this example shows, you can map the records you want to keep into multiple target elements and filter out the ones you don't want to keep at the same time using a single `flatMap()` transformation.

DataFrame Solution

Spark has an `RDD.map()` function, but it does not have this `map()` function for DataFrames. Spark's DataFrame does not have an explicit `map()` function, but we can achieve the `map()` equivalency in many ways: we can add new columns by applying `DataFrame.withColumn()` and drop existing columns by `DataFrame.drop()`.

Consider a DataFrame as:

```
tuples3 = [ ('alex', 800, 8), ('jane', 420, 4),
            ('bob', 380, 5), ('betty', 700, 10),
            ('ted', 480, 10), ('mary', 500, 0) ]
>>> column_names = ["name", "weekly_pay", "overtime_hours"]
>>> df = spark.createDataFrame(tuples3, column_names)
>>> df.show(truncate=False)
+-----+----------+--------------+
|name |weekly_pay|overtime_hours|
+-----+----------+--------------+
|alex |800       |8             |
|jane |420       |4             |
|bob  |380       |5             |
|betty|700       |10            |
|ted  |480       |10            |
|mary |500       |0             |
+-----+----------+--------------+
```

Suppose we want to calculate total weekly pay by adding `overtime_hours` to `weekly_pay`. Therefore, we want to create a new column `total weekly pay` based on the values of two columns: `overtime_hours` and `weekly_pay`. Assume that over time rate is $20 per hour.

```
def compute_total_pay(weekly_pay, overtime_hours):
    return (weekly_pay + (overtime_hours * 20))
#end-def
```

To keep all the columns, do the following:

```
>>> df2 = df.rdd.map(lambda x: (x["name"], x["weekly_pay"], x["overtime_hours"],
    compute_total_pay(x["weekly_pay"], x["overtime_hours"])))
    .toDF(["name", "weekly_pay", "overtime_hours", "total_pay"])
>>> df2.show(truncate=False)
+-----+----------+--------------+---------+
|name |weekly_pay|overtime_hours|total_pay|
+-----+----------+--------------+---------+
|alex |800       |8             |960      |
|jane |420       |4             |500      |
|bob  |380       |5             |480      |
|betty|700       |10            |900      |
|ted  |480       |10            |680      |
|mary |500       |0             |500      |
+-----+----------+--------------+---------+
```

Essentially you have to map the row to a tuple containing all of the existing columns and add in the new column(s).

If your columns are too many to enumerate, you could also just add a tuple to the existing row.

```
>>> df3 = df.rdd.map(lambda x: x + (str(compute_total_pay(x["weekly_pay"],
   x["overtime_hours"])),)).toDF(df.columns + ["total_pay"])
>>> df3.show(truncate=False)
+-----+----------+--------------+---------+
|name |weekly_pay|overtime_hours|total_pay|
+-----+----------+--------------+---------+
|alex |800       |8             |960      |
|jane |420       |4             |500      |
|bob  |380       |5             |480      |
|betty|700       |10            |900      |
|ted  |480       |10            |680      |
|mary |500       |0             |500      |
+-----+----------+--------------+---------+
```

You can also add a `total_pay` column using `DataFrame.withColumn()`:

```
>>> import pyspark.sql.functions as F
>>> df4 = df.withColumn("total_pay",
   F.lit(compute_total_pay(df.weekly_pay, df.overtime_hours)))
>>> df4.show(truncate=False)
+-----+----------+--------------+---------+
|name |weekly_pay|overtime_hours|total_pay|
+-----+----------+--------------+---------+
|alex |800       |8             |960      |
|jane |420       |4             |500      |
|bob  |380       |5             |480      |
|betty|700       |10            |900      |
```

```
|ted  |480        |10            |680       |
|mary |500        |0             |500       |
+-----+----------+-------------+---------+
```

Flat Mapper functionality

Spark's DataFrame does not have a `flatMap()` transformation (to flatten one element into many target elements), but instead it offers the `explode()` function, which returns a new row for each element in the given `column` (expressed as a list or dictionary) and uses the default column name `col` for elements in the array and key and value for elements in the dictionary unless specified otherwise.

Below is a complete example, which shows how to use `explode()` function as an equivalent to `RDD.flatMap()` transformation.

Let's first create a DataFrame, where two column are lists.

Next, we look at exploding multiple columns for a given DataFrame. Note that only one generator is allowed per `select` clause: this means that you can not explode two columns at the same time (but you can explode them iteratively one-by-one). The following example shows how to explode two columns:

```
>>> some_data = [
...     ('alex', ['Java','Scala', 'Python'], ['MS', 'PHD']),
...     ('jane', ['Cobol','Snobol'], ['BS', 'MS']),
...     ('bob', ['C++'], ['BS', 'MS', 'PHD']),
...     ('ted', [], ['BS', 'MS']),
...     ('max', ['FORTRAN'], []),
...     ('dan', [], [])
... ]
>>>
>>> df = spark.createDataFrame(data=some_data,
   schema = ['name', 'languages', 'education'])
>>> df.show(truncate=False)
+----+--------------------+-------------+
|name|languages           |education    |
+----+--------------------+-------------+
|alex|[Java, Scala, Python]|[MS, PHD]    |
|jane|[Cobol, Snobol]      |[BS, MS]     |
|bob |[C++]                |[BS, MS, PHD]|
|ted |[]                   |[BS, MS]     |
|max |[FORTRAN]            |[]           |
|dan |[]                   |[]           |
+----+--------------------+-------------+
```

Next we explode on the `languages` column, which is an array:

```
>>> exploded_1 = df.select(df.name,
   explode(df.languages).alias('language'), df.education)
>>> exploded_1.show(truncate=False)
+----+--------+-------------+
```

```
|name|language|education    |
+----+--------+------------+
|alex|Java    |[MS, PHD]   |
|alex|Scala   |[MS, PHD]   |
|alex|Python  |[MS, PHD]   |
|jane|Cobol   |[BS, MS]    |
|jane|Snobol  |[BS, MS]    |
|bob |C++     |[BS, MS, PHD]|
|max |FORTRAN |[]          |
+----+--------+------------+
```

As you can see, when exploding a column, if a column is a empty list, then that is dropped from exploding result (`tex` and `max` are dropped since they have an associated empty lists). Note that `ted` and `dan` were dropped since the exploded column value was an empty list.

Next, we explode on the `education` column:

```
>>> exploded_2 = exploded_1.select(exploded_1.name, exploded_1.language,
   explode(exploded_1.education).alias('degree'))
>>> exploded_2.show(truncate=False)
+----+--------+------+
|name|language|degree|
+----+--------+------+
|alex|Java    |    MS|
|alex|Java    |   PHD|
|alex|Scala   |    MS|
|alex|Scala   |   PHD|
|alex|Python  |    MS|
|alex|Python  |   PHD|
|jane|Cobol   |    BS|
|jane|Cobol   |    MS|
|jane|Snobol  |    BS|
|jane|Snobol  |    MS|
|bob |C++     |    BS|
|bob |C++     |    MS|
|bob |C++     |   PHD|
+----+--------+------+
```

Note that name `max` is dropped since the exploded column value was an empty list.

Input-Filter-Output

The Input-Filter-Output data design pattern, illustrated in Figure 9-2, is a simple pattern that lets you keep records that satisfy your data requirements while removing the unwanted records. You read the input from a set of files, then apply one or more filter functions to each record, keeping the records that satisfy the Boolean predicate and dropping the others.

Figure 9-2. The Input-Filter-Output design pattern

This is a useful design pattern for situations in which your dataset is large and you want to take a subset of this data to focus in on and maybe perform a follow-on analysis.

A simple scenario is reading input records consisting of URLs, keeping the valid ones while discarding the nonvalid URLs. This design pattern can be implemented with RDDs and DataFrames.

Here are a few sample records:

```
http://cnn.com ❶
htp://mysite.com ❷
http://www.oreilly.com ❸
https:/www.oreilly.com ❹
```

❶ Valid URL

❷ Invalid URL

❸ Valid URL

❹ Invalid URL

RDD Solution

This design pattern can be easily implemented using the `RDD.filter()` function:

```
data = ['http://cnn.com', 'htp://mysite.com',
  'http://www.oreilly.com', 'https:/www.oreilly.com' ]

urls = spark.sparkContext.parallelize(data)

# return True if a given URL is valid, otherwise return False
def is_valid_URL(url_as_str):
  if url_as_str is None: return False
  lowercased = url_as_str.lower()
  if (lowercased.startswith('http://') or
      lowercased.startswith('https://')):
    return True
  else:
    return False
#end-def

# return a new RDD containing only the
# elements that satisfy a predicate
```

```
valid_urls = urls.filter(is_valid_URL)
valid_urls.collect()
[ 'http://cnn.com', 'http://www.oreilly.com' ]
```

DataFrame Solution

Alternatively, you can use the `DataFrame.filter()` function to keep the desired records and drop the undesired records:

```
>>> data = [('http://cnn.com',), ('htp://mysite.com',),
    ('http://www.oreilly.com',), ('https:/www.oreilly.com',)]

# create a single-column DataFrame
>>> df = spark.createDataFrame(data, ['url'])

>>> df.show(truncate=False)
+----------------------+
|url                   |
+----------------------+
|http://cnn.com        |
|htp://mysite.com      |
|http://www.oreilly.com|
|https:/www.oreilly.com|
+----------------------+

# filter out undesired records
>>> df.filter(df.url.startswith('http://') |
              df.url.startswith('https://'))
      .show(truncate=False)
+----------------------+
|url                   |
+----------------------+
|http://cnn.com        |
|http://www.oreilly.com|
+----------------------+
```

DataFrame Filter

Spark's `filter()` function is used to filter the elements/rows from RDD/DataFrame based on the given condition. For DataFrames, you may also use a `where()` clause instead of the `filter()` function if you are coming from a SQL background. Both of these functions (`filter()` and `where()`) operate exactly the same. The goal of `filter()` and `where()` are to keep the desired elements/rows.

Consider a DataFrame as:

```
tuples3 = [ ('alex', 800, 8), ('jane', 420, 4),
            ('bob', 380, 5), ('betty', 700, 10),
            ('ted', 480, 10), ('mary', 500, 0) ]
>>> column_names = ["name", "weekly_pay", "overtime_hours"]
>>> df = spark.createDataFrame(tuples3, column_names)
```

```
>>> df.show(truncate=False)
+-----+----------+--------------+
|name |weekly_pay|overtime_hours|
+-----+----------+--------------+
|alex |800       |8             |
|jane |420       |4             |
|bob  |380       |5             |
|betty|700       |10            |
|ted  |480       |10            |
|mary |500       |0             |
+-----+----------+--------------+
```

Suppose we want to keep rows where `weekly_pay` is greater than 490.

Let's first use `filter()`:

```
>>> df.filter(df.weekly_pay > 490).show(truncate=False)
+-----+----------+--------------+
|name |weekly_pay|overtime_hours|
+-----+----------+--------------+
|alex |800       |8             |
|betty|700       |10            |
|mary |500       |0             |
+-----+----------+--------------+
```

We can achieve the same functionality by the `where` clause:

```
>>> df.where(df.weekly_pay > 490).show(truncate=False)
+-----+----------+--------------+
|name |weekly_pay|overtime_hours|
+-----+----------+--------------+
|alex |800       |8             |
|betty|700       |10            |
|mary |500       |0             |
+-----+----------+--------------+
```

The `filter()` can be used on single and multiple conditions:

```
>>> df.filter(df.weekly_pay > 400).show(truncate=False)
+-----+----------+--------------+
|name |weekly_pay|overtime_hours|
+-----+----------+--------------+
|alex |800       |8             |
|jane |420       |4             |
|betty|700       |10            |
|ted  |480       |10            |
|mary |500       |0             |
+-----+----------+--------------+

>>> df.filter((df.weekly_pay > 400) &
   (df.overtime_hours > 5)).show(truncate=False)
+-----+----------+--------------+
|name |weekly_pay|overtime_hours|
+-----+----------+--------------+
```

```
|alex |800       |8            |
|betty|700       |10           |
|ted  |480       |10           |
+-----+----------+-------------+
```

Input-Map-Reduce-Output

The Input-Map-Reduce-Output design pattern, illustrated in Figure 9-3, is the most common design pattern for aggregation operations, such as finding the sum or average of values by key.

RDD Solution

Spark offers the following powerful solutions for implementing this design pattern, many different combinations of which can be used to solve data problems:

- Map phase: `map()`, `flatMap()`, `mapPartitions()`, `filter()`
- Reduce phase: `reduceByKey()`, `groupByKey()`, `aggregateByKey()`, `combineByKey()`

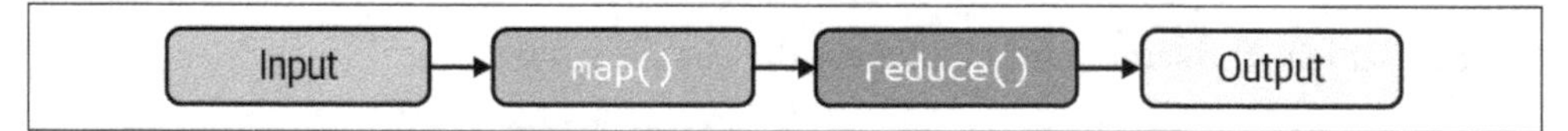

Figure 9-3. The Input-Map-Reduce-Output design pattern

This is the simplest MapReduce design pattern: read data, perform a map transformation—usually creating (key, value) pairs—aggregate (sum, average, etc.) all of the values for the same key, then save the output.

Suppose you have records with the format `<name><,><age><,><salary>` and you want to compute the average salary per age group, where the age groups are defined as `0-15`, `16-20`, `21-25`, ..., `96-100`. First, you need to read the input and create an RDD/DataFrame. The mapper will then process one record at a time and create (key, value) pairs, where the key is an age group and the value is a salary. For example, if our record is `alex,22,45000`, then the mapper will create the pair `('21-25', 45000)` since the age 22 falls into the age group `'21-25'`. The mapper function can be expressed as:

```
# rec: <name><,><age><,><salary>
def create_key_value_pair(rec):
  tokens = rec.split(",")
  age = int(tokens[1])
  salary = tokens[2]
  if age < 16: return ('0-15', salary)
  if age < 21: return ('16-20', salary)
  ...
```

```
    if age < 91: return ('85-90', salary)
    if age < 96: return ('91-95', salary)
    return ('96-100', salary)
#end-def
```

Then, the reducer will group the keys by age groups (`0-15`, `16-20`, etc.), aggregate the values in each group, and find the average salary per group.

Say you have the following input:

```
alex,22,45000
bob,43,50000,
john,23,65000
jane,41,48000
joe,44,66000
```

The mapper will generate the following (key, value) pairs:

```
('21-25', 45000)
('41-45', 54000)
('21-25', 67000)
('41-45', 68000)
('41-45', 70000)
```

Then the reducer will group the values for each key:

```
('21-25', [45000, 67000])
('41-45', [54000, 68000, 70000])
```

Grouping by key can be easily implemented with Spark's `groupByKey()` transformation. Using `groupByKey()`, we cay write the reducer as:

```
# rdd: RDD[(age-group, salary)]
grouped_by_age_group = rdd.groupByKey()
```

Finally, we can calculate the average per age group:

```
('21-25', 56000)
('41-45', 64000)
```

This can be accomplished by another simple mapper:

```
# grouped_by_age_group: RDD[(age-group, [salary-1, salary-2, ...])]
age_group_average = grouped_by_age_group.mapValues(lambda v: sum(v)/len(v))
```

If you want to use combiners (Spark uses combiners automatically in `reduceBy Key()`), the mapper will instead generate the following (key, value) pairs, where the value is `(sum, count)`:

```
('21-25', (45000, 1))
('41-45', (54000, 1))
('21-25', (67000, 1))
('41-45', (68000, 1))
('41-45', (70000, 1))
```

The reason for creating `(sum, count)` as a value is to guarantee that the reducer function is associative and commutative. If your reducer function does not follow these two algebraic rules, then Spark's `reduceByKey()` will not produce the correct semantics when the input data is spread across multiple partitions.

Given an `RDD[(key, (sum, count))]`, using Spark's `reduceByKey()`—note that this reducer works on a partition-by-partition basis and uses combiners as well—we may write the reducer as:

```
# rdd: RDD[(key, (sum, count))]
reduced_by_age_group = rdd.reduceByKey(
  lambda x, y: (x[0]+y[0], x[1]+y[1]))
```

The reducer will group the values by their associated keys:

```
('21-25', (112000, 2))
('41-45', (192000, 3))
```

Then, the average per age group can be caluculated by another simple mapper:

```
('21-25', 56000)
('41-45', 64000)
```

It's also possible to implement this design pattern using a combination of Spark's `map()` and `combineByKey()` transformations. The map phase is exactly as presented previously. Using the `create_key_value_pair()` function, it will create the following (key, value) pairs:

```
('21-25', 45000)
('41-45', 54000)
('21-25', 67000)
('41-45', 68000)
('41-45', 70000)
```

Let's assume that these (key, value) pairs are denoted by `age_group_rdd`. Then we can perform the reduction using a pair of `combineByKey()` and `mapValues()` transformations:

```
# C denotes (sum-of-salaries, count-of-salaries)
combined = age_group_rdd.combineByKey(
  lambda v : (v, 1), ❶
  lambda C, v: (C[0]+v, C[1]+1), ❷
  lambda C1,C2: (C1[0]+C2[0], C1[1]+C2[1]) ❸
)

# C denotes (sum-of-salaries, count-of-salaries)
avg_per_age_group = combined.mapValues(
  lambda C : C[0]/C[1]
)
```

❶ Create `C` as `(sum-of-salaries, count-of-salaries)`.

❷ Merge a salary into C.

❸ Combine two Cs (from different partitions) into a single C.

Notice that reduceByKey() is a special case of combineByKey(). For reduceByKey(), the source and target RDDs must be of the form RDD[(K, V]), while for combineByKey() the source RDD can be RDD[(K, V)] and the target RDD can be RDD[(K, C)], where V and C may be different data types. For example, V can be Integer, while C can be (Integer, Integer). In Spark, the combineByKey() transformation is the most general and powerful reducer for (key, value) datasets.

DataFrame Solution

PySpark's Dataframe offers comprehensive functionality for reduction transformations. You may use Dataframe.groupby(*cols), which groups the DataFrame using the specified columns so we can run aggregation on them. The other option is to register your Dataframe as a table (of rows and named columns) and then use the power of SQL to GROUP BY and aggregate the dsired columns.

The following example shows how to use the groupBy() function.

First, let's create a DataFrame:

```
>>> tuples4 = [("Illumina", "Alex", "San Diego", 100000),
...            ("Illumina", "Bob", "San Diego", 220000),
...            ("Illumina", "Jane", "Foster City", 190000),
...            ("Illumina", "Ted", "Foster City", 230000),
...            ("Google", "Rafa", "Menlo Park", 250000),
...            ("Google", "Roger", "Menlo Park", 160000),
...            ("Google", "Mona", "Menlo Park", 120000),
...            ("IBM", "Joe", "San Jose", 160000),
...            ("IBM", "Alex", "San Jose", 170000),
...            ("IBM", "George", "San Jose", 180000),
...            ("IBM", "Barb", "San Jose", 190000)]
>>> df = spark.createDataFrame(tuples4,
   ["company", "employee", "city", "salary"])
>>> df.show(truncate=False)
+--------+--------+-----------+------+
|company |employee|city       |salary|
+--------+--------+-----------+------+
|Illumina|Alex    |San Diego  |100000|
|Illumina|Bob     |San Diego  |220000|
|Illumina|Jane    |Foster City|190000|
|Illumina|Ted     |Foster City|230000|
|Google  |Rafa    |Menlo Park |250000|
|Google  |Roger   |Menlo Park |160000|
```

```
|Google  |Mona    |Menlo Park |120000|
|IBM     |Joe     |San Jose   |160000|
|IBM     |Alex    |San Jose   |170000|
|IBM     |George  |San Jose   |180000|
|IBM     |Barb    |San Jose   |190000|
+--------+--------+-----------+------+
```

Next, we apply grouping and aggregation functions:

- Describe your DataFrame:

```
>>> df.describe().show()
+-------+--------+--------+-----------+-----------------+
|summary| company|employee|       city|           salary|
+-------+--------+--------+-----------+-----------------+
|  count|      11|      11|         11|               11|
|   mean|    null|    null|       null|179090.9090909091|
| stddev|    null|    null|       null|44822.88376589473|
|    min|  Google|    Alex|Foster City|           100000|
|    max|Illumina|     Ted|   San Jose|           250000|
+-------+--------+--------+-----------+-----------------+
```

- Use `groupBy()` on a DataFrame:

```
>>> df.groupBy('company').max().show()
+--------+-----------+
| company|max(salary)|
+--------+-----------+
|Illumina|     230000|
|  Google|     250000|
|     IBM|     190000|
+--------+-----------+

>>> df.groupBy('Company').sum().show()
+--------+-----------+
| Company|sum(salary)|
+--------+-----------+
|Illumina|     740000|
|  Google|     530000|
|     IBM|     700000|
+--------+-----------+

>>> df.groupBy("company").agg({'salary':'sum'}).show()
+--------+-----------+
| company|sum(salary)|
+--------+-----------+
|Illumina|     740000|
|  Google|     530000|
|     IBM|     700000|
+--------+-----------+

>>> import pyspark.sql.functions as F
```

```
>>> df.groupby('company')
.agg(F.min("salary").alias("minimum_salary"),
F.max("salary").alias("maximum_salary")).show()
+--------+--------------+--------------+
| company|minimum_salary|maximum_salary|
+--------+--------------+--------------+
|Illumina|        100000|        230000|
|  Google|        120000|        250000|
|     IBM|        160000|        190000|
+--------+--------------+--------------+
```

Input-Multiple-Maps-Reduce-Output

The Input-Multiple-Maps-Reduce-Output design pattern involves multiple maps, joins, and reductions. This design pattern is also known as the *reduce-side join*, because the reducer is responsible for performing the join operation. To help you understand this design pattern, let me provide an example. Suppose we have the following two inputs, a Movies table and a Ratings table:

Movie-ID	Movie-Name
100	Lion King
200	Star Wars
300	Fiddler on the Roof
...	...

Movie-ID	Rating	User-ID
100	4	USER-1234
100	5	USER-3467
200	4	USER-1234
200	2	USER-1234
...	...	...

The final goal is to produce the following output, the AVG Rating table. This is a join of the Movies and Ratings tables, but after the join operation is completed, we still need to perform another reduction to find the average rating per Movie-ID:

Movie-ID	Movie-Name	AVG Rating
100	Lion King	4.5
200	Star Wars	3.0
...	...	...

This data design pattern is illustrated by Figure 9-4.

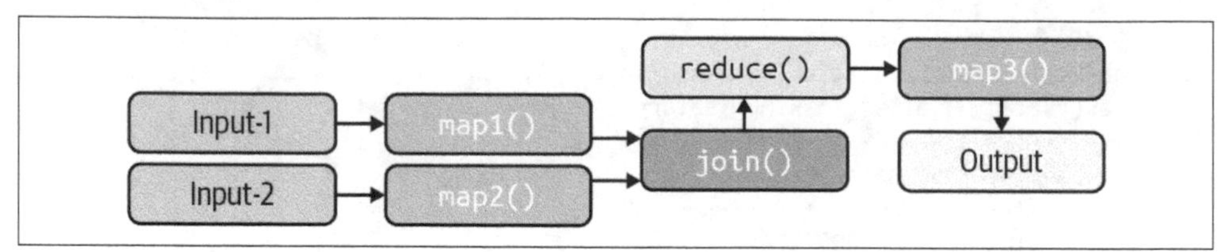

Figure 9-4. The Input-Map-Reduce-Output (reduce-side join) design pattern

Let's walk through it step by step:

1. The mapper reads the input data that is to be combined based on a common column or join key. We read `Input-1`, then apply `map1()` as a mapper and create `(<Common-Key>, <Rest-of-Attributes>)` pairs. Applying this to the Movies table will create `(Movie-ID, Movie-Name)` pairs, where `Movie-ID` is a key and `Movie-Name` is a value.
2. Next, we read `Input-2`, then apply `map2()` as a mapper and create `(<Common-Key>, <Rest-of-Attributes>)` pairs. Applying this to the Ratings table will create `(Movie-ID, (Movie-Name, Rating))` pairs, where `Movie-ID` is a key and `(Movie-Name, Rating)` is a value.
3. We now perform a `join()` operation between the outputs of `map1()` and `map2()`. Therefore, the goal is to join `(Movie-ID, Movie-Name)` pairs with `(Movie-ID, (Movie-Name, Rating))` pairs on the common key, `Movie-ID`. The result of this join is `(Movie-ID, (Rating, Movie-Name))` pairs.
4. The next step is to reduce and aggregate the output of the `join()` operation by using `Movie-ID` as a key: we need all ratings per `Movie-ID` to find the average of the ratings.
5. Finally, we have a simple mapper (`map3()`) calculate the average of the ratings and produce the final output.

For this design pattern, I will provide two PySpark solutions: one using RDDs and another using DataFrames.

RDD Solution

First, I'll present a simple PySpark solution using RDDs. The first step is to prepare the inputs. We'll create two RDDs to represent our two inputs. For this, I'll define two simple tokenization functions:

```
def create_movie_pair(rec):
  tokens = rec.split(",")
  return (tokens[0], tokens[1])
#end-def
```

```
def create_rating_pair(rec):
  tokens = rec.split(",")
  # we drop User_ID here (not needed)
  return (tokens[0], int(tokens[1]))
#end-def
```

Next, we use these functions in the mapper transformations:

```
# spark: SparkSession
movies_by_name = ["100,Lion King", "200,Star Wars",
                  "300,Fiddler on the Roof", "400,X-Files"]
movies = spark.sparkContext.parallelize(movies_by_name)
movies.collect()
['100,Lion King', '200,Star Wars',
 '300,Fiddler on the Roof', '400,X-Files']

movies_rdd = movies.map(create_movie_pair)
movies_rdd.collect()
[('100', 'Lion King'), ('200', 'Star Wars'),
 ('300', 'Fiddler on the Roof'), ('400', 'X-Files')]

ratings_by_users = ["100,4,USER-1234", "100,5,USER-3467",
                    "200,4,USER-1234", "200,2,USER-1234"]

ratings = spark.sparkContext.parallelize(ratings_by_users)
ratings.collect()
['100,4,USER-1234', '100,5,USER-3467',
 '200,4,USER-1234', '200,2,USER-1234']

ratings_rdd = ratings.map(create_rating_pair)
ratings_rdd.collect()
[('100', 4), ('100', 5), ('200', 4), ('200', 2)]
```

So far we have created two RDDs:

- `movies_rdd`: `RDD[(Movie-ID, Movie-Name)]`
- `ratings_rdd`: `RDD[(Movie-ID, Rating)]`

Now, we'll use these two RDDs to perform the join operation on the common key, `Movie-ID`:

```
joined = ratings_kv.join(movies_kv)
joined.collect()
[ ('200', (4, 'Star Wars')),
  ('200', (2, 'Star Wars')),
  ('100', (4, 'Lion King')),
  ('100', (5, 'Lion King'))]

grouped_by_movieid = joined.groupByKey()
                            .mapValues(lambda v: list(v))
grouped_by_movieid.collect()
```

```
[ ('200', [(4, 'Star Wars'), (2, 'Star Wars')]),
  ('100', [(4, 'Lion King'), (5, 'Lion King')])]
```

The last step is to use a simple mapper to prepare the final output, which includes the average rating per `Movie-ID`:

```
def find_avg_rating(values):
  total = 0
  for v in values:
    total += v[0]
    movie_name = v[1]
  return (movie_name, float(total)/len(values))
#end-def

grouped_by_movieid.mapValues(
   lambda values: find_avg_rating(values)).collect()
[
 ('200', ('Star Wars', 3.0)),
 ('100', ('Lion King', 4.5))
]
```

DataFrame Solution

The solution using DataFrames is quite straightforward: we create a DataFrame per input and then join them on the common key, `Movie-ID`.

First let's create the DataFrames:

```
movies_by_name = [('100', 'Lion King'), ('200', 'Star Wars'),
                  ('300', 'Fiddler on the Roof'), ('400', 'X-Files')]
movies_df = spark.createDataFrame(movies_by_name,
                  ["movie_id", "movie_name"])
movies_df.show()
+--------+-------------------+
|movie_id|         movie_name|
+--------+-------------------+
|     100|          Lion King|
|     200|          Star Wars|
|     300|Fiddler on the Roof|
|     400|            X-Files|
+--------+-------------------+

ratings_by_user = [('100', 4, 'USER-1234'),
                   ('100', 5, 'USER-3467'),
                   ('200', 4, 'USER-1234'),
                   ('200', 2, 'USER-1234')]

ratings_df = spark.createDataFrame(ratings_by_user,
                   ["movie_id", "rating", "user_id"]).drop("user_id")
ratings_df.show()
+--------+------+
|movie_id|rating|
```

```
+--------+------+
|     100|     4|
|     100|     5|
|     200|     4|
|     200|     2|
+--------+------+
```

Then all we have to do is perform the join operation. This is easy with DataFrames:

```
joined = ratings_df.join(movies_df, "movie_id")
joined.show()
+--------+------+----------+
|movie_id|rating|movie_name|
+--------+------+----------+
|     200|     4| Star Wars|
|     200|     2| Star Wars|
|     100|     4| Lion King|
|     100|     5| Lion King|
+--------+------+----------+

output = joined.groupBy("movie_id", "movie_name").avg()
output.show()
+--------+----------+-----------+
|movie_id|movie_name|avg(rating)|
+--------+----------+-----------+
|     200| Star Wars|        3.0|
|     100| Lion King|        4.5|
+--------+----------+-----------+
```

Input-Map-Combiner-Reduce-Output

The Input-Map-Combiner-Reduce-Output design pattern is very similar to Input-Map-Reduce-Output. The main difference is that combiners are used as well, to speed up the transformation. In the MapReduce paradigm (implemented in Apache Hadoop), a combiner—also known as a semi-reducer—is an optional function that works by accepting the outputs from the mapper function for each partition on a worker node, aggregating the results per key, and finally passing the output (key, value) pairs to the reducer function. In Spark, combiners are automatically executed on each worker node and partition, and you do not have to write any special combiner functions. An example of such a transformation is the `reduceByKey()` transformation, which merges the values for each key using an associative and commutative reduce function.

The main function of a combiner is to summarize and aggregate the mapper's output records as (key, value) pairs, with the same key per partition. The purpose of this design pattern is to make sure that combiners can be used and that your data algorithm will not deliver incorrect results. For example, the goal is to sum up values per key and we have the following (key, value) pairs:

```
(K1, 30), (K1, 40),
(K2, 5), (K2, 6), (K2, 7)
```

in the same partition, then, the job of a combiner is to summarize these as `(K1, 70)`, `(K2, 18)`.

This data design pattern is illustrated by Figure 9-5.

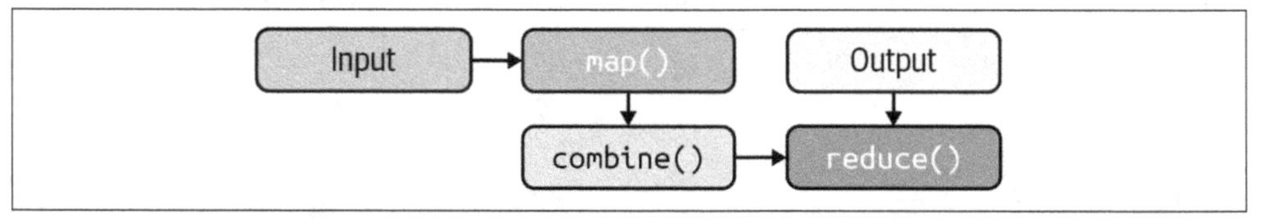

Figure 9-5. The Input-Map-Combine-Reduce-Output design pattern

Suppose we have input representing cities and their associated temperatures, and our goal is to find the average temperature for each city. `source_rdd` has the format `RDD[(String, Double)]` for our data, where the key is the city name and the value is the associated temperature. To find the average temperature per city, you might attempt to write:

```
# WARNING: THIS WILL NOT WORK
# let t1, t2 denote temperatures for the same city
avg_per_city = source_rdd.reduceByKey(
  lambda t1, t2: (t1+t2)/2
)
```

But this is not the right transformation, so it will not compute the average per city. The problem is that, as we know, the average function is not associative:

```
AVG(1, 2, 3, 4, 5) != AVG(AVG(1, 2), AVG(3, 4, 5))
```

That is, the average of averages is not an average. Why not? The following example illustrates. Suppose we have this data, on two partitions:

```
Partition-1:
  (Paris, 20)
  (Paris, 30)

Partition-2:
  (Paris, 40)
  (Paris, 50)
  (Paris, 60)
```

Our transformation will create:

```
Partition-1:
  (Paris, (20+30)/2) = (Paris, 25)

Partition-2:
  (Paris, (40+50)/2) = (Paris, 45)
  (Paris, (45+60)/2) = (Paris, 52.5)
```

Finally, combining the results of the two partitions will produce:

```
(Paris, (25+52.5)/2)) = (Paris, 38.75)
```

Is 38.75 the average of (20, 30, 40, 50, 60)? Of course not! The correct average is (20 + 30 + 40 + 50 + 60) / 5 = 200 / 5 = 40.

Because the average function is not associative, our reducer function is not correct—but with a minor modification, we can make the output of the mappers commutative and associative. This will give us the correct averages per unique city.

Say we have the following data in an RDD:

```
sample_cities = [('Paris', 20), ('Paris', 30),
  ('Paris', 40), ('Paris', 50), ('Paris', 60),
  ('Cupertino', 40), ('Cupertino', 60)]

cities_rdd = spark.sparkContext.parallelize(sample_cities)
```

Now, we'll create a new RDD from `cities_rdd` to make sure that its values comply with the laws of commutativity and associativity:

```
cities_sum_count = cities_rdd.mapValues(lambda v: (v, 1))
```

`cities_sum_count` is an `RDD[(city, (sum-of-temp, count-of-temp))`. Since we know that addition is a commutative and associative operation over a `(sum, count)` tuple, we can write our reduction as:

```
cities_reduced = cities_sum_count.reduceByKey(
  lambda x, y: (x[0]+y[0], x[1]+y[1])
)
```

We then need one final mapper to find the temperature average per city:

```
avg_per_city = cities_reduced.mapValues(
  lambda v: v[0]/v[1]
)
```

Another solution for this design pattern is to use Spark's `combineByKey()` transformation. If `cities_rdd` is our source RDD, then we can find the average temperature per city as follows:

```
avg_per_city = cities_rdd.combineByKey(
  lambda v: (v, 1), ❶
  lambda C, v: (C[0]+v, C[1]+1) ❷
  lambda C1, C2: (C1[0]+C2[0], C1[1]+C2[1]) ❸
).mapValues(lambda v: v[0]/v[1])
```

❶ Create C as `(sum, count)`.

❷ Merge values per partition.

❸ Combine two partitions (combine two `C`s into one).

For your combiners to work properly and be semantically correct, the intermediate values output by your mappers must be monoids and follow the algebraic laws of commutativity and associativity. To learn more about this design pattern, see Chapter 4 and the paper "Monoidify! Monoids as a Design Principle for Efficient MapReduce Algorithms" (*https://oreil.ly/kWNDP*) by Jimmy Lin.

Input-MapPartitions-Reduce-Output

Input-MapPartitions-Reduce-Output is a very important data design pattern in which you apply a function to each partition—each of which may have thousands or millions of elements—as opposed to each element. We discussed this design pattern in Chapters 2 and 3, but because of its importance I wanted to cover it here in more detail. Imagine that you have billions of records and you want to summarize all of these records into a compact data structure such as a list, array, tuple, or dictionary. You can do that with the Input-MapPartitions-Reduce-Output design pattern, illustrated in Figure 9-6.

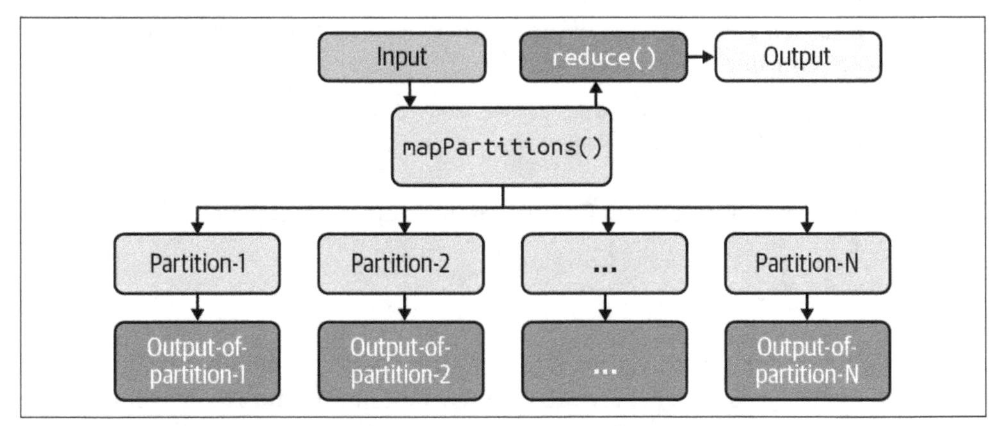

Figure 9-6. The Input-MapPartitions-Reduce-Output design pattern

The general scenario can be summarized as follows:

Input
: Billions of records.

Processing
: Use `mapPartitions()` as a summarization design pattern.

  Split the input into *N* partitions, then analyze/process each partition using a custom function, independently and concurrently, and produce a compact data structure (CDS) such as an array, list, or dictionary. We can label these outputs as CDS-1, CDS-2, ..., CDS-*N*.

Reducer
: The final reducer works on the generated values CDS-1, CDS-2, ..., CDS-*N*. The output of this step is a single compact data structure, such as an array, list, or dictionary.

Spark's `mapPartitions()` is a specialized `map()` that is called only once for each partition. The entire content of the partition is available as a sequential stream of values via the input argument (`Iterator[V]`, where `V` is the data type of the source RDD elements). The custom function must return an `Iterator[T]`, where `T` is the data type of the target RDD elements.

To understand this design pattern, you must understand the difference between `map()` and `mapPartitions()`. The method `map()` converts each element of the source RDD into a single element of the target RDD by applying a function. On the other hand, `mapPartitions()` converts each partition—comprised of thousands or millions of elements—of the source RDD into multiple elements of the result (possibly none).

Suppose we have billions of records of the form:

```
<name><,><gender><,><salary>
```

and our goal is to sum up the salaries of employees based on their gender. We want to find the following three (key, value) tuples from all the input records:

```
("male", (total-number-of-males, sum-of-salaries-for-males))
("female", (total-number-of-females, sum-of-salaries-for-females))
("unknown", (total-number-of-unknowns, sum-of-salaries-for-unknowns))
```

As we can observe from the expected output, there are only three keys: `"male"`, `"female"`, and `"unknown"`.

Here are a few examples of the input records, which I'll use to illustrate how this design pattern behaves:

```
alex,male,22000
david,male,45000
jane,female,38000
mary,female,39000
max,male,55000
nancy,female,67000
ted,x,45000
sam,x,32000
rafa,male,100000
```

A naive solution would be to generate (key, value) pairs, where the key is a gender and the value is a salary and then aggregate the results using the `groupByKey()`

transformation. However, this solution is not efficient and has the following potential problems, which we can avoid by using Spark's `mapPartitions()` transformation:

- It will create billions of (key, value) pairs, which will clutter the cluster network.
- Since there are only three keys, if you use the `groupByKey()` transformation each key will have billions of values, which might cause OOM errors.
- Since there are only three keys, the cluster might not be utilized efficiently.

The Input-MapPartitions-Reduce-Output design pattern comes to our rescue and offers an efficient solution. First, we partition the input into *N* partitions, each containing thousands or millions of records. The value *N* can be determined based on the input size (`N=200, 400, 1000, 20000, ...`). The next step is to apply the `mapPartitions()` transformation: we map each partition and create a very small dictionary per partition with three keys: `"male"`, `"female"`, and `"unknown"`. The final reduction will be to aggregate these *N* dictionaries.

Let's partition our sample input into two partitions:

```
Partition-1:
   alex,male,22000
   david,male,45000
   jane,female,38000
   mary,female,39000
   max,male,55000

Partition-2:
   nancy,female,67000
   ted,x,45000
   sam,x,32000
   rafa,male,100000
```

The main idea behind this design pattern is to partition the input and then process the partitions independently and concurrently. For example, if `N=1000` and you have *N* mappers, then all of them can be executed concurrently. Applying the basic mapping using `mapPartitions()`, we will generate the following dictionaries per partition:

```
Partition-1:
{
  "male": (122000, 3),
  "female": (77000, 2)
}

Partition-2:
{
  "male": (100000, 1),
  "female": (67000, 1),
  "unknown": (77000, 2)
}
```

Next, we will apply the final reduction to aggregate the output of all the partitions into a single dictionary:

```
final output:
{
  "male": (222000, 4),
  "female": (144000, 3),
  "unknown": (77000, 2)
}
```

When the Input-MapPartitions-Reduce-Output design pattern is used to summarize data, there is no scalability issue since we are creating one simple, small data structure (such as a dictionary) per partition. If even we set `N=100,000`, the solution is efficient, since processing 100,000 small dictionaries will not cause any OOM problems.

The most important reason to use the `mapPartitions()` transformation is performance. By having all the data (as a single partition) that we need to perform calculations on a single server node, we reduce the overhead of the shuffle (the need for serialization and network traffic).

An additional advantage of using Spark's `mapPartitions()` transformation to implement the Input-MapPartitions-Reduce-Output design pattern is that it allows you to perform heavyweight initialization per partition (rather than per element). The following example illustrates this. `mapPartitions()` provides for the initialization to be done once per worker task/thread/partition instead of once per RDD data element:

```
# source_rdd: RDD[V]
# source_rdd.count() in billions

# target_rdd: RDD[T]
# target_rdd.count() in thousands

# apply transformation
target_rdd = source_rdd.mapPartitions(custom_func)

def custom_func(partition):
  database_connection = <heavyweight-operation-initialization>
  target_data_structure = <initialize>
  for element in partition
    target_data_structure = update(element,
                                   target_data_structure,
                                   database_connection)
  #end-for
  close(database_connection)

  return target_data_structure
#def
```

Inverted Index

In computer science, an inverted index is a database index that stores a mapping from content—such as words or numbers—to its location(s) in a table, a document, or a set of documents. For example, consider the following input:

```
doc1: ant, dog
doc2: ant, frog
doc3: dog
doc4: ant
```

The goal of an inverted index is to create this index:

```
frog: [doc2]
ant: [doc1, doc2, doc4]
dog: [doc1, doc3]
```

Now, if you want to search for "dog," you know that it is in `[doc1, doc3]`. The Inverted Index design pattern generates an index from a dataset to allow for faster searches. This type of index is the most popular data structure used in document retrieval systems, and is used on a large scale in search engines.

The inverted index design pattern has advantages and disadvantages. Advantages include that it enables us to perform fast full-text searches (at the cost of increased processing when a document is added to the database), and that it is easy to develop. Using PySpark, we can implement this design pattern with a series of `map()`, `flatMap()`, and reduction transformations.

However, there is also a large storage overhead and high maintenance costs associated with update, delete, and insert operations.

Problem Statement

Suppose we have a dataset that consists of the works of Shakespeare, split among many files. We want to produce an index that contains a list of all the words, the file(s) in which each one occurs, and the number of times it occurs.

Input

Sample input documents for creating the inverted index can be downloaded from GitHub (*https://oreil.ly/5nD9H*). The documents consist of a series of 35 text files:

```
0ws0110.txt
0ws0210.txt
...
0ws4210.txt
```

Output

The output will be an inverted index created from all the documents read in the input phase. This output will have the following format:

```
(word, [(filename1, frequency1), (filename2, frequency2), ...])
```

which indicates that *word* is in *filename1* (with a frequency of *frequency1*), in *filename2* (with a frequency of *frequency2*), and so on.

PySpark Solution

Our PySpark implementation of this design pattern consists of the following steps:

1. Read the input files, filtering all stopwords (`a`, `of`, `the`, etc.) and apply stemming algorithms if desired (for example, converting `reading` to `read` and so on). This step creates pairs of `(path, text)`.
2. Create tuples with count 1. That is, the expected output would be `((word, document), 1)`.
3. Group all `(word, document)` pairs and sum the counts (reduction is required).
4. Transform each tuple of `((word, document), frequency)` into `(word, (document, count))` so that we can count `word`(s) per `document`.
5. Output the sequence of `(document, count)` pairs into a comma-separated string.
6. Save the inverted index.

Suppose we have the following three documents as input:

```
$ ls -l /tmp/documents/
file1.txt
file2.txt
file3.txt

$ cat /tmp/documents/file1.txt
fox jumped
fox jumped high
fox jumped and jumped

$ cat /tmp/documents/file2.txt
fox jumped
fox jumped high
bear ate fox
bear ate honey

$ cat /tmp/documents/file3.txt
fox jumped
bear ate honey
```

Step 1 is to read the input files and create pairs of `(path, text)`, where `path` is the full name of the input file and `text` is the content of the file. For example, if `path` denotes the file */tmp/documents/file1.txt*, then `text` is the content of the file *file1.txt*. Spark's `wholeTextFiles(`*`path`*`)` function reads a directory of text files from a filesystem URI. Each file is read as a single record and returned in a (key, value) pair, where the key is the path to the file and the value is the content of the file:

```
docs_path = '/tmp/documents/'
rdd = spark.sparkContext.wholeTextFiles(docs_path)
rdd.collect()
[('file:/tmp/documents/file2.txt',
   'fox jumped\nfox jumped high\nbear ate fox \nbear ate honey\n'),
  ('file:/tmp/documents/file3.txt',
   'fox jumped\nbear ate honey\n'),
  ('file:/tmp/documents/file1.txt',
   'fox jumped\nfox jumped high\nfox jumped and jumped\n')]
```

Step 2 is to map each `text` into a set of `((word, document), 1)` pairs. We start by splitting the texts on newlines:

```
def get_document_name(path):
  tokens = path.split("/")
  return tokens[-1]
#end-def

rdd2 = rdd.map(lambda x : (get_filename(x[0]), x[1]))
rdd2.collect()
[('file2.txt',
   'fox jumped\nfox jumped high\nbear ate fox \nbear ate honey\n'),
  ('file3.txt',
   'fox jumped\nbear ate honey\n'),
  ('file1.txt',
   'fox jumped\nfox jumped high\nfox jumped and jumped\n')]

rdd3 = rdd2.map(lambda x: (x[0], x[1].splitlines()))
rdd3.collect()
[('file2.txt',
  ['fox jumped', 'fox jumped high', 'bear ate fox ', 'bear ate honey']),
  ('file3.txt',
   ['fox jumped', 'bear ate honey']),
  ('file1.txt',
   ['fox jumped', 'fox jumped high', 'fox jumped and jumped'])]
```

Next, we create `(word, document)` pairs and map them into tuples of `((word, document), 1)`, which indicates that the `word` belongs to the `document` with a frequency of 1:

```
def create_pairs(tuple2):
  document = tuple2[0]
  records = tuple2[1]
  pairs = []
```

```
    for rec in records:
      for word in rec.split(" "):
        pairs.append((word, document))
    return pairs
#end-def

rdd4 = rdd3.flatMap(create_pairs)
rdd4.collect()
[('fox', 'file2.txt'), ('jumped', 'file2.txt'),
 ('fox', 'file2.txt'), ('jumped', 'file2.txt'), ... ]

rdd5 = rdd4.map(lambda x: (x, 1))
rdd5.collect()
[(('fox', 'file2.txt'), 1), (('jumped', 'file2.txt'), 1),
 (('fox', 'file2.txt'), 1), (('jumped', 'file2.txt'), 1), ...]
```

Step 3 is to perform a simple reduction to group all the `((word, document), 1)` pairs and sum the counts:

```
frequencies = rdd5.reduceByKey(lambda x, y: x+y)
frequencies.collect()
[(('fox', 'file2.txt'), 3), (('jumped', 'file2.txt'), 2),
 (('ate', 'file2.txt'), 2), (('bear', 'file3.txt'), 1), ...]
```

In step 4, we perform a very simple `map()` transformation that moves the `path` into the value part of the tuple:

```
((word, path), frequency) => (word, (path, frequency))
```

We do this as follows:

```
mapped = frequencies.map(lambda v: (v[0][0], (v[0][1], v[1])))
>>> mapped.collect()
[('fox', ('file2.txt', 3)), ('jumped', ('file2.txt', 2)),
 ('ate', ('file2.txt', 2)), ('bear', ('file3.txt', 1)), ...]
```

Next, in step 5 we output the sequence of `(document, count)` pairs into a comma-separated string:

```
inverted_index = mapped.groupByKey()
inverted_index.mapValues(lambda values: list(values)).collect()
[('fox', [('file2.txt', 3), ('file1.txt', 3), ('file3.txt', 1)]),
 ('bear', [('file3.txt', 1), ('file2.txt', 2)]),
 ('honey', [('file3.txt', 1), ('file2.txt', 1)]), ...]
```

To implement this step, I used the `groupByKey()` transformation. You may use other reduction transformations, such as `reduceByKey()` or `combineByKey()`, to accomplish the same task. For example, you could implement this step with the `combineByKey()` transformation as follows:

```
# convert a tuple into a list
def to_list(a):
  return [a]
```

```
# append a tuple to a list
def append(a, b):
  a.append(b)
  return a

# merge two lists from partitions
def extend(a, b):
  a.extend(b)
  return a

inverted_index = rdd6.combineByKey(to_list, append, extend)
```

Finally, step 6 is to save your created inverted index:

```
inverted_index.saveAsTextFile("/tmp/output/")
```

Summary

This chapter presented some of the most common and fundamental data analysis design patterns with simple examples, demonstrating implementations using PySpark. Before you invent a new custom data transformation, you should study the available PySpark APIs and use them if possible (since these APIs are tested rigorously, you can use them with confidence). Using combinations of Spark transformations will enable you to solve just about any data problem.

The next chapter introduces some practical data design patterns for production environments.

CHAPTER 10

Practical Data Design Patterns

The goal of this chapter is to introduce some practical data design patterns that are useful in solving common data problems. We will focus on actual design patterns that are used in big data solutions and deployed in production environments.

As in the previous chapter, I'll provide simple examples to illustrate the use of each one and show you how to use Spark's transformations to implement them. I'll also talk more about the concept of monoids, to help you better understand reduction transformations.

The best design patterns book available is the iconic computer science book *Design Patterns: Elements of Reusable Object-Oriented Software* by Erich Gamma, Richard Helm, Ralph Johnson, and John Vlissides (known as The "Gang of Four"). Rather than present data design patterns similar to those in the "Gang of Four" book, I will focus on practical, informal data design patterns that have been used in production environments.

The data design patterns that we'll cover in this chapter can help us to write scalable solutions to be deployed on Spark clusters. However, be aware that when it comes to adopting and using design patterns, there is no silver bullet. Every pattern should be tested for performance and scalability using real data, in an environment similar to your production environment.

For a general introduction to design patterns in software engineering, see the aforementioned *Design Patterns: Elements of Reusable Object-Oriented Software* by Erich Gamma, Richard Helm, Ralph Johnson, and John Vlissides (Addison-Wesley). To learn more about design patterns in MapReduce, see *MapReduce Design Patterns* by Donald Miner and Adam Shook and my book *Data Algorithms* (both published by O'Reilly).

The design patterns that I will cover in this chapter include:

- In-mapper combining
- Top-10
- MinMax
- The composite pattern/monoids
- Binning
- Sorting

We'll start with a useful summarization design pattern, using an in-mapper combiner.

> **Source Code**
>
> Complete programs for this chapter are available in the book's GitHub repository (*https://oreil.ly/TO5ji*).

In-Mapper Combining

In the MapReduce paradigm, a combiner (also known as a semi-reducer) is a process that runs locally on each worker to aggregate data before it's sent across the network to the reducer(s). In frameworks like Hadoop, this is typically viewed as an optional local optimization. An *in-mapper combiner* performs a further optimization by performing the aggregation in memory as it receives each (key, value) pair from the mapper, rather than writing them all to to the local disk and then aggregating the values by key. (Spark performs all its processing in memory, so this is how it operates by default.) The aim of the in-mapper combining design pattern is for the mapper to efficiently combine and summarize its output as much as possible, so it emits fewer intermediate (key, value) pairs for the sort and shuffle and reducers (such as `reduceByKey()` or `groupByKey()`) to handle. For example, for a classic word count problem, given an input record such as:

```
"fox jumped and fox jumped again fox"
```

without using the in-mapper combining design pattern we would generate the following (key, value) pairs to send to the reducers:

```
(fox, 1)
(jumped, 1)
(and, 1)
(fox, 1)
(jumped, 1)
(again, 1)
(fox, 1)
```

The problem is that for a very large dataset this approach would generate a huge number of `(word, 1)` pairs, which would be inefficient and keep the cluster network too busy. Using the in-mapper combining design pattern, we aggregate the data by key before sending it across the network, summarizing and reducing the mapper's output before the shuffle is performed. For example, as in this case there are three instances of `(fox, 1)` and two instances of `(jumped, 1)`, these (key, value) pairs will be combined into the following output:

```
(fox, 3)
(jumped, 2)
(and, 1)
(again, 1)
```

While the reduction is not significant in this toy example, if we have a large dataset with a lot of repeated words this design pattern can help us to achieve significantly better performance by generating far fewer intermediate (key, value) pairs.

To further demonstrate the concept behind this design pattern, the following sections will present three solutions to the problem of counting the frequency of characters in a set of documents. In simple terms, we want to find how many times each unique character appears in a given corpus. We will discuss the following solutions:

- Basic MapReduce algorithm
- In-mapper combining per record
- In-mapper combining per partition

Basic MapReduce Algorithm

To count the characters in a set of documents, we split each input record into a set of words, split each word into a character array, then (key, value) pairs where the key is a single character from the character array and the value is 1 (the frequency count of one character). This is the basic MapReduce design pattern that does not use any custom data types, and the reducer simply sums up the frequencies of each single unique character. The problem with this solution is that for large datasets it will emit a large number of (key, value) pairs, which can overload the network and harm the performance of the overall solution. The large number of (key, value) pairs emitted can also slow down the sort and shuffle phase (grouping values for the same key). The different stages of this approach are illustrated in Figure 10-1.

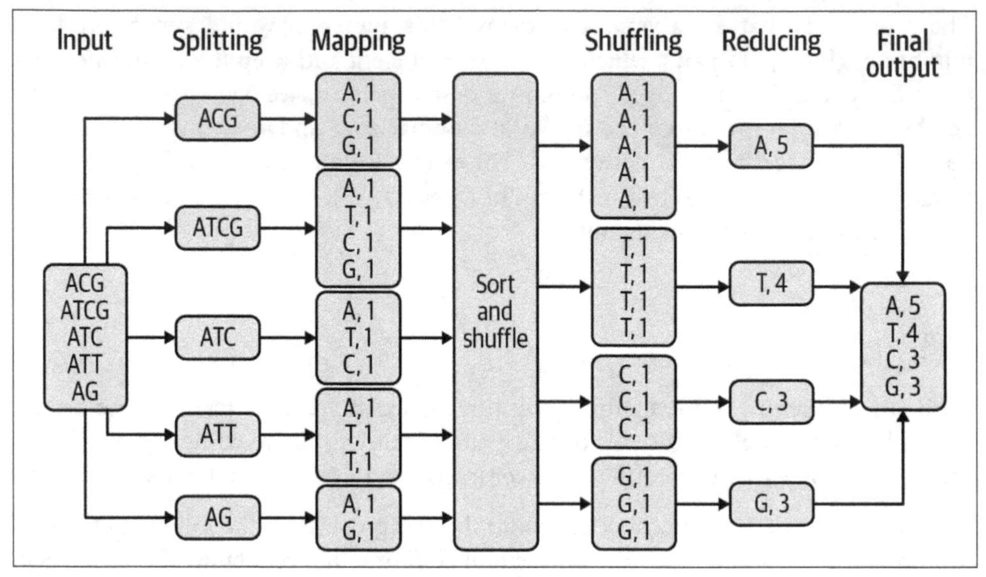

Figure 10-1. Character count: basic MapReduce algorithm

Given an `RDD[String]`, a PySpark implementation of this algorithm is provided next.

First we define a simple function that accepts a single `String` record and returns a list of (key, value) pairs, where the key is a character and the value is 1 (the frequency of that character):

```
def mapper(rec):
    words = rec.lower().split() ❶
    pairs = [] ❷
    for word in words: ❸
        for c in word: ❹
           pairs.append((c, 1)) ❺
        #end-for
    #end-for
    return pairs ❻
#end-def
```

❶ Tokenize a record into an array of words.

❷ Create an empty list as `pairs`.

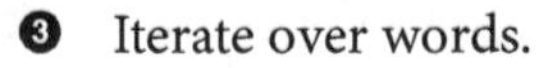

❸ Iterate over words.

❹ Iterate over a single word.

❺ Add each character (`c`) as `(c, 1)` to `pairs`.

❻ Return a list of (c, 1) for all characters in a given record.

This mapper() function can be simplified as:

```
def mapper(rec):
    words = rec.lower().split()
    pairs = [(c, 1) for word in words for c in word]
    return pairs
#end-def
```

Next, we use the mapper() function to count the frequencies of unique characters:

```
# spark: an instance of SparkSession
rdd = spark.sparkContext.textFile("/dir/input") ❶
pairs = rdd.flatMap(mapper) ❷
frequencies = pairs.reduceByKey(lambda a, b: a+b) ❸
```

❶ Create an RDD[String] from the input data.

❷ Map each record into a collection of characters and flatten it as a new RDD[Character, 1].

❸ Find the frequency of each unique character.

Next, we'll look at a more efficient implementation that uses the in-mapper combining design pattern.

In-Mapper Combining per Record

This section introduces the in-mapper combining per record design pattern, also known as local aggregation per record solution. It's similar to the basic Spark Map-Reduce algorithm, with the exception that for a given input record we aggregate frequencies for each character before emitting (key, value) pairs. In other words, in this solution we emit (key, value) pairs where the key is a unique character within a given input record and the value is the aggregated frequency of that character within that record. Then we use reduceByKey() to aggregate all the frequencies for each unique character. This solution uses local aggregation by leveraging the associativity and commutativity of the reduce() function to combine values before sending them across the network. For example, for the following input record:

```
foxy fox jumped over fence
```

we will emit the following (key, value) pairs:

```
(o, 3)  (m, 1)  (v, 1)
(x, 2)  (p, 1)  (r, 1)
(y, 1)  (e, 4)  (n, 1)
(j, 1)  (d, 1)  (c, 1)
```

Given an RDD[String], a PySpark solution is provided next.

First we define a simple function that accepts a single `String` record (an element of the input `RDD[String]`) and returns a list of (key, value) pairs, where the key is a unique character and the value is the aggregated frequency of that character:

```
import collections ❶
def local_aggregator(record):
    hashmap = collections.defaultdict(int) ❷
    words = record.lower().split() ❸
    for word in words: ❹
        for c in word: ❺
            hashmap[c] += 1 ❻
        #end-for
    #end-for
    print("hashmap=", hashmap)

    pairs = [(k, v) for k, v in hashmap.iteritems()] ❼
    print("pairs=", pairs)
    return  pairs ❽
#end-def
```

 The `collections` module provides high-performance container data types.

❷ Create an empty `dict[String, Integer]`. `defaultdict` is a `dict` subclass that calls a factory function to supply missing values.

❸ Tokenize the input record into an array of words.

❹ Iterate over words.

❺ Iterate over each word.

❻ Aggregate characters.

❼ Flatten the dictionary into a list of `(character, frequency)`.

❽ Return the flattened list of `(character, frequency)`.

Next, we use the `local_aggregator()` function to count the frequencies of unique characters:

```
input_path = '/tmp/your_input_data.txt'
rdd = spark.sparkContext.textFile(input_path)
pairs = rdd.flatMap(local_aggregator)
frequencies = pairs.reduceByKey(lambda a, b: a+b)
```

This solution will emit many fewer (key, value) pairs, which is an improvement over the previous solution. This means there will be less load on the network and the sort and shuffle will execute faster than with the basic algorithm. However, there's still a potential problem with this implementation: although it will scale out if we don't have too many mappers, because we instantiate and use a dictionary per mapper, if we have a lot of mappers we might run into OOM errors.

Next, I'll present another version of this design pattern that avoids this problem and is even more efficient.

In-Mapper Combining per Partition

This final solution aggregates the frequencies of each character per partition (rather than per record) of input data, where each partition may be comprised of thousands or millions of input records. To do this, we will again build a hash table of `dict[Character, Integer]`, but this time for the characters of a given input partition instead of an input record. The mapper will then emit (key, value) pairs comprised of entries from the hash table, where the key is `dict.Entry.getKey()` and the value is `dict.Entry.getValue()`. This is a very compact data representation, since every entry of `dict[Character, Integer]` is equivalent to *N* basic (key, value) pairs, where *N* is equal to `dict.Entry.getValue()`.

So, in this solution we use a single hash table per input partition to keep track of the frequencies of all characters in all records in that partition. After the mapper finishes processing the partition (using PySpark's `mapPartitions()` transformation), we emit all the (key, value) pairs from the frequencies table (the hash table we built). Then the reducers will sum up the frequencies from all the partitions and find the final count of characters. This solution is more efficient than the previous two because it emits even fewer (key, value) pairs, resulting in even less load on the network and less work for the sort and shuffle phase. It will also scale out better than the previous two solutions, because using a single hash table per input partition eliminates the risk of OOM problems. Even if we partition our input into thousands of partitions, this solution scales out very well.

As an example, for the following input partition (as opposed to a single record):

```
foxy fox jumped over fence
foxy fox jumped
foxy fox
```

we will emit the following (key, value) pairs:

```
(f, 7)  (u, 2)  (v, 1)  (j, 2)  (y, 3)
(o, 7)  (m, 1)  (r, 1)  (d, 2)  (e, 5)
(x, 6)  (p, 2)  (n, 1)  (c, 1)
```

One consideration when using this design pattern is that you need to be careful about the size of the hash table, to be sure it will not cause bottlenecks. For the character count problem, the size of the hash table for each mapper (per input partition) will be very small (since we have a limited number of unique characters), so there's no danger of a performance bottleneck.

Given an `RDD[String]`, the PySpark solution is provided next.

First we define a simple function that accepts a single input partition (comprised of many input records) and returns a list of (key, value) pairs, where the key is a character and the value is the aggregated frequency of that character:

```
def inmapper_combiner(partition_iterator): ❶
    hashmap = defaultdict(int) ❷
    for record in partition_iterator: ❸
        words = record.lower().split() ❹
        for word in words: ❺
            for c in word: ❻
                hashmap[c] += 1 ❼
            #end-for
        #end-for
    #end-for
    print("hashmap=", hashmap)
    #
    pairs = [(k, v) for k, v in hashmap.iteritems()] ❽
    print("pairs=", pairs)
    return  pairs ❾
#end-def
```

 `partition_iterator` represents a single input partition comprised of a set of records.

❷ Create an empty `dict[String, Integer]`.

❸ Get a single record from a partition.

❹ Tokenize the record into an array of words.

❺ Iterate over words.

❻ Iterate over each word.

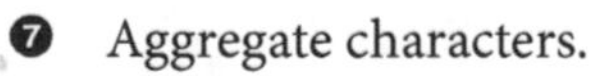
❼ Aggregate characters.

❽ Flatten the dictionary into a list of `(character, frequency)`.

❾ Return the flattened list of (character, frequency).

Next, we use the inmapper_combiner() function to count frequencies of unique characters:

```
rdd = spark.sparkContext.textFile("/.../input") ❶
pairs = rdd.mapPartitions(inmapper_combiner) ❷
frequencies = pairs.reduceByKey(lambda a, b: a+b)
```

❶ Create an RDD[String] from input file(s).

❷ The mapPartitions() transformation returns a new RDD by applying a function to each input partition (as opposed to a single input record) of this RDD.

This solution will emit far fewer (key, value) pairs than the previous ones. It's quite efficient, since we instantiate and use a single dictionary per input partition (rather than per input record). This greatly reduces the amount of data that needs to be transferred between the mappers and reducers, easing the load on the network and speeding up the sort and shuffle phase. The in-mapper combining algorithm makes good use of combiners as optimizers, and this solution scales out extremely well. Even if we have a large number of mappers, this will not cause OOM errors. However, it should be noted that this algorithm may run into a problem if the number of unique keys grows too large for the associative array to fit in memory, as memory paging will significantly affect performance. If this is the case, you will have to revert to the basic MapReduce approach.

In implementing the in-mapper combining per partition design pattern, we use Spark's powerful mapPartitions() transformation to transform each input partition into a single dict[Character, Integer], and then we aggregate these into a single final dict[Character, Integer]. For character counting and other applications where you want to extract a small amount of information from a large dataset, this algorithm is efficient and faster than other approaches. In the case of the character counting problem, the size of the associative array (per mapper partition) is bounded by the number of unique characters, so there are no scalability bottlenecks when using this design pattern.

To recap, the in-mapper combining per partition design pattern offers several important advantages in terms of efficiency and scalability:

- Greatly reduces the number of (key, value) pairs emitted
- Requires far less sorting and shuffling of (key, value) pairs
- Makes good use of combiners as optimizers
- Scales out very well

But there are also a few disadvantages to be aware of:

- More difficult to implement (requires custom functions for handling each partition)
- Underlying object (per mapper partition) is more heavyweight
- Fundamental limitation in terms of size of the underlying object (for the character count problem, an associative array per mapper partition)

Next, we'll look at a few other common use cases where you want to extract a small amount of information from a large dataset, and see what the best approaches are.

Top-10

Creating a top-10 list is a common task in many data-intensive operations. For example, we might ask the following questions:

- What were the top 10 URLs visited during the last day/week/month?
- What were the top 10 items purchased from Amazon during the last day/week/month?
- What were the top 10 search queries on Google in the last day/week/month?
- What were the top 10 most liked items on Facebook yesterday?
- What are the top 10 cartoons of all time?

A simple design pattern for answering these kinds of questions is illustrated in Figure 10-2.

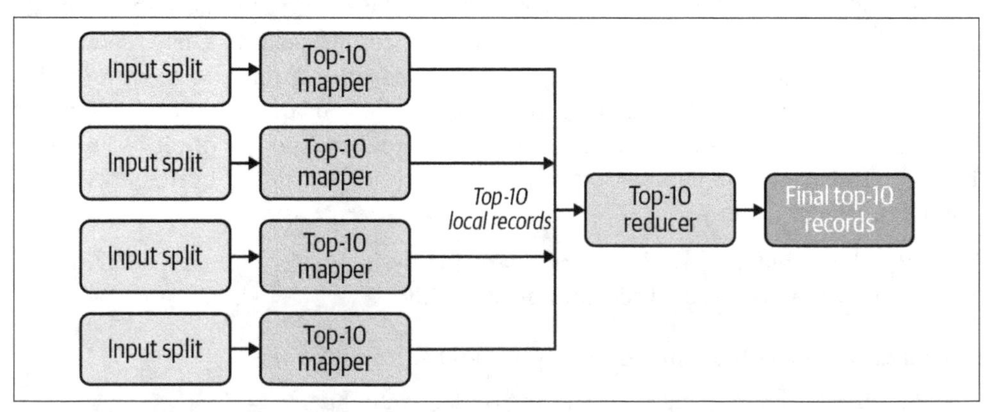

Figure 10-2. The top-10 design pattern

For example, say we have a table with two columns, `url` and `frequency`. Finding the top 10 most visited URLs with a SQL query is straightforward:

```
SELECT url, frequency
   FROM url_table
      ORDER BY frequency DESC
         LIMIT 10;
```

Finding the top *N* (where $N > 0$) records in Spark is also easy. Given an `RDD[(String, Integer)]` where the key is a string representing a URL and the value is the frequency of visits to that URL, we can use `RDD.takeOrdered(N)` to find the top-*N* list. The general format of `RDD.takeOrdered()` is:

```
takeOrdered(N, key=None)
Description:
   Get the N elements from an RDD ordered in ascending
   order or as specified by the optional key function.
```

Assuming that *N* is an integer greater than 0, we have various options for finding a top-N list efficiently with `RDD.takeOrdered()`:

```
# Sort by keys (ascending):
RDD.takeOrdered(N, key = lambda x: x[0])

# Sort by keys (descending):
RDD.takeOrdered(N, key = lambda x: -x[0])

# Sort by values (ascending):
RDD.takeOrdered(N, key = lambda x: x[1])

# Sort by values (descending):
RDD.takeOrdered(N, key = lambda x: -x[1])
```

For the sake of argument, let's assume that `takeOrdered()` does not perform optimally with large datasets. What other options do we have?

Given a large set of (key, value) pairs where the key is a `String` and the value is an `Integer`, we want an independent, reusable solution to the problem of finding the top *N* keys (where $N > 0$)—that is, a design pattern that enables us to produce reusable code to answer questions like the ones mentioned earlier when working with big data. This kind of question is common for data consisting of (key, value) pairs. This is essentially a filtering task: you filter out unwanted data and keep just the top *N* items. The top 10 function is also a function that is commutative and associative, and therefore using partitioners, combiners, and reducers will always produce correct results.

That is, given a top-10 function `T` and a set of values (such as frequencies) `{a, b, c}` for the same key, then we can write:

- Commutative

```
T(a, b) = T(b, a)
```

- Associative

```
T(a, T(b, c)) = T(T(a, b), c)
```

For additional details on the top-10 list design pattern, refer to *MapReduce Design Patterns* by Donald Miner and Adam Shook.

This section provides a complete PySpark solution for the top-10 design pattern. Given an `RDD[(String, Integer)]`, the goal is to find the top-10 list for that RDD. In our solution, we assume that all keys are unique. If the keys are not unique, then you may use the `reduceByKey()` transformation (before finding the top-10) to make them unique.

Our solution will generalize the problem and will be able to find a top-*N* list (for $N > 0$). For example, we will be able to find the top 10 cats, top 50 most visited websites, or top 100 search queries.

Top-N Formalized

Let's start by formalizing the problem. Let *N* be an integer number greater than 0. Let `L` be a list of pairs of `(T, Integer)`, where `T` can be any type (such as `String`, `Integer`, etc.), `L.size() = s`, and `s > N`. The elements of `L` are:

$$\{(K_i, V_i), i = 1, 2, \ldots, s\}$$

where K_i has a data type of `T` and V_i is an `Integer` type (this is the frequency of K_i). Let `{sort(L)}` be a sorted list where the sorting is done by using frequency as a key. This gives us:

$$\{(A_j, B_j), 1 \leq j \leq S, B_1 \geq B_2 \geq \ldots \geq B_s\}$$

where (A_j, B_j) are in L. Then, the top-N of list L is defined as:

$$\text{top-N(L)} = \left\{ \left(A_j, B_j\right), 1 \le j \le N,\ B_1 \ge B_2 \ge \ldots \ge B_N \ge B_{N+1} \ge \ldots \ge B_s \right\}$$

For our top-N solution, we will use Python's `SortedDict`, a sorted mutable mapping. The design of this type is simple: `SortedDict` inherits from `dict` to store items and maintains a sorted list of keys. Sorted dict keys must be hashable and comparable. The hash and total ordering of keys must not change while they are stored in the sorted dict.

To implement top-N, we need a hash table data structure whose keys can have a total order, such as `SortedDict` (in our case, keys represent frequencies). The dictionary is ordered according to the natural ordering of its keys. We can build this structure with `sortedcontainer.SortedDict()`. We will keep adding `(frequency, url)` pairs to the `SortedDict`, but keep its size at N. When the size is N+1, we will pop out the smallest frequency using `SortedDict.popitem(0)`.

An example of how this works is shown here:

```
>>> from sortedcontainers import SortedDict
>>> sd = SortedDict({10: 'a', 2: 'm', 3: 'z', 5: 'b', 6: 't', 100: 'd', 20: 's'})
>>> sd
SortedDict({2: 'm', 3: 'z', 5: 'b', 6: 't', 10: 'a', 20: 's', 100: 'd'})
>>> sd.popitem(0)
(2, 'm')
>>> sd
SortedDict({3: 'z', 5: 'b', 6: 't', 10: 'a', 20: 's', 100: 'd'})
>>> sd[50] = 'g'
>>> sd
SortedDict({3: 'z', 5: 'b', 6: 't', 10: 'a', 20: 's', 50: 'g', 100: 'd'})
>>> sd.popitem(0)
(3, 'z')
>>> sd
SortedDict({5: 'b', 6: 't', 10: 'a', 20: 's', 50: 'g', 100: 'd'})
>>> sd[9] = 'h'
>>> sd
SortedDict({5: 'b', 6: 't', 9: 'h', 10: 'a', 20: 's', 50: 'g', 100: 'd'})
>>> sd.popitem(0)
(5, 'b')
>>> sd
SortedDict({6: 't', 9: 'h', 10: 'a', 20: 's', 50: 'g', 100: 'd'})
>>>
>>> len(sd)
6
```

Next, I'll present a top-10 solution using PySpark.

PySpark Solution

The PySpark solution is pretty straightforward. We use the `mapPartitions()` transformation to find the local top *N* (where $N > 0$) for each partition, and pass these to a single reducer. The reducer then finds the final top-*N* list from all the local top-*N* lists passed from the mappers. In general, in most MapReduce algorithms having a single reducer is problematic and will cause a performance bottleneck if one reducer on one server receives all the data—potentially a very large volume—and all the other nodes are doing nothing, all the pressure and load will be on that one node, causing a bottleneck). However, in this case, our single reducer will not cause a performance problem. Why not? Let's assume that we have 5,000 partitions. Each mapper will only generate 10 (key, value) pairs, which means our single reducer will only get 50,000 records—a volume of data that's not likely to cause performance bottleneck in a Spark cluster.

A high-level overview of the PySpark solution for the top-10 design pattern is presented in Figure 10-3.

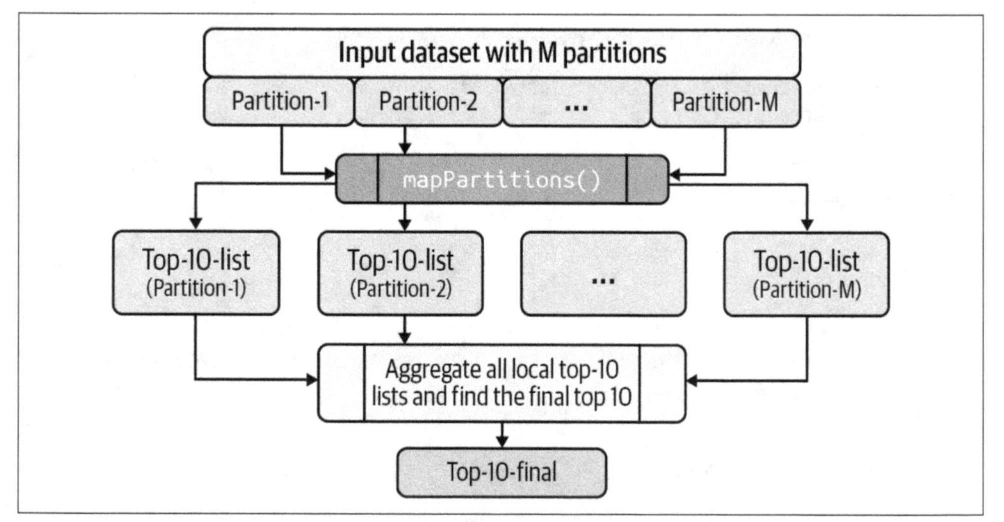

Figure 10-3. PySpark implementation of the Top-10 design pattern

Input is partitioned into smaller chunks, and each chunk is sent to a mapper. Each mapper emits a local top-10 list to be sent to the reducer(s). Here, we use a single reducer key so that the output from all mappers will be consumed by a single reducer.

Let `spark` be an instance of `SparkSession`. This is how the top-10 problem is solved by using the `mapPartitions()` transformation and a custom Python function named `top10_design_pattern()`:

```
pairs = [('url-1', 10), ('url-2', 8), ('url-3', 4), ...]
rdd = spark.sparkContext.parallelize(pairs)
```

```
# mapPartitions(f, preservesPartitioning=False)
# Return a new RDD by applying a function
# to each partition of this RDD.
top10 = rdd.mapPartitions(top10_design_pattern)
```

To complete the implementation, here I'll present the `top10_design_pattern()` function, which finds the top-10 for each partition (containing a set of (key, value) pairs):

```
from sortedcontainers import SortedDict

def top10_design_pattern(partition_iterator): ❶
    sd = SortedDict() ❷
    for url, frequency in partition_iterator: ❸
        sd[frequency] = url ❹
        if (len(sd) > 10):
            sd.popitem(0) ❺
    #end-for
    print("local sd=", sd)

    pairs = [(k, v) for k, v in sd.items()] ❻
    print("top 10 pairs=", pairs)
    return  pairs ❼
#end-def
```

❶ `partition_iterator` is an iterator for a single partition; it iterates over a set of `(URL, frequency)` pairs.

❷ Create an empty `SortedDict` of `(Integer, String)` pairs.

❸ Iterate over a set of `(URL, frequency)` pairs.

❹ Put the `(frequency, URL)` pairs into a `SortedDict`.

❺ Limit the size of the sorted dictionary to 10 (remove the lowest frequencies).

❻ Convert the `SortedDict` (which is a local top-10 list) into a list of `(k, v)` pairs.

❼ Return a local top-10 list for a single partition.

Each mapper accepts a partition of elements, where each element is a pair of `(URL, frequency)`. The number of partitions is typically determined by the data size and the available resources in the cluster (nodes, cores, memory, etc.), or it can be set explicitly by the programmer. After the mapper finishes creating its local top-10 list as a `SortedDict[Integer, String]`, the function returns that list. Note that we use a single dictionary (such as a `SortedDict`) per partition, and not per element of the source RDD. As described in "In-Mapper Combining per Partition" on page 309, this greatly improves the efficiency of the operation by reducing the network load and the work to be done in the sort and shuffle phase.

A complete solution using `mapPartitions()` is provided in the book's GitHub repository.

Finding the Bottom 10

In the previous section, I showed you how to find the top-10 list. To find the bottom-10 list, we just need to replace this line of code:

```
# find top 10
if (len(sd) > 10): ❶
    sd.popitem(0) ❷
```

❶ If the size of the `SortedDict` is larger than 10...

❷ ...then remove the URL with the lowest frequency from the dictionary.

with this:

```
# find bottom 10
if (len(sd) > 10): ❶
    sd.popitem(-1) ❷
```

❶ If the size of the `SortedDict` is larger than 10...

❷ ...then remove the URL with the highest frequency from the dictionary.

Next let's discuss how to partition your input. Partitioning RDDs is a combination of art and science. What is the right number of partitions for your cluster? There is no magic formula for calculating this; it depends on the number of cluster nodes, the number of cores per server, and the amount of RAM available. There's some trial and error involved, but a good rule of thumb is to start with the following:

```
2 * num_executors * cores_per_executor
```

When you create an RDD, if you do not set the number of partitions explicitly, the Spark cluster manager will set it to a default number (based on the available resources). You can also set the number yourself, as shown here:

```
input_path = "/data/my_input_path"
desired_num_of_partitions = 16
rdd = spark.sparkContext.textFile(input_path, desired_num_of_partitions)
```

This creates an `RDD[String]` with 16 partitions.

For an existing RDD, you can reset the new number of partitions by using the `coalesce()` function:

```
# rdd: RDD[T]
desired_number_of_partitions = 40
rdd2 = rdd.coalesce(desired_number_of_partitions)
```

The newly created rdd2 (another RDD[T]) will have 40 partitions. The coalesce() function is defined as follows:

```
pyspark.RDD.coalesce:
coalesce(numPartitions, shuffle=False)

Description:
  Return a new RDD that is reduced into numPartitions partitions.
```

Unlike repartition(), which can be used to increase or decrease the number of partitions but involves shuffling across the cluster, coalesce() can only be used to decrease the number of partitions and in most cases does not require a shuffle.

Next, I'll introduce the MinMax design pattern, which is used to distill a small amount of information from a large dataset of numbers.

MinMax

MinMax is a numerical summarization design pattern. Given a set of billions of numbers, the goal is to find the minimum, maximum, and count of all of the numbers. This pattern can be used in scenarios where the data you are dealing with or you want to aggregate is of a numerical type and the data can be grouped by specific fields. To help you understand the concept of the MinMax design pattern, I am going to present three different solutions with quite different performance.

Solution 1: Classic MapReduce

The naive approach is to emit the following (key, value) pairs:

```
("min", number)
("max", number)
("count", 1)
```

The sort and shuffle will then group all values by three keys, min, max, and count, and finally we can use a reducer to iterate through all the numbers and find the global min, max, and count. The problem with this approach is that we have to move potentially millions of (key, value) pairs across the network and then create three huge Iterable<T> data structures (where T is a numeric type, such as Long or Double). This solution might run into serious performance problems and will not scale. Furthermore, in the reduction phase it will not effectively utilize all of the cluster resources due to having only three unique keys.

Solution 2: Sorting

The next solution is to sort all the numbers and then find the top (max), bottom (min), and count of the dataset. If the performance is acceptable, this is a valid solution;

however, for a large dataset the sorting time might be unacceptably long. In other words, this solution will not scale out either.

Solution 3: Spark's mapPartitions()

The final solution, which is the most efficient from a performance and scalability point of view, splits the data into *N* chunks (partitions) and then uses Spark's `mapPartitions()` transformation to emit three (key, value) pairs from each partition:

```
("min", minimum-number-in-partition)
("max", maximum-number-in-partition)
("count", count-of-numbers-in-partition)
```

Finally, we find the global `min`, `max`, and `count` from all partitions. This solution scales out very well. No matter how many partitions you have, this will work and will not create OOM errors. For example, suppose you have 500 billion numbers in your dataset (assume one or more numbers per record), and you partition it into 100,000 chunks. In the worst case (one number per record), each partition will have 5 million records. Each of these partitions will emit the three pairs shown above. Then, you just need to find the `min`, `max`, and `count` of 100,000 x 3 pairs = 300,000 numbers. This is a trivial task that will not cause any scalability problems.

A high-level view of this solution is illustrated in Figure 10-4.

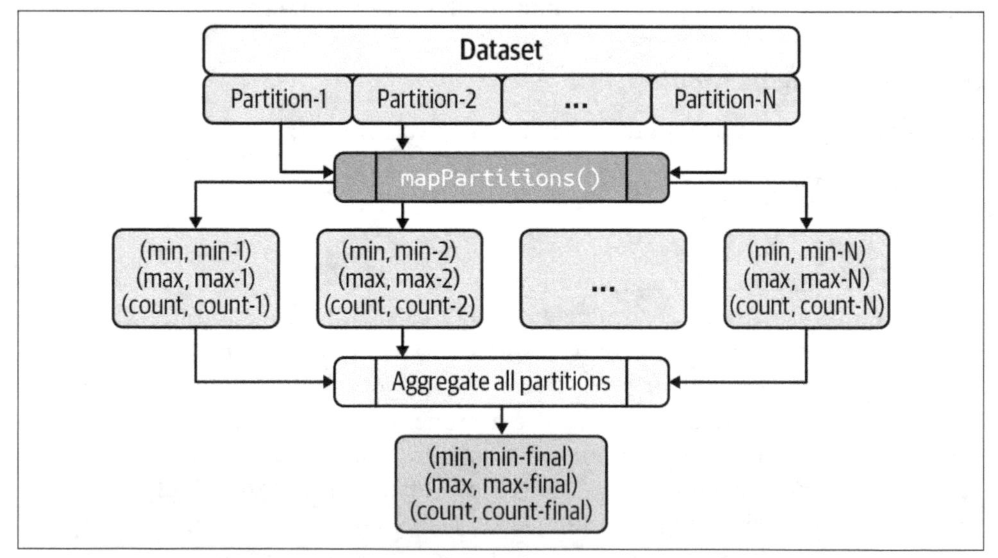

Figure 10-4. A PySpark implementation of the MinMax design pattern

Let's assume that our input records have the following format:

```
<number><,><number><,><number>...
```

Here are a few sample records:

```
10,345,24567,2,100,345,9000,765
2,34567,23,13,45678,900
...
```

Here's the PySpark solution for solving the MinMax problem (the complete program with sample input is available on GitHub (*https://oreil.ly/TO5ji*), in the file *minmax_use_mappartitions.py*):

```
input_path = <your-input-path>
rdd = spark.sparkContext.textFile(input_path) ❶
min_max_count = rdd.mapPartitions(minmax) ❷
min_max_count_list = min_max_count.collect() ❸
final_min_max_count = find_min_max_count(min_max_count_list) ❹
```

❶ Return a new RDD from the given input.

❷ Return an RDD of `(min, max, count)` from each partition by applying the `minmax()` function.

❸ Collect `(min, max, count)` from all partitions as a list.

❹ Find the `(final_min, final_max, final_count)` by calling the function `find_min_max_count()`.

I've defined the `minmax()` function as follows:

```
def minmax(iterator): ❶

    first_time = True

    for record in iterator: ❷
        numbers = [int(n) for n in record.split(",")] ❸
        if (first_time): ❹
            # initialize count, min, max to the 1st record values
            local_min = min(numbers)
            local_max = max(numbers)
            local_count = len(numbers)
            first_time = False
        else: ❺
            # update count, min, and max
            local_count += len(numbers)
            local_max = max(max(numbers), local_max)
            local_min = min(min(numbers), local_min)
    #end-for
    return [(local_min, local_max, local_count)] ❻
#end-def
```

❶ The `iterator` is of type `itertools.chain`.

❷ Iterate the `iterator` (`record` holds a single record).

❸ Tokenize the input and build an array of numbers.

❹ If this is the first record, find the `min`, `max`, and `count`.

❺ If this is not the first record, update `local_min`, `local_max`, and `local_count`.

❻ Finally, return a triplet from each partition.

What if some of the partitions are empty (i.e., contain no data)? There are many reasons that this can occur, and it's important to handle empty partitions gracefully (for more on this, see Chapter 3).

I'll show you how to do this next. Error handling in Python is done through the use of exceptions that are caught in `try` blocks and handled in `except` blocks. In Python, if an error is encountered in a `try` block, code execution is stopped and control is transferred down to the `except` block. Let's see how we can implement this in our MinMax solution:

```
def minmax(iterator): ❶

    print("type(iterator)=", type(iterator)) ❷
#   ('type(iterator)=', <type 'itertools.chain'>)

    try:
        first_record = next(iterator) ❸
    except StopIteration: ❹
        return [ None ] # We will filter out None values by filter()

    # initialize count, min, max to the 1st record values
    numbers = [int(n) for n in first_record.split(",")] ❺
    local_min = min(numbers)
    local_max = max(numbers)
    local_count = len(numbers)

    for record in iterator: ❻
        numbers = [int(n) for n in record.split(",")]
        # update min, max, count
        local_count += len(numbers)
        local_max = max(max(numbers), local_max)
        local_min = min(min(numbers), local_min)
#   end-for
    return [(local_min, local_max, local_count)] ❼
```

❶ The `iterator` is of type `itertools.chain`.

❷ Print the type of the `iterator` (for debugging only).

3. Try to get the first record from the `iterator`. If successful, then `first_record` is initialized to the first record of a partition.

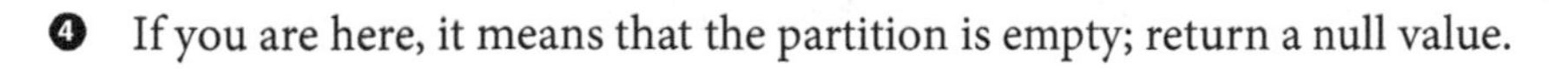

4. If you are here, it means that the partition is empty; return a null value.

5. Set `min`, `max`, and `count` from the first record.

6. Iterate the `iterator` for records 2, 3, etc. (`record` holds a single record).

7. Finally, return a triplet from each partition.

How should we test the handling of empty partitions? The program *min-max_force_empty_partitions.py* (available in the book's GitHub repository) forces the creation of empty partitions and handles them gracefully. You can force the creation of empty partitions by setting the number of partitions higher than the number of input records. For example, if your input has *N* records, setting the number of partitions to *N*+3 will cause the partitioner to create up to three empty partitions.

The Composite Pattern and Monoids

This section explores the concept of the composite pattern and monoids, introduced in Chapter 4, and delves into how to use them in the context of Spark and PySpark.

The composite pattern is a structural design pattern (also called a partitioning design pattern) that can be used when a group of objects can be treated the same as a single object in that group. You can use it to create hierarchies and groups of objects, resulting in a tree-like structure with leaves (objects) and composites (subgroups). This is illustrated in UML notation in Figure 10-5.

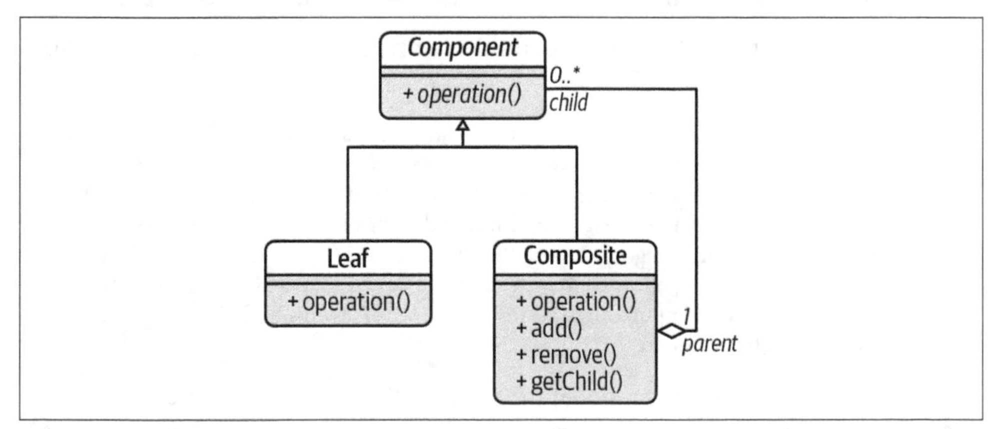

Figure 10-5. UML diagram of the Composite design pattern

With this design pattern, once you've composed objects into this tree-like structure, you can work with that structure as if it were a singular object. A key feature is the ability to run methods recursively over the whole tree structure and sum up the results. This pattern can be implemented with PySpark reducers.

A simple example of the use of the composite pattern is adding a set of numbers (over a set of keys), as illustrated in Figure 10-6. Here, the numbers are the leaves and the composites are the addition operator.

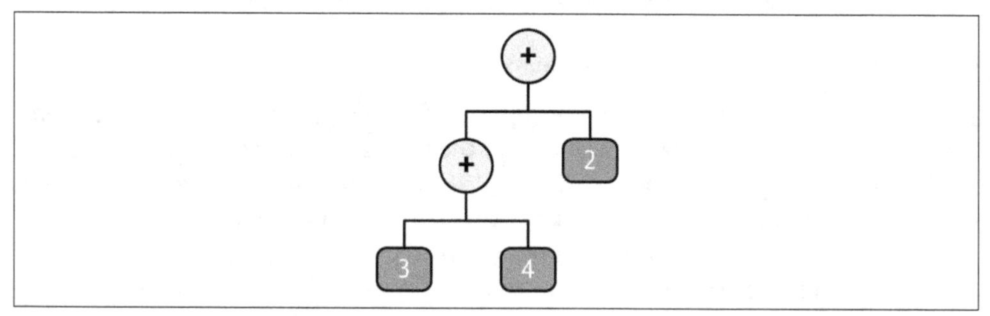

Figure 10-6. Composite pattern example: addition

Next, I'll discuss the concept of monoids in the context of the composite pattern.

Monoids

In Chapter 4, we discussed the use of monoids in reduction transformations. Here, we will look at monoids in the context of the composite pattern, which is commonly used in big data for composing (such as through addition and concatenation operators) and aggregating sets of data points. From the pattern's definition, it should be obvious that there is a commonality between monoids and the composite pattern.

As a refresher, let's take a look at the definition of monoids from Wikipedia (*https://oreil.ly/5TXsW*):

> In abstract algebra, a branch of mathematics, a monoid is a set equipped with an associative binary operation and an identity element. Monoids are semigroups with identity. Such algebraic structures occur in several branches of mathematics. For example, the functions from a set into itself form a monoid with respect to function composition. More generally, in category theory, the morphisms of an object to itself form a monoid, and, conversely, a monoid may be viewed as a category with a single object. In computer science and computer programming, the set of strings built from a given set of characters is a free monoid.

The MapReduce programming model is an application of monoids in computer science. As we've seen, it consists of three functions: `map()`, `combine()`, and `reduce()`. These functions are very similar to the `map()` and `flatMap()` functions (`combine()` is an optional operation) and reduction transformations in Spark. Given a dataset, `map()` maps arbitrary data to elements of a specific monoid, `combine()` aggregates/folds data at a local level (worker nodes in cluster), and `reduce()` aggregates/folds those elements, so that in the end we produce just one element.

So, in terms of programming language semantics, a monoid is just an interface with one abstract value and one abstract method. The abstract method for a monoid is the append operation (it can be an addition operator on integers or a concatenation operator on string objects). The abstract value for a monoid is the identity value, defined as the value you can append to any value that will always result in the original value, unmodified. For example, the identity value for collection data structures is the empty collection, because appending a collection to an empty collection will typically produce the same collection unmodified. For adding a set of integers, the identity value is zero, and for concatenating strings it's an empty string (a string of length zero).

Next, we will briefly review MapReduce's combines and abstract algebra's monoids and see how they are related to each other. As you'll see, when your MapReduce operations (e.g., `map()` and `reduceByKey()` transformations in Spark) are not monoids, it is very hard (if not impossible) to use combiners efficiently.

In the MapReduce paradigm, the mapper is not constrained, but the reducer is required to be (the iterated application of) an associative operation. The combiner (as an optional plug-in component) is a "local reducer" process that operates only on data generated by one server. Successful use of combiners reduces the amount of intermediate data generated by the mappers on a given single server (that is why it is called local). Combiners can be used as a MapReduce optimization to reduce network traffic by decreasing the amount of (key, value) pairs sent from mappers to reducers. Typically, combiners have the same interface as reducers. A combiner must have the following characteristics:

- Receives as input all the data emitted by the mapper instances on a given server (this is called a local aggregation)
- Sends its output to the reducers
- Side-effect free (combiners may run an indeterminate number of times)
- Has the same input and output key and value types
- Runs in memory after the map phase

We can define a combiner skeleton as follows:

```
# key: as KeyType
# values: as Iterable<ValueType>
def combine(key, values):
   ...
   # use key and values to create new_key and new_value
   new_key = <a-value-of-KeyType>
   new_value = <a-value-of-ValueType>
```

```
    ...
    return (new_key, new_value);
    ...
#end-def
```

This template illustrates that the (key, value) pairs generated by a combiner must be of the same type as the (key, value) pairs emitted by the mapper. For example, if a mapper outputs (T_1, T_2) pairs (where the key is of type T_1 and the value is of type T_2), then a combiner has to emit (T_1, T_2) pairs as well.

The Hadoop MapReduce framework does not have an explicit `combine()` function, but a `Combiner` class can be added between the `Map` and `Reduce` classes to reduce the amount of data transferred to the reducer. The combiner is specified with the `Job.setCombinerClass()` method.

The goal of the combiner should be to "monoidify" the intermediate value emitted by the mapper—as we saw in Chapter 4, this is the guiding principle for designing efficient MapReduce algorithms.

Some programming languages, like Haskell, have direct support for monoids. In Haskell, a monoid is "a type with a rule for how two elements of that type can be combined to make another element of the same type." We'll look at some examples in the following sections, but first let's have a quick refresher on monoids.

A monoid is a triplet (`S`, `f`, `e`), where:

- `S` is a set (called the underlying set of the monoid).
- `f` is a mapping called the binary operation of the monoid (`f : S x S → S`).
- `e` is the identity operation of the monoid (`e` ∈ `S`).

A monoid with binary operation + (note that here + denotes the binary operation, not a mathematical addition operator) satisfies the following three axioms (note that `f(a,b) = a + b`):

Closure
: For all `a`, `b` in `S`, the result of the operation `(a + b)` is also in `S`.

Associativity
: For all `a`, `b`, and `c` in `S`, the following equation holds:

```
((a + b) + c) = (a + (b + c))
```

Identity element
: There exists an element `e` in `S` such that for all elements `a` in `S`, the following two equations hold:

```
e + a = a
a + e = a
```

In mathematical notation, we can write these as follows:

Closure

```
∀a,b∈S: a + b∈S
```

Associativity

```
for all a,b,c in S: ((a + b) + c) = (a + (b + c))
```

Identity element

```
{
  exists e in S:
    for all a in S:
       e + a = a
       a + e = a
}
```

A monoid operation might (but isn't required to) have other properties, such as:

Idempotency

```
for all a in S: a + a = a
```

Commutativity

```
for all a, b in S: a + b = b + a
```

To form a monoid, first we need a type *S*, which can define a set of values such as integers: `{0, -1, +1, -2, +2, ...}`. The second component is a binary function:

$$+ : S \times S \rightarrow S$$

Then we need to make sure that for any two values *x* and *y* in *S*:

$$x + y : S$$

For example, if type *S* is a set of integers, then the binary operation may be addition (+), multiplication (*), or division (/). Finally, as the third and most important ingredient, we need the binary operation to follow the specified set of laws. If it does, then we say (*S*, +, *e*) is a monoid, where *e* in *S* is the identity element (such as 0 for addition and 1 for multiplication).

Note that the binary division operation (/) over a set of real numbers is not a monoid:

```
((12 / 4) / 2) != (12 / (4 / 2))
((12 / 4) / 2) =  (3 / 2) = 1.5
(12 / (4 / 2)) =  (12 / 2) = 6.0
```

In a nutshell, monoids capture the notion of combining arbitrarily many things into a single thing, together with a notion of an empty thing called the identity element or value. One simple example is addition of natural numbers `{1, 2, 3, ...}`. The addition function + allows us to combine arbitrarily many natural numbers into a single natural number, the sum. The identity value is the number 0. Another example is string concatenation, where the concatenation operator allows us to combine arbitrarily many strings into a single string; in this case the identity value is the empty string.

Monoidal and Non-Monoidal Examples

Spark uses combiners in the `reduceByKey()` transformation, so to use this transformation effectively you must be sure that the reduction function is a monoid—that is, a monoid is a set (denoted by `S`) that is closed under an associative binary operation (`f`) and has an identity element `I` in `S` such that for all `x` in `S`, `f(I, x)` = `x` and `f(x, I)` = `x`. To help you understand the concept of monoids, here I provide some monoidal and non-monoidal examples.

Maximum over a set of integers

The set `S = {0, 1, 2, ...}` is a commutative monoid for the `MAX` (maximum) operation, whose identity element is 0:

```
MAX(a, MAX(b, c)) = MAX(MAX(a, b), c)}
MAX(a, 0) = a
MAX(0, a) = a
MAX(a, b) in S
```

Subtraction over a set of integers

Subtraction (`-`) over a set of integers does not define a monoid; this operation is not associative:

```
(1 - 2) -3 = -4
1 - (2 - 3) = 2
```

Addition over a set of integers

Addition (+) over a set of integers defines a monoid; this operation is commutative and associative and the identity element is 0:

```
(1 + 2) + 3 = 6
1 + (2 + 3) = 6
n + 0 = n
0 + n = n
```

We can formalize this as follows, where `e(+)` defines an identity element:

```
S = {0, -1, +1, -2, +2, -3, +3, ...}
e(+) = 0
f(a, b) = f(b, a) = a + b
```

Union and intersection over integers

Union or intersection over a set of integers forms a monoid. The binary function is union/intersection and the identity element is an empty set, {}.

Multiplication over a set of integers

The set of natural numbers `N = {0, 1, 2, 3, ...}` forms a commutative monoid under multiplication (the identity element is 1).

Mean over a set of integers

On the other hand, the set of natural numbers, `N = {0, 1, 2, 3, ...}` does not form a monoid under the `MEAN` (average) function. The following example shows that the mean of means of an arbitrary subset of a set of values is not the same as the mean of the complete set of values:

```
MEAN(1, 2, 3, 4, 5)
-- NOT EQUAL --
MEAN( MEAN(1,2,3), MEAN(4,5) )

MEAN(1, 2, 3, 4, 5) = (1+2+3+4+5)/5
                    = 15/5
                    = 3

MEAN( MEAN(1,2,3), MEAN(4,5) ) = MEAN(2, 4.5)
                               = (2 + 4.5)/2
                               = 3.25
```

Therefore, if you want to find the average of values for an `RDD[(key, integer)]`, you may not use the following transformation (which might yield the incorrect value due to partitioning):

```
# rdd: RDD[(key, integer)]
average_per_key = rdd.reduceByKey(lambda x, y: (x+y)/2)
```

The correct way to find the average per key is to make that function a monoid:

```
# rdd: RDD[(key, integer)]
# create value as (sum, count) pair: this makes a monoid
rdd2 = rdd.mapValues(lambda n: (n, 1))
# find (sum, count) per key
sum_count = rdd2.reduceByKey(lambda x, y: (x[0]+y[0], x[1]+y[1]))
# now, given (sum, count) per key, find the average per key
average_per_key = sum_count.mapValues(lambda x: x[0]/x[1])
```

Median over a set of integers

The set of natural numbers likewise does not form a monoid under the `MEDIAN` function:

```
MEDIAN(1, 2, 3, 5, 6, 7, 8, 9)
-- NOT EQUAL --
MEDIAN( MEDIAN(1,2,3), MEDIAN(5,6,7,8,9) )

MEDIAN(1, 2, 3, 5, 6, 7, 8, 9)
  = (5 + 6) / 2
  = 11 / 2
  = 5.5

MEDIAN( MEDIAN(1,2,3), MEDIAN(5,6,7,8,9) )
  = MEDIAN(2, 7) =
  = (2 + 7) / 2
  = 9 / 2
  = 4.5
```

Concatenation over lists

List concatenation (+) with an empty list (`[]`) is a monoid. For any list `L`, we can write:

```
L + [] = L
[] + L = L
```

Also, note that the concatenation function is associative. Given two lists, say `[1,2,3]` and `[7,8]`, we can join them together using + to get `[1,2,3,7,8]`. However, except in the case of concatenation with the empty list (or string, set, etc.), it is not commutative: `[1,2,3]+[7,8] = [1,2,3,7,8]` while `[7,8]+[1,2,3] = [7,8,1,2,3]`.

Matrix example

Let `N = {1, 2, 3, ...}`, and let $m, n \in N$. Then the set of $m \times n$ matrices with integer entries, written as $Z^{m \times n}$, satisfies properties that make it a monoid under addition:

- Closure is guaranteed by the definition.
- The associative property is guaranteed by the associative property of its elements.
- The additive identity is `0`, the zero matrix.

These examples should help you understand what it means for a reduction function to be a monoid. Spark's `reduceByKey()` is an efficient transformation that merges the values for each key using an associative and commutative reduce function. We have to make sure that its reduce function is a monoid, or we might not get correct reduction results.

Non-Monoid MapReduce Example

Given a large number of (key, value) pairs where the keys are strings and the values are integers, the goal for this non-monoid example is to find the average of all the values by key. Suppose we have the following data in a table called `mytable`, with `key` and `value` columns:

```
SELECT key, value FROM mytable

key    value
---    -----
key1   10
key1   20
key1   30
key2   40
key2   60
key3   20
key3   30
```

In SQL, this is accomplished as follows:

```
SELECT key, AVG(value) as avg FROM mytable GROUP BY key

key    avg
---    ---
key1   20
key2   50
key3   25
```

Here's an initial version of a MapReduce algorithm, where the mapper is not generating monoid outputs for the mean/average function:

Mapper function

```
# key: a string object
# value: a long associated with key
map(key, value) {
   emit(key, value);
}
```

Reducer function

```
# key: a string object
# values: a list of long data type numbers
reduce(key, values) {
   sum = 0
   count = 0
   for (i : list) {
      sum += i
      count += 1
   }
   average = sum / count
```

```
        emit(key, average)
    }
```

There are a few problems with this first attempt at a MapReduce algorithm:

- The algorithm is not very efficient; it will require a lot of work to be done in the sort and shuffle phase.
- We cannot use the reducer as a combiner, because we know that the mean of means of arbitrary subsets of a set of values is not the same as the mean of the complete set of values.

What changes can we make to enable us to use our reducer as a combiner, so that we can lessen the load on the network and speed up the sort and shuffle phase? We need to change the output of the mapper, so that it's a monoid. This will ensure that our combiners and reducers will behave correctly.

Let's take a look at how we can do that.

Monoid MapReduce Example

In this section, I'll revise the mapper to generate (key, value) pairs where the key is a string and the value is a pair `(sum, count)`. The `(sum, count)` data structure is a monoid, and the identity element is `(0, 0)`. The proof is given here:

```
Monoid type is (N, N) where N = {set of integers}

Identity element is (0, 0):
(sum, count) + (0, 0) =  (sum, count)
(0, 0) + (sum, count) =  (sum, count)

Let a = (sum1, count1), b = (sum2, count2), c = (sum3, count3)
Then associativity holds:
(a + (b + c)) = ((a + b) + c)

+ is the binary function:
a + b = (sum1+sum2, count1+count2) in (N, N)
```

Now, let's write a mapper for our monoid data type:

```
# key: a string object
# value: a long data type associated with key
# emits (key, (sum, count))
map(key, value) {
   emit (key, (value, 1))
}
```

As you can see, the key is the same as before, but the value is a pair of `(sum, count)`. Now, the output of the mapper is a monoid where the identity element is `(0, 0)`. The element-wise sum operation can be performed as:

```
element1 = (key, (sum1, count1))
element2 = (key, (sum2, count2))

==> values for the same key are reduced as:

 element1 + element2
   = (sum1, count1) + (sum2, count2)
   = (sum1+sum2, count1+count2)
```

Because the mappers output monoids, the mean function will now be calculated correctly. Suppose the values for a single key are `{1, 2, 3, 4, 5}`, and `{1, 2, 3}` go to partition 1 and `{4, 5}` go to partition 2:

```
MEAN(1, 2, 3, 4, 5)
  = MEAN( MEAN(1,2,3), MEAN(4,5) )}
  = (1+2+3+4+5) / 5
  = 15 / 5
  = 3

Partition 1:
  MEAN(1,2,3) = MEAN(6, 3)

Partition 2:
  MEAN(4,5) = MEAN(9, 2)

Merging partitions:
MEAN( MEAN(1,2,3), MEAN(4,5) )
  = MEAN( MEAN(6, 3), MEAN(9, 2))
  = MEAN(15, 5)
  = 15 / 5
  = 3
```

The revised algorithm is as follows, where for a given pair `(sum, count)`, `pair.1` refers to `sum` and `pair.2` refers to `count`. Here is our combiner:

```
# key: a string object
# values: a list of pairs as [(s1, c1), (s2, c2), ...]
combine(key, values) {
   sum = 0
   count = 0
   for (pair : values) {
      sum += pair.1
      count += pair.2
   }
   emit (key, (sum, count))
}
```

And here is our reducer:

```
# key: a string object
# values: a list of pairs as [(s1, c1), (s2, c2), ...]
reduce(key, values) {
   sum = 0
```

```
        count = 0
        for (pair : values) {
           sum += pair.1
           count += pair.2
        }
        average = sum / count
        emit (key, average)
    }
```

Since our mapper is generating a monoidal data type, we know that our combiner will execute properly and our reducer will produce the correct results.

PySpark Implementation of Monoidal Mean

The goal of this section is to provide a solution that will enable us to use combiners to aggregate values when the goal is to find the mean across partitions. To compute the mean of all values for the same key, we can group the values using Spark's `groupByKey()` transformation, then find the sum and divide by the count of number (per key). However, this is not an optimal solution because, as we've seen in earlier chapters, for a large dataset using `groupByKey()` can lead to OOM errors.

For the solution presented here, for a given `(key, number)` pair we will emit a tuple of `(key, (number, 1))`, where the associated value for a key denotes a pair of `(sum, count)`:

```
(key, value1) = (key, (sum1, count1))
(key, value2) = (key, (sum2, count2))
```

Earlier, I demonstrated that using `(sum, count)` as the value will enable us to use combiners and reducers to properly calculate the mean. Instead of `groupByKey()` we will use the very efficient `reduceByKey()` transformation. This is how the reduction function will work:

```
value1 + value2 =
(sum1, count1) + (sum2, count2) =
(sum1+sum2, count1+count2)
```

Once the reduction is done, we'll use an additional mapper to find the average by dividing the sum by the count.

The input record format will be:

```
<key-as-string><,><value-as-integer>
```

For example:

```
key1,100
key2,46
key1,300
```

At a high level, the PySpark solution is comprised of the following four steps:

1. Read the input and create the first RDD as an RDD[String].
2. Apply map() to create an RDD[key, (number, 1)].
3. Perform the reduction with reduceByKey(), which will create an RDD[key, (sum, count)].
4. Apply mapValue() to create the final RDD as an RDD[key, (sum / count)].

The complete PySpark program (*average_monoid_driver.py*) is available on GitHub.

First, we need two simple Python functions to help us in using Spark transformations. The first function, create_pair(), accepts a String object as "key,number" and returns a (key, (number, 1)) pair:

```
# record as String of "key,number"
def create_pair(record):
  tokens = record.split(",")
  key = tokens[0]
  number = int(tokens[1])
  return (key, (number, 1))
# end-def
```

The second function, add_pairs(), accepts two pairs,(sum1, count1) and (sum2, count2), and returns their sum as (sum1+sum2, count1+count2):

```
# a = (sum1, count1)
# b = (sum2, count2)
def add_pairs(a, b):
    # sum = sum1+sum2
    sum = a[0] + b[0]
    # count = count1+count2
    count = a[1] + b[1]
    return (sum, count)
# end-def
```

Here is the complete PySpark solution:

```
from __future__ import print_function ❶
import sys ❷
from pyspark.sql import SparkSession ❸

if len(sys.argv) != 2: ❹
    print("Usage: average_monoid_driver.py <file>", file=sys.stderr)
    exit(-1)

spark = SparkSession.builder.getOrCreate() ❺

#  sys.argv[0] is the name of the script
#  sys.argv[1] is the first parameter
input_path = sys.argv[1] ❻
print("input_path: {}".format(input_path))
```

```
# read input and create an RDD[String]
records = spark.sparkContext.textFile(input_path) ❼

# create a pair of (key, (number, 1)) for "key,number"
key_number_one = records.map(create_pair) ❽

# aggregate the (sum, count) of each unique key
sum_count = key_number_one.reduceByKey(add_pairs) ❾

# create the final RDD as an RDD[key, average]
averages =  sum_count.mapValues(lambda (sum, count): sum / count) ❿
print("averages.take(5): ", averages.take(5))

# done!
spark.stop()
```

❶ Import the `print()` function.

❷ Import system-specific parameters and functions.

❸ Import `SparkSession` from the `pyspark.sql` module.

❹ Make sure that we have two parameters in the command line.

❺ Create an instance of `SparkSession` using the builder pattern.

❻ Define the input path (this can be a file or a directory containing any number of files).

❼ Read the input and create the first RDD as an `RDD[String]`, where each object has the format `"key,number"`.

❽ Create the `key_number_one` RDD as an `RDD[key, (number, 1)]`.

❾ Aggregate `(sum1, count1)` with `(sum2, count2)` and create `(sum1+sum2, count1+count2)` as values.

❿ Apply the `mapValues()` transformation to find the final average per key.

Functors and Monoids

You've now seen several examples of monoids and their use in the MapReduce framework—but we can even apply higher-order functions (like functors) to monoids. A functor is an object that is a function (it's a function and an object at the same time).

First, I'll present the use of a functor on a monoid through a simple example. Let `MONOID = (t, e, f)` be a monoid, where `T` is a type (set of values), `e` is the identity element, and `f` is the + binary plus function:

```
MONOID = {
   type T
   val e : T
   val plus : T x T -> T
}
```

Then we can define a functor `Prod` as follows:

```
functor Prod (M : MONOID) (N : MONOID) = {
   type t = M.T * N.T
   val e = (M.e, N.e)
   fun plus((x1,y1), (x2,y2)) = (M.plus(x1,x2), N.plus(y1,y2))
}
```

And we can define other functors, such as `Square`, as follows:

```
functor Square (M : MONOID) : MONOID = Prod M M
```

We can also define a functor between two monoids. Let (M_1, f_1, e_1) and (M_2, f_2, e_2) be monoids. A functor:

$$F : (M_1, f_1, e_1) \rightarrow (M_2, f_2, e_2)$$

is specified by an object map (monoids are categories with a single object) and an arrow map $F : M_1 \rightarrow M_2$. and the following conditions will hold:

$$\forall a,b \in M_1,\ F(f_1(a,b)) = f_2(F(a), F(b))$$
$$F(e_1) = e_2$$

A functor between two monoids is just a monoid homomorphism (a map between monoids that preserves the monoid operation and maps the identity element of the first monoid to that of the second monoid). For example, for the `String` data type, a function `Length()` that counts the number of letters in a word is a monoid homomorphism:

- `Length("") = 0` (the length of an empty string is 0).
- If `Length(x) = m` and `Length(y) = n`, then concatenation `x + y` of strings has `m + n` letters. For example:

```
Length("String" + "ology")
    = Length("Stringology")
    = 11
    = 6 + 5
    = Length("String") + Length("ology")
```

Again, having mappers create monoids guarantees that the reducers can take advantage of using combiners effectively and correctly.

Conclusion on Using Monoids

As we've observed, in the MapReduce paradigm (which is the foundation of Hadoop, Spark, Tez, and other frameworks), if your mapper generates monoids you can utilize combiners for optimization and efficiency purposes. Using combiners reduces network traffic and speeds up MapReduce's sort and shuffle phase, because there's less data to process. You also saw some examples of how to monoidify MapReduce algorithms. In general, combiners can be used when the function you want to apply is both commutative and associative (properties of a monoid). For example, the classic word count function is a monoid over a set of integers with the + operation (here you can use a combiner). However, the mean function (which is not associative) over a set of integers does not form a monoid. To use combiners effectively in a case like this, we need to ensure that the output from the mappers is monoidal. Next, we'll turn our attention to a few important data organization patterns: binning and sorting.

Binning

Binning is a way to group a number of more or less continuous values into a smaller number of "bins," or buckets. For example, if you have census data about a group of people, you might want to map their individual ages into a smaller number of age intervals, such as `0-5`, `6-10`, `11-15`, ..., `96-100+`. An important advantage of binning is that it narrows the range of the data you need to search for a specific value. For example, if you know that someone is 14 years old, to find them you only need to search in the bin labeled `11-15`. In other words, binning can help us to do faster queries by examining a slice of the data rather than the whole dataset. The binning design pattern moves the records into categories (bins) irrespective of the initial order of the records.

Figure 10-7 illustrates another example. In genomics data, chromosomes are labeled as `{chr1, chr2, ..., chr22, chrX, chrY, chrMT}`. A human being has 3 billion pairs of chromosomes, where `chr1` has about 250 million positions, `chr7` has 160 million positions, and so on. If you want to find a variant key of `10:100221486:100221486:G`, you'll have to search billions of records, which is very inefficient. Binning can help speed up the process: if we group the data by chromosomes, to find this variant key we can just look in the bin labeled `chr10` rather than searching all of the data.

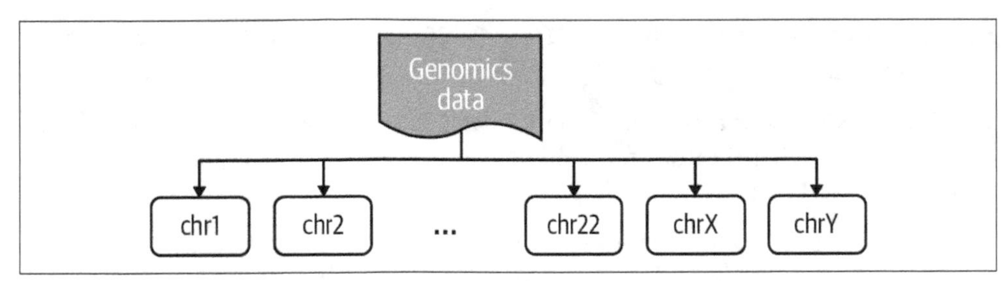

Figure 10-7. Binning by chromosome

To implement the binning algorithm in PySpark, first we read our input and create a DataFrame with the proper columns. Then, we create an additional column, called `chr_id`, which will denote a bin for a chromosome. The `chr_id` column will have values in the set `{chr1, chr2, ..., chr22, chrX, chrY, chrMT}`.

It is possible to implement binning in several layers—for example, first by chromosome and then by the modulo of the start position—as illustrated in Figure 10-8.

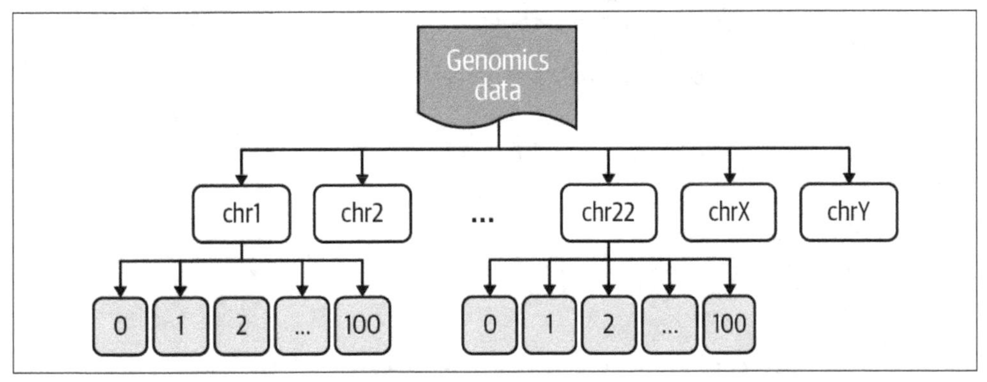

Figure 10-8. Binning by chromosome

This will be quite helpful because we might have millions of variants per chromosome; an additional layer of binning can help us to further reduce the query time by allowing us to examine an even thinner slice of the data. Before I show you how to implement binning by start position, let's take a look at the variant structure:

```
<chromosome><:><start_position><:><stop_position><:><allele>
```

A simple binning algorithm will be to partition the `start_position` into 101 bins (depending on the volume of data you may select a different number, but it should be a prime number). Therefore, our bin values will be `{0, 1, 2, ..., 100}`. We'll then create another new column called `modulo`, and its value will be defined as:

```
modulo = start_position % 101
```

For example, for a variant of `10:100221486:100221486:G`, the `module` value will be `95` (`100221486 % 101 = 95`).

Continuing with the example of genomics data, suppose we have the following data (note that I've included only a few columns here, to keep the example simple). First, we create a DataFrame from this data:

```
variants = [('S-100', 'Prostate-1', '5:163697197:163697197:T', 2),
            ('S-200', 'Prostate-1', '5:3420488:3420488:C', 1),
            ('S-100', 'Genome-1000', '3:107988242:107988242:T', 1),
            ('S-200', 'Genome-1000', '3:54969706:54969706:T', 3)]

columns = ['SAMPLE_ID', 'STUDY_ID', 'VARIANT_KEY', 'ZYGOSITY' ]

df = spark.createDataFrame(variants, columns)
df.show(truncate=False)
+---------+-----------+-----------------------+--------+
|SAMPLE_ID|STUDY_ID   |VARIANT_KEY            |ZYGOSITY|
+---------+-----------+-----------------------+--------+
|S-100    |Prostate-1 |5:163697197:163697197:T|2       |
|S-200    |Prostate-1 |5:3420488:3420488:C    |1       |
|S-100    |Genome-1000|3:107988242:107988242:T|1       |
|S-200    |Genome-1000|3:54969706:54969706:T  |3       |
+---------+-----------+-----------------------+--------+
```

Next, we create a binning function for a `chr_id`, to be extracted from a given `variant_key`:

```
def extract_chr(variant_key):
  tokens = variant_key.split(":")
  return "chr" + tokens[0]
#end-def
```

To use the `extract_chr()` function, first we have to create a UDF:

```
from pyspark.sql.functions import udf
from pyspark.sql.types import StringType
extract_chr_udf = udf(extract_chr, StringType())

binned_by_chr = df.select("SAMPLE_ID", "STUDY_ID", "VARIANT_KEY",
    "ZYGOSITY", extract_chr_udf("VARIANT_KEY").alias("CHR_ID"))

binned_by_chr.show(truncate=False)
+---------+-----------+-----------------------+--------+------+
|SAMPLE_ID|STUDY_ID   |VARIANT_KEY            |ZYGOSITY|CHR_ID|
+---------+-----------+-----------------------+--------+------+
|S-100    |Prostate-1 |5:163697197:163697197:T|2       |chr5  |
|S-200    |Prostate-1 |5:3420488:3420488:C    |1       |chr5  |
|S-100    |Genome-1000|3:107988242:107988242:T|1       |chr3  |
|S-200    |Genome-1000|3:54969706:54969706:T  |3       |chr3  |
+---------+-----------+-----------------------+--------+------+
```

To create a second level of binning, we need another Python function to find `start_position % 101`:

```
# 101 is the number of bins per chromosome
def create_modulo(variant_key):
  tokens = variant_key.split(":")
  start_position = int(tokens[1])
  return start_position % 101
#end-def
```

We then define another UDF to use this function to create the `modulo` column:

```
from pyspark.sql.functions import udf
from pyspark.sql.types import IntegerType
create_modulo_udf = udf(create_modulo, IntegerType())

binned_by_chr_and_position = df.select("SAMPLE_ID", "STUDY_ID", "VARIANT_KEY",
   "ZYGOSITY", extract_chr_udf("VARIANT_KEY").alias("CHR_ID"),
   create_modulo_udf("VARIANT_KEY").alias("modulo"))

binned_by_chr_and_position.show(truncate=False)
+---------+----------+---------------------+--------+-----+------+
|SAMPLE_ID|STUDY_ID  |VARIANT_KEY          |ZYGOSITY|CHR_ID|modulo|
+---------+----------+---------------------+--------+-----+------+
|S-100    |Prostate-1 |5:163697197:163697197:T|2       |chr5  |33    |
|S-200    |Prostate-1 |5:3420488:3420488:C    |1       |chr5  |22    |
|S-100    |Genome-1000|3:107988242:107988242:T|1       |chr3  |52    |
|S-200    |Genome-1000|3:54969706:54969706:T  |3       |chr3  |52    |
+---------+----------+---------------------+--------+-----+------+
```

We can save our DataFrame in Parquet format without binning as follows:

```
binned_by_chr_and_position.write.mode("append")\
                          .parquet(/tmp/genome1/)

$ ls -l /tmp/genome1/
-rw-r--r-- ...     0 Jan 18 14:34 _SUCCESS
...
-rw-r--r-- ...  1382 Jan 18 14:34 part-00007-....snappy.parquet
```

Or, to save the data with binning information, we can use the `partitionBy()` function:

```
binned_by_chr_and_position.write.mode("append")\
                          .partitionBy("CHR_ID", "modulo")\
                          .parquet(/tmp/genome2/)

$ ls -R /tmp/genome2/
CHR_ID=chr3 CHR_ID=chr5 _SUCCESS

/tmp/genome2//CHR_ID=chr3:
modulo=52

/tmp/genome2//CHR_ID=chr3/modulo=52:
```

```
part-00005-....snappy.parquet
part-00007-....snappy.parquet

/tmp/genome2//CHR_ID=chr5:
modulo=22 modulo=33

/tmp/genome2//CHR_ID=chr5/modulo=22:
part-00003-....snappy.parquet

/tmp/genome2//CHR_ID=chr5/modulo=33:
part-00001-....snappy.parquet
```

Sorting

Sorting of data records is a common task in many programming languages, such as Python and Java. Sorting refers to any process of arranging records systematically, and can involve ordering (arranging records in a sequence ordered by some criterion) or categorizing (grouping items with similar properties). With ordering, the sorting can be done either in the normal order of low to high (ascending) or the normal order of high to low (descending). There are many well-known sorting algorithms—such as quick sort, bubble sort, and heap sort—with different time complexities.

PySpark offers several functions for sorting RDDs and DataFrames, here are a few of them:

```
pyspark.RDD.repartitionAndSortWithinPartitions()
pyspark.RDD.sortBy()
pyspark.RDD.sortByKey()
pyspark.sql.DataFrame.sort()
pyspark.sql.DataFrame.sortWithinPartitions()
pyspark.sql.DataFrameWriter.sortBy()
```

Use of these sorting functions is straightforward.

Summary

MapReduce design patterns are common patterns in data analytics. These design patterns enable us to solve similar data problems in an efficient manner.

Data design patterns can be classified into several different categories, such as:

Summarization patterns
: Get a top-level view by summarizing and grouping data. Examples include in-mapper combining (which we used to solve the word count problem) and MinMax.

Filtering patterns
: View data subsets by using predicates. An example is the top-10 pattern.

Data organization patterns
: Reorganize data to work with other systems, or to make MapReduce analysis easier. Examples include binning and sorting algorithms.

Join patterns
: Analyze different datasets together to discover interesting relationships.

Meta patterns
: Piece together several patterns to solve multistage problems, or to perform several analytics in the same job.

Input and output patterns
: Customize the way you use a persistent store (such as HDFS or S3) to load or store data.

In the next chapter we'll look at design patterns for performing joins, which is an important transformation between two large datasets.

CHAPTER 11

Join Design Patterns

In this chapter we will examine practical design patterns for joining datasets. As in the previous chapters, I will focus on patterns that are useful in real-world environments. PySpark supports a basic join operation for RDDs (`pyspark.RDD.join()`) and DataFrames (`pyspark.sql.DataFrame.join()`) that will be sufficient for most use cases. However, there are circumstances where this join can be costly, so I'll also show you some special join algorithms that may prove useful.

This chapter introduces the basic concept of joining two datasets, and provides examples of some useful and practical join design patterns. I'll show you how the join operation is implemented in the MapReduce paradigm and how to use Spark's transformations to perform a join. You'll see how to perform map-side joins with RDDs and DataFrames, and how to perform an efficient join using a Bloom filter.

Source Code

Complete programs for this chapter are available in the book's GitHub repository (*https://oreil.ly/2XaBi*).

Introduction to the Join Operation

In the relational database world, joining two tables (aka "relations") with a common key—that is, an attribute or set of attributes in one or more columns that allow the unique identification of each record (tuple or row) in the table—is a frequent operation.

Consider the following two tables, T1 and T2:

```
T1 = {(k1, v1)}
T2 = {(k2, v2)}
```

where:

- k1 is the key for T1 and v1 are the associated attributes.
- k2 is the key for T2 and v2 are the associated attributes.

A simple inner join, which creates a new table by combining rows that have matching keys in two or more tables, can be defined as:

```
T1.join(T2) = {(k, (v1, v2))}
T2.join(T1) = {(k, (v2, v1))}
```

where:

- k = k1 = k2.
- (k, v1) is in T1.
- (k, v2) is in T2.

To illustrate how this works, let's create two tables, populating them with some sample data, and then join them. First we'll create our tables, T1 and T2:

```
>>> d1 = [('a', 10), ('a', 11), ('a', 12), ('b', 100), ('b', 200), ('c', 80)]
>>> T1 = spark.createDataFrame(d1, ['id', 'v1'])
>>> T1.show()
+---+---+
| id| v1|
+---+---+
|  a| 10|
|  a| 11|
|  a| 12|
|  b|100|
|  b|200|
|  c| 80|
+---+---+

>>> d2 = [('a', 40), ('a', 50), ('b', 300), ('b', 400), ('d', 90)]
>>> T2 = spark.createDataFrame(d2, ['id', 'v2'])
>>> T2.show()
+---+---+
| id| v2|
+---+---+
|  a| 40|
|  a| 50|
|  b|300|
|  b|400|
```

```
|  d| 90|
+---+---+
```

Then we'll join them with an inner join (the default join type in Spark). Notice that the rows with an `id` of `c` (from `T1`) and `d` (from `T2`) are dropped, since there are no matching rows for these in the other table:

```
>>> joined = T1.join(T2, (T1.id == T2.id))
>>> joined.show(100, truncate=False)
+---+---+---+---+
|id |v1 |id |v2 |
+---+---+---+---+
|a  |10 |a  |50 |
|a  |10 |a  |40 |
|a  |11 |a  |50 |
|a  |11 |a  |40 |
|a  |12 |a  |50 |
|a  |12 |a  |40 |
|b  |100|b  |400|
|b  |100|b  |300|
|b  |200|b  |400|
|b  |200|b  |300|
+---+---+---+---+
```

There are many types of joins that can be performed on two tables with a common key, but in practice, three types of join are the most common:

`INNER JOIN(T1, T2)`
: Combines records from two tables, T1 and T2, whenever there are matching values in a key common to both tables.

`LEFT JOIN(T1, T2)`
: Returns all records from the left table (T1) and the matched records from the right table (T2) table. If there is no match for a specific record, you'll get `NULL`s in the corresponding columns of the right table.

`RIGHT JOIN(T1, T2)`
: Returns all the rows of the table on the right side of the join (T2) and matching rows for the table on the left side (T1) of the join. The rows for which there is no matching row on left side, the result-set will contain null.

All of these join types are supported in PySpark, as well as some other types that are less frequently used. For an introduction to the different types of joins PySpark supports, see the tutorial "PySpark Join Types" (*https://oreil.ly/JoIUD*) on the Spark by {Examples} website.

Joining two tables is potentially an expensive operation, as it can require finding the Cartesian product (for two sets A and B, the set of all ordered pairs (x, y) where x is in A and y is in B). In the example just shown this would not be problematic, but consider a big data example: if table T1 has three billion rows and table T2 has one million rows, then the Cartesian product of these two tables will have three quadrillion (3 followed by 15 zeros) data points. In this chapter, I cover some basic design patterns that can help to simplify the join operation, to reduce this cost. As usual, when it comes to selecting and using join design patterns, there is no silver bullet: be sure to test your proposed solution for performance and scalability using real data.

Join in MapReduce

This section is presented for pedagogical purposes, to show you how a `join()` function can be implemented in a distributed computing environment. Suppose we have two relations, `R(k, b)` and `S(k, c)`, where `k` is a common key and `b` and `c` represent attributes of `R` and `S`, respectively. How do we find the join of `R` and `S`? The goal of the join operation is to find tuples that agree on their key `k`. A MapReduce implementation of the natural join for `R` and `S` can implemented as follows. First, in the map phase:

- For a tuple `(k, b)` in `R`, emit a (key, value) pair as `(k, ("R", b))`.
- For a tuple `(k, c)` in `S`, emit a (key, value) pair as `(k, ("S", c))`.

Then, in the reduce phase:

- If a reducer key `k` has the value list `[("R", v),("S", w)]`, then emit a single (key, value) pair as `(k, (v, w))`. Note that `join(R, S)` will produce `(k, (v, w))`, while `join(S, R)` will produce `(k, (w, v))`.

So, if a reducer key `k` has the value list `[("R", v1), ("R", v2), ("S", w1), ("S", w2)]`, then we will emit four (key, value) pairs:

```
(k, (v1, w1))
(k, (v1, w2))
(k, (v2, w1))
(k, (v2, w2))
```

Therefore, to perform a natural join between two relations `R` and `S`, we need two map functions and one reducer function.

Map Phase

The map phase has two steps:

1. Map relation `R`:

```
# key: relation R
# value: (k, b) tuple in R
map(key, value) {
```

```
      emit(k, ("R", b))
    }
```

2. Map relation S:

```
# key: relation S
# value: (k, c) tuple in S
map(key, value) {
  emit(k, ("S", c))
}
```

The output of the mappers (provided as input to the sort and shuffle phase) will be:

```
(k1, "R", r1)
(k1, "R", r2)
...
(k1, "S", s1)
(k1, "S", s2)
...
(k2, "R", r3)
(k2, "R", r4)
...
(k2, "S", s3)
(k2, "S", s4)
...
```

Reducer Phase

Before, we write a reducer function, we need to understand the magic of MapReduce, which occurs in the sort and shuffle phase. This is similar to SQL's `GROUP BY` function; once all the mappers are done, their output is sorted and shuffled and sent to the reducer(s) as input.

In our example, the output of the sort and shuffle phase will be:

```
(k1, [("R", r1), ("R", r2), ..., ("S", s1), ("S", s2), ...]
(k2, [("R", r3), ("R", r4), ..., ("S", s3), ("S", s4), ...]
...
```

The reducer function is presented next. For each key `k`, we build two lists: `list_R` (which will hold the values/attributes from relation `R`) and `list_S` (which will hold the values/attributes from relation `S`). Then we identify the Cartesian product of `list_R` and `list_S` to find the join tuples (pseudocode):

```
# key: a unique key
# values: [(relation, attrs)] where relation in {"R", "S"}
# and  attrs are the relation attributes
reduce(key, values) {
  list_R = []
  list_S = []
  for (tuple in values) {
    relation = tuple[0]
```

```
        attributes = tuple[1]
        if (relation == "R") {
           list_R.append(attributes)
        }
        else {
           list_S.append(attributes)
        }
     }

     if (len(list_R) == 0) OR (len(list_S) == 0) {
        # no common key
        return
     }

     # len(list_R) > 0 AND len(list_S) > 0
     # perform Cartesian product of list_R and list_S
     for (r in list_R) {
       for (s in list_S) {
          emit(key, (r, s))
       }
     }

  }
```

Implementation in PySpark

This section shows how to implement the natural join of two datasets (with some common keys) in PySpark without using the join() function. I present this solution to show the power of Spark, and how it can be used to perform custom joins if required.

Suppose we have the following datasets, T1 and T2:

```
d1 = [('a', 10), ('a', 11), ('a', 12), ('b', 100), ('b', 200), ('c', 80)]
d2 = [('a', 40), ('a', 50), ('b', 300), ('b', 400), ('d', 90)]
T1 = spark.sparkContext.parallelize(d1)
T2 = spark.sparkContext.parallelize(d2)
```

First, we map these RDDs to include the name of the relation:

```
t1_mapped = T1.map(lambda x: (x[0], ("T1", x[1])))
t2_mapped = T2.map(lambda x: (x[0], ("T2", x[1])))
```

Next, in order to perform a reduction on the generated (key, value) pairs by mappers, we combine these two datasets into a single dataset:

```
combined  = t1_mapped.union(t2_mapped)
```

Then we perform the groupByKey() transformation on a single combined dataset:

```
grouped  = combined.groupByKey()
```

And finally, we find the Cartesian product of the values of each grouped entry:

```
# entry[0]: key
# entry[1]: values as:
# [("T1", t11), ("T1", t12), ..., ("T2", t21), ("T2", t22), ...]
import itertools
def cartesian_product(entry):
  T1 = []
  T2 = []
  key = entry[0]
  values = entry[1]
  for tuple in values:
    relation = tuple[0]
    attributes = tuple[1]
    if (relation == "T1"): T1.append(attributes)
    else: T2.append(attributes)
  #end-for

  if (len(T1) == 0) or (len(T2) == 0):
     # no common key
     return []

  # len(T1) > 0 AND len(T2) > 0
  joined_elements = []
  # perform Cartesian product of T1 and T2
  for element in itertools.product(T1, T2):
    joined_elements.append((key, element))
  #end-for
  return joined_elements
#end-def

joined = grouped.flatMap(cartesian_product)
```

Map-Side Join Using RDDs

As we've seen, a join is a potentially expensive operation used to combine records from two (or more) datasets based on a common key between them. In a relational database, indexing can help to reduce the cost of a join operation; however, big data engines like Hadoop and Spark do not support indexing of data. So what can we do to minimize the cost of a join between two distributed datasets? Here, I'll introduce a design pattern that can completely eliminate the need for the shuffle and sort phase in the MapReduce paradigm: the *map-side join*.

A map-side join is a process where two datasets are joined by the mapper rather than using the actual join function (which is performed by a combination of a mapper and a reducer). In addition to decreasing the cost incurred for sorting and merging in the shuffle and reduce stages, this can speed up the execution of the task, improving performance.

To help you understand how this works, let's start with a SQL example. Suppose we have two tables in a MySQL database, EMP and DEPT, and we want to perform a join between them. The two tables are defined as follows:

```
mysql> use testdb;
Database changed

mysql> select * from emp;
+--------+----------+---------+
| emp_id | emp_name | dept_id |
+--------+----------+---------+
|   1000 | alex     | 10      |
|   2000 | ted      | 10      |
|   3000 | mat      | 20      |
|   4000 | max      | 20      |
|   5000 | joe      | 10      |
+--------+----------+---------+
5 rows in set (0.00 sec)

mysql> select * from dept;
+---------+------------+--------------+
| dept_id | dept_name  | dept_location |
+---------+------------+--------------+
|      10 | ACCOUNTING | NEW YORK, NY  |
|      20 | RESEARCH   | DALLAS, TX    |
|      30 | SALES      | CHICAGO, IL   |
|      40 | OPERATIONS | BOSTON, MA    |
|      50 | MARKETING  | Sunnyvale, CA |
|      60 | SOFTWARE   | Stanford, CA  |
+---------+------------+--------------+
6 rows in set (0.00 sec)
```

Next, we join two tables (using an INNER JOIN) on the dept_id key:

```
mysql> select e.emp_id, e.emp_name, e.dept_id, d.dept_name, d.dept_location
         from emp e, dept d
            where e.dept_id = d.dept_id;
+--------+----------+---------+------------+---------------+
| emp_id | emp_name | dept_id | dept_name  | dept_location |
+--------+----------+---------+------------+---------------+
|   1000 | alex     | 10      | ACCOUNTING | NEW YORK, NY  |
|   2000 | ted      | 10      | ACCOUNTING | NEW YORK, NY  |
|   5000 | joe      | 10      | ACCOUNTING | NEW YORK, NY  |
|   3000 | mat      | 20      | RESEARCH   | DALLAS, TX    |
|   4000 | max      | 20      | RESEARCH   | DALLAS, TX    |
+--------+----------+---------+------------+---------------+
5 rows in set (0.00 sec)
```

A map-side join is similar to an inner join in SQL, but the task is performed by the mapper alone (note that the result of an inner join and a map-side join must be identical).

In general, joins on large datasets are expensive, but rarely do you want to join the entire contents of one large table A with the entire contents of another large table B. Given two tables A and B, a map-side join will be most suitable when table A (called the *fact table*) is large and table B (the *dimension table*) is small to medium. To perform this type of join, we first create a hash table from B and broadcast it to all nodes. Next, we iterate all elements of table A with a mapper and then access the relevant information from table B through the broadcasted hash table.

Two demonstrate, we'll create two RDDs from our EMP and DEPT tables. First, we create EMP as an RDD[(dept_id, (emp_id, emp_name))]:

```
EMP = spark.sparkContext.parallelize(
[
  (10, (1000, 'alex')),
  (10, (2000, 'ted')),
  (20, (3000, 'mat')),
  (20, (4000, 'max')),
  (10, (5000, 'joe'))
])
```

Next, we create DEPT as an RDD[(dept_id, (dept_name, dept_location))]:

```
DEPT= spark.sparkContext.parallelize(
[ (10, ('ACCOUNTING', 'NEW YORK, NY')),
  (20, ('RESEARCH', 'DALLAS, TX')),
  (30, ('SALES', 'CHICAGO, IL')),
  (40, ('OPERATIONS', 'BOSTON, MA')),
  (50, ('MARKETING', 'Sunnyvale, CA')),
  (60, ('SOFTWARE', 'Stanford, CA'))
])
```

EMP and DEPT have a common key, dept_id, so we can join the two RDDs as follows:

```
>>> sorted(EMP.join(DEPT).collect())
[
 (10, ((1000, 'alex'), ('ACCOUNTING', 'NEW YORK, NY'))),
 (10, ((2000, 'ted'), ('ACCOUNTING', 'NEW YORK, NY'))),
 (10, ((5000, 'joe'), ('ACCOUNTING', 'NEW YORK, NY'))),
 (20, ((3000, 'mat'), ('RESEARCH', 'DALLAS, TX'))),
 (20, ((4000, 'max'), ('RESEARCH', 'DALLAS, TX')))
]
```

How does a map-side join optimize this task? Suppose EMP is a large dataset and DEPT is a relatively small dataset. Using a map-side join to join EMP with DEPT on dept_id, we will create a broadcast variable from the small table (using the custom function to_hash_table()):

```
# build a dictionary of (key, value),
# where key = dept_id
#       value = (dept_name , dept_location)
```

```
def to_hash_table(dept_as_list):
  hast_table = {}
  for d in dept_as_list:
    dept_id = d[0]
    dept_name_location = d[1]
    hash_table[dept_id] = dept_name_location
  return hash_table
#end-def

dept_hash_table = to_hash_table(DEPT.collect())
```

Alternatively, you may build the hash table using the Spark action `collectAsMap()`, which returns the (key, value) pairs in this RDD (`DEPT`) to the master as a dictionary:

```
dept_hash_table = DEPT.collectAsMap()
```

Now, using `pyspark.SparkContext.broadcast()`, we can broadcast the read-only variable `dept_hash_table` to the Spark cluster, making it available for all kinds of transformations (including mappers and reducers):

```
sc = spark.sparkContext
hash_table_broadcasted = sc.broadcast(dept_hash_table)
```

To perform the map-side join, in the mapper we can access this variable via:

```
dept_hash_table = hash_table_broadcasted.value
```

Using the function `map_side_join()`, defined as follows:

```
# e as an element of EMP RDD
def map_side_join(e):
  dept_id = e[0]
  # get hash_table from broadcasted object
  hash_table = hash_table_broadcasted.value
  dept_name_location = hash_table[dept_id]
  return (e, dept_name_location)
#end-def
```

we can then perform the join using a `map()` transformation:

```
joined = EMP.map(map_side_join)
```

This allows us to not shuffle the dimension table (i.e., `DEPT`) and to get quite good join performance.

With a map-side join, we just use the `map()` function to iterate through each row of the `EMP` table, and retrieve the dimension values (such as `dept_name` and `dept_location`) from the broadcasted hash table. The `map()` function will be executed concurrently for each partition, which will have its own copy of the hash table.

To recap, the map-side join approach has the following important advantages:

- It reduces the cost of the join operation by minimizing the amount of data that needs to be sorted and merged in the shuffle and reduce stages. We do this by making the smaller RDD/table a broadcast variable and thus avoiding a shuffle.
- It improves the performance of the join operation by avoiding significant network I/O. The main disadvantage is that the map-side join design pattern is appropriate only when one of the RDDs/tables on which you wish to perform the join operation is small enough to fit into memory. If both tables are large, it's not a suitable choice.

Map-Side Join Using DataFrames

As I discussed in the preceding section, a map-side join makes sense when one of the tables (the fact table) is large and the other (the dimension table) is small enough to be broadcast.

In the following example (inspired by Dmitry Tolpeko's article "Map-Side Join in Spark" (*https://oreil.ly/2sHBy*)), I will show how to use DataFrames along with broadcast variables to implement a map-side join. Suppose we have the fact table shown in Table 11-1, and the two dimension tables shown in Tables 11-2 and 11-3.

Table 11-1. `Flights` (fact table)

from	to	airline	flight_number	departure
DTW	ORD	SW	225	17:10
DTW	JFK	SW	355	8:20
SEA	JFK	DL	418	7:00
SFO	LAX	AA	1250	7:05
SFO	JFK	VX	12	7:05
JFK	LAX	DL	424	7:10
LAX	SEA	DL	5737	7:10

Table 11-2. `Airports` (dimension table)

code	name	city	state
DTW	Detroit Airport	Detroit	MI
ORD	Chicago O'Hare	Chicago	IL
JFK	John F. Kennedy Airport	New York	NY
LAX	Los Angeles Airport	Los Angeles	CA
SEA	Seattle-Tacoma Airport	Seattle	WA
SFO	San Francisco Airport	San Francisco	CA

Table 11-3. `Airlines` (dimension table)

code	airline_name
SW	Southwest Airlines
AA	American Airlines
DL	Delta Airlines
VX	Virgin America

Our goal is to expand the `Flights` table, replacing the airline codes with the actual airline names and the airport codes with the actual airport names. This operation requires a join of `Flights`—the facts table—with two dimension tables (`Airports` and `Airlines`). Since the dimension tables are small enough to fit in memory, we can broadcast these to all the mappers in all the worker nodes. Table 11-4 shows the desired joined output.

Table 11-4. Joined table

from city	to city	airline	flight number	departure
Detroit	Chicago	Southwest Airlines	225	17:10
Detroit	New York	Southwest Airlines	355	8:20
Seattle	New York	Delta Airlines	418	7:00
San Francisco	Los Angeles	American Airlines	1250	7:05
San Francisco	New York	Virgin America	12	7:05
New York	Los Angeles	Delta Airlines	424	7:10
Los Angeles	Seattle	Delta Airlines	5737	7:10

To achieve this result, we need to do the following:

1. Create a broadcast variable for `Airports`. First, we create an RDD from the `Airports` table and save it as a `dict[(key, value)]`, where the key is an airport code and the value is the name of the airport.
2. Create a broadcast variable for `Airlines`. Next, we create an RDD from the `Airlines` table and save it as a `dict[(key, value)]`, where the key is an airline code and the value is the name of the airline.
3. Create a DataFrame from the `Flights` table, to be joined with the cached broadcast variables created in steps 1 and 2.
4. Map each record of the `Flights` DataFrame and perform a simple join by looking up values in the cached dictionaries created in steps 1 and 2.

Next, I'll discuss another design pattern, joining using Bloom filters, that can be used for efficient joining of two tables.

Step 1: Create Cache for Airports

This step creates a broadcast variable from the `Airports` table (as a dictionary) to be cached on all worker nodes:

```
>>> airports_data = [
...   ("DTW", "Detroit Airport", "Detroit", "MI"),
...   ("ORD", "Chicago O'Hare", "Chicago",  "IL"),
...   ("JFK", "John F. Kennedy Int. Airport", "New York", "NY"),
...   ("LAX", "Los Angeles Int. Airport", "Los Angeles", "CA"),
...   ("SEA", "Seattle-Tacoma Int. Airport", "Seattle", "WA"),
...   ("SFO", "San Francisco Int. Airport", "San Francisco", "CA")
... ]
>>>
>>> airports_rdd = spark.sparkContext.parallelize(airports_data)\
...   .map(lambda tuple4: (tuple4[0], (tuple4[1],tuple4[2],tuple4[3])))

>>> airports_dict = airports_rdd.collectAsMap()
>>>
>>> airports_cache = spark.sparkContext.broadcast(airports_dict)
>>> airports_cache.value
{'DTW': ('Detroit Airport', 'Detroit', 'MI'),
 'ORD': ("Chicago O'Hare", 'Chicago', 'IL'),
 'JFK': ('John F. Kennedy Int. Airport', 'New York', 'NY'),
 'LAX': ('Los Angeles Int. Airport', 'Los Angeles', 'CA'),
 'SEA': ('Seattle-Tacoma Int. Airport', 'Seattle', 'WA'),
 'SFO': ('San Francisco Int. Airport', 'San Francisco', 'CA')}
```

Step 2: Create Cache for Airlines

This step creates a broadcast variable from the `Airlines` table to be cached on all worker nodes:

```
>>> airlines_data = [
...   ("SW", "Southwest Airlines"),
...   ("AA", "American Airlines"),
...   ("DL", "Delta Airlines"),
...   ("VX", "Virgin America")
... ]

>>> airlines_rdd = spark.sparkContext.parallelize(airlines_data)\
...   .map(lambda tuple2: (tuple2[0], tuple2[1]))

>>> airlines_dict = airlines_rdd.collectAsMap()
>>> airlines_cache = spark.sparkContext.broadcast(airlines_dict)
>>> airlines_cache
>>> airlines_cache.value
{'SW': 'Southwest Airlines',
 'AA': 'American Airlines',
 'DL': 'Delta Airlines',
 'VX': 'Virgin America'}
```

Step 3: Create Facts Table

This step creates a DataFrame from the `Flights` table to be used as a fact table and joined with the cached dictionaries created in steps 1 and 2:

```
>>> flights_data = [
...   ("DTW", "ORD", "SW", "225",  "17:10"),
...   ("DTW", "JFK", "SW", "355",  "8:20"),
...   ("SEA", "JFK", "DL", "418",  "7:00"),
...   ("SFO", "LAX", "AA", "1250", "7:05"),
...   ("SFO", "JFK", "VX", "12",   "7:05"),
...   ("JFK", "LAX", "DL", "424",  "7:10"),
...   ("LAX", "SEA", "DL", "5737", "7:10")
... ]
>>> flight_columns = ["from", "to", "airline", "flight_number", "departure"]
>>> flights = spark.createDataFrame(flights_data, flight_columns)
>>> flights.show(truncate=False)

+----+---+-------+-------------+---------+
|from|to |airline|flight_number|departure|
+----+---+-------+-------------+---------+
|DTW |ORD|SW     |225          |17:10    |
|DTW |JFK|SW     |355          |8:20     |
|SEA |JFK|DL     |418          |7:00     |
|SFO |LAX|AA     |1250         |7:05     |
|SFO |JFK|VX     |12           |7:05     |
|JFK |LAX|DL     |424          |7:10     |
|LAX |SEA|DL     |5737         |7:10     |
+----+---+-------+-------------+---------+
```

Step 4: Apply Map-Side Join

Finally, we iterate the fact table and perform the map-side join:

```
>>> from pyspark.sql.functions import udf
>>> from pyspark.sql.types import StringType
>>>
>>> def get_airport(code):
...   return airports_cache.value[code][1]
...
>>> def get_airline(code):
...   return airlines_cache.value[code]

>>> airport_udf = udf(get_airport, StringType())
...
>>> airport_udf = udf(get_airport, StringType())
>>>
>>> flights.select(
        airport_udf("from").alias("from_city"), ❶
        airport_udf("to").alias("to_city"), ❷
        airline_udf("airline").alias("airline_name"), ❸
        "flight_number", "departure").show(truncate=False)
```

```
+-------------+----------+-----------------+------------+---------+
|from_city    |to_city   |airline_name     |flight_number|departure|
+-------------+----------+-----------------+------------+---------+
|Detroit      |Chicago   |Southwest Airlines|225        |17:10    |
|Detroit      |New York  |Southwest Airlines|355        |8:20     |
|Seattle      |New York  |Delta Airlines   |418         |7:00     |
|San Francisco|Los Angeles|American Airlines |1250       |7:05     |
|San Francisco|New York  |Virgin America   |12          |7:05     |
|New York     |Los Angeles|Delta Airlines   |424        |7:10     |
|Los Angeles  |Seattle   |Delta Airlines   |5737        |7:10     |
+-------------+----------+-----------------+------------+---------+
```

❶ Map-side join for airport

❷ Map-side join for airport

❸ Map-side join for airline

Efficient Joins Using Bloom Filters

Given two RDDs, a larger `RDD[(K, V)]` and a smaller `RDD[(K, W)]`, Spark enables us to perform a join operation on the key `K`. Joining two RDDs is a common operation when working with Spark. In some cases, a join is used as a form of filtering: for example, if you want to perform an operation on a subset of the records in the `RDD[(K, V)]`, represented by entities in another `RDD[(K, W)]` you can use an inner join to achieve that effect. However, you may prefer to avoid the shuffle that the join operation introduces, especially if the `RDD[(K, W)]` you want to use for filtering is significantly smaller than the main `RDD[(K, V)]` on which you will perform your further computation.

You could do a broadcast join using a set (as a Bloom filter) constructed by collecting the smaller RDD you wish to filter by, but this requires collecting the entire `RDD[(K, W)]` in driver memory, and even if it is relatively small (several thousand or million records) that can still lead to some undesirable memory pressure. If you want to avoid the shuffle introduced by the join operation, then you may use the Bloom filter. This reduces the problem of joining the `RDD[(K, V)]` with the `RDD[(K, W)]` into a simple `map()` transformation, where we check the key `K` against the Bloom filter constructed from the smaller `RDD[(K, W)]`.

Introduction to Bloom Filters

A Bloom filter (*https://oreil.ly/sFnRT*) is a space-efficient probabilistic data structure that can be used to test whether an element is a member of a set. It may return true for elements that are not actually members of the set (i.e., false positives are possible), but it will never return false for elements that are in the set; queries return either "possibly in set" or "definitely not in set." Elements can be added to the set, but not removed. The more elements that are added to the set, the larger the probability of false positives.

In a nutshell, we can summarize the Bloom filter's properties as follows:

- Given a large set $S = \{x_1, x_2, \ldots, x_n\}$, a Bloom filter is a probabilistic, fast, and space-efficient cache builder. It does not store the items in the set itself, and uses less space than is theoretically required to store the data correctly; this is the source of its potential inaccuracy.
- It basically approximates the set membership operation and tries to answer questions of the form "Does item `x` exist in set `S`?
- It allows false positive errors. This means that for some `x` that is not in the set, a Bloom filter might indicate that `x` is in the set.
- It does not allow false negative errors. This means that if `x` is in the set, the Bloom filter will never indicate that `x` is not in the set.

To make this clearer, let's look at a simple join example between two relations, or tables. Suppose we want to join `R=RDD(K, V)` and `S=RDD(K, W)` on a common key `K`. Further assume that the following is true:

```
count(R) = 1000,000,000  (larger dataset)
count(S) =   10,000,000  (smaller dataset)
```

To do a basic join, we would need to check 10 trillion (10^{12}) records, which is a huge and time-consuming process. One way to reduce the required time and the complexity of the join operation between `R` and `S` is to use a Bloom filter on relation `S` (the smaller dataset) and then use the built Bloom filter data structure on relation `R`. This can eliminate the unneeded records from `R` (perhaps reducing its size to 20,000,000 records), making the join faster and more efficient.

Now, let's semi-formalize the Bloom filter data structure. How do we construct one? What is the probability of false positive errors, and how we can decrease their probability? This is how a Bloom filter works. Given a set $S = \{x_1, x_2, \ldots, x_n\}$:

- Let `B` be an `m`-bit array (`m` > 1), initialized with 0s. `B`'s elements are `B[0]`, `B[1]`, `B[2]`, …, `B[m-1]`. The amount of memory required for storing array `B` is only a fraction of that needed for storing the whole set `S`. The probability of false positives is inversely proportional to the size of the bit vector (the array `B`).
- Let $\{H_1, H_2, \ldots, H_k\}$ be a set of `k` hash functions. If $H_i(x_j) = a$, then set `B[a] =` 1. You may use SHA1, MD5, and Murmer as hash functions. For example:

  — $H_i(x)$ `= MD5(x+i)`

  — $H_i(x)$ `= MD5(x || i)`

- To check if $x \in S$, check B at $H_i(x)$. All k values must be 1.
- It is possible to have a false positive, where all k values are 1, but x is not in S. The probability of false positives is:

$$\left(1 - \left[1 - \frac{1}{m}\right]^{kn}\right)^k \approx \left(1 - e^{-kn/m}\right)^k$$

- What is the optimal number of hash functions? For a given *m* (number of bits selected for the Bloom filter) and *n* (size of the dataset), the value of *k* (the number of hash functions) that minimizes the probability of false positives is (*ln* stands for "natural logarithm"):

$$k = \frac{m}{n} ln(2)$$

$$m = -\frac{n\ ln(p)}{(ln(2))^2}$$

- Therefore, the probability that a specific bit has been flipped to 1 is:

$$1 - \left(1 - \frac{1}{m}\right)^{kn} \approx 1 - e^{-\frac{kn}{m}}$$

Next, let's take a look at a Bloom filter example.

A Simple Bloom Filter Example

This example shows how to insert elements into and perform queries on a Bloom filter of size 10 (m = 10) with three hash functions $H = \{H_1, H_2, H_3\}$, where H(x) denotes the result of these three hash functions. We start with a 10-bit-long array B initialized to 0:

```
Array B:
   initialized:
         index  0  1  2  3  4  5  6  7  8  9
         value  0  0  0  0  0  0  0  0  0  0

   insert element a,  H(a) = (2, 5, 6)
         index  0  1  2  3  4  5  6  7  8  9
         value  0  0  1  0  0  1  1  0  0  0

   insert element b,  H(b) = (1, 5, 8)
         index  0  1  2  3  4  5  6  7  8  9
         value  0  1  1  0  0  1  1  0  1  0
```

```
query element c
H(c) = (5, 8, 9) => c is not a member (since B[9]=0)

query element d
H(d) = (2, 5, 8) => d is a member (False Positive)

query element e
H(e) = (1, 2, 6) => e is a member (False Positive)

query element f
H(f) = (2, 5, 6) => f is a member (Positive)
```

Bloom Filters in Python

The following code segment shows how to create and use a Bloom filter in Python (you may roll your own Bloom filter library, but as a general rule if a library already exists, you should use it):

```
# instantiate BloomFilter with custom settings
>>> from bloom_filter import BloomFilter
>>> bloom = BloomFilter(max_elements=100000, error_rate=0.01)

# Test whether the Bloom-filter has seen a key
>>> "test-key" in bloom
False

# Mark the key as seen
>>> bloom.add("test-key")

# Now check again
>>> "test-key" in bloom
True
```

Using Bloom Filters in PySpark

A Bloom filter is a small, compact, and fast data structure for set membership testing. It can be used to facilitate the join of two RDDs/relations/tables such as `R(K, V)` and `S(K, W)` where one of the relations has huge number of records and the other relation has a smaller number of records (for example, `R` might have 1,000,000,000 records and `S` might have 10,000,000 records).

Performing a traditional join on the key field `K` between `R` and `S` would take a long time and be inefficient. We can speed things up by building a Bloom filter out of relation `S(K, W)`, and then testing the values in `R(K, V)` for membership using the built data structure (with Spark's broadcast mechanism). Note that for reduce-side join optimization we use a Bloom filter in the map tasks, which will force an I/O cost reduction for the PySpark job. How do we do this? The following steps show how to use a Bloom filter (representation of S) in mappers, which will be a substitute for the join operation between R and S:

1. Build the Bloom filter, using the smaller of the two relations/tables. Initialize the Bloom filter (create an instance of `BloomFilter`), then build the data structure with `BloomFilter.add()`. We'll call the built Bloom filter `the_bloom_filter`.
2. Broadcast the built Bloom filter. Use `SparkContext.broadcast()` to broadcast `the_bloom_filter` to all worker nodes, so that it's available to all Spark transformations (including mappers):

```
# to broadcast it to all worker nodes for read-only purposes
sc = spark.sparkContext
broadcasted_bloom_filter = sc.broadcast(the_bloom_filter)
```

3. Use the broadcasted object in mappers. Now, we can use the Bloom filter to get rid of the unneeded elements in R:

```
# e is an element of R(k, b)
def bloom_filter_function(e):
  # get a copy of the Bloom filter
  the_bloom_filter = broadcasted_bloom_filter.value()
  # use the_bloom_filter for element e
  key = e[0]
  if key in the_bloom_filter:
    return True
  else:
    return False
#end-def
```

We use the `bloom_filter_function()` for `R=RDD[(K, V)]` to keep the elements if and only if the key is in `S=RDD[(K, W)]`:

```
# R=RDD[(K, V)]
# joined = RDD[(K, V)] where K is in S=RDD[(K, W)]
joined = R.filter(bloom_filter_function)
```

Summary

This chapter introduced some design patterns that can be used in situations where optimizing the cost of a join operation is essential. I showed you how joins are implemented in the MapReduce paradigm and presented the map-side join, which reduces the join operation to a simple mapper with a lookup operation to a built dictionary (avoiding the actual `join()` function). This design pattern completely eliminates the need to shuffle any data to the reduce phase. Then I showed you a more efficient alternative to using a join as a filter operation. As you saw, by using a Bloom filter you can avoid the shuffle that the join operation results in. Next, we'll wrap up the book with a look at design patterns for feature engineering.

CHAPTER 12

Feature Engineering in PySpark

This chapter covers design patterns for working with features of data—any measurable attributes, from car prices to gene values, hemoglobin counts, or education levels —when building machine learning models (also known as *feature engineering*). These processes (extracting, transforming, and selecting features) are essential in building effective machine learning models. Feature engineering is one of the most important topics in machine learning, because the success or failure of a model at predicting the future depends mainly on the features you choose.

Spark provides a comprehensive machine learning API for many well-known algorithms including linear regression, logistic regression, and decision trees. The goal of this chapter is to present fundamental tools and techniques in PySpark that you can use to build all sorts of machine learning pipelines. The chapter introduces Spark's powerful machine learning tools and utilities and provides examples using the PySpark API. The skills you learn here will be useful to an aspiring data scientist or data engineer. My goal is not to familiarize you with famous machine learning algorithms such as linear regression, principal component analysis, or support vector machines, since these are already covered in many books, but to equip you with tools (normalization, standardization, string indexing, etc.) that you can use in cleaning data and building models for a wide range of machine learning algorithms.

No matter which algorithm you use, feature engineering is important. Machine learning enables us to find patterns in data—we find the patterns by building models, then we use the built models to make predictions about new data points (i.e., query data). To get those predictions right, we must construct the dataset and transform the data correctly. This chapter covers these two key steps.

> **Source Code**
>
> Complete programs for this chapter are available in the book's GitHub repository (*https://oreil.ly/11XWm*).

Topics we will discuss include:

- Adding a new derived feature
- Creating and applying UDFs
- Creating pipelines
- Binarizing data
- Data imputation
- Tokenization
- Standardization
- Normalization
- String indexing
- Vector assembly
- Bucketing
- Logarithm transformation
- One-hot encoding
- TF-IDF
- Feature hashing
- Applying SQL transformations

First, though, let's take a more in-depth look at feature engineering.

Introduction to Feature Engineering

In his excellent blog post (*https://oreil.ly/IO6T6*) on mastering feature engineering, Jason Brownlee defines it as "the process of transforming raw data into features that better represent the underlying problem to the predictive models, resulting in improved model accuracy on unseen data." In this chapter, my goal is to present generic feature engineering techniques available in PySpark that you can use to build better predictive models.

Let's say that your data is represented in a matrix of rows and columns. In machine learning, columns are called features (such as age, gender, education, heart rate, or blood pressure), and each row represents an instance of the dataset (i.e., a record).

The features in your data will directly influence the predictive models you build and use and the results you can achieve. Data scientists spend around half their time on data preparation, and feature engineering is an important part of this.

Where does feature engineering fit in with building machine learning models? When do you apply these techniques to your data? Let's take a look at the key steps in building and using a machine learning model:

1. Gather requirements for machine learning data and define the problem.
2. Select data (collect and integrate the data, then denormalize it into a dataset).
3. Preprocess data (format, clean, and sample the data so you can work with it).
4. Transform data (perform feature engineering).
5. Model data (split the data into training and test sets, use the training data to create models, then use the test data to evaluate the models and tune them).
6. Use the built model to make predictions on query data.

Feature engineering happens right before you build a model from your data. After selecting and cleansing the data (for example, making sure that null values are replaced with proper values), you transform the data by performing feature engineering: this might involve converting string into numeric data, bucketizing the data, normalizing or standardizing the data, etc.

The part of the overall process that this chapter covers is illustrated in Figure 12-1.

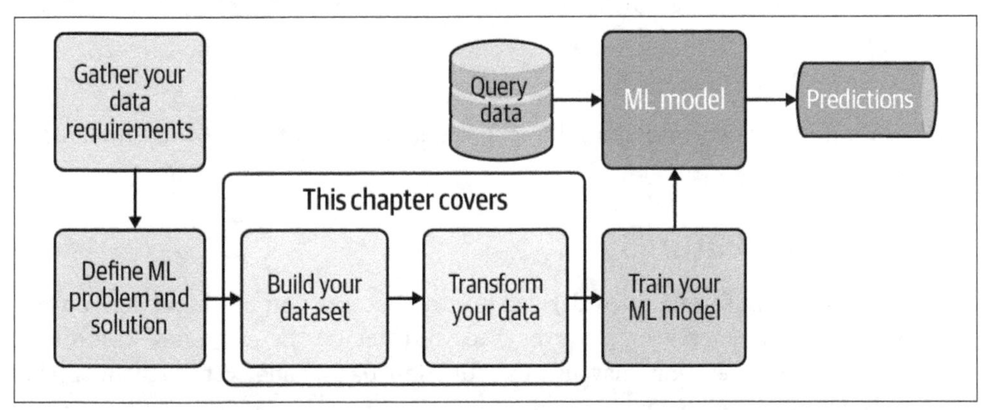

Figure 12-1. Feature engineering

The Spark API provides various algorithms (*https://oreil.ly/butJ1*) for working with features, which are roughly divided into these groups:

- Extraction (algorithms for extracting features from "raw" data)
- Transformation (algorithms for scaling, converting, or modifying features)

- Selection (algorithms for selecting a subset from a larger set of features)
- Locality-sensitive hashing (LSH); algorithms for grouping similar items)

There can be many reasons for data transformation and feature engineering, either mandatory or optional:

Mandatory transformations
: These transformations are necessary to solve a problem (such as building a machine learning model) for data compatibility reasons. Examples include:

  - Converting non-numeric features into numeric features. For example, if a feature has non-numeric values, then average, sum, and median calculations will be impossible; likewise, we cannot perform matrix multiplication on a string but must convert it to some numeric representation first.
  - Resizing inputs to a fixed size. Some linear models and feed-forward neural networks have a fixed number of input nodes, so your input data must always have the same size. For example, image models need to reshape the images in their dataset to a fixed size.

Optional transformations
: Optional data transformations may help the machine learning model to perform better. These transformations might include:

  - Changing text to lowercase before applying other data transformations
  - Tokenizing and removing nonessential words, such as "of," "a," "and," "the," and "so"
  - Normalizing numeric features

We'll examine both types in the following sections. Let's dive into our first topic, adding a new feature.

Adding New Features

Sometimes you want to add a new derived feature (because you need that derived feature in your machine learning algorithm) to your dataset, to add a new column or feature to your dataset, you may use the function `DataFrame.withColumn()`. This concept is demonstrated below:

```
# SparkSession available as 'spark'
>>> column_names = ["emp_id", "salary"]
>>> records = [(100, 120000), (200, 170000), (300, 150000)]
>>> df = spark.createDataFrame(records, column_names)
>>> df.show()
+------+------+
|emp_id|salary|
+------+------+
```

```
|   100|120000|
|   200|170000|
|   300|150000|
+------+------+
```

You may use Spark's `DataFrame.withColumn()` to add a new column/feature:

```
>>> df2 = df.withColumn("bonus", df.salary * 0.05)
>>> df2.show()
+------+------+------+
|emp_id|salary| bonus|
+------+------+------+
|   100|120000|6000.0|
|   200|170000|8500.0|
|   300|150000|7500.0|
+------+------+------+
```

Applying UDFs

If PySpark does not provide the function you need, you can define your own Python functions and register them as user-defined functions (UDFs) with Spark SQL's DSL using `spark.udf.register()`. You can then apply these functions in your data transformations.

To make your Python functions compatible with Spark's DataFrames, you need to convert them to PySpark UDFs by passing them to the `pyspark.sql.functions.udf()` function. Alternatively, you can create your UDF in a single step using annotations, as shown here. Add `udf@` as a "decorator" of your Python function, and specify its return type as the argument:

```
from pyspark.sql.functions import udf

>>> @udf("integer") ❶
... def tripled(num):
...   return 3*int(num)
...
>>> df2 = df.withColumn('tripled_col', tripled(df.salary))
>>> df2.show()
+------+------+-----------+
|emp_id|salary|tripled_col| ❷
+------+------+-----------+
|   100|120000|     360000|
|   200|170000|     510000|
|   300|150000|     450000|
+------+------+-----------+
```

 The function `tripled()` is a UDF and its return type is `integer`.

❷ `tripled_col` is a derived feature.

Note that if your features are represented as an RDD (where each RDD element represents an instance of your features), you may use the `RDD.map()` function to add a new feature to your feature set.

Creating Pipelines

In machine learning algorithms, you can glue several stages together and run them in order. Consider three stages, called `{Stage-1, Stage-2, Stage-3}`, where the output of `Stage-1` is used as an input to `Stage-2` and the output of `Stage-2` is used as an input to `Stage-3`. These three stages form a simple pipeline. Suppose we have to transform the data in the order shown in Table 12-1.

Table 12-1. Pipeline stages

Stage	Description
`Stage-1`	Label encode or string index the column `dept` * (create `dept_index` column).
`Stage-2`	Label encode or string index the column `education` (create `education_index` column).
`Stage-3`	One-hot encode the indexed column `education_index` (create `education_OHE` column).

Spark provides a pipeline API, defined as `pyspark.ml.Pipeline(*, stages=None)`, which acts as an estimator (an abstraction of a learning algorithm that fits a model on a dataset). According to the Spark documentation:

> A `Pipeline` consists of a sequence of stages, each of which is either an `Estimator` or a `Transformer`. When `Pipeline.fit()` is called, the stages are executed in order. If a stage is an `Estimator`, its `Estimator.fit()` method will be called on the input dataset to fit a model. Then the model, which is a transformer, will be used to transform the dataset as the input to the next stage. If a stage is a `Transformer`, its `Transformer.transform()` method will be called to produce the dataset for the next stage. The fitted model from a `Pipeline` is a `PipelineModel`, which consists of fitted models and transformers, corresponding to the pipeline stages. If stages is an empty list, the pipeline acts as an identity transformer.

To illustrate the concept of pipelines, first we'll create a sample DataFrame with three columns to use as input data, as shown here, then we'll create a simple pipeline using `pyspark.ml.Pipeline()`:

```
# spark: an instance of SparkSession
# create a DataFrame
df = spark.createDataFrame([
    (1, 'CS', 'MS'),
    (2, 'MATH', 'PHD'),
    (3, 'MATH', 'MS'),
    (4, 'CS', 'MS'),
    (5, 'CS', 'PHD'),
    (6, 'ECON', 'BS'),
```

```
        (7, 'ECON', 'BS'),
    ], ['id', 'dept', 'education'])
```

We can view our sample data with `df.show()`:

```
>>> df.show()
+---+----+---------+
| id|dept|education|
+---+----+---------+
|  1|  CS|       MS|
|  2|MATH|      PHD|
|  3|MATH|       MS|
|  4|  CS|       MS|
|  5|  CS|      PHD|
|  6|ECON|       BS|
|  7|ECON|       BS|
+---+----+---------+
```

Now that we have created the DataFrame, suppose we want to transform the data through three defined stages, `{stage_1, stage_2, stage_3}`. In each stage, we will pass the input and output column names, and we'll set up the pipeline by passing the defined stages to the `Pipeline` object as a list.

Spark's pipeline model then performs specific steps one by one in a sequence and gives us the final desired result. Figure 12-2 shows the pipeline we will define.

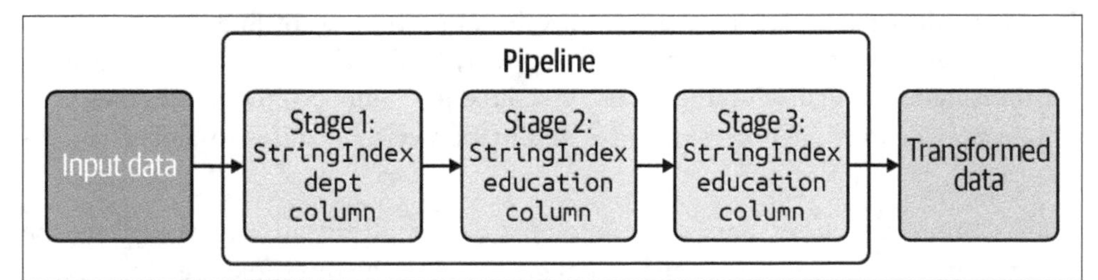

Figure 12-2. A sample pipeline with three stages

The three stages are implemented as follows:

```
from pyspark.ml import Pipeline
from pyspark.ml.feature import StringIndexer
from pyspark.ml.feature import OneHotEncoder

# Stage 1: transform the `dept` column to numeric
stage_1 = StringIndexer(inputCol= 'dept', outputCol= 'dept_index')
#
# Stage 2: transform the `education` column to numeric
stage_2 = StringIndexer(inputCol= 'education', outputCol= 'education_index')
#
# Stage 3: one-hot encode the numeric column `education_index`
stage_3 = OneHotEncoder(inputCols=['education_index'],
                        outputCols=['education_OHE'])
```

Next, we'll define our pipeline with these three stages:

```
# set up the pipeline: glue the stages together
pipeline = Pipeline(stages=[stage_1, stage_2, stage_3])

# fit the pipeline model and transform the data as defined
pipeline_model = pipeline.fit(df)

# view the transformed data
final_df = pipeline_model.transform(df)
final_df.show(truncate=False)
+---+----+---------+----------+---------------+-------------+
|id |dept|education|dept_index|education_index|education_OHE|
+---+----+---------+----------+---------------+-------------+
|1  |CS  |MS       |0.0       |0.0            |(2,[0],[1.0])|
|2  |MATH|PHD      |2.0       |2.0            |(2,[],[])    |
|3  |MATH|MS       |2.0       |0.0            |(2,[0],[1.0])|
|4  |CS  |MS       |0.0       |0.0            |(2,[0],[1.0])|
|5  |CS  |PHD      |0.0       |2.0            |(2,[],[])    |
|6  |ECON|BS       |1.0       |1.0            |(2,[1],[1.0])|
|7  |ECON|BS       |1.0       |1.0            |(2,[1],[1.0])|
+---+----+---------+----------+---------------+-------------+
```

Binarizing Data

Binarizing data means setting the feature values to 0 or 1 according to some threshold. Values greater than the threshold map to 1, while values less than or equal to the threshold map to 0. With the default threshold of 0, only positive values map to 1. Binarization is thus the process of thresholding numerical features to binary `{0, 1}` features.

Spark's `Binarizer` takes the parameters `inputCol` and `outputCol`, as well as the `threshold` for binarization. Feature values greater than the threshold are binarized to `1.0`; values equal to or less than the threshold are binarized to `0.0`.

First, let's create a DataFrame with a single feature:

```
from pyspark.ml.feature import Binarizer

raw_df = spark.createDataFrame([
    (1, 0.1),
    (2, 0.2),
    (3, 0.5),
    (4, 0.8),
    (5, 0.9),
    (6, 1.1)
], ["id", "feature"])
```

Next, we'll create a `Binarizer` with `threshold=0.5`, so any value less than or equal to `0.5` will map into `0.0` and any value greater than `0.5` will map into `1.0`:

```
>>> from pyspark.ml.feature import Binarizer
>>> binarizer = Binarizer(threshold=0.5, inputCol="feature",
                          outputCol="binarized_feature")
```

Finally, we apply the defined `Binarizer` to a feature column:

```
binarized_df = binarizer.transform(raw_df)

>>> print("Binarizer output with Threshold = %f" % binarizer.getThreshold())
Binarizer output with Threshold = 0.500000

>>> binarized_df = binarizer.transform(raw_df)
>>> binarized_df.show(truncate=False)
+---+-------+-----------------+
|id |feature|binarized_feature|
+---+-------+-----------------+
|1  |0.1    |0.0              |
|2  |0.2    |0.0              |
|3  |0.5    |0.0              |
|4  |0.8    |1.0              |
|5  |0.9    |1.0              |
|6  |1.1    |1.0              |
+---+-------+-----------------+
```

Imputation

Spark's `Imputer` is an imputation transformer for filling in missing values. Real-world datasets commonly contain missing values, often encoded as nulls, blanks, `NaN`s, or other placeholders. There are many methods to handle these values, including the following:

- Delete instances if there is any missing feature (this might not be such a good idea since important information from other features will be lost).
- For a missing feature, find the average value of that feature and fill in that value.
- Impute the missing values, (i.e., to infer them from the known part of the data). This is often the best strategy.

Spark's `Imputer` has the following signature:

```
class pyspark.ml.feature.Imputer(*, strategy='mean', missingValue=nan,
                                 inputCols=None, outputCols=None,
                                 inputCol=None, outputCol=None,
                                 relativeError=0.001)
```

It uses either the mean or the median of the columns in which the missing values are located. The input columns should be of numeric type; currently `Imputer` does not support categorical features and may create incorrect values for a categorical feature.

Note that the mean/median/mode value is computed after filtering out missing values. All `null` values in the input columns are treated as missing, and so are also imputed. For computing the median, `pyspark.sql.DataFrame.approxQuantile()` is used with a relative error of 0.001.

You can instruct the imputer to impute custom values other than `NaN` by using `.setMissingValue(`*`custom_value`*`)`. For example, `.setMissingValue(0)` tells it to impute all occurrences of `0` (again, `null` values in the input columns will be treated as missing and also imputed).

The following example shows how an imputer can be used. Suppose that we have a DataFrame with three columns, `id`, `col1`, and `col2`:

```
>>> df = spark.createDataFrame([
...     (1, 12.0, 5.0),
...     (2, 7.0, 10.0),
...     (3, 10.0, 12.0),
...     (4, 5.0, float("nan")),
...     (5, 6.0, None),
...     (6, float("nan"), float("nan")),
...     (7, None, None)
... ], ["id", "col1", "col2"])
>>> df.show(truncate=False)
+---+----+----+
|id |col1|col2|
+---+----+----+
|1  |12.0|5.0 |
|2  |7.0 |10.0|
|3  |10.0|12.0|
|4  |5.0 |NaN |
|5  |6.0 |null|
|6  |NaN |NaN |
|7  |null|null|
+---+----+----+
```

Next, let's create an imputer and apply it to our created data:

```
>>> from pyspark.ml.feature import Imputer
>>> imputer = Imputer(inputCols=["col1", "col2"],
                      outputCols=["col1_out", "col2_out"])
>>> model = imputer.fit(df)
>>> transformed = model.transform(df)
>>> transformed.show(truncate=False)
+---+----+----+--------+--------+
|id |col1|col2|col1_out|col2_out|
+---+----+----+--------+--------+
|1  |12.0|5.0 |12.0    |5.0     |
```

```
|2  |7.0 |10.0|7.0     |10.0    |
|3  |10.0|12.0|10.0    |12.0    |
|4  |5.0 |NaN |5.0     |9.0     |
|5  |6.0 |null|6.0     |9.0     |
|6  |NaN |NaN |8.0     |9.0     |
|7  |null|null|8.0     |9.0     |
+---+----+----+--------+--------+
```

How did we get the numbers to use for the missing values (`8.0` for `col1` and `9.0` for `col2`)? It's easy; since the default strategy is "mean," we simply compute the averages for each column and use those for the missing values:

```
col1: (12.0+7.0+10.0+5.0+6.0) / 5 = 40 / 5 = 8.0
col2: (5.0+10.0+12.0) / 3 = 27.0 / 3 = 9.0
```

Based on your data requirements, you may want to use a different strategy to fill in the missing values. You can instruct the imputer to use the median of available feature values instead as follows:

```
>>> imputer.setStrategy("median")
>>> model = imputer.fit(df)
>>> transformed = model.transform(df)
>>> transformed.show(truncate=False)
+---+----+----+--------+--------+
|id |col1|col2|col1_out|col2_out|
+---+----+----+--------+--------+
|1  |12.0|5.0 |12.0    |5.0     |
|2  |7.0 |10.0|7.0     |10.0    |
|3  |10.0|12.0|10.0    |12.0    |
|4  |5.0 |NaN |5.0     |10.0    |
|5  |6.0 |null|6.0     |10.0    |
|6  |NaN |NaN |7.0     |10.0    |
|7  |null|null|7.0     |10.0    |
+---+----+----+--------+--------+
```

To get these values (`7.0` for `col1` and `10.0` for `col2`), we just compute the median value for each column:

```
median(col1) =
median(12.0, 7.0, 10.0, 5.0, 6.0) =
median(5.0, 6.0, 7.0, 10.0, 12.0) =
7.0

median(col2) =
median(5.0, 10.0, 12.0) =
10.0
```

Tokenization

Tokenization algorithms are used to split a phrase, sentence, paragraph, or entire text document into smaller units, such as individual words, bigrams, or terms. These smaller units are called *tokens*. For example, the lexical analyzer (an algorithm used in compiler writing) breaks programming code into a series of tokens by removing any whitespace or comments. Therefore, you can think of tokenization more generally as the process of splitting a string into any kind of meaningful tokens.

In Spark, you can use the `Tokenizer` and `RegexTokenizer` (which allows you to define custom tokenization strategies through regular expressions) to tokenize strings.

Tokenizer

Spark's `Tokenizer` is a tokenizer that converts the input string to lowercase and then splits it by whitespace. To show how this works, let's create some sample data:

```
>>> docs = [(1, "a Fox jumped over FOX"),
            (2, "RED of fox jumped")]
>>> df = spark.createDataFrame(docs, ["id", "text"])
>>> df.show(truncate=False)
+---+---------------------+
|id |text                 |
+---+---------------------+
|1  |a Fox jumped over FOX|
|2  |RED of fox jumped    |
+---+---------------------+
```

Then apply the `Tokenizer`:

```
>>> tokenizer = Tokenizer(inputCol="text", outputCol="tokens")
>>> tokenized = tokenizer.transform(df)
>>> tokenized.select("text", "tokens")
        .withColumn("tokens_length", countTokens(col("tokens")))
        .show(truncate=False)
+---------------------+----------------------------+-------------+
|text                 |tokens                      |tokens_length|
+---------------------+----------------------------+-------------+
|a Fox jumped over FOX|[a, fox, jumped, over, fox]|5            |
|RED of fox jumped    |[red, of, fox, jumped]      |4            |
+---------------------+----------------------------+-------------+
```

RegexTokenizer

Spark's `RegexTokenizer` is a regular expression–based tokenizer that extracts tokens either by using the provided regex pattern to split the text (the default) or repeatedly matching the regex (if the optional `gaps` parameter, which is `True` by default, is `False`). Here's an example:

```
>>> regexTokenizer = RegexTokenizer(inputCol="text", outputCol="tokens",
                                    pattern="\\W", minTokenLength=3)
>>> regex_tokenized = regexTokenizer.transform(df)
>>> regex_tokenized.select("text", "tokens")
```

```
      .withColumn("tokens_length", countTokens(col("tokens")))
      .show(truncate=False)
+--------------------+--------------------------+------------+
|text                |tokens                    |tokens_length|
+--------------------+--------------------------+------------+
|a Fox jumped over FOX|[fox, jumped, over, fox]|4           |
|RED of fox jumped   |[red, fox, jumped]        |3           |
+--------------------+--------------------------+------------+
```

Tokenization with a Pipeline

We can also perform tokenization as part of a pipeline. Here, we create a DataFrame with two columns:

```
>>> docs = [(1, "a Fox jumped, over, the fence?"),
            (2, "a RED, of fox?")]
>>> df = spark.createDataFrame(docs, ["id", "text"])
>>> df.show(truncate=False)
+---+------------------------------+
|id |text                          |
+---+------------------------------+
|1  |a Fox jumped, over, the fence?|
|2  |a RED, of fox?                |
+---+------------------------------+
```

Next, we apply the `RegexTokenizer()` function to this DataFrame:

```
>>> tk = RegexTokenizer(pattern=r'(?:\p{Punct}|\s)+', inputCol="text",
                        outputCol='text2')
>>> sw = StopWordsRemover(inputCol='text2', outputCol='text3')
>>> pipeline = Pipeline(stages=[tk, sw])
>>> df4 = pipeline.fit(df).transform(df)
>>> df4.show(truncate=False)
+---+---------------+---------------+-------------+
|id | text          |text2          |text3        |
+---+---------------+---------------+-------------+
|1  |a Fox jumped,  |[a, fox, jumped, |[fox, jumped, |
|   |over, the fence?|over, the, fence]| fence]      |
|2  |a RED, of fox? |[a, red, of, fox]|[red, fox]   |
+---+---------------+---------------+-------------+
```

Standardization

One of the most popular techniques for scaling numerical data prior to building a model is standardization. Standardizing a dataset involves rescaling the distribution of values so that the mean of observed values (as a feature) is `0.00` and the standard deviation is `1.00`.

Many machine learning algorithms perform better when numerical input variables (features) are scaled to a standard range. For example, algorithms such as linear regression that use a weighted sum of the input and algorithms like k-nearest neighbors that use distance measures require standardized values, as otherwise the built models might underfit or overfit the training data and underperform.

A value is standardized as follows:

```
y = (x - mean) / standard_deviation
```

Where the mean is calculated as:

```
mean = sum(x) / count(x)
```

$$\bar{x} = \frac{1}{N}\sum_{i=1}^{N} x_i$$

And the standard deviation is calculated as:

```
standard_deviation = sqrt(sum( (x - mean)^2 ) / count(x))
```

$$sd = \sqrt{\frac{1}{N}\sum_{i=1}^{N}\left(x_i - \bar{x}\right)^2}$$

For example, if `X = (1, 3, 6, 10)`, the mean/average is calculated as:

```
mean = (1+2+6+10)/4 = 20/4 = 5.0
```

and the standard deviation is calculated as:

```
standard_deviation
= sqrt ( ((1-5)^2 + (3-5)^2 + (6-5)^2 + (10-5)^2)) / 4)
= sqrt ((16+4+1+25)/4)
= sqrt(46/4)
= sqrt(11.5) = 3.39116
```

So, the new standardized values will be :

```
y = (y1, y2, y3, y4) = (-1.1795, -0.5897, 0.2948, 1.4744)
```

where:

```
y1 = (1 - 5.0) / 3.39116
y2 = (3 - 5.0) / 3.39116
y3 = (6 - 5.0) / 3.39116
y4 = (10 - 5.0) / 3.39116
```

As you can see, the mean of the standardized values `(y)` is `0.00` and the standard deviation is `1.00`.

Let's go over how to perform standardization in PySpark. Let's say that we are trying to standardize (`mean = 0.00, stddev = 1.00`) one column in a DataFrame. First we'll create a sample DataFrame, then I'll show you two ways to standardize the `age` column:

```
features = [('alex', 1), ('bob', 3), ('ali', 6), ('dave', 10)]
columns = ("name", "age")
samples = spark.createDataFrame(features, columns)
>>> samples.show()
+----+---+
|name|age|
+----+---+
|alex|  1|
| bob|  3|
| ali|  6|
|dave| 10|
+----+---+
```

Method 1 is to use DataFrame functions:

```
>>> from pyspark.sql.functions import stddev, mean, col
>>> (samples.select(mean("age").alias("mean_age"),
...                 stddev("age").alias("stddev_age"))
...    .crossJoin(samples)
...    .withColumn("age_scaled",
       (col("age") - col("mean_age")) / col("stddev_age")))
...    .show(truncate=False)
+--------+------------------+----+---+-------------------+
|mean_age|stddev_age        |name|age|age_scaled         |
+--------+------------------+----+---+-------------------+
|5.0     |3.9157800414902435|alex|1  |-1.0215078369104984|
|5.0     |3.9157800414902435|bob |3  |-0.5107539184552492|
|5.0     |3.9157800414902435|ali |6  |0.2553769592276246 |
|5.0     |3.9157800414902435|dave|10 |1.276884796138123  |
+--------+------------------+----+---+-------------------+
```

or alternatively, we may write this as:

```
>>> mean_age, sttdev_age = samples.select(mean("age"), stddev("age"))
    .first()
>>> samples.withColumn("age_scaled",
    (col("age") - mean_age) / sttdev_age).show(truncate=False)
+----+---+-------------------+
|name|age|age_scaled         |
+----+---+-------------------+
|alex|1  |-1.0215078369104984|
|bob |3  |-0.5107539184552492|
|ali |6  |0.2553769592276246 |
|dave|10 |1.276884796138123  |
+----+---+-------------------+
```

Method 2 is to use functions from PySpark's `ml` package. Here, we use `pyspark.ml.feature.VectorAssembler()` to transform the `age` column into a vector, then standardize the values with Spark's `StandardScaler`:

```
>>> from pyspark.ml.feature import VectorAssembler
>>> from pyspark.ml.feature import StandardScaler
>>> vecAssembler = VectorAssembler(inputCols=['age'], outputCol="age_vector")
```

```
>>> samples2 = vecAssembler.transform(samples)
>>> samples2.show()
+----+---+----------+
|name|age|age_vector|
+----+---+----------+
|alex|  1|     [1.0]|
| bob|  3|     [3.0]|
| ali|  6|     [6.0]|
|dave| 10|    [10.0]|
+----+---+----------+

>>> scaler = StandardScaler(inputCol="age_vector", outputCol="age_scaled",
...   withStd=True, withMean=True)
>>> scalerModel = scaler.fit(samples2)
>>> scaledData = scalerModel.transform(samples2)
>>> scaledData.show(truncate=False)
+----+---+----------+---------------------+
|name|age|age_vector|age_scaled           |
+----+---+----------+---------------------+
|alex|1  |[1.0]     |[-1.0215078369104984]|
|bob |3  |[3.0]     |[-0.5107539184552492]|
|ali |6  |[6.0]     |[0.2553769592276246] |
|dave|10 |[10.0]    |[1.276884796138123]  |
+----+---+----------+---------------------+
```

Unlike normalization, which we'll look at next, standardization can be helpful in cases where the data follows a Gaussian distribution. It also does not have a bounding range, so if you have outliers in your data they will not be impacted by standardization.

Normalization

Normalization is a scaling technique often applied as part of data preparation for machine learning. The goal of normalization is to change the values of numeric columns in the dataset to use a common scale, without distorting differences in the ranges of values or losing information. Normalization scales each numeric input variable separately to the range `[0,1]`, which is the range for floating-point values, where we have the most precision. In other words, the feature values are shifted and rescaled so that they end up ranging between `0.00` and `1.00`. This technique is also known as *min-max scaling*, and Spark provides a transformer for this purpose called `MinMaxScaler`.

Here's the formula for normalization:

$$\tilde{X}_i = \frac{X_i - X_{min}}{X_{max} - X_{min}}$$

Note that X_{max} and X_{min} are the maximum and minimum values of the given feature, X_i, respectively.

To illustrate the normalization process, let's create a DataFrame with three features:

```
>>> df = spark.createDataFrame([ (100, 77560, 45),
                                 (200, 41560, 23),
                                 (300, 30285, 20),
                                 (400, 10345, 6),
                                 (500, 88000, 50)
                               ], ["user_id", "revenue","num_of_days"])

>>> print("Before Scaling :")
>>> df.show(5)
+-------+-------+-----------+
|user_id|revenue|num_of_days|
+-------+-------+-----------+
|    100|  77560|         45|
|    200|  41560|         23|
|    300|  30285|         20|
|    400|  10345|          6|
|    500|  88000|         50|
+-------+-------+-----------+
```

Next, we'll apply the `MinMaxScaler` to our features:

```
from pyspark.ml.feature import MinMaxScaler
from pyspark.ml.feature import VectorAssembler
from pyspark.ml import Pipeline
from pyspark.sql.functions import udf
from pyspark.sql.types import DoubleType

# UDF for converting column type from vector to double type
unlist = udf(lambda x: round(float(list(x)[0]),3), DoubleType())

# Iterating over columns to be scaled
for i in ["revenue","num_of_days"]:
    # VectorAssembler transformation - Converting column to vector type
    assembler = VectorAssembler(inputCols=[i],outputCol=i+"_Vect")

    # MinMaxScaler transformation
    scaler = MinMaxScaler(inputCol=i+"_Vect", outputCol=i+"_Scaled")

    # Pipeline of VectorAssembler and MinMaxScaler
    pipeline = Pipeline(stages=[assembler, scaler])

    # Fitting pipeline on DataFrame
    df = pipeline.fit(df).transform(df)
      .withColumn(i+"_Scaled", unlist(i+"_Scaled")).drop(i+"_Vect")

After scaling, we can create and execute the following pipelines:

for i in ["revenue","num_of_days"]:
```

```
assembler = VectorAssembler(inputCols=[i], outputCol=i+"_Vect")
scaler = MinMaxScaler(inputCol=i+"_Vect", outputCol=i+"_Scaled")
pipeline = Pipeline(stages=[assembler, scaler])
df = pipeline.fit(df)
         .transform(df)
         .withColumn(i+"_Scaled", unlist(i+"_Scaled"))
         .drop(i+"_Vect")
```

And examine the scaled values:

```
>>> df.show(5)
+-------+-------+-----------+--------------+------------------+
|user_id|revenue|num_of_days|revenue_Scaled|num_of_days_Scaled|
+-------+-------+-----------+--------------+------------------+
|    100|  77560|         45|         0.866|             0.886|
|    200|  41560|         23|         0.402|             0.386|
|    300|  30285|         20|         0.257|             0.318|
|    400|  10345|          6|           0.0|               0.0|
|    500|  88000|         50|           1.0|               1.0|
+-------+-------+-----------+--------------+------------------+
```

Normalization is a good technique to use when you know that your data does not follow a Gaussian distribution. This can be useful in algorithms that do not assume any distribution of the data, like linear regression, *k*-nearest neighbors, and neural networks. In the following sections, we'll walk through a few more examples.

Scaling a Column Using a Pipeline

As with tokenization, we can apply normalization in a pipeline. First, let's define a set of features:

```
>>> from pyspark.ml.feature import MinMaxScaler
>>> from pyspark.ml import Pipeline
>>> from pyspark.ml.feature import VectorAssembler
>>> triplets = [(0, 1, 100), (1, 2, 200), (2, 5, 1000)]
>>> df = spark.createDataFrame(triplets, ['x', 'y', 'z'])
>>> df.show()
+---+---+----+
|  x|  y|   z|
+---+---+----+
|  0|  1| 100|
|  1|  2| 200|
|  2|  5|1000|
+---+---+----+
```

We can now apply `MinMaxScaler` in a pipeline as follows to normalize the values of feature (column) `x`:

```
>>> assembler = VectorAssembler(inputCols=["x"], outputCol="x_vector")
>>> scaler = MinMaxScaler(inputCol="x_vector", outputCol="x_scaled")
>>> pipeline = Pipeline(stages=[assembler, scaler])
>>> scalerModel = pipeline.fit(df)
```

```
>>> scaledData = scalerModel.transform(df)
>>> scaledData.show(truncate=False)
+---+---+----+--------+--------+
|x  |y  |z   |x_vector|x_scaled|
+---+---+----+--------+--------+
|0  |1  |100 |[0.0]   |[0.0]   |
|1  |2  |200 |[1.0]   |[0.5]   |
|2  |5  |1000|[2.0]   |[1.0]   |
+---+---+----+--------+--------+
```

Using MinMaxScaler on Multiple Columns

We can also apply a scaler (such as `MinMaxScaler`) on multiple columns:

```
>>> triplets = [(0, 1, 100), (1, 2, 200), (2, 5, 1000)]
>>> df = spark.createDataFrame(triplets, ['x', 'y', 'z'])
>>> df.show()
+---+---+----+
|  x|  y|   z|
+---+---+----+
|  0|  1| 100|
|  1|  2| 200|
|  2|  5|1000|
+---+---+----+
>>> from pyspark.ml import Pipeline
>>> from pyspark.ml.feature import MinMaxScaler
>>> columns_to_scale = ["x", "y", "z"]
>>> assemblers = [VectorAssembler(inputCols=[col],
    outputCol=col + "_vector") for col in columns_to_scale]
>>> scalers = [MinMaxScaler(inputCol=col + "_vector",
    outputCol=col + "_scaled") for col in columns_to_scale]
>>> pipeline = Pipeline(stages=assemblers + scalers)
>>> scalerModel = pipeline.fit(df)
>>> scaledData = scalerModel.transform(df)
>>> scaledData.show(truncate=False)
+---+---+----+--------+--------+--------+--------+--------+-------------------+
|x  |y  |z   |x_vector|y_vector|z_vector|x_scaled|y_scaled|z_scaled           |
+---+---+----+--------+--------+--------+--------+--------+-------------------+
|0  |1  |100 |[0.0]   |[1.0]   |[100.0] |[0.0]   |[0.0]   |[0.0]              |
|1  |2  |200 |[1.0]   |[2.0]   |[200.0] |[0.5]   |[0.25]  |[0.1111111111111111]|
|2  |5  |1000|[2.0]   |[5.0]   |[1000.0]|[1.0]   |[1.0]   |[1.0]              |
+---+---+----+--------+--------+--------+--------+--------+-------------------+
```

You can do some postprocessing to recover the original column names:

```
from pyspark.sql import functions as f

names = {x + "_scaled": x for x in columns_to_scale}
scaledData = scaledData.select([f.col(c).alias(names[c]) for c in names.keys()])
```

The output will be:

```
>>> scaledData.show()
+------+-----+--------------------+
|     y|    x|                   z|
+------+-----+--------------------+
| [0.0]|[0.0]|               [0.0]|
|[0.25]|[0.5]|[0.1111111111111111]|
| [1.0]|[1.0]|               [1.0]|
+------+-----+--------------------+
```

Normalization Using Normalizer

Spark's `Normalizer` transforms a dataset of `Vector` rows, normalizing each `Vector` to have unit norm (i.e., a length of 1). It takes a parameter `p` from the user, which represents the p-norm. For example, you can set `p=1` to use the Manhattan norm (or Manhattan distance) or `p=2` to use the Euclidean norm:

```
L1: z = || x ||1 = sum(|xi|) for i=1, ..., n
L2: z = || x ||2 = sqrt(sum(xi^2)) for i=1,..., n

from pyspark.ml.feature import Normalizer
# Create an object of the class Normalizer
ManhattanDistance=Normalizer().setP(1)
  .setInputCol("features").setOutputCol("Manhattan Distance")
EuclideanDistance=Normalizer().setP(2)
  .setInputCol("features").setOutputCol("Euclidean Distance")
# Transform
ManhattanDistance.transform(scaleDF).show()
+---+--------------+--------------------+
| id|      features|  Manhattan Distance|
+---+--------------+--------------------+
|  0|[1.0,0.1,-1.0]|[0.47619047619047...|
|  1| [2.0,1.1,1.0]|[0.48780487804878...|
|  0|[1.0,0.1,-1.0]|[0.47619047619047...|
|  1| [2.0,1.1,1.0]|[0.48780487804878...|
|  1|[3.0,10.1,3.0]|[0.18633540372670...|
+---+--------------+--------------------+

EuclideanDistance.transform(scaleDF).show()
+---+--------------+--------------------+
| id|      features|  Euclidean Distance|
+---+--------------+--------------------+
|  0|[1.0,0.1,-1.0]|[0.70534561585859...|
|  1| [2.0,1.1,1.0]|[0.80257235390512...|
|  0|[1.0,0.1,-1.0]|[0.70534561585859...|
|  1| [2.0,1.1,1.0]|[0.80257235390512...|
|  1|[3.0,10.1,3.0]|[0.27384986857909...|
+---+--------------+--------------------+
```

String Indexing

Most machine learning algorithms require the conversion of categorical features (such as strings) into numerical ones. String indexing is the process of converting strings to numerical values.

Spark's `StringIndexer` is a label indexer that maps a string column of labels to a column of label indices. If the input column is numeric, we cast it to string and index the string values. The indices are in the range `[0, numLabels)`. By default, they are ordered by label frequency in descending order, so the most frequent label gets the index `0`. The ordering behavior is controlled by setting the `stringOrderType` option.

Applying StringIndexer to a Single Column

Suppose we have the following PySpark DataFrame:

```
+-------+--------------+----+----+
|address|          date|name|food|
+-------+--------------+----+----+
|1111111|20151122045510| Yin|gre |
|1111111|20151122045501| Yin|gre |
|1111111|20151122045500| Yln|gra |
|1111112|20151122065832| Yun|ddd |
|1111113|20160101003221| Yan|fdf |
|1111111|20160703045231| Yin|gre |
|1111114|20150419134543| Yin|fdf |
|1111115|20151123174302| Yen|ddd |
|2111115|      20123192| Yen|gre |
+-------+--------------+----+----+
```

If we want to transform it to use with `pyspark.ml`, we can use Spark's `StringIndexer` to convert the `name` column to a numeric column, as shown here:

```
>>> indexer = StringIndexer(inputCol="name", outputCol="name_index").fit(df)
>>> df_ind = indexer.transform(df)
>>> df_ind.show()
+-------+--------------+----+----------+----+
|address|          date|name|name_index|food|
+-------+--------------+----+----------+----+
|1111111|20151122045510| Yin|       0.0|gre |
|1111111|20151122045501| Yin|       0.0|gre |
|1111111|20151122045500| Yln|       2.0|gra |
|1111112|20151122065832| Yun|       4.0|ddd |
|1111113|20160101003221| Yan|       3.0|fdf |
|1111111|20160703045231| Yin|       0.0|gre |
|1111114|20150419134543| Yin|       0.0|fdf |
|1111115|20151123174302| Yen|       1.0|ddd |
|2111115|      20123192| Yen|       1.0|gre |
+-------+--------------+----+----------+----+
```

Applying StringIndexer to Several Columns

What if we want to apply `StringIndexer` to several columns at once? The simple way to do this is to combine several `StringIndexes` in a `list()` function and use a `Pipeline` to execute them all:

```
from pyspark.ml import Pipeline
from pyspark.ml.feature import StringIndexer

indexers = [ StringIndexer(inputCol=column, outputCol=column+"_index").fit(df)
  for column in list(set(df.columns)-set(['date'])) ]

pipeline = Pipeline(stages=indexers)
df_indexed = pipeline.fit(df).transform(df)

df_indexed.show()
+-------+--------------+----+----+----------+----------+-------------+
|address|          date|food|name|food_index|name_index|address_index|
+-------+--------------+----+----+----------+----------+-------------+
|1111111|20151122045510| gre| Yin|       0.0|       0.0|          0.0|
|1111111|20151122045501| gra| Yin|       2.0|       0.0|          0.0|
|1111111|20151122045500| gre| Yln|       0.0|       2.0|          0.0|
|1111112|20151122065832| gre| Yun|       0.0|       4.0|          3.0|
|1111113|20160101003221| gre| Yan|       0.0|       3.0|          1.0|
|1111111|20160703045231| gre| Yin|       0.0|       0.0|          0.0|
|1111114|20150419134543| gre| Yin|       0.0|       0.0|          5.0|
|1111115|20151123174302| ddd| Yen|       1.0|       1.0|          2.0|
|2111115|      20123192| ddd| Yen|       1.0|       1.0|          4.0|
+-------+--------------+----+----+----------+----------+-------------+
```

Next, I'll dig a little deeper into the `VectorAssembler`, introduced in "Standardization" on page 377.

Vector Assembly

The main function of the `VectorAssembler` is to concatenate a set of features into a single vector which can be passed to the estimator or machine learning algorithm. In other words, it's a feature transformer that merges multiple columns into a single vector column. Suppose we have the following DataFrame:

```
>>> df.show()
+----+----+----+
|col1|col2|col3|
+----+----+----+
| 7.0| 8.0| 9.0|
| 1.1| 1.2| 1.3|
| 4.0| 5.0| 6.0|
|   2|   3|   4|
| 5.0| NaN|null|
+----+----+----+
```

We can apply the VectorAssembler to these three features (col1, col2, and col3) and merge them into a vector column named features, as shown here:

```
from pyspark.ml.feature import VectorAssembler
input_columns = ["col1", "col2", "col3"]
assembler = VectorAssembler(inputCols=input_columns, outputCol="features")
# use the transform() method to transform the dataset into a vector
transformed = assembler.transform(df)
transformed.show()
+----+----+----+-------------+
|col1|col2|col3|     features|
+----+----+----+-------------+
| 7.0| 8.0| 9.0|[7.0,8.0,9.0]|
| 1.1| 1.2| 1.3|[1.1,1.2,1.3]|
| 4.0| 5.0| 6.0|[4.0,5.0,6.0]|
|   2|   3|   4|[2.0,3.0,4.0]|
| 5.0| NaN|null|[5.0,NaN,NaN]|
+----+----+----+-------------+
```

If you want to skip rows that have NaN or null values, you can do this by using VectorAssembler.setParams(handleInvalid="skip"):

```
>>> assembler2 = VectorAssembler(inputCols=input_columns, outputCol="features")
                 .setParams(handleInvalid="skip")

>>> assembler2.transform(df).show()
+----+----+----+-------------+
|col1|col2|col3|     features|
+----+----+----+-------------+
| 7.0| 8.0| 9.0|[7.0,8.0,9.0]|
| 1.1| 1.2| 1.3|[1.1,1.2,1.3]|
| 4.0| 5.0| 6.0|[4.0,5.0,6.0]|
|   2|   3|   4|[2.0,3.0,4.0]|
+----+----+----+-------------+
```

Bucketing

Data binning—also called discrete binning or bucketing—is a data preprocessing technique used to reduce the effects of minor observation errors. With this technique, the original data values that fall into a given small interval (a bin) are replaced by a value representative of that interval, often the central value. For example, if you have data on car prices where the values are widely scattered, you may prefer to use bucketing instead of the actual individual car prices.

Spark's Bucketizer transforms a column of continuous features to a column of feature buckets, where the buckets are specified by the user.

Consider this example: there's no linear relationship between latitude and housing values, but you may suspect that individual latitudes and housing values are related. To explore this, you might bucketize the latitudes, creating buckets like:

```
Bin-1:  32 < latitude <= 33
Bin-2:  33 < latitude <= 34
...
```

The binning technique can be applied on both categorical and numerical data. Table 12-2 shows a numerical binning example, and Table 12-3 shows a categorical binning example.

Table 12-2. Numerical binning example

Value	Bin
0-10	Very low
11-30	Low
31-70	Mid
71-90	High
91-100	Very high

Table 12-3. Categorical binning example

Value	Bin
India	Asia
China	Asia
Japan	Asia
Spain	Europe
Italy	Europe
Chile	South America
Brazil	South America

Binning is used with genomics data as well: we bucketize human genome chromosomes (1, 2, 3, ..., 22, X, Y, MT). For instance, chromosome 1 has 250 million positions, which we may bucketize into 101 buckets as follows:

```
for id in (1, 2, 3, ..., 22, X, Y, MT):
  chr_position = (chromosome-<id> position)
  # chr_position range is from 1 to 250,000,000
  bucket = chr_position % 101
  # where
  #      0 =< bucket <= 100
```

Bucketizer

Bucketing is the most straightforward approach for converting continuous variables into categorical variables. To illustrate, let's look at an example. In PySpark, the task of bucketing can be easily accomplished using the `Bucketizer` class. The first step is to define the bucket borders; then we create an object of the `Bucketizer` class and apply the `transform()` method to our DataFrame.

First, let's create a sample DataFrame for demo purposes:

```
>>> data = [('A', -99.99), ('B', -0.5), ('C', -0.3),
...   ('D', 0.0), ('E', 0.7), ('F', 99.99)]
>>>
>>> dataframe = spark.createDataFrame(data, ["id", "features"])
>>> dataframe.show()
+---+--------+
| id|features|
+---+--------+
|  A|  -99.99|
|  B|    -0.5|
|  C|    -0.3|
|  D|     0.0|
|  E|     0.7|
|  F|   99.99|
+---+--------+
```

Next, we define our bucket borders and apply the `Bucketizer` to create buckets:

```
>>> bucket_borders=[-float("inf"), -0.5, 0.0, 0.5, float("inf")]
>>> from pyspark.ml.feature import Bucketizer
>>> bucketer = Bucketizer().setSplits(bucket_borders)
   .setInputCol("features").setOutputCol("bucket")
>>> bucketer.transform(dataframe).show()
+---+--------+------+
| id|features|bucket|
+---+--------+------+
|  A|  -99.99|   0.0|
|  B|    -0.5|   1.0|
|  C|    -0.3|   1.0|
|  D|     0.0|   2.0|
|  E|     0.7|   3.0|
|  F|   99.99|   3.0|
+---+--------+------+
```

QuantileDiscretizer

Spark's `QuantileDiscretizer` takes a column with continuous features and outputs a column with binned categorical features. The number of bins is set by the `numBuckets` parameter, and the bucket splits are determined based on the data. It is possible that the number of buckets used will be smaller than the specified value, for example if there are too few distinct values in the input to create enough distinct quantiles (i.e., segments of the dataset).

You can use the `Bucketizer` and `QuantileDiscretizer` together, like this:

```
>>> from pyspark.ml.feature import Bucketizer
>>> from pyspark.ml.feature import QuantileDiscretizer
```

```
>>> data = [(0, 18.0), (1, 19.0), (2, 8.0), (3, 5.0), (4, 2.2)]
>>> df = spark.createDataFrame(data, ["id", "hour"])
>>> print(df.show())
+---+----+
| id|hour|
+---+----+
|  0|18.0|
|  1|19.0|
|  2| 8.0|
|  3| 5.0|
|  4| 2.2|
+---+----+

>>> qds = QuantileDiscretizer(numBuckets=5, inputCol="hour",
   outputCol="buckets", relativeError=0.01, handleInvalid="error")
>>> bucketizer = qds.fit(df)
>>> bucketizer.setHandleInvalid("skip").transform(df).show()
+---+----+-------+
| id|hour|buckets|
+---+----+-------+
|  0|18.0|    3.0|
|  1|19.0|    3.0|
|  2| 8.0|    2.0|
|  3| 5.0|    2.0|
|  4| 2.2|    1.0|
+---+----+-------+
```

Logarithm Transformation

In a nutshell, logarithm (commonly denoted by `log`) transformation compresses the range of large numbers and expands the range of small numbers. In mathematics, the logarithm is the inverse function to exponentiation and is defined as (where *b* is called the base number):

$$log_b(x) = y \rightarrow b^y = x$$

In feature engineering, log transformation is one of the most commonly used mathematical transformations. It helps us to handle skewed data by forcing outlier values closer to the mean, making the data distribution more approximate to normal (for example, the natural/base e logarithm of the number 4,000 is 8.2940496401). This normalization reduces the effect of the outliers, helping make machine learning models more robust.

The logarithm is only defined for positive values other than 1 (0, 1, and negative values cannot reliably be the base of a power function). A common technique for handling negative and zero values is to add a constant to the data before applying the log transformation (e.g., log(x+1)).

Spark provides the logarithm function in any base, defined as follows:

```
pyspark.sql.functions.log(arg1, arg2=None)

Description: Returns the first argument-based logarithm
of the second argument. If there is only one argument,
then this takes the natural logarithm of the argument.
```

Its use is illustrated in the following example. First, we create a DataFrame:

```
>>> data = [('gene1', 1.2), ('gene2', 3.4), ('gene1', 3.5), ('gene2', 12.6)]
>>> df = spark.createDataFrame(data, ["gene", "value"])
>>> df.show()
+-----+-----+
| gene|value|
+-----+-----+
|gene1|  1.2|
|gene2|  3.4|
|gene1|  3.5|
|gene2| 12.6|
+-----+-----+
```

Then we apply the logarithm transformation on a feature labeled `value`:

```
>>> from pyspark.sql.functions import log
>>> df.withColumn("base-10", log(10.0, df.value))
      .withColumn("base-e", log(df.value)).show()
+-----+-----+------------------+------------------+
| gene|value|           base-10|            base-e|
+-----+-----+------------------+------------------+
|gene1|  1.2|0.0791812460476248|0.1823215567939546|
|gene2|  3.4| 0.531478917042255|1.2237754316221157|
|gene1|  3.5|0.5440680443502756| 1.252762968495368|
|gene2| 12.6|1.1003705451175627| 2.533696813957432|
+-----+-----+------------------+------------------+
```

One-Hot Encoding

Machine learning models require that all input features and output predictions be numeric. This implies that if your data contains categorical features—such as education degree `{BS, MBA, MS, MD, PHD}`—you must encode it numerically before you can build and evaluate a model.

Figure 12-3 illustrates the concept of one-hot encoding, an encoding scheme in which each categorical value is converted to a binary vector.

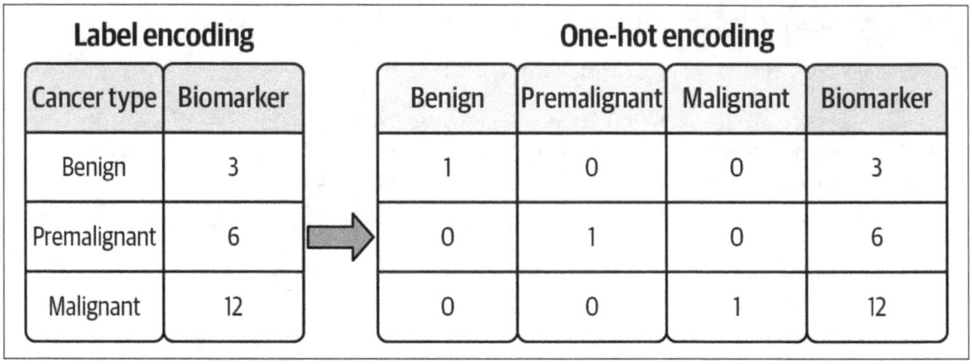

Label encoding

Cancer type	Biomarker
Benign	3
Premalignant	6
Malignant	12

One-hot encoding

Benign	Premalignant	Malignant	Biomarker
1	0	0	3
0	1	0	6
0	0	1	12

Figure 12-3. One-hot encoding example

A one-hot encoder maps the label indices to a binary vector representation with at most a single 1 value indicating the presence of a specific feature value from the set of all possible feature values. This method is useful when you need to use categorical features but the algorithm expects continuous features. To understand this encoding method, consider a feature called `safety_level` that has five categorical values (represented in Table 12-4). The first column shows the feature values and the rest of the columns show one-hot encoded binary vector representations of those values.

Table 12-4. Representing categorical values as binary vectors

safety_level (text)	Very-Low	Low	Medium	High	Very-High
`Very-Low`	1	0	0	0	0
`Low`	0	1	0	0	0
`Medium`	0	0	1	0	0
`High`	0	0	0	1	0
`Very-High`	0	0	0	0	1

For string type input data, it is common to encode categorical features using `StringIndexer` first. Spark's `OneHotEncoder` then takes the string-indexed label and encodes it into a sparse vector. Let's walk through an example to see how this works. First we'll create a DataFrame with two categorical features:

```
>>> from pyspark.sql.types import *
>>>
>>> schema = StructType().add("id","integer")\
...                      .add("safety_level","string")\
...                      .add("engine_type","string")
>>> schema
StructType(List(StructField(id,IntegerType,true),
                StructField(safety_level,StringType,true),
                StructField(engine_type,StringType,true)))
>>> data = [
```

```
...       (1,'Very-Low','v4'),
...       (2,'Very-Low','v6'),
...       (3,'Low','v6'),
...       (4,'Low','v6'),
...       (5,'Medium','v4'),
...       (6,'High','v6'),
...       (7,'High','v6'),
...       (8,'Very-High','v4'),
...       (9,'Very-High','v6')
... ]
>>>
>>> df = spark.createDataFrame(data, schema=schema)
>>> df.show(truncate=False)
+---+------------+-----------+
|id |safety_level|engine_type|
+---+------------+-----------+
|1  |Very-Low    |v4         |
|2  |Very-Low    |v6         |
|3  |Low         |v6         |
|4  |Low         |v6         |
|5  |Medium      |v4         |
|6  |High        |v6         |
|7  |High        |v6         |
|8  |Very-High   |v4         |
|9  |Very-High   |v6         |
+---+------------+-----------+
```

Next, we'll apply the `OneHotEncoder` transformation to the `safety_level` and `engine_type` features. In Spark, we cannot apply `OneHotEncoder` to string columns directly; we need to first convert them to numeric values, which we can do with Spark's `StringIndexer`.

First, we apply `StringIndexer` to the `safety_level` feature:

```
>>> from pyspark.ml.feature import StringIndexer
>>> safety_level_indexer = StringIndexer(inputCol="safety_level",
    outputCol="safety_level_index")
>>> df1 = safety_level_indexer.fit(df).transform(df)
>>> df1.show()
+---+------------+-----------+------------------+
| id|safety_level|engine_type|safety_level_index|
+---+------------+-----------+------------------+
|  1|    Very-Low|         v4|               3.0|
|  2|    Very-Low|         v6|               3.0|
|  3|         Low|         v6|               1.0|
|  4|         Low|         v6|               1.0|
|  5|      Medium|         v4|               4.0|
|  6|        High|         v6|               0.0|
|  7|        High|         v6|               0.0|
|  8|   Very-High|         v4|               2.0|
|  9|   Very-High|         v6|               2.0|
+---+------------+-----------+------------------+
```

Next, we apply `StringIndexer` to the `engine_type` feature:

```
>>> engine_type_indexer = StringIndexer(inputCol="engine_type",
    outputCol="engine_type_index")
>>> df2 = engine_type_indexer.fit(df).transform(df)
>>> df2.show()
+---+------------+-----------+-----------------+
| id|safety_level|engine_type|engine_type_index|
+---+------------+-----------+-----------------+
|  1|    Very-Low|         v4|              1.0|
|  2|    Very-Low|         v6|              0.0|
|  3|         Low|         v6|              0.0|
|  4|         Low|         v6|              0.0|
|  5|      Medium|         v4|              1.0|
|  6|        High|         v6|              0.0|
|  7|        High|         v6|              0.0|
|  8|   Very-High|         v4|              1.0|
|  9|   Very-High|         v6|              0.0|
+---+------------+-----------+-----------------+
```

We can now apply `OneHotEncoder` to the `safety_level_index` and `engine_type_index` columns:

```
>>> from pyspark.ml.feature import OneHotEncoder
>>> onehotencoder_safety_level = OneHotEncoder(inputCol="safety_level_index",
    outputCol="safety_level_vector")
>>> df11 = onehotencoder_safety_level.fit(df1).transform(df1)
>>> df11.show(truncate=False)
+---+------------+-----------+------------------+-------------------+
|id |safety_level|engine_type|safety_level_index|safety_level_vector|
+---+------------+-----------+------------------+-------------------+
|1  |Very-Low    |v4         |3.0               |(4,[3],[1.0])      |
|2  |Very-Low    |v6         |3.0               |(4,[3],[1.0])      |
|3  |Low         |v6         |1.0               |(4,[1],[1.0])      |
|4  |Low         |v6         |1.0               |(4,[1],[1.0])      |
|5  |Medium      |v4         |4.0               |(4,[],[])          |
|6  |High        |v6         |0.0               |(4,[0],[1.0])      |
|7  |High        |v6         |0.0               |(4,[0],[1.0])      |
|8  |Very-High   |v4         |2.0               |(4,[2],[1.0])      |
|9  |Very-High   |v6         |2.0               |(4,[2],[1.0])      |
+---+------------+-----------+------------------+-------------------+

>>> onehotencoder_engine_type = OneHotEncoder(inputCol="engine_type_index",
    outputCol="engine_type_vector")
>>> df12 = onehotencoder_engine_type.fit(df2).transform(df2)
>>> df12.show(truncate=False)
+---+------------+-----------+-----------------+------------------+
|id |safety_level|engine_type|engine_type_index|engine_type_vector|
+---+------------+-----------+-----------------+------------------+
|1  |Very-Low    |v4         |1.0              |(1,[],[])         |
|2  |Very-Low    |v6         |0.0              |(1,[0],[1.0])     |
|3  |Low         |v6         |0.0              |(1,[0],[1.0])     |
|4  |Low         |v6         |0.0              |(1,[0],[1.0])     |
```

```
|5  |Medium      |v4         |1.0             |(1,[],[])         |
|6  |High        |v6         |0.0             |(1,[0],[1.0])     |
|7  |High        |v6         |0.0             |(1,[0],[1.0])     |
|8  |Very-High   |v4         |1.0             |(1,[],[])         |
|9  |Very-High   |v6         |0.0             |(1,[0],[1.0])     |
+---+------------+-----------+----------------+------------------+
```

We can also apply this encoding to multiple columns at the same time:

```
>>> indexers = [StringIndexer(inputCol=column, outputCol=column+"_index")
    .fit(df) for column in list(set(df.columns)-set(['id'])) ]

>>> from pyspark.ml import Pipeline
>>> pipeline = Pipeline(stages=indexers)
>>> df_indexed = pipeline.fit(df).transform(df)
>>> df_indexed.show()
+---+------------+-----------+------------------+-----------------+
| id|safety_level|engine_type|safety_level_index|engine_type_index|
+---+------------+-----------+------------------+-----------------+
|  1|    Very-Low|         v4|               3.0|              1.0|
|  2|    Very-Low|         v6|               3.0|              0.0|
|  3|         Low|         v6|               1.0|              0.0|
|  4|         Low|         v6|               1.0|              0.0|
|  5|      Medium|         v4|               4.0|              1.0|
|  6|        High|         v6|               0.0|              0.0|
|  7|        High|         v6|               0.0|              0.0|
|  8|   Very-High|         v4|               2.0|              1.0|
|  9|   Very-High|         v6|               2.0|              0.0|
+---+------------+-----------+------------------+-----------------+

>>> encoder = OneHotEncoder(
...     inputCols=[indexer.getOutputCol() for indexer in indexers],
...     outputCols=[
...         "{0}_encoded".format(indexer.getOutputCol()) for indexer in indexers]
... )
>>>
>>> from pyspark.ml.feature import VectorAssembler
>>> assembler = VectorAssembler(
...     inputCols=encoder.getOutputCols(),
...     outputCol="features"
... )
>>>
>>> pipeline = Pipeline(stages=indexers + [encoder, assembler])
>>>
>>> pipeline.fit(df).transform(df).show()
+---+------------+-----------+------------------+-----------------+
| id|safety_level|engine_type|safety_level_index|engine_type_index|
+---+------------+-----------+------------------+-----------------+
|  1|    Very-Low|         v4|               3.0|              1.0|
|  2|    Very-Low|         v6|               3.0|              0.0|
|  3|         Low|         v6|               1.0|              0.0|
|  4|         Low|         v6|               1.0|              0.0|
|  5|      Medium|         v4|               4.0|              1.0|
```

```
|  6|        High|          v6|              0.0|              0.0|
|  7|        High|          v6|              0.0|              0.0|
|  8|   Very-High|          v4|              2.0|              1.0|
|  9|   Very-High|          v6|              2.0|              0.0|
+---+------------+------------+-----------------+-----------------+

+---+-------------+--------------------------+------------------+
| id| safety_level_|engine_type_index_encoded|          features|
|   | index_encoded|                         |                  |
+---+-------------+--------------------------+------------------+
|  1| (4,[3],[1.0])|                (1,[],[])|     (5,[3],[1.0])|
|  2| (4,[3],[1.0])|            (1,[0],[1.0])|(5,[3,4],[1.0,1.0])|
|  3| (4,[1],[1.0])|            (1,[0],[1.0])|(5,[1,4],[1.0,1.0])|
|  4| (4,[1],[1.0])|            (1,[0],[1.0])|(5,[1,4],[1.0,1.0])|
|  5|     (4,[],[])|                (1,[],[])|         (5,[],[])|
|  6| (4,[0],[1.0])|            (1,[0],[1.0])|(5,[0,4],[1.0,1.0])|
|  7| (4,[0],[1.0])|            (1,[0],[1.0])|(5,[0,4],[1.0,1.0])|
|  8| (4,[2],[1.0])|                (1,[],[])|     (5,[2],[1.0])|
|  9| (4,[2],[1.0])|            (1,[0],[1.0])|(5,[2,4],[1.0,1.0])|
+---+-------------+--------------------------+------------------+
```

There is another way to do all of the data transformations: we can use a pipeline to simplify the process. First, we create the required stages:

```
>>> safety_level_indexer = StringIndexer(inputCol="safety_level",
    outputCol="safety_level_index")
>>> engine_type_indexer = StringIndexer(inputCol="engine_type",
    outputCol="engine_type_index")
>>> onehotencoder_safety_level = OneHotEncoder(
    inputCol="safety_level_index",
    outputCol="safety_level_vector")
>>> onehotencoder_engine_type = OneHotEncoder(
    inputCol="engine_type_index",
    outputCol="engine_type_vector")
```

Then we create a pipeline and pass all the defined stages to it:

```
>>> pipeline = Pipeline(stages=[safety_level_indexer,
...                             engine_type_indexer,
...                             onehotencoder_safety_level,
...                             onehotencoder_engine_type
...                    ])
>>>
>>> df_transformed = pipeline.fit(df).transform(df)
>>> df_transformed.show(truncate=False)
+---+---------+------+------+------+------------+-----------------+
|id |   safety|engine|safety|engine| safety_level|      engine_type |
|   |   _level| _type|_level| _type|      _vector|          _vector |
|   |         |      |_index|_index|             |                  |
+---+---------+------+------+------+------------+-----------------+
|1  |Very-Low |v4    |3.0   |1.0   |(4,[3],[1.0])| (1,[],[])        |
|2  |Very-Low |v6    |3.0   |0.0   |(4,[3],[1.0])| (1,[0],[1.0])    |
|3  |Low      |v6    |1.0   |0.0   |(4,[1],[1.0])| (1,[0],[1.0])    |
```

```
|4  |Low      |v6   |1.0   |0.0   |(4,[1],[1.0])|  (1,[0],[1.0])    |
|5  |Medium   |v4   |4.0   |1.0   |(4,[],[])    |  (1,[],[])        |
|6  |High     |v6   |0.0   |0.0   |(4,[0],[1.0])|  (1,[0],[1.0])    |
|7  |High     |v6   |0.0   |0.0   |(4,[0],[1.0])|  (1,[0],[1.0])    |
|8  |Very-High|v4   |2.0   |1.0   |(4,[2],[1.0])|  (1,[],[])        |
|9  |Very-High|v6   |2.0   |0.0   |(4,[2],[1.0])|  (1,[0],[1.0])    |
+---+---------+-----+------+------+-------------+-------------------+
```

TF-IDF

Term frequency–inverse document frequency (TF-IDF) is a measure of the originality of a word (a.k.a. term) based on the number of times it appears in a document and the number of documents in a collection that it appears in. In other words, it's a feature vectorization method used in text mining to reflect the importance of a term to a document in a corpus (set of documents). The TF-IDF technique is commonly used in document analysis, search engines, recommender systems, and other natural language processing (NLP) applications.

Term frequency `TF(t,d)` is the number of times that term `t` appears in document `d`, while document frequency `DF(t, D)` is the number of documents that contain term `t`. If a term appears very often across the corpus, it means it does not carry special information about a particular document—usually these kinds of words (such as "of," "the," and "as") may be dropped from the text analysis. Before we go deeper into the TF-IDF transformation, let's define the terms used in the following equations (Table 12-5).

Table 12-5. TF-IDF notation

Notation	Description
`t`	Term
`d`	Document
`D`	Corpus (set of finite documents)
`|D|`	The number of documents in the corpus
`TF(t, d)`	Term Frequency: the number of times that term `t` appears in document `d`
`DF(t, D)`	Document Frequency: the number of documents that contain term `t`
`IDF(t, D)`	Inverse Document Frequency: a numerical measure of how much information a term provides

Inverse document frequency (IDF) is defined as:

$$IDF(t, D) = log\left(\frac{|D| + 1}{DF(t, D) + 1}\right)$$

Let's say `N` is the number of documents in a corpus. Since the logarithm is used, if a term appears in all documents, its `IDF` value becomes `0`:

$$IDF(t, D) = log\left(\frac{N+1}{N+1}\right) = log(1) = 0$$

Note that a smoothing term (`+1`) is applied to avoid dividing by zero for terms that do not appear in the corpus. The `TF-IDF` measure is simply the product of `TF` and `IDF`:

$$TF - IDF(t, d, D) = TF(t, d) \times IDF(t, D)$$

where:

- `t` denotes the term(s)
- `d` denotes a document
- `D` denotes the corpus
- `TF(t,d)` denotes the number of times that term `t` appears in document `d`

We can express TF as:

$$TF_{i,j} = \frac{n_{i,j}}{\Sigma_k n_{k,j}} IDF_i = \log\frac{|D|}{|d : t_i \in d|}$$

Before, I show you how Spark implements TF-IDF, let's walk through a simple example with two documents (corpus size is 2 and `D = {doc1, doc2}`). We start by calculating the term frequency and document frequency:

```
documents = spark.createDataFrame([
    ("doc1", "Ada Ada Spark Spark Spark"),
    ("doc2", "Ada SQL")],["id", "document"])

TF(Ada, doc1) = 2
TF(Spark, doc1) = 3
TF(Ada, doc2) = 1
TF(SQL, doc2) = 1

DF(Ada, D) = 2
DF(Spark, D) = 1
DF(SQL, D) = 1
```

Then we calculate the IDF and TF-IDF (note that the logarithm base is *e* for all calculations):

```
IDF(Ada, D) = log ( (|D|+1) / (DF(t,D)+1) )
            = log ( (2+1) / (DF(Ada, D)+1) )
            = log ( 3 / (2+1)) = log(1)
            = 0.00

IDF(Spark, D) = log ( (|D|+1) / (DF(t,D)+1) )
            = log ( (2+1) / (DF(Spark, D)+1) )
            = log ( 3 / (1+1) )
            = log (1.5)
            = 0.40546510811

TF-IDF(Ada, doc1, D) = TF(Ada, doc1) x IDF(Ada, D)
                     = 2 x 0.0
                     = 0.0

TF-IDF(Spark, doc1, D) = TF(Spark, doc1) x IDF(Spark, D)
                       = 3 x 0.40546510811
                       = 1.21639532433
```

In Spark, `HashingTF` and `CountVectorizer` are the two algorithms used to generate term frequency vectors. The following example shows how to perform the required transformations. First, we create our sample DataFrame:

```
>>> from pyspark.ml.feature import HashingTF, IDF, Tokenizer
>>>
>>> sentences = spark.createDataFrame([
...     (0.0, "we heard about Spark and Java"),
...     (0.0, "Does Java use case classes"),
...     (1.0, "fox jumped over fence"),
...     (1.0, "red fox jumped over")
... ], ["label", "text"])
>>>
>>> sentences.show(truncate=False)
+-----+-----------------------------+
|label|text                         |
+-----+-----------------------------+
|0.0  |we heard about Spark and Java|
|0.0  |Does Java use case classes   |
|1.0  |fox jumped over fence        |
|1.0  |red fox jumped over          |
+-----+-----------------------------+

>>> tokenizer = Tokenizer(inputCol="text", outputCol="words")
>>> words_data = tokenizer.transform(sentences)
>>> words_data.show(truncate=False)
+-----+-----------------------------+------------------------------------+
|label|text                         |words                               |
+-----+-----------------------------+------------------------------------+
|0.0  |we heard about Spark and Java|[we, heard, about, spark, and, java]|
```

```
|0.0  |Does Java use case classes    |[does, java, use, case, classes]    |
|1.0  |fox jumped over fence         |[fox, jumped, over, fence]          |
|1.0  |red fox jumped over           |[red, fox, jumped, over]            |
+-----+------------------------------+------------------------------------+
```

Next we, create raw features:

```
>>> hashingTF = HashingTF(inputCol="words", outputCol="raw_features",
  numFeatures=16)
>>> featurized_data = hashingTF.transform(words_data)
>>> featurized_data.select("label", "raw_features").show(truncate=False)
+-----+-------------------------------------------------+
|label|raw_features                                     |
+-----+-------------------------------------------------+
|0.0  |(16,[1,4,6,11,12,15],[1.0,1.0,1.0,1.0,1.0,1.0])|
|0.0  |(16,[2,6,11,13,15],[1.0,1.0,1.0,1.0,1.0])       |
|1.0  |(16,[0,1,6,8],[1.0,1.0,1.0,1.0])                |
|1.0  |(16,[1,4,6,8],[1.0,1.0,1.0,1.0])                |
+-----+-------------------------------------------------+
```

Then we apply the `IDF()` transformation:

```
>>> idf = IDF(inputCol="raw_features", outputCol="features")
>>> idf_model = idf.fit(featurized_data)
>>> rescaled_data = idf_model.transform(featurized_data)
>>> rescaled_data.select("label", "features").show(truncate=False)
+-----+-------------------------------------------------------------+
|label|features                                                     |
+-----+-------------------------------------------------------------+
|0.0  |(16,[1,4,6,11,12,15],[0.22314355131420976,0.5108256237659907, |
|     |0.0,0.5108256237659907,0.9162907318741551,0.5108256237659907])|
|0.0  |(16,[2,6,11,13,15],[0.9162907318741551,0.0,0.5108256237659907,|
|     | 0.9162907318741551,0.5108256237659907])                      |
|1.0  |(16,[0,1,6,8],[0.9162907318741551,0.22314355131420976,        |
|     |0.0,0.5108256237659907])                                      |
|1.0  |(16,[1,4,6,8],[0.22314355131420976,0.5108256237659907,        |
|     |0.0,0.5108256237659907])                                      |
+-----+-------------------------------------------------------------+
```

The next example shows how to do TF-IDF using `CountVectorizer`, which extracts a vocabulary from a document collection and generates a `CountVectorizerModel`. In this example, each row of the DataFrame represents a document:

```
>>> df = spark.createDataFrame(
...     [(0, ["a", "b", "c"]), (1, ["a", "b", "b", "c", "a"])],
...     ["label", "raw"]
... )
>>> df.show()
+-----+---------------+
|label|            raw|
+-----+---------------+
|    0|      [a, b, c]|
```

```
|    1|[a, b, b, c, a]|
+-----+---------------+

>>> from  pyspark.ml.feature import CountVectorizer
>>> cv = CountVectorizer().setInputCol("raw").setOutputCol("features")
>>> model = cv.fit(df)
>>> transformed = model.transform(df)
>>> transformed.show(truncate=False)
+-----+---------------+-------------------------+
|label|raw            |features                 |
+-----+---------------+-------------------------+
|0    |[a, b, c]      | (3,[0,1,2],[1.0,1.0,1.0])|
|1    |[a, b, b, c, a]| (3,[0,1,2],[2.0,2.0,1.0])|
+-----+---------------+-------------------------+
```

In the `features` column, taking the example of the second row:

- `3` is the vector length.
- `[0, 1, 2]` are the vector indices (`index(a)=0, index(b)=1, index(c)=2`).
- `[2.0,2.0,1.0]` are the vector values.

`HashingTF()` converts documents to vectors of fixed size:

```
>>> hashing_TF = HashingTF(inputCol="raw", outputCol="features", numFeatures=128)
>>> result = hashing_TF.transform(df)
>>> result.show(truncate=False)
+-----+---------------+-------------------------------+
|label|raw            |features                       |
+-----+---------------+-------------------------------+
|0    |[a, b, c]      |(128,[40,99,117],[1.0,1.0,1.0])|
|1    |[a, b, b, c, a]|(128,[40,99,117],[1.0,2.0,2.0])|
+-----+---------------+-------------------------------+
```

Note that the size of the vector generated through `CountVectorizer` depends on the training corpus and the document, whereas the one generated through `HashingTF` has a fixed size (we set it to 128). This means that when using `CountVectorizer`, each raw feature is mapped to an index, but `HashingTF` might suffer from hash collisions, where two or more terms are mapped to the same index. To avoid this, we can increase the target feature dimension.

FeatureHasher

Feature hashing projects a set of categorical or numerical features into a feature vector of specified dimension (typically substantially smaller than that of the original feature space). A hashing trick (*https://en.wikipedia.org/wiki/Feature_hashing*) is used to map features to indices in the feature vector.

Spark's FeatureHasher operates on multiple columns, which may contain either numeric or categorical features. For numeric features, the hash of the column name is used to map the feature value to its index in the feature vector. For categorical and Boolean features, the hash of the string "column_name=value" is used, with an indicator value of 1.0. Here's an example:

```
>>> from pyspark.ml.feature import FeatureHasher
>>> df = spark.createDataFrame([
...     (2.1, True, "1", "fox"),
...     (2.1, False, "2", "gray"),
...     (3.3, False, "2", "red"),
...     (4.4, True, "4", "fox")
... ], ["number", "boolean", "string_number", "string"])

>>> input_columns = ["number", "boolean", "string_number", "string"]

>>> featurized = hasher.transform(df)
>>> featurized.show(truncate=False)
+------+-------+------------+------+-------------------------------------+
|number|boolean|string_number|string|features                             |
+------+-------+------------+------+-------------------------------------+
|2.1   |true   |1           |fox   |(256,[22,40,71,156],[1.0,1.0,2.1,1.0]) |
|2.1   |false  |2           |gray  |(256,[71,91,109,130],[2.1,1.0,1.0,1.0])|
|3.3   |false  |2           |red   |(256,[71,91,130,205],[3.3,1.0,1.0,1.0])|
|4.4   |true   |4           |fox   |(256,[40,71,84,156],[1.0,4.4,1.0,1.0]) |
+------+-------+------------+------+-------------------------------------+
```

SQLTransformer

Spark's SQLTransformer implements the transformations that are defined by a SQL statement. Rather than registering your DataFrame as a table and then querying the table, you can directly apply the SQL transformations to your data represented as a DataFrame. Currently, SQLTransformer has limited functionality and can be applied to a single DataFrame as __THIS__, which represents the underlying table of the input dataset.

SQLTransformer supports statements like:

```
SELECT salary, salary * 0.06 AS bonus
   FROM __THIS__
      WHERE salary > 10000

SELECT dept, location, SUM(salary) AS sum_of_salary
   FROM __THIS__
      GROUP BY dept, location
```

The following example shows how to use `SQLTransformer`:

```
>>> from pyspark.ml.feature import SQLTransformer
>>> df = spark.createDataFrame([
...     (10, "d1", 27000),
...     (20, "d1", 29000),
...     (40, "d2", 31000),
...     (50, "d2", 39000)], ["id", "dept", "salary"])
>>>
>>> df.show()
+---+----+------+
| id|dept|salary|
+---+----+------+
| 10|  d1| 27000|
| 20|  d1| 29000|
| 40|  d2| 31000|
| 50|  d2| 39000|
+---+----+------+

query = "SELECT dept, SUM(salary) AS sum_of_salary FROM __THIS__ GROUP BY dept"
sqlTrans = SQLTransformer(statement=query)
sqlTrans.transform(df).show()
+----+-------------+
|dept|sum_of_salary|
+----+-------------+
|  d2|        70000|
|  d1|        56000|
+----+-------------+
```

Summary

The goal of machine learning algorithms is to use input data to create usable models that can help us to answer questions. The input data comprises features (such as education level, car price, glucose level, etc.) which are in the form of structured columns. In most cases the algorithms require features with some specific characteristics to work properly, which raises the need for feature engineering. Spark's machine learning library, MLlib (included in PySpark), has a set of high-level APIs that make feature engineering possible. Proper feature engineering helps to build semantically proper and correct machine learning models.

The following is a list of accessible resources that provide additional information on feature engineering and other topics covered in this book:

- "Getting Started with Feature Engineering" (*https://oreil.ly/GAlRk*), a blog post by Pravar Jain
- "Data Manipulation: Features" (*https://oreil.ly/Qc3sP*), by Wenqiang Feng
- "Representation: Feature Engineering" (*https://oreil.ly/eDeDr*) from Google's *Machine Learning Crash Course with TensorFlow APIs*

- "Want to Build Machine Learning Pipelines? A Quick Introduction Using PySpark" (*https://oreil.ly/kHLFL*), a blog post by Lakshay Arora
- TF-IDF, Term Frequency-Inverse Document Frequency (*https://oreil.ly/2WlgI*)—documentation by Ethen Liu

This concludes our journey through data algorithms with Spark! I hope you feel prepared to tackle any data problem, big or small. Remember my motto: keep it simple and use parameters so that your solution can be reused by other developers.

Index

D

N

O

P

Q

R

U

V

W

Z

About the Author

Dr. Mahmoud Parsian is a software architect and author. He leads Illumina's Big Data team, focused on large-scale genome analytics, where he develops scalable distributed algorithms for genomics data using Python, Java, MapReduce, Spark, and open source tools. Dr. Parsian is a practicing software professional with 30+ years of experience as a developer, designer, architect, and author. For the past 15 years, he has been involved in Python, Java server-side, databases, MapReduce, Spark, machine learning, and distributed computing.

Dr. Parsian has published four books: *Data Algorithms* (O'Reilly), *JDBC Metadata, MySQL, and Oracle Recipes* (Apress), *JDBC Recipes* (Apress), and *PySpark Algorithms* (Amazon).

He earned his MS and PhD in computer science from Iowa State University and is an adjunct faculty member at Santa Clara University, where he teaches courses on big data and machine learning.

Colophon

The animal on the cover of *Data Algorithms with Spark* is a thorn-tailed rayadito (*Aphrastura spinicauda*). This little bird is commonly found in the temperate forests and subtropical dry grass- and shrublands of Chile and Argentina. Thorn-tailed rayaditos have a black head and bill, a white throat and belly, and orange "eyebrows" that extend to the back of the neck. Their upper wings are black with white tips while the flight feathers are a reddish-orange banded with pale brown. The rayadito's body and distinctive tail is a mix of black, brown, and rust-colored feathers, with narrow protruding shafts that give it the "thorn-tailed" moniker.

These birds are only 13–14 centimeters long and weigh 10–13 grams—less than half an ounce! They are very active, inquisitive, and vocal, foraging for food in foliage, moss, lichen, tree branches and trunks, and occasionally on the ground. They breed during the austral spring and summer (Oct.–Jan.), nesting in tree trunks, crevices, and even under roofs. The female lays three to four eggs in a nest made of vines, roots, grasses, and feathers, and both parents incubate them for about two weeks. Unlike most birds, thorn-tailed rayaditos do not migrate, but they are monogamous and are often found in pairs or small groups of up to 15 birds. Their population is stable, and they are considered a species of least concern by the IUCN. Many of the animals on O'Reilly covers are endangered; all of them are important to the world.

The cover illustration is by Karen Montgomery, based on a black and white engraving from *British Birds*. The cover fonts are Gilroy Semibold and Guardian Sans. The text font is Adobe Minion Pro; the heading font is Adobe Myriad Condensed; and the code font is Dalton Maag's Ubuntu Mono.

Printed in the USA
CPSIA information can be obtained
at www.ICGtesting.com
JSHW052311280624
65591JS00005B/49

9 781492 082385